## BY THE SAME AUTHOR

*Reliques of the Rives,* 1929
*Before the Curtain Falls,* 1932
*German Military Ciphers,* 1935
*The Pageant of Persia,* 1936
*Escape to Cairo,* 1938
*American Foreign Service,* 1948
*Restif de la Bretonne,* 1949 (in French)
*Casanoviana: An Annotated World Bibliography of Casanova and of Works Concerning Him,* 1956
*Casanova Gleanings,* edited by the author from 1958 to 1973 (by F.L. Mars since 1974)
*Casanova: A Biography Based on New Documents,* 1961 (translated into German, 1960; Italian, 1962; French, 1962; and Japanese, 1968)
*Diplomatic and Literary Quests,* 1963
*Foreign Service Farewell,* 1969
*Collector's Quest: The Correspondence of Henry Miller and J. Rives Childs, 1947-1965,* 1968 (edited by Richard Clement Wood)
*Casanova: Eine Biographie,* 1977 (German translation of an earlier version of the manuscript from which the present work developed)
*Let the Credit Go: The Autobiography of J. Rivers Childs*

# Casanova

# Casanova

## A NEW PERSPECTIVE

### J. RIVES CHILDS

*A GINIGER BOOK*
*published in association with*
**PARAGON HOUSE PUBLISHERS**
*New York*

First U.S. Edition

Published in the United States by

Paragon House Publishers
90 Fifth Avenue
New York, New York 10011
in association with The K.S. Giniger Company, Inc.
1133 Broadway
New York, New York 10010

Edited by Walter Glanze

Designed by A. Christopher Simon

**Library of Congress Cataloging-in-Publication Data**

Childs, J. Rives (James Rives), 1893-1987
    Casanova, a new perspective

    "A Giniger book."
    Bibliography:
    Includes indexes.
    1. Casanova, Giacomo, 1725-1789.      2. Europe-Biography.
I. Title
D285.8.C4C448    1987      940.2'53'0924   [B]   87-8915
ISBN 0-913729-69-8

# Contents

# *Illustrations*

# *Introduction*

No man in history has probably left quite so sincere a record of his life as Casanova; no one has revealed the truth about himself and about his era with such telling effect as he. Where others have masked their lives and testimonies, he told all—or almost all. Such unparalleled procedure has proved too much for a world habituated to deceit; the consequence has been that Casanova has been damned incontinently for the best part of two centuries.

Upon the first appearance of the *Memoirs* in 1822, they were received for the most part with incredulity. The Italian poet and critic Ugo Foscolo, writing in the *Westminster Review* in April 1827, questioned not only their authenticity, but even the very existence of the purported writer. The chasm that the French Revolution had created between the eighteenth and nineteenth centuries had clouded the memory of happenings before that event. A French critic, Paul Lacroix in 1857, while acknowledging the existence of a Casanova, insisted that the *Memoirs* could only have been written by a writer of the distinction of Stendhal.

Germany was the first to appraise Casanova as an incomparable social historian; it is in Germany that the greatest number of editions of the *Memoirs* have been published. French recognition came somewhat later with the important studies of Armand Baschet, Charles Henry, Charles Samaran, Édouard Maynial, Octave Uzanne, Raoul Vèze, and Joseph Pollio. The fact that the *Memoirs* were not published in Italy until 1882 reflects the tardiness of Italian acclaim. Such distinguished scholars as Ademollo, d'Ancona, Valeri, Mola, Molmenti, Brunelli, Croce, Nicolini, Damerini, and Zottoli were, however, to make up for this initial neglect of one of their greatest compatriots. In more recent years, important contributions to Casanova studies by Edgecumbe, Symons, Havelock Ellis, and Bleackley have emerged from Great Britain; and in the United States Morris Bishop, Guy Endore, Edmund Wilson, and Lawrence Powell have produced valuable critical examinations. In addition, the *Memoirs* have been translated, in whole or in part, into at least twenty-four languages to date, including Arabic, Bengali, Croatian, Czech, Danish, Dutch, English, Finnish, German, Hebrew, Hungarian, Italian, Japanese, Lettish, Norwegian, Polish, Portuguese, Russian, Serbian, Slovenian, Spanish, Swedish, and Turkish.

The world commonly knows Casanova as an adventurer, lover, and author of the immortal *Memoirs*. What the world generally ignores is his erudition. There was scarcely a subject he did not touch upon in the twenty-four works he published during his lifetime, or in the vast accumulation of manuscripts left at his death. Many of the former represent fugitive pamphlets, and such was their neglect by his contemporaries that it is difficult to find any copies at all. Nor do we have the two university theses that were his first literary labors: one in civil law, *De testamentis*, and another in canon law, *Utrum Hebraei possint construere novas synagogas*, on whether Jews may build new synagogues.

Notwithstanding his prolific writings, Casanova's place in world literature rests on one book, and that was published a quarter of a century after his death: the *Memoirs*, or *Histoire de ma vie*, as he himself entitled his manuscript. But for it, his name would have long disappeared beneath the sediment of history. It is, of course, principally on this work that any biography of the man must be based.

Purposely avoiding a systematic paraphrasing of his autobiographical record, I have been governed by two considerations
in the choice of material from it: First, I have made use only of
those episodes and incidents that best contribute to an understanding of his character; and, second, I have included those
judged as important for the story of his life. In addition, I have
included those new discoveries in European archives that bring
valuable light to bear on his activities. Considering the extent to
which those archives have been combed for nearly a century, those
new findings are surprising in their number. That I and others
have been fortunate enough to break much new ground indicates
that, notwithstanding all that has been accomplished, the field of
explorations is so vast as to be far from exhausted.

It is possible that some may find that a certain disproportionate
emphasis has been given in this present study to the significance of
the new material in terms of a consideration of Casanova's life.
This may be found particularly the case in respect to the identifications of those persons of the *Memoirs,* who, until now, have been
legendary figures masked by the pseudonyms Casanova gave them
to conceal their identities—persons such as Lucrezia, Angelica,
Cecilia Monti, Don Francesco, Giacomo Castelli, Bellino, Henriette, M.M., and the Hanoverian sisters. If I have, perhaps, unduly
stressed this new material and these identifications, it has been in
the belief that these have a prime importance in substantiating the
essential veracity of the *Memoirs.* The end of the nineteenth
century and the beginning of our own had brought increasing
credit to the *Memoirs* as an incomparable source of knowledge of
both the surface and the seamy sides of the eighteenth century;
now critical scrutiny increasingly brought to bear on them rein-
forces the proof of their unequalled historic importance and
makes it impossible to ignore them any longer as a creditable
source of knowledge for the many subjects on which they touch.

Much has been made in the past of the untrustworthiness of
certain chronological confusions in the *Memoirs,* and of proven
inexactitudes in dates. Like many men of genius, Casanova was
deficient in a precise sense of time. If he reported an event in a
given month of the year, when we know by documentary evidence
that it took place in another month, the error was most probably
involuntary rather than intentional. As all memorialists have

done, he often recounted events out of their chronological sequence, and frequently confused those that involved successive visits to the same locality. In the chronology appearing as an appendix, it has been possible to reestablish this with a very fair degree of certainty, except for the years 1742-45. Here I must confess that the problems defy any satisfactory solution; in all other instances it has been possible to correct Casanova's often faulty chronology on the basis of documentary evidence. An attempt to justify the chronology offered would have unduly expanded this work to little advantage for anyone but the specialist. In certain instances, I have set forth the principal problems involved; so far as others are concerned, the assurance is given that there is valid evidence in support of the chronology proposed for the period 1725-42 and that subsequent to 1745.

A biography of Casanova would be incomplete if confined exclusively to an account of his life. For a proper understanding of him, it is essential that an endeavor be made to place him in the framework of his century and of the principal figures with whom his career was joined, including some historical background of the events with which he was connected and of those manners and customs with which he deals.

A fundamental word of caution to which reference is elsewhere made, but which cannot be overemphasized: no greater error can be made than to judge Casanova by present standards rather than by those of his own day. In many respects, the outlook of the eighteenth century is as far removed and as different from our own as that of the Middle Ages. It is inconceivable that he would have enjoyed the friendship of some of the most notable Europeans of his time if he had been to them the moral leper he appears today to some. He was no better and no worse than the majority of his contemporaries in the social circles in which he moved. If he has borne opprobrium from the moment of the publication of the *Memoirs*, it is not because he was any worse than others of his time, but because he was frankest in divulging the truth about himself. He literally damned himself by his sincerity.

Casanova's love affairs occupy about one third of the *Memoirs*, a far greater proportion than is ordinarily so allotted by other memorialists. In consequence, the majority of readers have their perspective so clouded that for some the *Memoirs* give the appearance of having to do with little else but love. In reality, Casanova was concerned constantly with intellectual matters. To restore a balance long overdue, I have eschewed mention in this biography of numerous love affairs that are concerned with minor figures, or which add nothing to the portrait of the man, even though they play prominent roles in the *Memoirs*. This biography is intended less for those interested in his erotic exploits than for those concerned with his serious significance.

The serious aspect of Casanova has been most neglected in previous assessments of him. It may be that, in endeavoring to restore the balance, I have given the impression of holding a brief in his defense. On the contrary, I have sought, to the best of my ability—taking into account human fallibility and the inherent difficulty of achieving perfect objectivity—to avoid the role of either prosecuting attorney or counsel for the defense. It has been my aim to conform rather to the role of judge, presenting to the jury all available testimony, whether favorable or unfavorable, leaving any final judgment to be rendered by the reader. It is on this account that I have deliberately abstained from a concluding estimate.

The occasional comments introduced have been by way of interpretation, with a view to defining the problem involved. It has seemed justifiable here and there to run up a storm warning against rejecting out of hand such justification of Casanova as may appear reasonable, or against accepting unquestionably all that may be adduced as detrimental to him. I have interpreted my task as that of examining the pros and cons, without undue emphasis on either, bearing in mind Rémy de Gourmont's remark: "He recounts so much that is unfavorable to himself that one must accept all those that are favorable."

That he was a genius is indisputable; that he wasted his extraordinary talents is equally unquestionable—which brings us to the curious paradox that had he not been an adventurer and, in many respects, a wastrel, he would be today completely forgotten. Had he led a conventional life, with regular employment, it is doubtful if the material or the occasion would have been given him to write the immortal *Memoirs*. When all is considered, there is a certain irrelevancy in essaying to pass judgment on the good or the evil character of either the writer or his work. The fundamental touchstone is rather: are the *Memoirs* true or false? With the extensive new evidence assembled in favor of their essential veracity, the verdict can only be in favor of their astonishing fidelity. This is their importance. If it may be said that they contain passages of cynical immorality, it is precisely in this respect that they are a faithful reflection of a certain society of their era.

Composed in French, in the declining years of his life, the *Memoirs* are addressed to Count Marcolini, prime minister of Saxony, on April 27, 1797, proposing trial publication of a first volume. Nothing came of the suggestion, however, but some time before Marcolini's death, he apparently reconsidered the matter and offered 2,500 thalers to Carlo Angiolini, nephew-in-law of Casanova to whom the manuscript had been bequeathed. Once again there was no agreement, and in the end Carlo's son of the same name disposed of the manuscript of the *Memoirs*, together with three brief essays included in the inheritance, to the German publishing firm of Brockhaus on January 18, 1821, for the derisory sum of 200 thalers.

Brockhaus submitted the text of the *Memoirs* to a number of eminent German critics, including Ludwig Tieck, who recommended publication. A German translation was entrusted to Wilhelm von Schütz (1776-1847), and twelve volumes entitled *Memoiren* appeared between 1822 and 1828. If many episodes were mitigated, the translation, so far as it went, was a faithful one. Such was its success that, between 1825 and 1829, a Paris publisher, Tournachon-Molin, brought out a pirated edition purporting to be a translation of the Schütz text. In reality, this translation of a translation not only omitted much of Schütz but introduced spurious interpolations. To take advantage of the interest aroused outside of Germany, Brockhaus thereupon decided to issue a French edition and commissioned Jean Laforgue, a French professor at Dresden, to edit it.

If Laforgue had confined himself to his proper task, which was to correct Casanova's awkward turns of expression and to remove the Italianisms that obscured the text, he would have earned the gratitude of posterity. Lacking, however, the high sense of scholar-ship that was possessed by few in the early nineteenth century, he undertook to embellish the *Memoirs* in a manner responsive to the preromantic movement. It was as if a sculptor, dissatisfied with the classic lines of an Ionic column, undertook to attach orna-ments to it of florid Corinthian design. Nor was this all. As Jacobin and freethinker, Laforgue so deformed Casanova's views as to represent him as irreligious, while suppressing or attentuating his unfavorable comments on the French Revolution.

If Laforgue had no sense of exact scholarship, he was equally lacking in a sense of history. As a result, he failed to conserve numerous details of places and persons, about which Schütz had been more scrupulous. Apparently it never occurred to Laforgue that certain minutiae would be of value to social historians; for him the story was everything, and the particulars of no im-portance.

While omitting a few episodes that he considered overly licen-tious, Laforgue also disfigured Casanova's generally chaste prose with offensively prurient details on other occasions. As Schütz's more conscientious German translation has been largely ignored all these years except by the German public, the world's judgment of Casanova since 1826, with the appearance of the first volume of the Laforgue adaptation, has been formed on the basis of a corrupt text that has represented in so many respects a disfigurement of Casanova.

To add to this textual miasma, account must be taken of still another text, that of the so-called Paulin or Busoni text, edited by Busoni. Desirous of profiting from the success of the Laforgue edition issued by Brockhaus, Paulin printed in Paris in 1833 a pirated textual reprint of the first eight volumes of the former, which had appeared by 1832. In that year, censorship difficulties had interrupted the appearance of the remaining four Brockhaus volumes edited by Laforgue. Busoni, confronted by the dilemma of delivering the remaining text, resolved it in a manner that remained a mystery for some time, and published two final volumes in 1837.

Upon the appearance in 1838 of the four remaining volumes of the Laforgue text, it was noted that there were extraordinary differences between the two final Paulin volumes and the four concluding ones of Laforgue. Some episodes appearing in the Laforgue text were missing from the Busoni edition, while certain episodes were to be found in the latter that were in the texts of neither Laforgue nor Schütz.

It has been suggested that Busoni had access to an original manuscript unknown to Brockhaus; others have argued that the two final volumes of the Paulin edition were the invention of Busoni. This last hypothesis has been proven untenable with the discovery of details in Busoni that were found in unpublished archives unavailable to him; they are indubitably authentic. Recent revelation that the manuscript acquired by Brockhaus in 1821 contains two variants of seven chapters has thrown a flood of light on a hitherto seemingly impenetrable mystery. The two last volumes of the Paulin-Busoni edition are now seen to possess more or less the same distinctive characteristics as these, to such an extent as to warrant the conclusion that the disputed Busoni text comprises variants left by Casanova other than those that entered into the possession of Brockhaus.[1]

My interest in Casanova goes back more than forty years. In Cairo in 1930, I ordered from a catalogue, for the satisfaction of my omnivorous reading, the twelve-volume set of Arthur Machen's translation of the *Memoirs*, then the most complete text available in English. For sheer entertainment there are few more fascinating works. As the Prince de Ligne before me, I found Casanova one of the most extraordinary characters ever met with in or out of books. There was, besides, an almost inexhaustible fund of information about the eighteenth century, together with psychological revelations of much of the same dramatic intensity as those found in *The Thousand Nights and One*. Not least appealing was the stark genuineness reflected by the narrative.

Years later, as I neared the end of my diplomatic career, I became intrigued by some of the challenging bibliographical problems presented by the variant texts. A number of papers on the subject were published by the Bibliographical Society of America beginning in 1952.

This inspired the resolve to assemble as complete a collection as possible of works by and about Casanova with the idea of publishing an annotated bibliography. Having realized this in 1956, the next step was the launching in 1958 of *Casanova Gleanings* as an outlet for the publication of contemporary Casanova studies. This subsequently made its modest way among subscribers as far afield as Japan and New Zealand and with an increasing number of learned contributions from distinguished foreign scholars. Then I was invited to write a brief biography of Casanova by Rowohlt for its monograph series in German. This was subsequently translated into Italian and Japanese and was expanded and published in English in London, the English text being in turn revised and extended and published in French in Paris. The present text represents a considerably revised and extended one, based on further important new material subsequently brought to light.

By far the most important development in the Casanova world was the decision by F.A. Brockhaus, after almost 150 years, to reveal the integral text of the *Mémoires* which that German firm had acquired in 1821 from Casanova's heirs. Victorian inhibitions had precluded publication of the original complete French text. By 1960 Casanova's frank but never prurient or offensive language had become acceptable to changing standards. On February 23 of that year, Mr. F.A. Brockhaus made public announcement at Wiesbaden to a select group of German writers and journalists of the firm's intention. It was my privilege to be the only foreigner present on the occasion.

An edition in twelve volumes, under the work's original title, *Histoire de ma vie*, with the scholarly annotations of Mrs. and Dr. Arthur Hübscher, appeared from 1960 to 1962. One consequence was a fresh stimulus to Casanova research. This brought to light a not inconsiderable amount of archival material in France, Germany, Italy, Great Britain, and Poland in particular that adds much to our knowledge of the man and has gone far in substantiating his fundamental truthfulness. The few important areas that remain largely unexplored are Russia, Spain, and Portugal. Whatever these may yield, they are unlikely to disturb the image of one of the most exceptionally gifted and authoritative social historians of his age.

# CHAPTER 1

## Early Years     ·

He was born in Venice on April 2, 1725, this Jacques[1] Casanova, outstanding in a long line of Italian adventurers, writers, and condottiere, one of the most prodigious figures of his century. Two world personalities have sprung from the city of lagoons: Marco Polo and Casanova. Yet one will look in vain for the name of the latter in a Venetian guidebook; not the least memorial to him is to be found. As Frenzi has said, "The bad reputation of Casanova is due in great part to the sincerity of his confessions," which is to say that nothing is so indigestible as truth.

Born of an actor and an actress, he had the theater in his blood, and the world became his stage. The Venice of his time was given over to the pursuit of pleasure. Theaters numbered no less than seven; prostitutes enjoyed both governmental subvention and social favor; carnival, when everyone went masked, extended over half the year. Gambling assumed such proportions that in 1774 the *ridotto*, given to it, had to be closed. Life was a round of pleasure with satisfaction of the senses a principal objective of artisans, patricians, abbés and bishops, monks and nuns. So it was for Casanova:

> To cultivate the pleasures of my senses was throughout my life my main preoccupation; I have never had any more important objective.

It was in such an atmosphere that his youth was spent, and it became an inseparable part of him. Destined to become one of the most cosmopolitan men of his time, he never ceased to be a Venetian, transporting with him, whether in Paris, London, St. Petersburg, or Madrid, that "pleasant place of all festivity," as it was so aptly described by Byron.

Probably no man so epitomized his century as Casanova; certainly no one has given us so comprehensive a picture of it as he. As F.W. Barthold wrote in 1846:

> The *Memoirs* of Casanova are not alone the most complete and detailed picture of the customs and conditions of a society in the century preceding the French Revolution, but are as well a mirror of the life of the State and its various divisions—in short, the innermost secrets of the life of an era.

The importance of the *Memoirs* does not end here. What has been commonly overlooked is the filiation of their pagan frankness with such typically Italian writers as Boccaccio, Masuccio, and Straparola. An Italian scholar has remarked that these writers are "bereft of pity for the weak" and "directed against the gullible and naive." We shall find examples in Casanova that reflect this same kind of exploitation: his tricking of Panagiotti with the adulteration of mercury, the advantages taken of Capitani's credulity at Cesena, as well as of Bragadin and the Marquise d'Urfé.

And Casanova's treatment of love is no less characteristic of the Italian novella.

> It is a love, with a few rare exceptions, of sensual reality—transport of the senses, possession, enjoyment, satisfaction of an ardent need—which finds fulfillment only in union. It is not treated as a sin, nor anything to be ashamed of; it is a manifestation of nature.[2]

Thus Casanova may be said to project into the eighteenth century the literary traditions and spirit of his Renaissance predecessors. In this projection, and in his incomparable depiction of his century are to be found his two-fold importance.

Casanova's acknowledged father was Gaetano Giuseppe Giacomo, of Parma, who was drawn to a theatrical career through an attachment to an actress, Giovanna Balletti, better known as the Fragoletta. On February 27, 1724, Gaetano, then playing at the Grimani's S. Samuele Theater in Venice, married the daughter of a shoemaker, Zanetta Farussi, whom he in turn introduced to the stage. The following year, after the birth of Jacques, the couple sought their fortune on the boards in London, where Zanetta made her debut in 1727 or 1728. Jacques had been left behind in care of his grandmother, Marzia. A second child, Francesco, who became a famous painter of battle pictures, was born in London, June 1, 1727. It has been said that he had for father so illustrious a personage as the Prince of Wales, future George II; what we do know is that, in common with most actresses of her time, Zanetta was, as the saying went, not cruel to her admirers.

Casanova offers us, in his *Memoirs*, an elaborate genealogy of his paternal lines, beginning with Don Jacob Casanova, born in 1428 at Saragossa in Spain, natural son of Don Francisco, Secretary of King Alphonso (1396-1458), who is stated to have persuaded the inmate of a convent, Donna Anna Palafox, to run off with him on the day after the taking of her vows. The two escaped to Rome, where they spent a year in prison until Pope Martin V gave the couple nuptial benediction on the recommendation of Don Juan Casanova, the uncle, a Spanish Dominican who had been made cardinal in 1430. Don Juan, a son, married in 1475 but was obliged to flee from Rome after killing an officer of the King of Naples, and, seeking his fortune in a voyage with Christopher Columbus, died in 1493.[3] This companion of Columbus left one son, Mark Anthony, brought up at Como, who became a poet and was secretary of Cardinal Pompeo Colonna (1479-1532). For the same reason that his illustrious descendant was compelled to quit Venice in 1783, Mark Anthony was obliged to leave Rome after writing a satire, but, eventually permitted to return, he died there in 1526 of the plague. A posthumous child, Giacomo Casanova, born of his widow, died in France a colonel in the Spanish Army fighting against Henry IV, leaving a child at Parma, who was married and to whom was born a son, Giacomo. This last married

Anne Roli in 1680 and was the grandfather of the adventurer.

The genealogy Casanova offers of his paternal line, as doubtful as its integral authenticity may be, is interesting in containing some of the seeds of his own career. There are strong reasons for believing, however, that he may not have been the son of Gaetano, but issue of the Venetian patrician Michele Grimani, whose brother, Abbé Alvise Grimani, became Casanova's guardian. In the *Commediante in fortuna* (1755), Abbé Chiari represented Casanova as a bastard, while he himself in *Né amori, né donne*, written in 1782, ascribed his origin to Michele Grimani.

Casanova's putative father Gaetano, while highly esteemed by the patricians of Venice, left no mark of his talents as an actor. With his wife, whom he had induced to go on the stage, it was quite otherwise. Upon the death of Gaetano in 1733, at the early age of thirty-six, she entered the renowned theatrical troupe of Joseph Imer and appears to have become his mistress. Having attracted the attention of the famous playwright and poet Carlo Goldini, the Italian Molière, she is mentioned admirably in his *Memoirs* as a pretty and talented widow who played the young sweethearts in comedies and for whom he especially wrote *La Pupilla*. In 1735 she was engaged by Pedrillo with a troupe to play in Russia, where she remained until early in 1737, when she returned to Venice, entered a company formed by Andrea Bertoldi, and went to Dresden. She played there under the patronage of the Elector of Saxony for almost thirty years, retiring in 1764 with a pension of 400 thalers. She died November 29, 1776, aged sixty-eight.[4]

Casanova exhibited little filial affection for his mother or for his brothers other than Francesco, whose fame so exceeded that of Jacques until well into the nineteenth century that the date of the death of the former, in 1803, was frequently mistaken for that of the latter. Of his other brothers, Giovanni, born in 1730 in Venice, was the most notable and, to some extent, notorious. Having accompanied his mother to Dresden, he bagan the study of painting at an early age and pursued it under Piazetta in Venice in 1746, and subsequently under Guariente. Between 1750 and 1764 he was under the apprenticeship of Raphael Mengs in Rome, where Jacques found him on a visit there in 1760. The only girl in the family to live to maturity, Maria Magdelena Antonia, born in Venice in 1732, was engaged as a dancer for a time in Dresden, where she married Peter August, a court musician, and where she died in 1800.

It is noteworthy of one who was to reveal so exceptional an intelligence, that Jacques Casanova did not develop the faculty of memory or learn to read until eight years of age, nor to write until he was nine. He was to make up for his arrested development; his many published works other than the *Memoirs* attest an extra-ordinary range of reading, which embraced both the classics and all contemporary literature of importance. His favorite authors were Horace and Ariosto, whose works he learned by heart.

At the age of eight, still in the care of his grandmother Marzia while Zanetta pursued her theatrical career, he was taken to a sorcerer in Murano, in the hope of curing his nosebleeds. The performance of her rites made a profound impression, and he was to take advantage of an attachment to the occult throughout his life. A year later, in 1734, his grandmother placed him in a boarding house in Padua, where he was to study under Abbé Gozzi. After six months, half starved on the short rations given him, he obtained, upon appeal to his grandmother, transfer to the Gozzi home. There he remained, first under the tutelage of his preceptor, and then as a student at the University of Padua until awarded the degree of doctor *in utroque jure* at the age of seventeen.

Doubt of Casanova's claim to have been a student at Padua subsisted until 1923, when the late Count Bruno Brunelli discovered a record in the archives of that University of his matriculation on November 28, 1737, and again on November 27, 1738. In both those years, Casanova is recorded as residing with "the priest, Gozzi." President de Brosses has left a description of the University in 1739 that portrays it during the time of Casanova's study there:

> Today when universities have declined it is the case of this one still more than others. The students, so impressive in number and strength, now are only in small numbers, and most of the time the professors lecture to empty benches. However, there are always a large number of talented teachers and among them many persons

of good family, who are not ashamed, as in France, to make their
talents useful to society, nor to pass for knowing something. Of all
the colleges that were at Padua there remains only one named the
Boeuf.[5]

Among Casanova's professors were Giacomo Giacometta, professor
of moral philosophy, Guiseppe Suzzi, of mathematics; and Count
Dandini, of law. Casanova was to have an extended correspondence
in later years with a professor of theoretical medicine, Count
Simeon Stratico, one of the most accomplished scientists of his
day.[6] It was Casanova's keen regret that he had not been permitted
to study medicine, for which he had a strong penchant; instead he
had to devote himself to law to become an ecclesiastical advocate.
In the end he never pursued this calling, but all his life he
exhibited an unusual knowledge of the medical art. He frequently
prescribed for his friends, or took his own treatment out of the
hands of doctors to deal with himself. The details he has left us on
the state of medicine in the eighteenth century are such as to have
provoked long commentaries by physicians of many nations.

From Abbé Gozzi he learned to play the violin. But although he
was to leave a veritable encyclopedia on eighteenth-century music
and musicians, he professed, strangely enough, an indifference to
music all his life.

It was in Padua also that he acquired his first knowledge of
chemistry, a science he was to put to advantageous use.

A distinguished scholar, Dr. Giovanni Moggi, has made a
searching examination of the almost precocious extent of Casanova's grasp of the subject. He has concluded that, for him,
chemistry was a science whose possibilities opened new paths, the
mastery of which permitted the man of intelligence to raise
himself above the ignorant masses. It is apparent from his
*Icosameron* (1788) that chemical knowledge constituted an exact
science destined to serve man by its practical applications, a
conception that does not differ from that which we hold of it
today. His affirmation of the superiority of experimentation over
theoretical considerations revealed how much he was in advance
of his age.[7]

His knowledge was not all dry-as-dust; it was in Dr. Gozzi's

library that he read in Latin his first erotic work, *Aloysea Sigeia*.[8]
It was to lead to his reading of *Thérèse philosophe*, Aretino, and
similar books, for one of his most distinguishing characteristics
was an insatiable curiosity. Yet in his sexual relations he never
exhibited evidence of perversity: sadism, masochism, or fetishism.
And his rare acts of pederasty were provoked less by inclination
than the curiosity that was one of his impelling characteristics.

It was also at Dr. Gozzi's that he had his first love affair, with the
abbé's sister Bettina, four years older than he, *une fine mouche*
who kept him in a continual state of excitement while withholding satisfaction of his passion. This was his introduction to
women's wiles, the study of which became one of the principal
preoccupations of his life. He was to prove adept in not being
imposed upon thereafter, with but rare exceptions. With the Gozzi
family he maintained a lifelong attachment, and he was at Bettina's
bedside when she died in 1777. Dr. Gozzi was one of the subscribers
to Casanova's translation of Homer's *Iliad* in 1775.

Returning to Venice in 1739, he continued his studies. Versifica-
tion was an essential mark of the well-rounded man, and he gave
himself to it, practicing it first in Italian and later in French until
the end of his days.

Destined, willy-nilly, for an ecclesiastical career, the most common to men of talent without fortune, he received the tonsure, and
became an abbé on February 17, 1740, and, eleven months later,
received the four minor orders. His second ecclesiastical act ended
in disaster. Charged with delivering a panegyric at S. Samuele on
March 19, 1741, he dined so well that, once in the pulpit, his
carefully prepared text was forgotten. Fainting, he was borne to
the sacristy and, recovering, made his escape. Three years elapsed
before his clerical career was finally abandoned.

His initial knowledge of society was gained in the home of a
wealthy bachelor, Senator Malipiero, whose palace on the Grand
Canal was but a few steps from his home. There he was a constant
visitor, sharing the meals of this patrician who indoctrinated him
in an epicurean philosophy. Thus Casanova gave early evidence
of an ability to ingratiate himself with the great, which was to
serve him later in good stead. The favor of this *grand seigneur* was
abruptly withdrawn when Malipiero surprised his protegé taking

liberties with young Thérèse Imer, another ward of a different degree in Malipiero's affections. We shall find Thérèse recrossing Casanova's path for another score of years as Thérèse Pompeati and Mme. Cornelys.

According to the *Memoirs,* after his unfortunate clerical experience at S. Samuele, Casanova left at once for Padua to qualify for the university certificate marking completion of "the third part of his studies." As this was customarily awarded in January, March, and June, it was evidently in March 1741 that he received it. His own account indicates that he returned after Easter to Venice. On the contrary, he appears to have proceeded at this time to Corfu, and from there to Constantinople. Corfu was then Venetian territory, and contact between Venice and that island, as well as with Constantinople, was anything but uncommon.

It has been hitherto generally believed that if Casanova did, indeed, visit Turkey, of which some doubt has been expressed, it was in 1745. However, the discovery by Charles Samaran in 1961, of documents having to do with a curious episode of Casanova's life in Corfu, considered in conjunction with other circumstances, offers convincing reasons for placing him in Corfu and Constantinople as early as 1741.

The adventurer himself tells us he had an orderly in Corfu a French soldier, aged twenty-five, whom he calls La Valeur and describes as a hairdresser of peasant origin from Picardy. When La Valeur fell ill of an inflammation of the lungs and his superior, Captain Camporese, was notified by Casanova, the soldier was removed to a hospital. On the fourth day, he called for a priest who gave him extreme unction. Later the priest delivered to Camporese a package from the apparently dying man. Sealed with ducal arms, it contained a baptismal certificate indicating his parents François V and Gabrielle Plessis, together with a sheet of paper in "execrable French" signed "François VI, Charles Philippe, Louis Foucauld, Prince de La Rochefoucauld," requesting that the whole be conveyed to the duke his father through the French ambassador in Venice. According to Casanova, he was the only one in Corfu not taken in by the hoax, having gained knowledge of the ducal family's pedigree while with the Cardinal Acquaviva in Rome, through Abbé Liancourt of the same princely line.

Captain Camporese, however, was so far impressed that he went at once with the news to the commanding general, who ordered that "the prince" should be transferred to proper quarters and given honors befitting his rank, including visits by the principal officers on the island.

A royal almanac, which might have exposed La Valeur's pretensions, was unavailable, while the French consul, described as "a booby of the first water," was of no assistance in determining the degree of credit to be given the pretender. Upon recovery, La Valeur, making an appearance at a gathering of the distinguished company in Corfu, and informed that the Venetian doubted his bona fides, struck him insolently with the back of his hand. To avoid a scene before the ladies present, Casanova left unobtrusively to await La Valeur's departure. When the latter emerged, the Venetian attacked him, while the poltroon made no attempt to defend himself. When the news of the punishment thus administered to "the prince" became known, Casanova was ordered to present himself under arrest to a galley in which local prisoners were confined. Instead of obeying, he proceeded to the wharf where, finding an empty boat, he made for open seas, was taken aboard a sailing vessel, and disembarked at Casopo. There, enlisting twenty-four peasants as bodyguards, he passed his time tranquilly in the midst of pretty seamstresses engaged to provide him with clothes and to beguile his time. His life as a petty sovereign was soon interrupted with the appearance of an officer from Corfu who had been charged to bring him back. His consent was given only upon the assurance that his contentions regarding La Valeur had been in every particular confirmed on the receipt of dispatches from Venice, and that his return would be a triumph rather than imprisonment.

Not the least remarkable feature of this curious episode has been the uncovering of documentary evidence that it has a solid basis of fact. When Charles Samaran examined the dispatches of the French consul at Corfu, he found several letters, the first dated June 30, 1741, to the French authorities in Paris that support in many particulars the account given by Casanova. The correspondence is inclusive of two letters in that "execrable" French imputed to the imposter, addressed by him to a member of the La

Rochefoucauld family, and one from a Captain Felice de Aldeman, presumably Casanova's "Camporese." This last, dated June 16, 1741, recorded the arrival "recently" of a recruit (age twenty-one according to the consul) who, having fallen ill, had been transported to a hospital. Upon claiming to be one of the La Rochefoucauld family he had been removed, with the approval of General Loredan, to the home of Aldeman. The consul's first letter on the subject had only reached Paris on August 26 when the Minister, himself a member of the La Rochefoucauld family, had replied that the soldier was an imposter. In an acknowledgment of November 10 the consul noted that the false prince had "so far deceived everyone as to cut a considerable figure among the notables," adding that he had been reintegrated in the company of a Major Broschi and embarked for Venice.[9]

The details of the official correspondence are in general agreement with those of Casanova except that the name of the captain is given as Aldeman instead of Camporese, and inquiries to determine the bona fides of the alleged prince were made to Paris rather than to Venice. The absence of mention of Casanova in the reports would seem to have no special significance as it is unlikely that if everyone were taken in by the imposter the contradictory opinion of a young man would have been considered worth recording.

But there is still other evidence in support of Casanova's presence in Corfu in 1741. He himself states that he served there as adjutant to "M.D.R.," initials representing Giacomo da Riva. In Casanova's *Confutazione*, published in 1769, there is a significant entry:

Twenty-seven years ago, in my earliest youth, I was the prey to an error and he (da Riva) prevented me from succumbing. He did not despair of me but saw in my faults the weakness of inexperience. He kept me a year with him and conducted me from the Levant to Venice.[10]

The year in question would seem most likely to have been that of 1741-42.

There is equally persuasive testimony corroborative of Casanova's presence in Constantinople in 1741. He mentions having seen Antonio Pocchini at Cerigo, while en route from Corfu to

Constantinople, who was sent there after March 3, 1741, and remained there until 1743. De Ligne, in his "Fragment sur Casanova," cites an extract from the latter's *capitulaires* dated June 2, 1741, relating to Turkey. A memorandum found in Casanova's papers states that "the French ambassador in Constantinople in my time was M. Villeneuve." His mission is known to have ended in May 1741. In the *Memoirs* Casanova mentions having met at Bonneval's in Turkey a former minister for foreign affairs, Ismail Effendi, who appears to have died in 1741.[11]

But how are we to reconcile the anachronisms contained in the account of his presumed initial visit to Corfu and Constantinople, which apparently took place between about April 1741 and March 1742? In the La Valeur episode he has interwoven the development of a love affair he had with a certain Mme. F. She has been identified as Andreana Longo, who, on December 4, 1742, married Sopracomito Vicenzo Foscarini. According to Casanova she left Venice on the day of her marriage for Corfu, in which case she obviously could not have been there when the La Rochefoucauld pretender was exposed, some days before November 10, 1741. The Venetian could only have known her on his later visit in 1745. Nor could Casanova have exercised knowledge of the La Rochefoucauld pedigree in 1741, if he obtained it, as he states, from Abbé Liancourt at Rome, when his first extended sojourn in that city was not until 1744, unless he had gained this information under other circumstances before June 1741.

From the details given of the false prince by Casanova it is difficult to avoid the conclusion that he was most probably in Corfu when the incident occurred. He could have been there as early as April 1741, in time for La Valeur to have entered his service as orderly. As he would seem to have been in Constantinople on June 2, it is more difficult to account for his presence in Corfu when La Valeur put forth his claim, some time before June 15, unless several weeks had elapsed before the French consul saw fit to report it. From the documents found by Charles Samaran, we now know that some five months intervened before the assertion of La Valeur's pedigree and his exposure. The Venetian would thus have had ample time in which to return from Constantinople shortly after the false representations were made, to have been involved in an imbroglio with the pretender, say in October, and to have escaped to Casopo and been brought back to Corfu after La Valeur's true identification some time before November 10. It cannot, of course, be excluded that Casanova found the story so entertaining that he appropriated it for his particular purposes and, *inter alia,* to cast himself in the role of one who saw through a fraud that had deceived the leading officials of Corfu. Such a conclusion, however, does not necessarily follow from his confusion of events occurring in different years (1741-42 and 1745-46), concerned with successive sojourns at Corfu, as this was not uncommon with him on other occasions, which were obviously involuntary errors.

It is evident that Casanova had returned to Venice by April 2, 1742, as he witnessed a notarial act there on that date.

These early days of his youth were marked by an episode destined to have a decisive influence on his relations with women. On a visit to nearby Pasean, in September 1742, he met fourteen-year-old Lucie, whom he was too conscientious to sully. Returning to Pasean the following year, he found she had yielded to the blandishments of a rascal with whom she had run off. Casanova accepted it as a lesson to be less scrupulous in future matters of this nature. Sixteen years later, he found Lucie a prostitute in Amsterdam. As cynical as he had become, the contrast between her former purity and the degradation into which she had fallen horrified him. Of the countless women he eventually met, he could number only two, Lucie and the Corticelli, who suffered through him. We must rely largely on his testimony in this matter, but from such letters as have survived he does seem to have had the faculty of bringing unalloyed happiness to the women whose favors he enjoyed, however fleeting the relationship.

What was the secret of Casanova's extraordinary success with women, and how can it be explained that, as volatile as he was, they consistently cherished his memory? In the eighteenth century, love was a game, not taken with the seriousness later given it by the romantic movement. In his youth he must have been exceptionally handsome; Frederick the Great remarked upon it. Of swarthy complexion, he was of commanding presence, perhaps close to six feet in height; that he was unusually virile, there can be no question. His prodigality endeared him to a sex impressed always by that trait. He was attentive to every want of the women he knew, anticipating their smallest desires, outfitting them sumptuously when they were in need of wardrobes, and never bargaining over his purchases.

> There exists no honest woman with an uncorrupted heart whom a man is not sure of conquering by dint of gratitude. It is one of the surest and shortest means.

On another occasion he observes: "A man who makes known his love by words is a fool; he should only thus reveal himself by his attentiveness." and again, "When a man is given the time, he achieves his aim by attentions, and when he is pressed. . .he makes use of presents and gold."

Nor may we overlook the emphasis Casanova placed on the spiritual side of a relationship. He encouraged self-expression in his women; and because he was unfamiliar with her language, he declined to sleep with one of the most famous courtesans in England, Kitty Fisher, of whom he remarked that the enjoyment of all his senses was essential to him. Explaining his lack of pleasure in an episodic liaison with a German Swiss girl at Zurich in 1760, with whom he had a similar language barrier, he concluded that "without speech, the pleasure of love is diminished by at least two-thirds." In short, he sought in women something more than a source of carnal satisfaction, and this did not fail to be extremely flattering to them.

Shortly after his meeting with Lucie, late in 1742, he himself lost his innocence at the age of seventeen. Two sisters, Nanette and Marton Savorgnan, of a noble Venetian family, bestowed upon him their first favors. They swore a pact of eternal friendship, which endured for three years, longer than most such youthful compacts. The coincidental seduction of two women was often to mark his subsequent career, and induced on one such occasion these reflections:

> In my long and profligate career, in which I have turned the heads of some hundreds of women, I have become familiar with all the

methods of seduction; but my guiding principle has been never to direct my attack against novices or those whose prejudices were likely to prove an obstacle except in the presence of another woman. I soon found that timidity makes a girl averse to being seduced, while in company of another girl she is easily conquered; the weakness of the one brings on the fall of the other. . . .The girl grants some small favor, and immediately makes her friend grant a much greater one to hide her own blushes. . . .Before she has had time to think, pleasure attracts her, curiosity draws her a little farther, and opportunity does the rest.

This is one of the rare instances when Casanova lets us into the secrets of his successful conquests. Of his methods to that end we must generally rely on the details casually introduced in the *Memoirs*. We know that the use of violence was quite repugnant to him. "I am not brutal," he told a woman when refusing her favors offered in financial extremity, but whom he assisted nonetheless. Such an importance did he attach to the free consent of his partner that he refused more than once to profit from the willing submission of women excited by alcohol.

From the manner in which she conducted herself I saw that there was no question but that she would abandon herself. I feared to take advantage of the occasion. It offered too attractive a victory to be due to drunkenness.

On another occasion, when a companion proposed that they intoxicate a girl on whom they both had designs, Casanova protested that "it would be a pity" to employ such a device. A mutuality of inclination, freely expressed, was essential to him for any real satisfaction. This point of view is summed up in his observation: "in the absence of love, what is essential in affairs of this kind is submission," and, on another occasion, when compelled to share a woman's bed against his will, "without love this great act is a sordid thing." Neither facile conquests nor overly prolonged suits had great appeal for him. He cites Martial as his mentor in this respect: *nolo nimis facilem difficilem que nimis* (I care neither for that which is too easy nor what is too difficult). The occasional orgies in which he indulged left him "disgusted" with himself. Let us never forget that he was a man of keen sensibility, and not without delicacy of feeling.

For all his interest in women, he already had another passion almost equally as strong: that of learning. He remained only two weeks in St. Cyprien Seminary, where he was placed in March 1743, but this was due more to the poor understanding of his teachers than to an indifference to study. On his own, he was to pursue his education ceaselessly for the rest of his life.

On March 18, 1743, he suffered the loss of his beloved grandmother and, for reasons he does not make altogether clear, was incarcerated late that month in Fort Saint André, where he remained until the last days of July. It was during his stay on this island that he conceived the project of wreaking vengeance on a Venetian enemy, Razzetta, who had sought to dispossess him of his belongings, in an imbroglio that might have occasioned Casanova's imprisonment. He observed that he could elude all surveillance, slip into Venice, and return by night, if he could find a boatman who might be bribed to run the risk. Having made his arrangements, he ventured into a boat by climbing down the mast from his window, went into Venice, and there ascertained from observation by what street and at what hour Razzetta returned home in the evening. With this information, he returned to the Fort and reentered his room unobserved.

Having fixed on an evening with the boatman for the return expedition, Casanova stumbled while walking with a friend in the Fort, and complained of having sprained his ankle. He was transported to his room, a doctor was summoned, and he was ordered to keep to his bed. To have someone to look after him and at the same time to corroborate the alibi he was taking pains to establish, he insisted that his servant sleep in his room. Dismissing the doctor and the chaplain of the Fort who had rooms above his own and who had visited him in their solicitude for his welfare, he plied his servant with brandy, and, after seeing him fast asleep, he entered the boat awaiting him. In Venice he purchased a stout stick and, upon Razzetta's appearance, he assailed him with blows on his head and arms, administered with such force that Razzetta fell into a canal. At the same instant, a man with a lantern emerged from a house. To avoid recognition, Casanova struck the man's arm with such force that he was compelled to drop the light. Discarding his stick, Casanova sped off to rejoin his boat. The clock was striking midnight as he reentered the Fort. Undressing in a flash and hastening to bed, he began shouting in pain, calling upon his servant to summon the doctor to relieve a colic that he pretended had overcome him. When he had been administered to, and professed to have found relief, he was left to resume his rest.

The next morning, the major of the Fort, having been to Venice, returned with the news. The talk of the town was the attack on Razzetta at midnight the previous evening, after which he and a witness, the lantern bearer, had complained that Casanova was the culprit. The major added that he had been able to assure the authorities that Casanova had been confined to bed with a sprained ankle, and that precisely at midnight he had suffered a violent colic, the truth of which numerous persons at the Fort could testify. An official was sent to investigate, and after Casanova's alibi had been established by the doctor, the chaplain and the servant, as well as by others, Razzetta suffered the chagrin at the recognition of Casanova's innocence, while compelled himself to pay the costs of the inquiry.

Casanova at this time was but eighteen years of age. The incident demonstrates both that he could move mountains to satisfy his sense of vengeance once aroused, and, more important, that he was capable of exceptional imagination in thought, and of marked decisiveness in action.

Although Casanova's mother, having left him in care of his grandmother, exhibited apparently little maternal affection for her offspring, she offered evidence of her concern for him at this time. Probably disturbed about finding a permanent post for her son, she addressed herself to Bernardin de Bernardis, a monk in Warsaw seeking appointment as bishop in his native land of Calabria. Bernardis seems to have promised to accept Casanova into his service if Zanetta were able to persuade the Queen of Poland to induce her daughter, the Queen of Naples, to bring about the appointment. Nominated by the Pope on May 6, 1743, through Zanetta's intervention with her influential friends, Bernardis arrived in Venice early in August, where he received

Casanova a few days after the latter's release at the end of July from Fort Saint André.

Setting out for his new bishopric at Martirano, Bernardis promised to await Casanova in Rome. The latter left some weeks later, about October 18, 1743, accompanying Da Lezze, Venetian ambassador at Rome, as far as Ancona. His accumulation of papers, together with his forbidden books, were left in the care of Mme. Manzoni, one of his most faithful friends. It is the first reference among many in the *Memoirs* to the notes he had begun intermittantly to make. With the passing years, he became more methodical in preserving memoranda of his life, termed by him his *capitulaires*. This is evident both from the occasional reference to these, as well as from the more accurate chronology presented as the years advance.

Two misfortunes that were to be frequently his fate befell him at Chioggia: Fleeced by gamblers, he had to pawn his effects, while suffering a renewal of a gonorrhea contracted earlier that year. At Ancona he was quarantined for twenty-eight days in a pest house, owing, as he states, to the prevalence of plague at Messina and the fact that ships from there had touched at Venice. Contemporary accounts confirm the presence of plague at Messina at this time. In the course of his sojourn at Ancona, Casanova mentions that he observed a Turkish merchant celebrating "little Bairam," the Moslem religious feast of three days after the fast of Ramadan. The detail enables us to establish the approximate period of his stay at Ancona, from the end of October to about November 24, 1743, as "little Bairam" fell that year on November 18. Casanova was in general so careless of his chronology that the dates that can be fixed in his narrative with exactitude are as valuable to us as astronomical sightings to a mariner.

During his sojourn in the pest house he carried on an inconclusive intrigue with a beautiful Greek slave belonging to the Turkish merchant and made the acquaintance of an unprincipled monk, Steffano, who conducted him to Rome on foot, providing for the two of them with the alms he contrived to collect with Casanova's reluctant assistance. The latter was frequently appalled by the monk's unchristian behavior, and especially by his theft of a bag of truffles in Soma, a region still reputed for this delicacy, from an attractive young woman who had offered them the free hospitality of her inn. Casanova was so indignant when he discovered the theft after their departure that he set upon the monk, seized his stick, and belabored him unmercifully. Abandoning him to his own devices, Casanova stopped at the next town, and from there sent back the truffles with a note of excuse. While we must rely upon his own testimony for this, there is no suggestion anywhere in the *Memoirs* that he was guilty of theft, or that he ever condoned stealing. The Greek slave he had met at Ancona had offered to appropriate a box of diamonds belonging to her master and, from the sale, to escape with Casanova and live a life of ease.

> I was enamored of this creature, her proposal disquieted me, but the next day on awaking I hesitated no longer. She came with the box in the evening, and, when I told her I could not bring myself to become an accomplice of the theft, she said, while crying, that I did not love her as she loved me, but that I was a true Christian.

If he were guilty of many questionable practices in his life, he did draw the line at barefaced misappropriation.

Arriving in Rome, Casanova found, to his extreme discomfiture, that the bishop had already departed for his diocese at Martirano, leaving no word for him. Taking stock of his reduced resources, he discovered only a few pennies. And now his innate capacity for extricating himself from any difficulty asserted itself. He encountered a Greek merchant with a stock of wines and minerals, including mercury. Casanova recalled his lessons in chemistry and disclosed to his chance acquaintance the formula for augmenting that liquid with lead and bismuth, proceeding on his way well supplied with funds. When we analyze Casanova's procedure, his account of it shows that he knew precisely the role of each ingredient employed in the preparation of the amalgam. Thus the quantity of lead that Casanova added was practically the maximum compatible with the necessity of not altering exaggeratedly the density of the amalgam. "Thus, at eighteen years of age, Casanova possessed a serious and not negligible theoretic and practical acquaintanceship with technical chemistry."[12] Casanova's fertile imagination, united with an unusual ability to adapt himself to the most unfavorable circumstances, were to be evidenced in the years ahead.

Of this deal with the merchant he observed:

> Cheating is wrong, but honest deceit is nothing other than prudence of character. It is a virtue. It resembles, it is true, dishonesty, but one must pass by there. Whoever does not resort to it is a fool.

Nothing, of course, could be more casuistical and, at the same time, nothing more honest by way of confession. These eternal paradoxes in him—or shall we say rather in all humans?—are illuminative of his curiously amoral character.

At Martirano, remarking the absence of good books, men of letters, and pretty women, he asked for the bishop's benediction and permission to leave. He set out to return to Rome by way of Naples with no notion of what he would do. It was enough for him to follow his demon and trust to Providence in whose guidance he placed implicit confidence. Even in his illicit love-making he acknowledged the inscrutable ways of God, not in a spirit of cynicism, but with complete sincerity. There is no trace of impiety in his reflection that all is God's will. It is inconceivable to him that what happens can be contrary to the dictates of Providence.

Besides funds that Bernardis had provided for him, he had what to him was of perhaps even greater importance, letters of recommendation to two eminent Neopolitans. Casanova was always particular, in accordance with the custom prevailing in the eighteenth century when human relations were still highly formalized, about obtaining such letters. He sought them from people of prominence to those with whom he was already acquainted in order to give him added prestige. With the backing thereby given him in Naples, he made such influential acquaintances as the Marquis de Galiani, brother of the famous abbé, and Lelio Caraffa, Duke of Matalone, one of the leading families of Naples, who, in turn, gave him letters of introduction to Cardinal Acquaviva, one of the great personages of Rome, into whose service he was to enter for a time. It was perhaps for the excellent relations he formed at Naples that this city became one of his favorites.

# CHAPTER 2

# Ancona, Rome, Corfu, and Constantinople

I t has been remarked that the chronology of Casanova's life for the years 1742-45 is of great obscurity. That he was at Martirano in December 1743 is fairly certain. Although Bernardis was not consecrated bishop there until December 22, 1743, too much importance need not be attached to this date because he could have assumed his funcions before consecration. As Casanova did not leave Ancona for Rome until late in November 1743, he could not have reached Martirano before the following month. Happily, we have at least a few precise dates to guide us through what is at best a labyrinth: He is in Rimini in February 1744, is again in Venice on April 26, and is in Marino between Naples and Rome on May 31. There are his several references to the months of October, November (1744), and January (1745) in Rome, followed by his celebration of Easter Friday, April 16, 1745, in Corfu. According to his own account, he passed through Martirano, Naples, and Marino in that order en route to Rome, remained there for some months, proceeding thence to Ancona, Rimini, Bologna, and Venice, and from there to Corfu. It is manifest, however, from the dates cited, that he has confounded the processus of events, as these could not possibly have occurred in the order he gives. It is obvious that he has fallen into the same chronological confusion here as on a number of other occasions when dealing with successive visits to the same localities. These particular years, 1743-45, have been the despair of many commentators; it is all the more important that we thread our way out of so tangled a maze.

A first and important deduction: To have sojourned many months in Rome after leaving Martirano at the end of 1743 and to have spent some weeks in the vicinity of Ancona and Rimini before February 18, 1744, Casanova must have proceeded, after a brief stay in Naples, directly to Ancona before taking up residence in the papal capital.

Ancona was marked by his meeting of Bellino (to whom he later gave the name Thérèse), which was to be memorable to him for many years. He encountered her in a theatrical troupe, where she was representing herself as a male singer in order to be permitted to appear on the stage. Until the end of the eighteenth century, women were forbidden to exercise their theatrical talents in the Papal States. As a result, many singers in Italy were castrates. Dr. Burney sought in vain, when visiting that country in 1770, to obtain precise information about so abhorrent a practice. All that he could learn was that death was the penalty imposed on those performing the operation and that excommunication was incurred by those concerned with it. Yet it was widely practiced, as we know, both from him as well as from Casanova. According to Lalande, "all castrates who sing in Italy are fashioned at Naples, as that is the locality where this operation is most skillfully made."[1]

For all Bellino's persistence in claiming to be a boy, Casanova, with his already extensive knowledge of female anatomy, was not deceived. When closer examination proved his surmise of her true sex correct, he became so enamored of her charms that he offered to marry her. He was to offer marriage to many women, a tie from which he was invariably spared at the decisive moment.

> I have loved women even to madness, but I have always loved liberty more; and, whenever I have been in danger of losing it, I have only been spared by chance.

Hugo von Hofmannsthal has dramatized in *Der Abenteurer und die Sängerin* one episode in Thérèse's life when Casanova met her again in Florence in 1760, while Balzac is believed to have been inspired by her story to write *Sarrasine*.

If Thérèse has captured the imaginations of two such world-famous writers as Hofmannsthal and Balzac, she has likewise incited students of the *Memoirs* to endeavor to pierce the veil of mystery that Casanova cast about her. She possesses the distinction of being perhaps the only actress in the *Memoirs* to whom Casanova gave a fictitious name. Although he was scrupulous in protecting the identities of those women of position with whom he had affairs by attributing false names to them, he had no similar compunction generally about women of the stage; they themselves rarely, if ever, were concerned about the concealment of their peccadillos.

The Italian philosopher Benedetto Croce and others who have fallen under Casanova's spell have vainly sought to identify Thérèse Lanti. Her true name has finally been brought to light with the publication of the integral text of *Histoire de ma vie*. The annotators, Mrs. and Dr. Arthur Hübscher, succeeded in distinguishing the stricken out letters "Cal. . ." and "Ca. . . ." in two separate references to Thérèse, as well as the full name, Angiola Calori, in "a long, canceled but clearly legible passage" when Casanova wrote of her in Prague in 1766. It is through him alone that we have many details of the career of one of the most successful Italian sopranos of the eighteenth century. The earliest biographical mention of her (*Elenco dei signori virtuosi de canto e di danze*, Milan, 1775, p.8) states that she was born in 1732 at Valenza Pò (Alessandria), a date accepted both by Grove (Dictionary of Music and Musicians) and by Fétis (*Dictionnaire des musiciens*) both of whom, however, give Milan as her birthplace. Casanova would have us believe she was born in Bologna about 1728, perhaps the better to conceal her identity. Grove notes that nothing is known of her career before her appearance in Cocchi's *Zenobia* in London on January 10, 1758, where she was singing as late as April 28, 1761. According to Grove, she had a soprano voice of great range, a profound knowledge of music, and extraordinary rapidity of execution.

Grove's incomplete account of her career is considerably supplemented by Casanova. We learn that she was trained by the well-known singer Felice Salimbeni (1712-51), and that from Ancona and Rimini she went in 1744 to fill an engagement in Naples. Croce was unable to find any singer in Naples during that period answering her description. It is not improbable that Casanova may have deliberately misled us as to her engagements to protect her identity. Thus he claims to have met her unexpectedly in Florence in December 1760, when Grove shows her singing in London on November 22 of that year, and on January 6, 1761. It is possible that the meeting Casanova depicts in Florence in 1760 actually took place in 1762 in Turin or nearby Alessandria. A letter has survived, dated October 20, 1762, addressed to him at Alessandria from Count Trana at Turin, wishing him "much pleasure with the beautiful Calori," presumably singing in Piedmont at this time.[2] By reason of both time and place it is easier to credit his meeting with her again in February 1763 in Milan. There was another encounter in London later that year when he reported her singing at the Haymarket Theater and married to Xavier Constantini. On this occasion he gives her name as Angiola Calori with no reference to her as Thérèse or any previous meeting. From his reserved impersonal account it appears that since Milan they had had serious differences. They met again at Prague in 1766 where Angiola is known to have sung from that year until 1768. From 1770 to 1774, she was singing in Dresden with great success, where Dr. Burney heard her; he wrote:

> The best singer in this placid pastoral was Signora Calori, who, twelve or fourteen years ago, when in England, wanted only spirit to make her an excellent performer: for there her voice, her shake [trill], and execution were good; her person elegant, and features regular.[3]

Returning thereafter to Italy she continued to sing in operas until 1783 and died about 1790, according to Grove.

Once again Casanova has added to our knowledge of music and musicians of the eighteenth century, of the importance of which many critics have testified, including notably Cucuel, Nettl, Dent, and others.

In Pesaro, to which Casanova had proceeded from Ancona with Thérèse, they were asked for their passports by an officer of the Spanish army then in a protracted struggle with Austrian forces for the possession of this part of Italy. Thérèse produced her passport, but Casanova discovered to his chagrin that he had lost his own. Brought before General Gages, whose troops were in occupancy of Pesaro, he was ordered held until he could obtain another passport from Rome. He observes:

A young man who has once lost his purse, and another time his passport, will not again lose either. These two misfortunes did not happen to me again. They would have happened if I had not feared that they would do so. A heedless person has never fear.

Thérèse was allowed to continue to Rimini where she had a theatrical engagement. This fixes the date as some time before February 18, 1744, whe the season in Rimini closed until the autumn of 1745.[4] While awaiting his passport, Casanova was enticed into a game of faro by a Neopolitan adventurer, Giuseppe d'Afflisio, known also as Don Bepe di Cadetto, Mercati, or Marrati. Casanova met him again in 1750 at Lyons, and in 1753 in Vienna. D'Afflisio's career reflects the adventurous and equivocal character of large segments of European society before the French Revolution. In 1754 he purchased the rank of captain-lieutenant in an Austrian regiment. In 1761 Casanova found him in Munich, aide-de-camp of Duke Frederick des Deux Ponts. In 1768 he was named director of Viennese theaters. A year and a half later, leaving a deficit of 200,000 florins, he disappeared. Their paths crossed again in Bologna in 1772. There D'Afflisio was arrested as a counterfeiter in 1778, and again the following year for false bills of exchange. At Leghorn, he was condemned to the galleys, where he died in 1787. Casanova's account of his end is confirmed by Michael Kelly who, in the early 1780s visited Pisa where "the well-known" Afflisio, whose name he transcribed as "Giuseppe Afrissa," was pointed out to him, "in the dress of a galley slave sweeping the baths." He colorful history was recounted to and recorded by Kelly.[5] In addition to those friends who were among the most distinguished Europeans of his day, Casanova had equally wide acquaintance with some of the greatest rascals.

At the end of nine or ten days, while awaiting his passport, Casanova was taking an early morning walk when he saw an officer stop and leave his horse by the road. When the officer had disappeared from sight, Casanova approached and "without any end in view" he mounted the animal, the first time he had ever been on horseback. When he touched the steed with his cane or his heels, it dashed off, and passed the last post of the Spanish Army, which was then separated from the opposing Austrian troops by only a brief distance. He was challenged to stop and was fired on when unable to do so, but was not hit. At the first Austrian post he was held up and was able to dismount. After explaining his plight to Prince Lobkowitz, the commander, he was given an officer to escort him to a road outside Rimini leading to Cesena. On entering a café on the outskirts, he recognized Thérèse's pretended brother, who informed him of where she might be found in Rimini. Before he could devise a means of reentering the town without being detected, his difficulty was resolved by the sight of a file of mules headed in the direction of the city. Having hastily turned his coat inside out, he placed his hand on the neck of one of the mules, passed undisturbed by the Austrian guard, found Thérèse, informed her that he would return as soon as he had his passport, slipped out of the town by the same means with which he had reentered it, made his way to Bologna, and from there wrote to Pesaro that his passport be forwarded when received.

In Bologna, the fancy took him to abandon the ecclesiastical garb he had previously worn as an abbé and to attire himself as an officer. In the eighteenth century there was nothing unusual about the assumption of a military uniform by a civilian. It is probable that Casanova did so at this time to permit his readier passage through military lines to Venice, and that, once there, he wore civilian clothes until his departure for Corfu a year later.

While awaiting his passport in Bologna he received word from Thérèse that she had been offered an excellent contract to sing at the famous San Carlo theater in Naples. Before accepting it, she sought to learn his wishes, adding that they could go together to Naples, or she would join him where he wished. Casanova was never an irresolute character, but this occasion brought the following response from him:

This letter having compelled me to think, I ordered the messenger to return the next day. I found myself in the greatest uncertainty. It was the first time in my life that I found myself powerless to reach a decision.

He is speaking from the heart, not only here, but where he analyzes his irresolution:

Two motives of equal weight in the balance prevented me from inclining to one or the other. I could not advise Thérèse to reject such good fortune, nor to allow her to go to Naples without me, nor decide to go to Naples with her. The very thought of placing an obstacle in the way of Thérèse's success made me shudder, and what prevented me from going to Naples with her was my *amour-propre*, even stronger than the fire that enamoured me of her. How could I decide to return to Naples seven or eight months after I had left, appearing there without any other status than that of a dastard who lived at the expense of his wife or his mistress? . . . The reflection that, in the most promising moment of my youth, I was going to renounce all hope of that great fortune for which I appeared to have been born, gave to the balance such a violent blow that my reason enforced silence on my heart.

Whatever grave faults of character Casanova may have been guilty of in his life, he cannot be accused of exploiting the women to whom he became sentimentally attached. Here, as in many other instances, we have evidence of that genuine concern he consistently displayed for the individual personalities of his loves and for their own welfare. Egoist he was, certainly, but it was an egoism tempered by an indisputable regard for those women with whom fate joined him. In this he was the antithesis of the fictitious Don Juan for whom the seduction of women was a game in which love did not enter and with whom his name is often associated by uncritical writers who, in doing so, give the most striking possible evidence of their complete misconception of Casanova's character.

Casanova states that to gain time he wrote Thérèse to go to Naples, promising to join her there in July and that, on reaching Venice, she informed him that she had proceeded there in company of a duke who had made arrangements for her theatrical engagement. This may be a confusion of memory, as there is also reference to her intention to leave Rimini only at the beginning of May.

There are good grounds for placing Casanova's return to Venice shortly before February 26, 1744. At the entrance to Revere, he informed a guard who questioned him that he was on his way to Venice to speak to the Duke of Modena, who is known to have gone there on a mission early in 1744 and to have left on February 26.

One of Casanova's first visits on returning to his native city was to Nanette and Marton, the two sisters who had initiated him in 1742 as their joint lover. He states that they welcomed him joyfully after an absence of nine months; in fact, it had been but little more than four. The lapse of time mentioned is revealing because he has evidently confused this shorter absence with a later one of nine months' duration. He has likewise evidently confused, as was his custom, certain encounters in Venice in the early spring of 1745 with those of 1744. Aside from the renewal of intimacy with the two sisters, all that can be said with certainty is that he was still in Venice on April 26, 1744, when he witnessed a contract in the office of the procurator, Marco Leze, of S. Samuele Parish, where he may have been temporarily employed as he was in 1746.

From Venice Casanova must have returned to Naples in May 1744 if the events he records are to fall into place. He does not speak of two separate visits to Naples in the same year; he has presumably confounded them as in the case of his two sojourns in Corfu and Constantinople. Seeking some stable situation, he may have returned to renew the promising acquaintances made in Naples a few months previous, or perhaps on the strength of promises then extended of an introduction to the powerful Cardinal Acquaviva at Rome. It is highly unlikely that he went to Naples with Thérèse or that he would have met her there. In any case, it seems incontestable that he did return, for one of the most memorable incidents in his narrative took place while he was en route from Naples to Rome. It concerned the breaking of a bed in which two sisters slept, at an inn in Marino. During the night of May 31, 1744, a Neopolitan lawyer, with whom Casanova had left

Naples by coach for Rome, was awakened by a street combat between Austrian and Spanish forces, and went out to inquire about the disorder. After the custom of the time, Casanova occupied a bed with the lawyer, whose wife and sister shared another bed in the same room. He was quick to take advantage of the husband's absence, and when Casanova slipped into bed beside the wife, she offered no resistance. Nor did the flimsy couch. When it collapsed under the weight of the bold lover, the wife, and her sister, a sudden end was put to his enterprise on this occasion.

Casanova gives the name of Giacomo Castelli to the husband, that of Lucrezia to the wife, and Angelica to the sister. During the ensuing twenty-six years, "Lucrezia" was to occupy, at intervals, an important place in his affections. Their love manifested itself in a manner that affords a curious commentary on the lightness of the morals of those times. On another occasion, "Lucrezia" readily admitted Casanova to the bed she was sharing with her sister. Only nineteen years of age, and still of relative innocence, he was keenly embarrassed the next morning when she thrust him into the arms of "Angelica." His reluctance to make love to the sister was only overcome when he was satisfied that his compliance would afford gratification rather than chagrin to "Lucrezia" who, on the point of returning to Naples, was desirous of passing him on to "Angelica" to serve the happiness of both.

"Lucrezia's" behavior in this instance and the lightness with which she treated Casanova's attachment become considerably more understandable in view of the fact that, far from being about his own age, as he represented her, she was actually ten years older. Seventeen years later, when he encountered her with a daughter, Leonilda, fruit of their love in 1744, the mother found nothing untoward in going to bed with the child and Casanova. On this occasion, his love for Leonilda did not exceed the bounds of paternal affection. It was quite a different story, however, ten years later. This was not a unique case of incest for him; Irene Rinaldi, or Balzale, another mistress, may have also been his daughter, and he avows quite frankly that he had carnal knowledge of a niece at Rome in 1771. The relative frequency of incest, and the facility with which men and women went to bed together in the eighteenth century, are strongly suggestive of the inference that, in that era, differing so radically in many ways from our own, sexual intercourse had hardly greater significance than the act of eating or drinking; it was a bodily function to which scant importance was attached. In London in 1763, Casanova was offered by a woman of position a seat in her coach to return to London from Ranelagh. With Casanova the sequel is easily imagined. Some days later, when they met at a social gathering, he was quite taken aback when he received no sign of recognition from her. When he pressed her for an explanation, she replied coldly: "I recall you perfectly, but a folly does not carry with it a claim to acquaintanceship."

Such distinguished Italian savants as Benedetto Croce, Fausto Nicolini, and A. Zottoli, sought unremittingly but in vain to establish the identity of Giacomo Castelli, his wife, and family. Their search was made the more difficult by their acceptance of the names offered by Casanova as genuine. In 1959, after long study, I became convinced that these and many other names in the *Memoirs* were fictitious. In the case of "Lucrezia" and "Angelica," Casanova himself left one precious clue when stating that the two sisters were daughters of "Cecilia Monti," residing in the Minerva quarter of Rome. There was another in his statement that "Angelica" was married in January 1745 in Rome, to "Don Francesco." An examination was made of the parish records of S. Maria sopra Minerva. Happily for the search, but one marriage was celebrated in the month indicated, that on January 17, 1745, between a Lucrezia d'Antoni, born in 1725, and a Filippo Tomasi. The date fitted perfectly, and the name of the bride was highly suggestive. But there was more: This Lucrezia (presumably "Angelica" of the *Memoirs*) named her first-born child Angelica. Were we on the right track? It seemed increasingly so as we pursued the search, particularly when records revealed that the mother of the two sisters bore the given name of Cecilia, ascribed to her by Casanova. It is true her family name was d'Antoni and not Monti, and that she was fifty-two years in 1744 and the wife of a painter, being neither young nor a widow as Casanova had represented her. But those particular details might well have been introduced to baffle and deceive the overly curious.

If Casanova's "Angelica" bore, in fact, the name of Lucrezia,

there remained the task of finding record of her sister, said to have
been married before 1742, as well as of their young brother, an
abbé, described by Casanova as fifteen in 1744. The young brother
was the first thereafter to be brought to light, Giuseppe, born in
1729, the precise age attributed him. The name of the sister, Anna
Maria, born in 1715, as well as record of her marriage in 1734 to
one Alessio Vallati, was at length uncovered after long and patient
research. Anna Maria d'Antoni (evidently the Lucrezia of the
*Memoirs*), who perhaps bore the full name of Anna Maria Angelica, was long since a bride in 1742. Critics have remarked that
Casanova persistently rejuvenated his heroines. May it not rather
be that, at least in some instances, it was they who out of feminine
coquetry misrepresented their ages? Instead of detracting from the
truth of the narrative, such discrepancies, as in this case, reinforce
it.

The importance of these identifications is that characters in the
*Memoirs*, considered by some incorrigible scoffers as fictitious,
prove to be, here and elsewhere, persons of flesh and blood. From
these and other recent identifications it may now be safely affirmed
that, contrary to the skepticism voiced by Gugitz, Curiel, and one
or two other scholars, probably *not one figure in the Memoirs is
the product of Casanova's imagination.*

The procedure he followed to conceal the identity of the "Monti"
family is illustrative both of a common practice on his part and
his scrupulous care to protect the women of any social position
with whom he had affairs. That he was deeply concerned with this
problem, while engaged in the composition of *Histoire de ma vie*,
is clearly indicated in a passage from a letter of January 10, 1791,
to J.F. Opiz:

> What afflicts me is the duty I am under to conceal the names as I
> have no right to publish the affairs of others.

He was working at this time on a first draft. Beginning with the
events he narrates from the year 1744, he veiled his characters when
this became necessary by reason of the delicate situations in which
they were involved; as of that year and thereafter, when the names
of these are given in full, the surname is invariably fictitious and

the given name either replaced or, where sisters are involved (those of the families d'Antoni, Muralt, and Schwicheldt), interchanged.

In the case of the "Monti" family, he altered the surname from d'Antoni and switched the given names of the sisters, leaving the mother's name of Cecilia unchanged. "Giacomo Castelli," name of the husband of one sister, and "Don Francesco," fiancé of the other, were alike fictitious. Another practice Casanova occasionally employed was the use of initials. When not obviously arbitrary, as Mme. X or Mme. Z, they may be accepted as genuine. Two examples are C.C. and M.M. of the Murano convent. It is evident that Casanova had every confidence when making use of these initials that they would suffice to protect the identities of the women whose favors he enjoyed; he could not have anticipated the research that would one day be undertaken by scholars to establish fact.[6]

In Rome, Casanova might have made his fortune in the Spanish secretariat of Cardinal Acquaviva, then more renowned than Casanova for affairs of the heart, had he not become involuntarily involved in the romantic adventure of an acquaintance. Bent on learning French, essential to his career, he engaged a Roman lawyer, Delacqua, as his teacher. Delacqua's daughter Barbara occasionally acted as substitute. When Barbara was on the point of being seized by the authorities to prevent her abduction by an unidentified lover, Casanova, yielding to a generous impulse, hid her in the cardinal's palace, outside the jurisdiction of the Roman police.[7] He was to befriend disinterestedly more than one young woman in distress. While he was candid in admitting that their good looks were the initial title to his sympathy, his sense of real chivalry cannot well be disputed.

The cardinal, while recognizing that Casanova's conduct, however indiscreet, had been wholly honorable, risked being compromised by an inference that he had connived at Casanova's action. To ease the pain of his dismissal, the cardinal offered him letters of recommendation assuring him employment in any country he might choose. On the spur of the moment he named Constantinople. A letter was thereupon given him to Bonneval Pasha, former French nobleman, who, after a distinguished military career under Louis XV, had become an apostate in disillusionment over his treatment, and had entered the Turkish service.

It has always appeared strange that Casanova should have chosen, seemingly arbitrarily, Constantinople. It becomes less so if he had previously visited that city, in 1741, and was already acquainted with Bonneval. We have noted earlier that it was far from unusual for letters of introduction to be borne to persons already known. A greater incongruity in Casanova's recital, one indeed almost unbelievable, is the intimation that a prince of the Church of Rome should have been in contact with a heretic and more particularly one who had abjured the Christian faith. As to this, we are not dependent upon Casanova's sole testimony. In a letter to his brother, Bonneval wrote:

> But what will appear to you even more surprising is that various cardinals, archbishops, and bishops, my former friends, give me, when they have occasion, very sincere evidence of the continuance of their esteem and of their friendship.[8]

Casanova's punishment for the offense committed seems unduly severe. The Prince de Ligne, in a summary of the *Memoirs*, issued before their publication, based on a reading of the manuscript and perhaps conversations with Casanova, gives another version: "He takes away a mistress of the nephew of the Pope and, about to be assassinated, makes his escape."[9] Whatever the facts, he appears to have left Rome for Venice not later than the end of January or early February 1745, and arrived there in the first half of that month.

It was probably at this time, if not in 1741, that he purchased the rank of ensign in a regiment stationed in Corfu, with leave to proceed thence to Constantinople. It seems much more probable for him to have made his way from Rome to Constantinople without undue delay, rather than to have spent, according to his own account, aimless weeks at Ancona and Rimini. He himself states that he left for Corfu in May, but as he describes the celebration of Easter week there (in 1745 Easter Friday fell on April 16), it is probable that his departure from Venice was several weeks before that date. It must have been before March 2, 1745. On his return from Corfu in 1746 he found his old love, Nanette, a bride whose marriage appears to have taken place on that date.

On board the vessel bound for Corfu he barely escaped with his life from a situation that points up two of his distinguishing characteristics: his bravado and, at the same time, calm resolution in face of the greatest peril. Outraged by the invocations of a priest, in the midst of a tempest that had cast despair in the hearts of the sailors, the intrepid Venetian, feeling that the priest's task should have been more properly that of encouragement, took over:

> Climbing myself on the ropes I incited the sailors to pursue their work and to brave the danger, telling them there were no devils and that the priest, proclaiming them, was mad.

When the storm continued unabated for two days, the priest, alleging that Casanova was an atheist, persuaded the crew that unless he were got rid of, they were lost. He was promptly seized and thrown overboard, but his life was spared when his clothes were caught on the arm of an anchor. When Casanova was rescued, the priest was not appeased until the Venetian handed over, for burning, a parchment bought before embarking, which the religious fanatic claimed was a diabolical charm. According to Casanova, its only pretended virtue was to make women fall in love with its possessor. As to this he observed:

> I hope the reader will believe that I put no faith in any philtres and that I had only bought the parchment for a half écu as a joke. There are everywhere in Italy, and in both ancient and modern Greece, Greeks, Jews, and astrologers who sell to the credulous documents whose virtues are prodigious.

For all his skepticism of the efficacy of such charms, he was not one who would fail to take advantage of the faith of others in them.

Casanova arrived in Corfu some time in March, where he participated in the Eastern ceremonies of April 16 and 19, 1745. He tells us that he sailed from Corfu to Constantinople on the *Europe* with Francesco Venier, Venetian ambassador to Turkey, who is known to have arrived in Corfu in the middle of June and to have set sail for Turkey on July 1, 1745. Casanova records Annibal Gambara and Carlo Zenobio as being in the ambassador's suite. These names have been confirmed in contemporary official accounts.

En route, according to Casanova, a stop was made at Cerigo, a call unreported in Venier's records. It has been noted that this visit must have been made by Casanova in 1741. Though his chronology may be incorrect, the circumstances are not in dispute. On the island, Casanova was accosted by a prisoner, condemned with his companions, for living on the charms of women. He was Antonio Pocchini, a gentleman of Padua, one of many adventurers who were to cross Casanova's path repeatedly in subsequent years. His imprisonment did nothing to correct his ways. Casanova encountered him again in Amsterdam in 1760, pimping for two women represented as his nieces, and again that same year in Stuttgart, where Pocchini was instrumental in fleecing him, in a house of ill fame, of promissory notes for 4,000 gold louis. In 1763 they met in London, where Casanova roundly trounced him in Hyde Park; in Vienna in 1767, Casanova found him exploiting the charms of his own daughter. Pocchini was responsible for Casanova's expulsion from that city. They met again in Venice in 1780 and, for the last time, at Aix-la-Chapelle in 1783, date of Pocchini's death according to the memorialist.[10]

Many like adventurers stalk Casanova's pages, including d'Afflisio, Count Medin, Viscount Talvis de la Perrine, Antonio Croce, Baron Wiedau, Charles Iwanoff, Giacomo Passano, Ange Goudar, and the Zannovich brothers, Stefano and Premislas, to name a few of the many who make their appearance on the vast panorama of Casanova's portrait gallery. Most of them were gamesters living by their wits, and some as Medin and Goudar, also by their pens. They include also Count de Saint-Germain and Cagliostro, who achieved a European reputation exceeding in their time that of Casanova; and those who had arisen above their origins such as Mme. de Pompadour, Count Du Barry, and Mme. Du Barry. They had, whatever their rank, one characteristic in common: They were one and all symptomatic of a society in a profound state if dissolution, which was to reach its climax in the French Revolution. It is precisely in some of the lesser figures of the *Memoirs* that the character of that society, hastening headlong to its ruin, is most intimately revealed.

Casanova's stay at Constantinople was to be of some three months: from the middle of July to October 12. No portion of the *Memoirs* has been more disputed than this. More recent examination warrants the conclusion that he visited Turkey not only once but on two occasions. To anyone acquainted with the Near East, the casual details he lets drop of daily life give his account persuasive verisimilitude. He tells us he was warned upon his arrival never to venture forth without being accompanied by a janissary. Until our own day, the presence of a janissary or dragoman was essential to a Westerner walking abroad in the Near East. There is reference to the fondness of the Turks for pipe smoking, that is to say, the narghile or hubble-bubble, and even to the brand of tobacco current among smokers, *zapandi*, a leaf tobacco still used in Iraq under the name of *zamanda*. But what has tended most to confirm Casanova's telescoped recital of his two Turkish visits is his description of Bonneval Pasha, which is completely supported by recently discovered documents unavailable to him when the *Memoirs* were written.[11] That Casanova may have given his Constantinople recital color by romanticizing certain incidents, seems altogether possible. The division of the sexes in Turkey in the eighteenth century, as in many parts of the Near East today, was absolute. Yet if we are to believe Casanova, he was received on one occasion by the wife of Yussef, a Turkish acquaintance made in Bonneval's home, and was permitted to converse with her alone. Before making love to her, Casanova sought to remove her veil, which so aroused her ire that he found himself checkmated. Recounting the story later to Bonneval, Casanova was laughed at for his ignorance of Muslim female psychology, being reminded that a Turkish woman would reveal any part of her body sooner than her face. Casanova was highly chagrined when informed that he had lost an easy victory but for the misdirection of his attack.

Nothing could be truer than Bonneval's observations and, at the same time, nothing probably further from the truth than the occasion described by Casanova as provoking them. It is quite inconceivable that a Turk of any class or condition would have allowed Casanova access to a female member of his family.

Casanova also tells us that he met in Bonneval's home Ismail Effendi, a former Turkish minister for Foreign Affairs. This Ismail had never been identified until we addressed ourselves to Professor Norman Itzkowitz, a leading student of Turkish history, and elicited from him the information that an Ismail Effendi had indeed served as Turkish foreign minister from 1730 to 1736. Such records as are available indicate that Ismail died in 1740-41 on a pilgrimage to Mecca. If Casanova took sufficient pains to give us the correct name of a foreign minister, it seems most probable that he was personally known to him, a fact strongly suggestive that he paid a first visit to Constantinople in 1741. There are even more compelling reasons to conclude that he visited that city in 1741 rather than 1745. One might be tempted to exclude a second sojourn but for the circumstantial details, confirmed by contemporary records, of the voyage in 1745, and his statement of a meeting with George Keith there, known to have been in Constantinople that year.

Casanova claims to have returned from Constantinople with Donà, retiring Venetian ambassador, who embarked there on October 12, 1745, and arrived in Corfu on November 1. Casanova's pretension that, after making the voyage with Donà, he sailed with Renier from Corfu for Venice at the end of September, when records show him to have left there on October 25, has aroused doubts in the minds of many that the Venetian ever set foot in Turkey. This discrepancy in dates is clarified if it is accepted that he confused the circumstances of his several visits.

The presumption that he did leave Constantinople with Donà in 1745 and that he may not have returned to Venice until late February 1746 is supported by his reference to a carnival passed in Corfu. He states that it was unusually long "that year." He adds that in undertaking the role of impresario for a troupe of actors he stipulated that the receipts for two days each week, totaling seventeen days, would be his. Between 1740 and 1746, only one carnival period conforms with his description, that of 1745-46. This lasted from December 26, 1745, to February 23, 1746, or precisely eight and one half weeks, for which he would have been entitled to seventeen days of receipts. The strong inference is that he remained in Corfu until the end of February 1746 and did not reach Venice again until early in March of that year.

There is no gainsaying that Casanova's account of his life for the years 1741-45, including in particular visits to Constantinople and Corfu in 1741-42 and in 1745-46, represents a telescoping of events, not unusual with him, with consequent occasional anachronisms and anomalies not always easy to interpret. So perverse is the character of some of them at times that there is the temptation to conclude that the adventurer introduced them here and there as if to mock us from the grave.

But let us beware of treating him lightly. When the nature of some unusual episode leaves us most disposed to question its truth, documentary evidence has a bewildering way of turning up, as in the case of the false prince at Corfu, in support, if not of every detail, at least of the fundamentals. In assaying the historical value of *Histoire de ma vie*, we would do well to bear in mind both the number of seemingly dubitable facts that have been confirmed and the many other memorialists of indisputable integrity who have been equally guilty of the same occasional anachronisms and confused chronology.

# CHAPTER 3

## He Finds a Patron and Goes to Paris

Until 1745 Casanova lived largely by the wits with which he was so plentifully endowed, and which were to sustain him in many moments of adversity. The question arises how a young man of such modest background could so readily gain admittance to and enjoy the confidence of such distinguished figures as Cardinal Acquaviva, Bonneval, Bragadin, Crébillon, Cardinal de Bernis, Pope Clement XIII, Marquis de Caraccioli, Frederick the Great, Catherine the Great, Count Lamberg, Prince de Ligne, and Benjamin Franklin, to name some of the most outstanding. In an age of erudition Casanova possessed a great fund; in an era when the art of conversation was developed to a supreme degree he was reputed for the brilliance of his wit. It is perhaps not too much to say that he was one of the most notable conversationalists of Europe. The Prince de Ligne, perhaps the most distinguished European of his day, wrote of him: "His every word is a revelation and every thought a book," adding that he was the most interesting odd character that he had ever met. Such qualifications constituted a passport that admitted him everywhere.

But upon his return to Venice, about March of 1746, from Constantinople and Corfu, he was still obscure, with no financial resources. To support himself, he became a violinist at the S. Samuele theater. In the early hours of April 20, 1746, emerging from the wedding festivities where he had been engaged to play, he noticed a patrician drop a letter on entering his gondola. Casanova restored the letter to the owner, who offered to conduct him home. En route, his host suffered a stroke. Never at a loss in an emergency, and with the decisiveness that marked his character, he accompanied the stricken man to his palace, ordered him bled, overruled with authority the doctor summoned, and announced he would remain until the patient had recovered. The patrician proved to be Matteo Bragadin, former Inquisitor of State, now senator, living with two other bachelors, Marco Dandolo and Marco Barbaro. Finding them given over to the occult, in which he himself was versed, along with most other branches of knowledge, Casanova imposed upon their credulity by proposing to consult the cabalistic oracle, imparted to him, so he said, by a hermit, to obtain answers to any questions they had to propose. Upon emerging successfully with his usual ingenuity from the tests given him, he assured himself of their lifelong attachment. Bragadin proposed to adopt him as his son and to provide him with a monthly allowance of ten sequins,[1] which he received until his protector's death in 1767. Casanova confesses that:

> Had I desired to conform to a strict morality I should have, one may say, either have held myself aloof or have disabused them. As for the latter my reply is 'no' for I did not consider myself strong enough. They would have laughed at me, have treated me as an ignoramus and dismissed me. They would not have thanked me for that, and I had no mission to assume the role of apostle. As for taking the heroic resolution to leave them as soon as I had recognized their visionary character, to have done so I would have needed the morality of a misanthrope, as well as displaying indifference to my own interest. As a young man desirous of living well and enjoying those pleasures that such an age demands, should I have risked allowing M. de Bragadin to die and to have been so indifferent as to leave those honest persons a prey to some rascal who might have introduced himself in their midst and ruined them in inducing

them to undertake the chimerical operation of the great work? Apart from these considerations, an invincible *amour-propre* prevented me from declaring myself unworthy of their friendship on the score of my ignorance, price, or lack of politeness, of which I would have been manifestly guilty in rejecting their overtures.

How was it possible that men of the distinction of Casanova's patrons could have been so easily imposed upon? If the eighteenth century was an age of enlightenment, it was marked at the same time by a spirit of great credulity. Scientists could accept the theory of gravitation and at the same time believe in the philosophers' stone. Women as notable as the Duchess of Chartres, Countess du Rumain, and the Marquise d'Urfé clamored to enjoy Casanova's cabalistic powers, and the Marquise contributed to his fortunes even more extravagantly than Bragadin.

What was the principle that Casanova employed when consulting his oracle, of which we are to hear so much in his *Memoirs*, and when constructing the pyramids of numbers from which he drew his sibylline replies? The *Memoirs* are silent as to the details, but a partial explanation is found in a letter he wrote in 1793 to Mlle. Eva Frank, in the interpretation of which, however, even experts differ.[2] All that can be reasonably concluded is that the pyramid consisted of twenty-one numbers formed from the number of letters of each word contained in the question put to the oracle. In the reply each letter was given a numerical value corresponding to its order in the alphabet. As Casanova had memorized from his youth these numerical values, it was easy for him to draw instantly from the pyramid the number representing the letter he sought when framing the words of the oracular answer. In this and all comparable mystifications, the means were attained less by any strictly logical system than by that hocus-pocus in which he was so supremely adept.

Through Bragadin's patronage Casanova pursued for three years in Venice the life of ease of a nobleman. He was nominally employed in the office of a lawyer, Marco Leze, and a large part of his time was devoted to gambling and making love. He befriended a beautiful young countess, A.S., with much the same knight errantry he had shown to Barbara Delacqua, although the sequel, if uncontemplated, was this time more satisfactory. For another girl he met by accident, Christine, he found a husband after making love to her himself, a practice often repeated with others. If guileful in his promises, he was gallant in seeing that his loves were provided with husbands—other than himself.

Compelled to leave Venice early in 1749 after several peccadillos, he visited Milan and Mantua. There he made the acquaintance of a credulous character who displayed a knife with which he claimed St. Peter had cut off the ear of Malchus on the Mount of Olives. Seeing that he had to do with one easily duped, Casanova proposed to sell him for a thousand sequins the missing scabbard to complete an instrument giving access to a hidden treasure. Casanova improvised a scabbard out of old leather, and the deal was concluded and arrangements made for the magical rites on the property of a certain Francia at Cesena where, according to legend, such a treasure was to be found. The ceremony instituted to bring it to light, involving the virgin daughter Javotte, was interrupted by a terrific thunderstorm which struck terror in the heart even of one so unabashed as Casanova. His description of the magic rites makes it evident that he was familiar with the practice of magic, as he was with other occult sciences. It is also clear that he was as astute in exploiting human cupidity as the most accomplished confidence man of our day.

Intending to return to Naples, he allowed a chance encounter with a beautiful young woman in the inn where he lodged at Cesena to change his plans. Aroused by a disturbance in the room adjoining his, he ventured out to investigate the cause. From the innkeeper, whom Casanova's neighbor was apostrophizing for having opened his door, he learned that the complainant, who apparently spoke only Latin, was in bed with a girl, and that the police of the bishop had come to ascertain whether she was his wife.

The two persons in question proved to be a Hungarian officer and a girl dressed in men's clothes, calling herself Henriette. Casanova was outraged at the indignities offered the officer and his companion, and attracted by Henriette's beauty he took steps at once to obtain reparation for the Hungarian, who was traveling on an official mission. A friend, Count Spada, commanding the local troops, was persuaded to order the bishop to pay a compensation of thirty sequins to the Hungarian, while the innkeeper and the police, who had intruded upon the officer's privacy, were forced to beg his pardon on bended knees.

Two facts of some interest emerge from Casanova's narration: first the fluency of the Hungarian in Latin. In the eighteenth century Latin was an official language in Hungary, so much so that all official acts of the government were drafted in that language.[3] Also noteworthy is the surveillance exercised by the ecclesiastical authorities over the Hungarian officer to determine whether he was married to the woman occupying his room. This may appear to smack more of contemporary American practice than that now prevalent in Europe, but we shall find it characteristic in the eighteenth century of many parts of Italy as well as the whole of Spain and Austria, both from Casanova's testimony and that of other travelers.

Smitten at first sight with Henriette, Casanova was determined to possess her. He abandoned all thought of going to Naples when he learned that she and her cicerone were heading for Parma, and he proposed to accompany them there. He had no difficulty in persuading the Hungarian to give her up, especially since the officer knew only German, Hungarian, and Latin, and was thus unable to converse with her. Casanova's curiosity had been piqued when he learned from the Hungarian the circumstances under which he had met Henriette at Civitavecchia. From the window of his room there, he had been able to look into hers, where he observed her attired as an officer, dining with an elderly gentleman with whom she never exchanged a word. Mistaking her for an adventuress, the Hungarian sent his servant to offer her ten sequins for a rendezvous. She replied with word that they were leaving for Rome, where it would be possible for them to meet. There the servant found her at the appointed place outside the city on the road that the officer would use to make his definitive departure. Upon their meeting, she proposed that he permit her to accompany him as far as Parma, where she desired to proceed. They were en route there when Casanova made their acquaintance at Cesena.

Having obtained the Hungarian's acquiescence to relinquishing

Henriette, subject, of course, to her consent, Casanova's task was to win this. Using him as an interpreter, she made known to the Hungarian that she refused categorically to accept any money from him and insisted that once in Parma she be left to her own devices with no inquiry as to her whereabouts. Casanova found mixed in this woman "the most elevated sentiment with an appearance of great license," and could not make up his mind who she could be. When he unburdened himself to her, he expressed the hope that she would not seek from him the same ultimate indifference she had demanded from the officer. His attitude toward her is clarified in this spirited declaration:

> As I have friendship for you, you should understand that it is not possible for me to leave you alone, without funds and with nothing to sell in the middle of the street in a city where you cannot even make yourself understood. Do you find that a man whose friendship you have inspired can abandon you after having determined and learned from yourself your situation? If you think so, you do not have any conception of friendship, and if such a man accords you the request you make, he is not your friend.

Continuing his arguments he insisted that she should make her position toward him clear at once. Should he accompany her to Parma? Should he remain behind? "One of the two," he announced. "Make up your mind." Breaking into peals of laughter, she answered, "Come to Parma."

This was the beginning of the greatest romance of his checkered career, and the eminent American critic Edmund Wilson has referred to it as one of the most attractive love affairs in literature. The little we learn from Casanova's account of her is that she was from Aix-en-Provence, that her husband and father-in-law were "monsters" and that she had escaped from her father-in-law who had the intention of placing her in a convent. She declined to go into other particulars of her past aside from a reference to "three follies" she had committed in her life, of which the last would have been her ruin, so she stated, but for Casanova. We are left to surmise that the first folly was probably her marriage and the second that which had occasioned the break with her husband.

Parma, where they established themselves for three months, had passed, by the treaty of Aix-la-Chapelle in 1748, under the suzerainty of Don Philippe, Infante of Spain, along with Piacenza and Guastalla. This was a reflection of the constant struggle of France and Spain, on the one hand, and Austria on the other, for the extension of their influence in Italy. Casanova and Henriette arrived in Parma at the end of August, only a few months after Don Philippe's formal entry on March 7, 1749, and shortly before the appearance of his consort, Princess Louise Elizabeth, daughter of Louis XV, who joined her husband on November 23. Casanova offered us an interesting glimpse of the many changes that were being introduced at the time of his visit, with the presence of numerous Spanish and French courtiers, who were so turning the heads of the Italian populace that the latter were finding it difficult to adjust themselves to the new customs. Casanova's remarks have ample confirmation in a letter written by Sir Horace Mann, British minister at Florence, to Horace Walpole on April 18, 1749:

> The new Duke of Parma has disgusted all his new subjects. He is so horribly French that they cannot please him.[4]

Henriette's desire to lead a life of seclusion to avoid being recognized was in conflict with Casanova's own inclination to exhibit her in public. With some difficulty he overcame her scruples, but when attending the opera, they took a loge where there were no candles, and she went without rouge. It is evident that she did so to avoid being identified as of French origin. In the eighteenth century rouge was a distinguishing mark of aristocratic Frenchwomen who, without it, were not admitted to court, while its use was forbidden to the commonalty.[5] In other European countries, with the exception of Austria, its employment was limited largely to prostitutes. A French traveler visiting Genoa in 1785 remarked that the use of white was the mode there, as rouge was in Paris, but that the latter was compromising to Genoese ladies[6] Travelers to England offer like testimony, one observing that even street girls used rouge sparingly, and another, that no decent woman used it.[7]

Henriette's apprehensions were at length realized when she was recognized by M. d'Antoine-Blacas, a Provençal in the suite of Don Philippe, who induced her to return to Aix. Casanova was permitted to accompany her as far as Geneva. Before parting from him she traced unobserved, with the point of a diamond, on the window pane of their room at the Hotel des Balances. *"Tu oublieras aussi Henriette"* (You will forget Henriette, too), which he discovered after her departure. As late at 1828, the inscription was pointed out to Lord Malmesbury.

Perhaps no woman so captivated Casanova as Henriette; few women obtained so deep an understanding of him. She penetrated his outward shell early in their relationship, resisting the temptation to unite her destiny with his. She came to discern his volatile nature, his lack of social background, and the precariousness of his finances. Before leaving, she slipped into his pocket five hundred louis, mark of her evaluation of him.[8]

She encountered him again in 1763 and in 1769 but refrained from making herself known. She was aware that he loved her—after his fashion—but she was careful, after one experience, in 1749, to evade him thereafter. Casanova makes no serious attempt to analyze her attitude towards him or, when he does so briefly in 1763, he shows himself to be singularly obtuse. To gain an understanding of their relationship, we must read between the lines of his narrative. So taken up was he with his own feelings, supreme egoist that he was, he never appreciated the undertones of his own recital.

Upon returning to Venice from Geneva by way of Parma, where he tarried for some weeks, he left his native city again in June 1750, after a stay of only three months, to visit Paris. In Lyons, which he reached in August, he took a step that was to exercise a great influence on his life. He gained admission to a lodge of Freemasons there, perhaps that of the Grand Scottish lodge, *Amitié, amis choisis*, became an apprentice and, a few months later, companion in the "lodge of the Duke of Clermont" in Paris, where he was also Master Mason.[9] This position was to serve as a most useful open sesame, because Freemasonry in the eighteenth century was spreading widely in political and aristocratic circles, as well as in the world of letters. Many of the friends Casanova made, including Thomas Hope, the great merchant of Amsterdam;

Sir Horace Mann, British minister in Florence; the Duke de Matalone in Naples; Count de la Perouse, of Turin; Count Panin in Russia; the Prince de Ligne; and Count Waldstein, were Masons, not to mention Mozart, and many others. It is most probable that indeed many more of his friends and acquaintances than it has been possible so to identify were also Masons.

Casanova gives the following explanation of his decision to enter Freemasonry:

> There is no man in the world who succeeds in knowing everything, but every man should so aspire. Every young man who travels, who desires to know the great world, who does not wish to find himself inferior to another and excluded from the company of his equals in the age in which we live, should be initiated into what is called Freemasonry, if only to learn superficially what it is. He should, however, be careful to choose well the lodge in which he wishes to enter, for although bad company cannot have an activity in a lodge, it can nevertheless be found there, and the candidate should guard himself against dangerous connections.

Without attempting to enter here into a history of so important a movement, we should observe that the religious struggles that had stained both British and Continental history had given a marked impulse to the search for a means of reducing hate and discord by the uniting of men in fraternal association. Such a spirit had inspired the establishment in Paris, about 1727 or 1728, of the first Masonic lodge to hold regular meetings in France. English, Scottish, and Irish Jacobite refugees of the Roman Catholic faith were responsible for its inception. Similar lodges appeared thereafter in other parts of the country, including Lyons as early as 1739 and Bordeaux in 1743. Many of these French lodges offered degrees additional to the original three. In Italy, Masonry was introduced in Florence in 1733 by the Duke of Middlesex. The bull of excommunication issued five years later, on May 4, 1738, by Pope Clement XII against members of the order, had little effect in stemming its spread. For all Casanova's deep attachment to the Roman Catholic faith, he was no more influenced by papal disapproval of Masonry than many other Roman Catholics of the time.

At some time, about which he gives us no details, Casanova also became a Rosicrucian. The origin of this sect is highly obscure; some have traced the foundation to a German, Rosencreutz, of the fourteenth century, who seems, however, to have been a legendary figure. Spreading from Germany to France and England, the Rosicrucian movement was concerned with alchemy and the occult. About the beginning of the seventeenth century, members of it became connected with the beginnings of Speculative Masonry in England and with Masonry in Scotland. In France, the center of the Rosicrucian activities was Paris. Two of the most remarkable figures in the world of the occult in the eighteenth, Count de Saint-Germain and Cagliostro, were both Rosicrucian adepts as well as Freemasons.[10]

Casanova's journey from Italy to Paris was made in the company of Antoine Balletti, an actor, himself the son of renowned players, namely the famous Silvia and her husband, Giuseppe, a son of the Fragoletta, who had been mistress of Casanova's father. Silvia's daughter, Manon, later became enamoured of Casanova. Forty-one letters from her, dating between April 1757 and February 7, 1760, were found among his papers, and reveal a deep love on her part, and on his, the insouciance that generally marked his relations with women. The correspondence terminated on the eve of Manon's contract of marriage on July 20, 1760, with François Joseph Blondel, a well-known architect, after she had no doubt become convinced that she could not count on Casanova.

Much has been made of these letters by those aristarchs who are fond of exploiting the occasional discrepancies found in his narrative. In this instance, Casanova claimed to have disposed of Manon's letters when he learned of her marriage; nevertheless, they were found among his papers, while other letters he had received from women with whom he had affairs, according to the *Memoirs*, have never been found. There is no suggestion in the *Memoirs* that his relations with Manon Balletti exceeded certain bounds. As we now know that, contrary to popular belief, Casanova was of exemplary punctiliousness in protecting the identity of women of any social standing with whom he had liaisons, it is evident that the letters he received from these women were carefully destroyed by him before his death. No satisfactory explanation has ever been offered as to why he claimed not to have preserved Manon's letters, or for what reason, if any, he tells us that he heard of her marriage late in 1759, when it was not to take place for another six months. It is possible that he may have heard of her engagement or contemplated marriage and confused this later, when writing his *Memoirs*, with the actual event.

As an instance, among many, of our ability to bring verification to bear on some of the most minute details of the *Memoirs*, it may be noted here that upon returning from Holland in January 1759, Casanova states that he brought back, as a gift for Manon, earrings that cost him 6,000 florins. We do not have to take his word for this: in a letter of the Amsterdam bankers, Benjamin and Samuel Symons, addressed to him in Paris on March 5, 1759, there is mention of their operations on his behalf for what must have been these earrings.

A contemporary police report, that of Meusnier of July 17, 1752, noted that Casanova was living "currently at the charge of Mlle. Silvia, of the Italian Comedy." According to another report of the same inspector: "Mlle. Silvia lives with Casanova, an Italian, said to be the son of an Italian actress. It is she who keeps him."[11] Even Casanova's most hostile critics have been almost unanimous in rejecting the accusation. The report may have been occasioned by Casanova's presence in the Balletti household. He himself was always profuse in his eulogies of her character, and there is no testimony, other than Meusnier's, that would compromise her.

Through Silvia, at that time the idol of France, Casanova was introduced both to the theatrical and to the literary world of Paris. At her home, shortly after his arrival in August, he was so fortunate as to meet Crébillon, to whom he confided that his principal object in coming to France was to devote himself "with all his force" to the study of French literature and to that language.[12] Casanova informed him that he was looking for a teacher, but feared it would be difficult, because as a student he was "insupportable, questioning, curious, importunate, insatiable," an excellent self-analysis. Crébillon claimed that he had been seeking such a pupil for fifty years and that, rather than charge him for the lessons, he would be willing to pay him to accept him as his instructor. Crébillon's reaction indicates that

Casanova must have possessed an unusual mental endowment at so early an age as twenty-five, to have warranted this eminent writer's interest in him. Although Crébillon gave him three lessons weekly for about two years, Casanova confesses that he was never able to free himself from Italianisms, of which his published works offer abundant evidence. Other men of letters whose acquaintance he made included d'Alembert, with whom he appeared to have remained in contact until the latter's death on October 29, 1783, Fontenelle, and Abbé Voisenon. To Voisenon, on his second visit to Paris, he gave the idea of writing oratorios in verse, or so he states.

Grimm, in his correspondence, credits Voisenon with having created the first oratorio in the French language, while Voltaire also makes reference, in a letter, to Voisenon's important contribution. The development of the oratorio in France was comparatively late, and, while in England, Germany, Holland, and Italy oratorios were given at churches, in France they were to be heard only at what were known as sacred concerts. Casanova states that on his second visit to France he went to one at the Tuileries, where:

> A motet was given set to music by Mondonville, written by Abbé Voisenon entitled *Les Israelites sur la montagne d'Horeb*. It was a novelty. It was I who had given the idea to the amiable Abbé.

That this was not an idle boast on his part seems indicated by a memorandum in his handwriting:

> I wrote it in lyric Italian verses, and the Abbé, my friend, wrote it in French verses, not in translating but in imitating me and in embellishing my ideas by their union with his own. He gave it at the sacred concert during Easter 1758.

The exact date of its presentation was March 14, 1758. Although Casanova's contribution to the development of the oratorio in France is nowhere acknowledged by French or other historians, a Dutch writer, Fritz Heymann, not only credits it, but has claimed that the work of Casanova and Voisenon was appropriated by another and published in English.[13] Although Heine saw and commented on that text, no copy has ever been found in any of the world's libraries. Voisenon's oratorio was, however, published in the *Mercure de France* of April 1758, where it was given the greatest praise.[14] That Casanova should have interested himself in writing Italian verses for sacred music may at first thought appear highly incongruous to those entertaining the current superficial view of his light character. It was not more so, however, that the participation of Voisenon, a poet who, for all his clerical affiliations, is now best known for his licentious tales. The warning cannot be too often repeated that any judgment of Casanova and of his contemporaries must be made in the light of the supremely frivolous century in which they lived.

Casanova's study of the French language with Crébillon was not his only activity in 1750. He sought to make himself proficient in the minuet, and in the stately bows accompanying the dance, under the tutelage of Marcel, a former opera dancer who had gained renown with such instruction.

At this time, Casanova was also making his initial contribution to the theater with the translation into Italian of Cahusac's *Zoroastre*. This work, undertaken at the request of the ambassador of Saxony, presumably at the instigation of Casanova's mother, was produced at Dresden in February 1752, with both his mother and his sister in the cast. Some months later, on July 24, 1752, the Comédie Italienne in Paris produced *Les Thessaliennes*, in which he had collaborated with Le Prévost d'Exmes, but which were performed only four times. In perhaps the first printed notice of Casanova, an analysis of the play, it was remarked of him that he possessed a "competence allowing him to satisfy his love for literature and travel."[15]

As a devotee of the theater, he was charmed by the Comédie Française but found French opera less admirable. With a French friend, Claude Pierre Patu, a promising young author, he attended on December 10, 1750, Campra's *Les fetes venitiennes*, initially produced in 1710. The music, which struck him as old-fashioned, was novel enough to interest him at first, but soon became wearisome, the melody in particular being monotonous to him, and the singing of the performers ill-placed shouting. His reaction did not pass unnoticed, judging from an account published some years later, which obviously refers to him:

> A Venetian, who was present when *Les fêtes venitiennes* was given, asked of a Frenchman . . . a moment before the opera ended: "Sir, when does the singing begin?" "But, confound it, sir," replied the Frenchman with some annoyance, "Haven't you heard it? They have been singing for four hours." "I beg your pardon, sir," said the Venetian, "if I have asked the question, it is because in my country this is not called singing but declamation."[16]

Casanova was not alone in finding French music of this time not only old-fashioned but inferior to the Italian. After a visit to France in 1770, Dr. Burney concluded that French music had undergone few changes in a hundred years and that in melody and expression it was still in its infancy. These judgments were shared not only by Casanova, but by d'Alembert, Rousseau, and many others. What Casanova did admire was the novel rapidity in the change of scenery, as well as the silence of the spectators as compared with the noisy clamor of the crowd in Italy, where the opera was primarily a social gathering and occasion for conversation. He found curious the conducting of the orchestra with a baton, a practice then unknown in Italy, although it was to become universal.

Musically, France compared badly with both Italy and Germany, but it excelled in ballet. Casanova had the exceptional fortune of seeing two of the most famous dancers of the day, Louise Dupré and Maria Camargo, a Spaniard. The latter had introduced the *tutu* or ballet skirt, to replace the classic tunic, and is said also to have been the first to discard high heels when dancing. Altogether Casanova's description of the Paris opera is important testimony in the history of music.[17]

It was soon after his arrival in Paris that, while seated below the loge of the Marquise de Pompadour, unaware of her identity, he had the brashness to engage her in conversation, as he did the equally famous Duke de Richelieu. At Fontainebleau he had his first glimpse of Louis XV and the Queen. Observing her dining— a privilege given visitors—and served a fricassee of chicken, he was impressed when she sought confirmation that it was indeed such.

He does not interpret her curiosity as due to the recent introduction of this dish in France from Italy.

Residing opposite Casanova in Paris were the O'Murphy family, of which Marie-Louison was destined to become, in 1751, for a period of three years, the mistress of Louis XV. Casanova, who calls her Helen, was so taken with her beauty that he had a German miniaturist do her portrait, showing her outstretched on her stomach with her head sideways and her lower extremities exposed. According to his account, a copy of the miniature was shown by M. de Saint-Quentin to the King, who expressed a desire to see the original. Several days later, she was introduced to Louis XV by Lebel, his valet de chambre. She promptly became his mistress. The liaison lasted from 1751 to 1754. Casanova adds that she fell into disgrace when, inspired by Mme. de Valentinois, she made an inquiry concerning his treatment of the Queen and provoked the King's ire.

The ghost of Casanova seems present to mock malignantly those disposed to question even his most extravagant stories. Soulavie tells approximately the same story with no mention of Casanova or Saint-Quentin, who may have been, however, "the young courtier" to whom he attributes the showing of the miniature to Louis XV.[18] In Soulavie's account it was Mme. d'Estrées who prompted O'Murphy to inquire about the Marquise de Pompadour rather than the Queen. M. Jean Adhémar, latest to examine the details, credits Casanova's version, and suggests that the German miniaturist was probably Johan Anton Peters, residing at the time in Paris and known as a copyist of Boucher, whom two contemporary sources name as the author of O'Murphy's portrait.[19] One of these is in Munich, and the other at the Louvre, while two Peters miniatures, conformable in every detail with the Boucher portraits, are now in the Wallace Collection in London.[20]

Casanova's two-year sojourn in Paris afforded him full opportunity to observe the license of prevailing morals. When presented to a well-known opera singer, Marie Le Fel, he remarked upon the attractiveness of the three children who surrounded her. Informed that one was a son of the Duke d'Anneci (perhaps d'Ancenis), another of Count d'Egmont and still a third of Étienne de Maisonrouge, Casanova remarked that he thought she was the mother of the three. "But I am," she replied, bursting into a peal of laughter.

It was not the only faux pas his ignorance of Parisian manners led him to make. Calling on Lany, famous ballet master of the Opera, he found him surrounded by several young girls of thirteen or fourteen years in company of their mothers. When one of the girls, suffering from a headache, complained that she feared she was pregnant, Casanova observed that he never would have believed her married. His remark left him the butt of laughter.

Casanova has also left us an account of a visit, with his friend Patu, to one of the most elegant and renowned houses of prostitution, that of Mme. Pâris, the Hôtel du Roule. He describes the excellent taste of the furnishings and attire of the inmates, and the superior meals and wines provided. A fixed scale of prices was "not dear": six francs to breakfast with a girl, twelve to dine (to lunch) with her, and a louis to sup and spend the night. The relative exactitude of Casanova's information is confirmed in *Les cannevas de la Paris*.[21]

After Casanova and Patu had each chosen a girl, strolled in the garden while their rooms were being prepared, and duly paid their compliments to their companions, they were called to lunch. Coffee had hardly been served, when the mistress of the house, "watch in hand, summoned the two girls, declaring that the party was finished but that after paying another six francs we might amuse ourselves until the evening."

Two different companions were chosen, and towards evening the visitors decided upon a fresh selection and, with these, to spend the night.

> To render the occasion more lively, we asked for a room and two beds, and at supper we drank four bottles of champagne. After supper, each with his partner, we went to bed after having examined together our beauties in a state of nature. The Richemont made fun of my poor friend, who cursed the champagne which, he said, had robbed him of his amorous power. The St. Hilaire and I mingled our pleasures of lovemaking with shrieks of laughter, which excited the Richemont, who undertook the the impossible of bringing Patu to life without succeeding. The poor fellow having at length

fallen asleep, I enjoyed an incomparable scene. The Richemont left her bed, overcome with ardor, and came to lie down in mine at the moment when I held in my arms the St. Hilaire, who was indignant at the action. She told her to go away, the other jeered and tried to interfere with her rights: I laughed, but my sultana angrily pushed her out of the bed. Seeing that the other, who had gotten up, was going to avenge herself, I took, as was fitting, my partner's defense and represented to the Richemont, with honeyed words, that she was in the wrong. I explained that all my amorous strength belonged to the St. Hilaire and that, in honor bound, I could not give her a single kiss without offending the one whom fortune had given me to exploit.

Casanova became so captivated with the St. Hilaire that he returned to see her at least ten times. He adds that "shortly afterwards an Englishman took her from there, and thirteen years later I found her a Milady in London at the assembly of the Duchess of Northumberland."[22] When Casanova asked Mme. Pâris why she limited the number of her girls to fourteen, she produced a signboard she had intended to place outside her establishment until forbidden by the police. It read: *Sunt mihi bis septem praestanti corpore nymphae!* (I possess twice seven nymphs with enticing bodies). She disclosed the piquant detail that the verse from Virgil had been proposed to her by Voltaire, who had passed a night with Patu's Richemont. That there was such a girl at the Hôtel du Roule is confirmed by contemporary records, which reveal that she left the house in February 1751.

It is impossible not to be impressed by the extent to which details offered by Casanova of some of the obscurest figures in his *Memoirs* find confirmation where surviving records make possible their verification. Another example is afforded by the account he gives of a Mlle. Vesian and her brother, of Parma, whose acquaintance he made when they took lodgings at his hotel on their arrival in Paris from Italy. She represented herself as the orphan daughter of an officer who had served with French troops, and as having come to Paris to solicit a pension from the War Ministry; Casanova took an immediate interest in her, as a compatriot, and as well by reason of her beauty and need of aid. He persuaded his

friend Balletti to give her dancing lessons; she was received at the
Opera, and several months later retired from the boards at the
instance of a rich protector, while her brother found lucrative
employment.

When Casanova proposed to her that she enter the Opera, he
made it plain that, as the dancers received no salary, she would be
obliged to depend on some protector for her living, for, as he
remarked:

> . . . a girl who is there must through that circumstance renounce
> what ordinary people call chastity, for whoever would live virtu-
> ously would die of hunger. But if a newcomer has the ability to
> remain chaste for only a month, her fortune is certain to be made,
> for then the gentlemen who seek to take possession of this respect-
> able chastity are the most respected. A great nobleman is delighted
> that he is pointed out when the girl shows herself . . . What
> especially attracts French noblemen to acquire as mistress a girl of
> the Opera is that all these girls belong to the King in their capacity
> as agents of his Royal Academy of Music.

Casanova's report is confirmed and supplemented by contemporary police reports in which Vesian is described as Italian,
orphan daughter of 'a gentleman and officer of merit in the
engineers'; also confirmed is the fact that her brother did indeed
find a well-paying position while, in 1760, she had been during
some ten years the mistress of the Marquis d'Etrehan, whom
Casanova refers to as "de Trehan."[23] Casanova states that once he
had launched her on her career, he never attempted to speak with
her after she had left their hotel, but when he saw her "with
diamonds and she observed me, our souls spoke to one another." It
was one of the many examples of striking solicitude he showed for
women whose favors he enjoyed. It reveals also a certain delicacy,
of which he gave not infrequent evidence, in not standing in the
way of a lady's own interests.

Casanova's time was not taken up exclusively with women of
the theater. During this period of his first stay in Paris, he met the
Duke de Matalone, whom he recalled having seen in 1744 in the
home of his uncle, Don Lelio Caraffa. He was born in 1734, and
when Casanova met him again in Paris between 1751 and 1752, he

was only seventeen or eighteen. We have the testimony of Count Dufort de Cheverny[24] that the duke, whom he refers to as one of the most distinguished foreigners in Paris, was indeed there at this time. Casanova became intimate with him and received an invitation to visit him in Naples, which he did in 1761.

Although Casanova was to be received by many crowned heads, he makes no reference to having been presented to Louis XV, of whom, nevertheless, he has left this apposite sketch:

> He was the most polished of all French, particularly towards ladies, and towards his mistresses in public; he disgraced whoever dared neglect them in the least thing; and no one possessed more than he the royal virtue of dissimulation, faithful guardian of a secret, and enchanted when he was certain that he knew something ignored by all the world . . . Louis XV was great in everything, and he would have had no fault if flattery had not brought him to this. How could he realize his deficiencies when everyone told him he was the best of Kings?

If, as there are strong grounds for believing, Casanova was to become, on his second visit to Paris, a secret agent of the French court, it may be that his silence regarding his presentation to "Louis le Bien-Aimé" was the product of discretion.

If Casanova did not meet the King, he did make the acquaintance of Louise Henriette de Bourbon-Conti, who had married in 1743 a son of the former Regent, Louis Philippe, Duke de Chartres, later Duke d'Orleans. The Duchess of Chartres was notable both for the lightness of her morals and her interest in the occult. Perhaps she is best remembered as the mother of Philippe Egalité who, the sole member of the royal family having a seat in the National Convention, cast his vote on January 20, 1793, in favor of the death penalty for Louis XVI, who was decapitated the following day. This cousin of the King suffered himself the same penalty on November 6, 1793. To Casanova his action was so monstrous that he wrote it would have been better had he been stifled at his birth.

Casanova states that it was at the instance of the Count de Melfort, who contemporaries alleged was the lover of the Duchess de Chartres, that he was introduced to her apartment at the Palais Royal, because she wished to consult his oracle as to how she might cure herself of pimples that disfigured her skin. Casanova prescribed for her daily purges, a strict regime, the washing twice a day in plantain water, and discontinuance of the use of any pomades. In a week, her pimples had disappeared. However, when failing to observe his prescriptions, her afflictions reappeared, and she confessed that she had eaten ham and had drunk liqueurs, while asking him, "as she drew from her pocket a box of ivory," why "this pomade no longer is effective?"

August Hervey has left us descriptions in his *Journal* of a number of the persons mentioned in Casanova's *Memoirs*, including in particular the Duchess de Chartres. In his accounts of her, he offers details confirming Casanova's, when stating that, in 1764 "she had a breaking out on her face, for which she had taken something of a pomatum that very much disfigured her."[25] It is also from Hervey and Casanova that we learn that the ladies-in-waiting of the duchess included Mme. de Boufflers and Mme. de Blot. Few women of the court led so dissolute a life. The Marquis d'Argenson, writing of her in his own *Memoirs* on October 5, 1747, when she was only twenty-two, characterized her as a "great whore." If she was brought to the grave at the early age of thirty-two, it was as she had wished it. Casanova remarks that:

> . . . she was lively, without conventional restraints, gay, quick in repartee, addicted to pleasure, which she preferred to a long life. "Short and sweet" was an expression constantly on her lips.

The portrait Casanova gives of her could not be more faithful. He visited her a number of times to consult his oracle on her behalf, and before he left Paris, he received from her through the Count de Melfort a tortoise-shell box with her portrait and a hundred louis. In consideration of the temperaments of both, it has been suggested that he may have been her lover. He himself confesses that:

> I was madly in love with her, but I never would have allowed her to suspect my feelings. A comparable prize appeared too grand for me to aspire to it: I feared to be humiliated by too marked a scorn, and perhaps I was a fool. All that I know is that I have always repented

of not having declared my passion. It is true that I enjoyed certain privileges that she might not have allowed me to enjoy had she suspected that I loved her.

Casanova expressed this same sentiment on other occasions when he held back from opening his heart to a woman out of intense pride and fear of a refusal. "I had need of being sure that I would not find the least resistance, and I was not sure," he remarked at another time. However great a lover he may have been, contrary to the popular conception of him, he was far from possessing the same audacity with women that he showed in other aspects of his life. Despite, too, his clear disclaimer that he was never the duchess's lover, it cannot be accepted unquestioningly. Even if he had been, he had too much respect for the reputation of the women of the world with whom he had affairs to have compromised such a reputation as the duchess had by imputing to her a liaison with one so far beneath her rank as he.

There is hardly any aspect of Paris life that Casanova does not present in writing of his various visits there. It is, however, noteworthy that he does not appear to have had access to the fashionable literary salons of Mme. du Deffand or Mme. Geoffrin; at any rate, they are nowhere mentioned. Although he met many people of the highest rank, he frequented more particularly the world of the theater, where he was most at ease.

He did meet Mme. de Bocage, termed the "French Sappho" by Goldoni, attributing to her a *bon mot* that other chroniclers have ascribed to the wife of Louis XV. He has her relate this anecdote during his first visit in Paris anticipating events by some years.

> Not long ago, the King vaunted to a courtier whom I cannot name the joys that would be his if he passed the night with Mme. M. He claimed that hardly another woman on earth was capable of provoking like pleasures. The courtier replied that His Majesty was of that opinion for the reason perhaps that he had never visited a bordel.

A contemporary writer records almost the same words under the date of 1769, that, soon after Louis XV had made the acquaintance of Mme. Du Barry, the Duke de Noailles had such a conversation with the King as that registered by Casanova.[26] As is known, Mme. du Barry, whose fate it was to perish by the guillotine in 1793, made her debut in the notorious Parisian house of ill fame of Mme. Gourdan. Count Du Barry discovered her there, made her his mistress, became her pimp, and married her to his complaisant brother to give her a shroud of respectability before passing her into the arms of Louis XV. In Casanova's anecdote of her, he appears to be drawing on what he had read or what had been repeated to him. However that may be, it has been shown that it did not come from his imagination.

Leaving Paris in October 1752 in company of his brother Francesco, Casanova proceeded to Dresden, where his mother occupied a privileged position at the Elector's court. During his stay until March 1753, he wrote, to please her, *La Moluccheide*, a play produced there on February 22, 1753, of which only the program, containing a list of characters and summary of the plot, survives. Shortly thereafter, he visited Prague en route to Vienna, where he remained more than a month, amusing himself with gambling and a pretty Fräulein whom he calls "B.C.,"[27] and who had the advantage of being outside the jurisdiction of the commissioners of chastity appointed by Empress Maria Theresa to curb illicit lovemaking. Casanova recounts, with no little indignation, the inflexible pursuit by these commissioners of chastity of all women living by their charms, other than those, like B.C., who were of social standing, and their exile to Temesvar. There is confirmation by an English traveler, N.W. Wraxall, who reported from Vienna, in 1779:

> Women who are accused or convicted of devoting themselves, however secretly, to the pleasures of the public, are instantly taken up and confined. Many are annually transported down the Danube, into the Bannat of Temeswar, a marshy and unwholesome province on the frontier of the Turkish dominions.[28]

Alongside the repression of one form of vice, Casanova exhibits to us, in the course of a visit to Presbourg, during his stay in Vienna, the spectacle of a prince-bishop of the church giving a resplendent ball and presiding himself at one of the gambling tables.

It was not in Casanova's character, however, to neglect more serious matters. One of his most striking incongruities was to pass from gambling halls and the company of cutthroats and prostitutes to spiritual concerns. Vice, as he tells us, was not comparable to these last and he rarely neglected an opportunity to immure himself in a good library or to seek out the society of the intellectual giants of his day. It was quite in conformity, therefore, with his temperament, that he should have visited the Imperial Library, now the National Library of Vienna. A letter of recommendation to Metastasio enabled him to have extended conversation with that renowned court poet whose company he sought again thirteen years later upon returning to Vienna. On May 29, 1753, or perhaps even some days previous, he was back in Venice after three years absence, welcomed joyfully by his three patrician protectors.

# CHAPTER 4

## Adventures with Nuns; His Imprisonment

In common with many memorialists, Casanova confounded incidents of successive sojourns spent in the same localities. A further difficulty in following him is his indiscriminate
use of the Venetian calendar in which the year began on March 1.
These two circumstances have mystified those attempting to follow
the chronology of the events he records, particularly the period
1753-55, into which he has indifferently mingled several episodes
of 1748. The jigsaw puzzle thus presented can only be solved, here
and elsewhere in the *Memoirs,* when these factors are kept constantly in mind. A further peculiarity of the *Memoirs* is the
computation of the hours of the day. In Venice in the eighteenth
century, and elsewhere in Italy during a part of it, the setting of the
sun marked the beginning of the twenty-four hours, as it still does
in some Arabian countries.[1] The day was computed thus in the
Orient from immemorial times; it may have been the Crusaders or
early Venetian traders who introduced the Near Eastern practice in
Italy.

Perhaps no portion of the *Memoirs* has excited more curiosity
than that dealing with the two convent inmates C.C. and M.M.,

the stage for which was set by a chance meeting between Casanova and C.C.'s brother. According to the *Memoirs*, this meeting with P.C., identified as Pietro Capretta, occurred immediately after Casanova's return to Venice in 1753, when, out of love for P.C.'s sister, he agreed to accept a worthless letter of exchange from him. Documentary evidence proves that Casanova was involved with Pietro Capretta over such a letter, not in 1753, but already in August 1748. There is thus every reason to believe that he first met Capretta in 1748. The *Memoirs* leave the impression that Casanova's acquaintance with C.C., Caterina Capretta, came thereafter. Taking into account all of the facts at our disposal, the more reasonable date for Casanova's introduction to C.C. is May 1753. If this date is accepted, his courtship of her, and the discovery of it by her father, led to her confinement as a boarder in the convent of S. Angelo at Murano early in June 1753.

It is to a distinguished Italian Casanovist, the late Count Bruno Brunelli, that we owe the identification of C.C., P.C., and Ch.C. as Caterina Capretta, Pietro Capretta, and their father, Christoforo.[2] He also gave us the name of Caterina's husband, Sebastiano Marsigli, a Venetian lawyer.[3] Casanova tells us that she married the lawyer shortly after Casanova's escape from the Leads (November 1, 1756). Jacques Marsan recently uncovered the record of her marriage on February 5, 1758, and that of her birth on December 3, 1738, daughter of Christoforo Capretta and Maddalena Evick. To researchers, the *Memoirs* offer the same fascination as the parts of a picture puzzle, which, with infinite patience over the years, can be made to fall one by one into place, thus demonstrating with each new confirmatory detail their astonishing fidelity to fact.

If we know beyond dispute, now for more than thirty years, the name of one of the two convent inmates with whom Casanova became romantically involved between 1753 and 1755, the identity of the other has so far eluded incontrovertible substantiation. Casanovists as qualified as D'Ancona, Mola, Samaran, Gugitz, and others have, over the years, tentatively proposed Maria-Eleanora Michiel. On the basis of information supplied me by the Curia Patriarcale in Venice I found strong reasons for concurring in this hypothesis only to discover that the entries from the convent archives supplied me had been incorrectly transcribed. Subsequently Piero Chiara turned up a document of 1760 showing the presence in the convent of S. Maria degli Angeli of no less than eight nuns with the initials M. M. Of these, five from what is known of their ages would qualify as candidates for the elusive nun. Pierre Gruet, patron of Casanova studies, in 1975 published the apparently irrefutable proof of M. M.'s identity as Marina Maria Morosini.[4] The proof: She was born on September 11, 1731, so that she was twenty-two in 1753, and she came from a prominent patrician family of Venice. Both facts agree with the *Memoirs*.

Perhaps nothing in the *Memoirs* is more shocking to our conventional ideas than Casanova's account of his trysts with C. C. and M. M. during the period extending from November 1753 to the end of 1754. Almost every Sunday during the summer of 1753, Casanova visited the chapel of S. Angelo on the island of Murano opposite Venice, to be seen by C. C., that she might be convinced of his continuing attachment after he had seduced her on his promise of marriage. A fellow inmate, M. M., a great beauty and thorough voluptuary, observed him on his visits and sent him a message soliciting his acquaintance. On their meeting she disclosed herself as not only the mistress of the French ambassador, Abbé de Bernis, but, as well, the lesbian friend of C. C. De Bernis was in ill health and was no doubt making preparations in anticipation of his recall. Although Casanova's story does not suggest this, it seems fairly evident that the ambassador had encouraged M. M. to find another lover to reduce her pain at separation from him.

De Bernis had peculiar tastes which he satisfied as concealed spectator of Casanova's first night with M. M., passed in the retreat loaned her for that purpose by the ambassador. There followed a series of light-hearted supper parties in which the participants were Casanova, M. M., and de Bernis, another with the addition of C. C., one when Casanova spent the night with both M. M. and C. C., and still another when Casanova was maneuvered by de Bernis' skillful diplomacy into ceding his place to the ambassador. The content of these episodes is not of great importance, but their illumination of the manners and morals of the age merits particular examination, and from this comes the long-debated question of how much is fact and how much fiction. That certain nuns in Venice engaged in clandestine love affairs during this period is a matter of historical fact; [5] that some ecclesiastics of the Church of Rome were notorious for their dissolute conduct is likewise attested. Such conduct was not out of keeping with de Bernis' known character.

What is to be said of de Bernis who, while French ambassador in Venice, played so equivocal a role in those scenes of a rare voluptuousness recounted by Casanova?

Born in 1715, and therefore ten years Casanova's senior, François Joachim de Pierre de Bernis, of a very ancient but hardly wealthy family of the French nobility, was educated by the Jesuits in Paris, in anticipation of a career in the church. After the completion of his studies, de Bernis solicited in 1741 an ecclesiastical appointment from his father's friend, the all-powerful Cardinal de Fleury, first tutor and then prime minister of Louis XV. The aged cardinal, who did not look with a favorable eye on the worldly life his suppliant had been leading, informed de Bernis that as long as he lived he would receive no appointment at his hands. De Bernis, who enjoyed a reputation as a wit, rose to the occasion. "Very well, Your Grace, I shall wait."

While doing so he led an insouciant social life and published various works, including numerous lewd verses for which he blushed in later life, but which at the same time opened all doors to him, including those of the French Academy in 1744. His main chance came, however, through an acquaintanceship with Mme. d'Étoiles, before 1745 when she became mistress of Louis XV and, as Marquise de Pompadour, effective ruler of France for about twenty years. It has even been suggested that de Bernis was her lover. Through her he received a small pension, a lodging at the Louvre, and then appointment as ambassador to Venice, where he finally took priestly vows in April 1755. Having been named counselor of state during his stay in Venice, upon his return to Paris he was charged with negotiation of a treaty with Austria, concluded in 1756, which ended a 200-year-old rivalry between France and Austria. The negotiation, sponsored energetically by the Marquise de Pompadour, precipitated the Seven Years' War against France and Austria by England and Prussia, which proved a disaster for France. De Bernis, who had in the meanwhile become minister for foreign affairs on June 28, 1757, appalled by accumulative disasters, urged that steps be taken in favor of peace, thereby alienating the favor of the Marquise de Pompadour. Following his dismissal on October 4, 1758, after the most disinterested service, which particularly distinguished him at a court so thoroughly corrupt, he received the red hat of a cardinal on November 30, and was exiled ignominiously a few days later to his estates at Soissons. In an unpublished contemporary letter of January 29, 1759, it was remarked that "One speaks no more of de Bernis. . . . The bon mot current about him is that he was only given the (cardinal's) hat to make his reverence."[6] With the death of the Marquise de Pompadour in 1764 it was expected he might be recalled from banishment. The *London Chronicle* in its issue of January 14-17, 1764, speculating upon this, offered from a French correspondent an interesting sidelight into his disgrace in 1758:

> Mme. de Pompadour raised him to the Ministry, and afterwards got him to be dismissed and banished from Court, on pretense of his behaving ill towards her. He was very much beloved while in power. Mme. Pompadour pressed him to grant her a favor inconsistent with the good of the State, which he refused, saying, "Madam, I am infinitely attached to you, but still more to my country."

There were few at Versailles of whom the same could be said. In 1769, with the death of Pope Clement XIII, he was named ambassador to Rome, where he attained, as such, a unique position and influence, terminated only by the French Revolution and his death in 1794, in Rome.

There is every reason to believe that Casanova knew de Bernis in Venice.[7] A revealing passage of the *Memoirs* recounts the circumstances of their first Venetian meeting, which took place in M. M.'s presence at Casanova's casino on the evening of February 8, 1754. At this time, Casanova recalled that they had met in Paris at the Venetian ambassador's in the presence of Lord Marshal Keith, minister of Prussia, four days before de Bernis' departure from Paris from 1751 to 1754; de Bernis is known to have left Paris for

Venice a few days after September 9, 1752, at which time Casanova himself was there, as he did not leave until the middle of October of that year for Dresden. The pieces, therefore, fall admirably into place.

We do not have to rely on the *Memoirs* exclusively for testimony of Casanova's relations with de Bernis in Venice. In another work, written in 1796, Casanova makes this important disclosure:

> In the year 1754. . .a minister of France who resided at Venice and who died at Rome a cardinal two years ago, had in his service an excellent cook.
>
> This cook, who was called du Rosier, became my friend through an adventure I shall spare you, as it had nothing in common with the word *Franciade*.
>
> Being my friend, he had the kindness to give me supper prepared by him in a casino that belonged to his master, where at his pleasure I often passed delicious nights.
>
> At this supper, a Venetian lady whom the sovereign police of the Venetian government did not forbid to be the mistress of a foreign minister, found among others a dish so exquisite that she considered she would be unhappy for the rest of her days if she did not learn how to make it.
>
> I rose quickly and, plate in hand, went down to the kitchen, and having made the circumstances known to du Rosier, I asked for the recipe of this dish on which the happiness of an adorable being depended. He answered, with that composure which all accomplished chefs affect, that his dish was called the *Franciade*, and that instead of giving me the recipe, which in the absence of practice would serve me not at all, he would teach me to make it. He kept his word several days afterwards, and the lady was very satisfied.[8]

Casanova's references to the Venetian government's implicit sanction of M. M.'s relationship with the French ambassador is of particular interest on two counts. We know that that government was under heavy obligation to de Bernis, which would explain a connivance that has puzzled more than one commentator. There is also the clear intimation that M. M. was of a patrician family. As early as the fifteenth century, the strictest penalties had been imposed by Venice on any contact whatsoever between patricians and foreign representatives out of a desire to reduce to a minimum the spread of information about affairs of State, a policy that has parallels in modern times in the Soviet Union. Although Casanova was not a patrician and was therefore not punishable for contact with foreign diplomats, it may have been to avoid possible complaints against him or against his patrician protectors that he gave up, some time before March 15, 1754, residence in Bragadin's palace to take up quarters, first in the parish of S. Maria Formosa and later, in March 1755, in the house of a widow, Caterina dal Pozzo, situated in a street that now is the Calle della Gorna.[9]

What adds verisimilitude to Casanova's recital is a letter dated September 1, 1754, addressed by de Bernis to the Countess des Alleurs, wife of the French ambassador at Constantinople, in which he makes specific reference to a flirtation on his part with a Venetian nun at this precise time. He writes:

Your nun has evaded the walls of her convent to take refuge at Padua, which is the most sombre cloister that I know. I have been to see her, and she will come to dine at my house in the fields.[10] In speaking of her flirtations you cast in the most delightful possible manner some stones in my garden; you put to me questions of unfaithfulness which, happily or unhappily for me, can no longer embarrass me. I lead the life of a Carthusian friar, and I have all the more merit in that it is quite necessary that I possess some sanctity.[11]

The letter may mean nothing so far as M. M. is concerned as there is no evidence of any visit paid by her to a convent at Padua. Its importance is the proof it offers that de Bernis was not above engaging in an intrigue with a Venetian nun, on which there are two other contemporary testimonies that have never previously been cited. The first is that of the Prince de Ligne:

The Abbé de Bernis, with whom I was intimate in Vienna, was never, as M. de La Harpe states, minister at that court. If I dared to relate an adventure that he had with a nun in Venice, and quote the best verse that he ever made in his life, which he left one day at my table, the story would be more piquant than anything that has been said about him.[12]

The other is that of an anonymous writer, perhaps Ange Goudar:

> The Abbé de Bernis being of an amorous disposition, instead of concerning himself with affairs of state, gave himself up entirely to Venetian women. And he had effectively some adventures in Venice to which a man who only studies the interest of princes would never have exposed himself.[13]

That Casanova may have drawn upon his fertile imagination in depicting the voluptuous scenes he describes, involving de Bernis, M. M., C. C., and himself is entirely possible. They cannot, however, be shrugged off disdainfully as Masson, the ambassador's official apologist, has done. A jury weighing the evidence would more readily return the verdict of not proven than one of not guilty.

De Bernis was not the only foreign diplomatic representative at Venice with whom Casanova was involved in piquant adventures, according to his narrative. The British ambassador, John Murray, who had arrived on October 9, 1754, became his intimate soon after, and dumbfounded him when he disclosed that there was not a nun in Venice or Murano who could not be had for money, including M. M., mistress of the ambassador. When Casanova disputed the fact, Murray confided that he had already had her once for a hundred sequins. Casanova's offer to wager that it was quite impossible was accepted by Murray. To settle it to the satisfaction of both, it was agreed that Murray would arrange a rendezvous at the casino of Casanova with the nun he claimed was M. M. As soon as she was there, he would excuse himself, requesting her to await his return; he would then join Casanova and take him to the convent where Casanova would ask to speak to her. It was further agreed that her appearance under such circumstances in their presence would convince Murray that he had to do with an impostor. Matters passed as had been agreed, and to Casanova's infinite relief M. M. showed herself in the parlor of her convent when Casanova and Murray called, while the M. M. whom Murray had mistaken for her was waiting for him in Casanova's casino. Upon confronting the impostor, they were informed by her that she had been put up to it by a certain Count Francesco Capsocefalo, a notorious pimp. Casanova was subsequently assured by Murray that having communicated the entire story of the false nun to the secretary of the State Inquisitors, he had been promised full satisfaction, and that the miscreant had been sent to his native Cefalonia.

It is a matter of record that on March 29, 1755, Capsocefalo was indeed condemned to three years imprisonment at Corfu and perpetual banishment in the Ionian Islands after having been arrested the previous month for espionage and relations with a foreign ambassador. The judgment does not refer to any nun or to Murray by name, but as an Italian commentator has observed, the diplomatic immunity of Murray would have assured him the discretion of the Venetian authorities when delivering judgment.[14] The description Casanova gives of Murray, as consorting with pimps and prostitutes, is entirely conformable with testimony from other sources. Lady Mary Wortley Montagu, in a letter from Venice, May 30, 1757, wrote of Murray that he was:

> . . . a scandalous fellow in every sense of the word, he is not to be trusted to change a sequin, despised by this Government for his smuggling, which was his original profession, and always surrounded with pimps and brokers, who are his privy councillors.[15]

When the threads of these intrigues were being drawn, a storm was brewing over Casanova's head. While he was consorting with M. M., C. C., de Bernis, and Murray, the Venetian Inquisitors had charged one of their spies, C. B. Manuzzi, to observe him and report on his activities. Six of these reports have been discovered in the Venetian archives, extending from November 11, 1754, to July 24, 1755. They represent him as making a habit of living on others and of cultivating credulous persons, or those given to debauchery, with a view to furthering their dissolute ways. The reports said he caused the "ruin of Bragadin, from whom he has extracted much money," has traveled "under the title of man of letters" in various countries, has "through his skillful tongue" made the acquaintance of many patricians, and "to everyone's knowledge is considered as a cheater at cards." His friendship for the Memmo brothers is attributed to their common epicurean philosophy. He "is acquainted with many foreigners," as well as "the flower of youth," visits many females, including married women, is "always trying to bring off important strokes of fortune," with money "never lacking to him." In short, the figure drawn of him resembles that of the dissipated young man-about-town of a thousand cities since the days of Babylon.

But what excited Manuzzi above all else was a poem he had heard Casanova read that he considered reprehensible because of its mockery of religion. "The subject," he added, "is treated in an astonishing manner, for he speaks both directly and indirectly of copulation." It is clear that, as most spies, Manuzzi had singularly little sense of humor; he had interpreted a youthful metrical satire as expressive of Casanova's genuine convictions. But the light treatment of religious subjects was no trifling matter in eighteenth-century Venice.

On July 20, the Secretary of the Inquisitors ordered that Manuzzi "should procure the poem," while on the 24th Messer Grande was instructed "to arrest G. Casanova, to take all his papers and conduct him to the Leads," an order executed in the night of July 25-26, 1755. The immediate occasion for his arrest was recorded in the journal of the secretary of the Inquisitors of August 21, 1755: "The Tribunal, having taken cognizance of the grave faults committed by G. Casanova primarily in public outrages against the holy religion, their Excellencies have caused him to be arrested and imprisoned under the Leads." A note of September 12 mentions that he "has been condemned to five years." There was no trial, and Casanova was left unacquainted both with the reasons for his imprisonment and the duration of the sentence. As profligacy and cheating at cards were common practices, it may be that the controlling reason was the enmity of Antonio Condulmer, one of the three Inquisitors, to whose mistress Casanova was paying an assiduous court. Condulmer may have taken advantage of Manuzzi's reports, as well as the complaints of Mme. Memmo that Casanova was inculcating irreligious sentiments in her sons, to put out of the way so dangerous a rival. This, at least, was Casanova's opinion, expressed long afterwards.

Casanova was now in one of the most impregnable prisons of

the world, one from which no one had previously escaped. It comprised the attics of the ducal palace, and its name, the Leads, was derived from the lead plates with which the roof was covered. When some months had passed and he despaired of being released, he took stock of his situation, and with his plentiful courage and resourcefulness he set about plotting a means of attaining his freedom. As he observed:

> It has always been my opinion that when a man sets himself determinedly to do something, and thinks of nothing but his design, he must succeed despite all difficulties in his path; such a one may make himself Pope or Grand Vizier, he may overturn an ancient line of kings—provided that he knows how to seize on his opportunity.

He was to prove that he was such a man.

While exercising in the garret, he espied an iron bar a foot and half in length and of the thickness of his thumb. Examining it, he found he could conceal it under the seat of his armchair. With a fragment of marble, appropriated for use as a whetting stone, he fashioned out of the bar an octagonal-sided pike. His next problem was to provide a lamp with which to work in the obscurity of his cell. A porringer did for a vase. Oil was obtained for use with his salad; his cotton counterpane provided him with wicks. He simulated a toothache and asked Laurent, his jailer, for a flint on the plea that, soaked with vinegar, it would ease his pain. Supposedly to cure a rash, he obtained a doctor'sprescription for sulphur, which Laurent gave him in the form of matches. He recalled that he had had his tailor place tinder under the armpits of his coat as a protection against perspiration. With the material for his lamp thus ingeniously acquired, he set to work. Laboring for six hours daily, he had pierced the floor by August 23, 1756. He had fixed his escape for the 27th, but on the 25th, to his consternation, he heard the bolts of his cell being withdrawn. It was Laurent bringing what he thought would be welcome news, of his transfer to a more commodious cell. His only consolation was that he had time to conceal his dagger in the armchair. This and other personal belongings accompanied him to his new quarters, where he awaited the storm when the hole in the floor would be discovered.

For two hours he remained in the agony of suspense. At length, Laurent appeared, transfixed with rage, and demanded that the tools employed to pierce the floor be handed over. With perfect sangfroid Casanova professed complete ignorance. A search of his belongings failed to turn up the pike hidden in the armchair. When Laurent threatened him with means of compelling him to talk, Casanova cooly replied that he would do so only to the Inquisitors and would declare that the tools came from the jailer. Thus intimidated, Laurent feared to report the occurrence. His complaisance extended so far that shortly afterwards he allowed Casanova to exchange books with another prisoner. In this indulgence, cupidity played a part, as Casanova had ceded to Laurent any excess remaining from his monthly allowance, so that the jailer had a personal interest in reducing Casanova's expenditures for reading matter.

An exchange of books afforded opportunity for an exchange of messages. Casanova's correspondent was Marino Balbi, a dissolute monk. As Casanova's cell was under constant surveillance after his attempt to escape, he proposed to Balbi that he convey the pike to him, that he pierce the ceiling of his cell, then the wall that separated the space above them, when he would be over Casanova's cell, and that he would next make a hole in the ceiling above Casanova to enable them both to escape. To pass the pike to Balbi, Casanova had Laurent purchase him a large folio Bible, in the parchment binding of which the instrument could be concealed. The more effectively to hide the weapon in case the ends should be perceived, Casanova told Laurent he wanted to make a present to his fellow prisoner of both the Bible and a large plate of macaroni. The dish was placed on the Bible for the better concealment of the pike it contained, and the whole was dutifully conveyed to Casanova's conspirator by the dull-witted jailer.

In due course, the monk executed his task according to Casanova's instructions. When Balbi appeared in the aperture of the ceiling, Casanova hastily provided the necessary rope out of sheets. The two then removed one of the lead plates of the roof, through which they made their way to the summit to take stock of their situation. Casanova espied a dormer window above the gutter. He slid down the roof and got astride it, then, lying on his belly and using his pike he dislodged the grating. With the aid of their rope, Balbi was lowered into the loft below. Casanova found it too far to jump and had no other means of descent. Reconnoitering the roof, he found a ladder left by workmen, which, with great difficulty, he maneuvered through the window. In doing so he slipped and in an instant was over the parapet as far as his chest, sustained only by his elbows. With superhuman effort he extricated himself, regained the window, and made his way down the ladder.

The room in which he and Balbi found themselves had a door that was fortunately unlocked. In the adjoining room, they forced the keyhole of a locked door with the pike, and found themselves in the ducal chancery. The door was locked, but its wood was pierced in half an hour. After descending two flights of stairs, they came to the main door of the grand stairway, which was locked and impenetrable. They looked out of a window and were seen by loungers in the palace court who reported their presence to the doorkeeper. At the moment he opened the door, thinking they had been locked in overnight, Casanova and Balbi rushed past him down the stairs to the canal, entered a waiting gondola, and were off.

When set down in Mestre, they took a coach to Treviso. To throw off their pursuit, Casanova decided to follow the longest way to the frontier and to separate himself from Balbi, so that they would be less easily identified. He was so confident of his own resourcefulness that he abandoned to the monk the little money he had. Not the least astonishing part of the bold tactics characterizing his escape was his seeking refuge overnight in the home of the local chief of gendarmes who was absent in Casanova's pursuit.

Such are the bare details of one of the most remarkable prison escapes in history. Thirty years later he wrote an account of it in *Histoires de ma fuite,* published in Prague in 1787. It has since gone through more than fifty editions in a score of languages. At a time when it was the fashion to suspect in general the authenticity of the *Memoirs,* Casanova's account of his escape did not escape distrust. Critics began to sing another tune when substantiating records were discovered in the Venetian archives. Contemporary confirmation was likewise found in Gradenigo's manuscript journal of December 4, 1759, and August 13, 1766, in which full weight was given to the escape, described as "prodigious."

Casanova's mother, La Zanetta (silhouette)

The Piazza di Spagna: Casanova lived in the third house to the right of the
Spanish Steps (engraving by Giuseppe Vasi)

Paris around 1790: The Quai Saint Paul

Casanova's escape from the Leads (after an
engraving by Johann Berka, 1788)

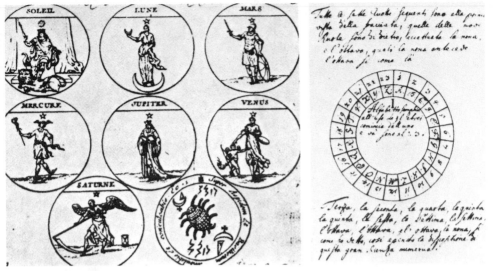

[1] Zodiac and astrological talismans [2] Cabalistic arrangement
(notes made by Casanova)

Casanova at thirty

Voltaire as guest of Frederick the Great (after a painting by A. Neumann)

Mlle. Roman-Coupier (painting by François Herbert Drouais)

Anton Raphael Mengs (self-portrait)

Count Cagliostro (Joseph Balsamo)

Card players, 1783 (engraving by Jean Dambrun, after Jean
Michel Moreau the Younger)

Departure of a gondola (painting by Giandomenico Tiepolo)

Dux Castle (18th-century painting)

Casanova (painting by Alessandro Longhi)

Mme. Cornelys (the only known painting)

# CHAPTER 5

# Lottery and Black Magic

I t was on November 1, 1756, that Casanova made his escape. Pausing at Bolzano long enough to obtain funds from Bragadin, Casanova proceeded to Munich. From there he made his way by easy stages through Augsburg and Strasbourg to Paris, arriving there on January 5, 1757, the day of Damiens' attempt on the life of Louis XV. A few months later, he witnessed Damiens' execution on the Place de Grève, now Place de l'Hôtel de Ville, where he engaged a window overlooking the spectacle to please certain female acquaintances. During the victim's agony while being drawn and quartered, Casanova was forced to turn away his eyes and stop his ears at the heartrending cries of Damiens, although the women present were unaffected. That Casanova was a singularly faithful observer is attested by a contemporary description of the same scene:

> What was most impressive was the eagerness of sensitive compassionate women to attend this spectacle, to satiate themselves with it, to support it in all its horror, with dried eyes, without the

slightest emotion, when almost all the men shuddered and turned away their gaze.[1]

Casanova's first visit after his arrival as to de Bernis who, through the favor of the Marquise de Pompadour, was now a powerful minister, about to be named minister for foreign affairs. De Bernis, one of whose most admirable traits was loyalty to his friends, welcomed Casanova cordially, procuring his introduction to the influential M. de Boulogne, whose appointment on August 25, 1757, as financial controller was brought about by de Bernis. The foreign minister, with the heedlessness that marked the era, represented Casanova as a man well versed in financial matters. Calling at de Boulogne's residence, Casanova was presented as such to one of the great financial figures of France, Pâris-Duverney, who in 1751 had been responsible for the establishment of the École Militaire, and was now seeking means of raising funds for that institution without unduly burdening the French treasury. Let us note in the colloquy that followed how astutely Casanova, a perfect tyro in things financial, held his own with such a master as Duverney:

"It is God alone, sir, who has the creative power," Casanova sententiously observed.

"I am not God," replied Duverney, "but for all that I have now and then created—but the times have changed."

Casanova parried: "Everything is more difficult than it used to be; but in spite of difficulties I have a plan that would give the King an interest of a hundred million."

"What expense would there be to the Crown?" Duverney inquired.

"Merely the cost of receiving," was Casanova's cautious answer.

"The nation, then, would furnish the sum in question?"

"Undoubtedly, but voluntarily." Casanova refused to commit himself to anything specific.

"I know what you are thinking of," Duverney countered, seeking to draw him out. But Casanova declined to show his hand, remarking, "You astonish me, sir, as I have told nobody of my plan."

He could have told no one of his plan, for he had none. On the promise that the plan would be revealed, Duverney was sufficiently impressed to invite him to lunch. The following day, in the presence of a large number of people, including Jean Calzabigi, another Italian, Duverney exhibited the latter's project for a lottery. When he added that this was the plan that Casanova had undoubtedly had in mind, the Venetian glibly responded that such indeed was the fact. With his usual aplomb and nimble tongue, he had extricated himself successfully.

Calzabigi, who had been in Paris since 1756 as secretary of legation of the Kingdom of the Two Sicilies, no doubt sensing in his fellow countryman a shrewdness and craftiness equal to if not surpassing his own, decided that it would be wise to make an associate of him. The decision may have been reinforced by his knowledge that Casanova had influencial friends, such as de Bernis and others who would be useful allies. According to Casanova, d'Alembert, in his capacity as eminent mathematician, assisted in at least one of the deliberations leading to the establishment of the lottery. There is reason to believe that Diderot may also have had a hand in its organization, since a prospectus about it in his own handwriting once existed among his papers.[2]

With the adoption of the lottery project by decrees of August 15 and October 15, 1757, Ranieri Calzabigi, elder brother of Jean, was named administrator and Casanova director. It appears from his account that he was given six lottery offices, of which he sold five at once for 2,000 francs each, retaining but one which was to prove a lucrative source of income until his departure in 1759, when he made a present of it to his manager. Contemporary records mention one of Casanova's offices, perhaps the single one he retained, but its location is given as the rue Saint-Martin and not the rue Saint-Denis. He is correct in stating that the headquarters of the lottery were in the rue Montmartre. From other sources we learn that already on September 27, 1757, Ranieri Calzabigi, his brother Jean's wife, and a certain Abraham Rame, whom Casanova does not mention, had leased the premises.

The lottery operation involved the drawing of five numbers from a total of ninety. Participants might select a single number (*par extrait*), two numbers (*par ambe*), or three (*par terne*). Single numbers paid fifteen times the amount of the purchase price, double numbers 270, and triple numbers 5,200 times. The winning numbers on the first drawing, April 18, 1758, were 83, 4, 51, 27, and 15. There were four other drawings in 1758 and ten in 1759. The connection of the Calzabigis with the lottery was terminated about the same time as that of Casanova in 1759; he was to meet Jean five years later in Berlin, occupied with a lottery for Frederick the Great.[3]

It may appear curious that three Italians should have laid the basis of a French enterprise initially undertaken to provide funds for the École Militaire, and subsequently transformed into the French National Lottery that exists today. It was in Italy, however, and more particularly in Venice and Genoa, that the lottery had evolved in the form that had become known in Europe. Both Casanova and the Calzabigis had long been familiar with the operation of lotteries; once the French considered introducing one, it was natural that advice on its establishment should be sought from Italians. If we are left in ignorance of the means by which the Calzabigis obtained preferment in the undertaking, a glance at Casanova's past and the friendship formed at Venice in 1754 with Abbé de Bernis throw a flood of light on the support given the former upon his arrival in France in 1757. While we have to rely exclusively on Casanova for the details of his relations with de Bernis, unsupported as they are by any published papers of the latter, it remains inexplicable that Casanova could have obtained an entrée to important French financial circles, permitting his association with the French lottery, of which there is corroborative contemporary evidence, unless he had powerful protection. De Bernis was an intimate friend of Pâris-Duverney. Casanova's access to him could have been readily had through de Bernis, and the former's account is a persuasive one.

The favor that Casanova enjoyed at the hands of the foreign minister was not limited to the lottery. A few months after Casanova's arrival, de Bernis proposed that he undertake a secret mission to Dunkirk to report on the state of the French navy there, vessels of which were assembled, in concert with Sweden, for a descent on England. Casanova was informed that because his task was a secret one he could not be given a passport by de Bernis and that he would be instantly disavowed if any mischance befell him. With his insinuating ability and facile speech he was successful in making friends with the naval officers and in obtaining full information for which he was rewarded with five hundred louis. Reflecting upon the folly of the mission entrusted to him, he observes:

> The mission cost the Ministry twelve thousand francs, and the minister might easily have procured all the information I gave him without spending a penny. Any intelligent young naval officer would have done it just as well and would have acquitted himself with zeal and discretion, to gain the good opinion of the ministers. But all the French ministers were the same. They lavished money which came out of other people's pockets to enrich their creatures, and they were absolute: The down-trodden people counted for nothing, and, through this, the indebtedness of the State and the confusion of finances were the inevitable results. A Revolution was necessary. It is the language of the representatives who reign today in France, pretending to be the faithful ministers of the people, masters of the Republic. Poor people! Foolish people who die of hunger and misery or who go to be massacred by all Europe to enrich those who have deceived them.[4]

It is one of the rare occasions when he had a good word to say for the French Revolution; in his outlook he was the antithesis of the *sans-culottes*, and a stout defender of the *ancien régime*.

As in the case of his adventures in Venice between 1753 and 1755, when events were often chronologically confused, Casanova has reported certain of his Parisian experiences in the years 1757 to 1759 in an unlikely sequence. It is known that his visit to Dunkirk occurred between the end of August and the middle of September 1757, and that it preceded his appointment to the French lottery, which took place after his return from this first French mission. This does not, however, preclude the possibility that conversations looking to the establishment of the Ecole Militaire lottery may well have been begun shortly after his arrival.

In this period, 1757-59, he had been admitted into some of the most exclusive social circles of Paris. On his first visit he had acquired a reputation for his cabalistic powers, and now certain women of high rank, taken up with the occult, sought his acquaintance. Two of these, Countess du Rumain, of his own age, and the Marquise d'Urfé, twenty years older than he, were to play important roles in his life. Although he remained silent as to the amorous relationship with the first, correspondence of hers indicates he was her lover. Her attachment to him endured ten years during which she aided him from time to time financially. A more important source of revenue from 1757 to 1763 was the Marquise d'Urfé whose relations with Casanova, until a rupture interevened, form some of the most extraordinary pages of the *Memoirs*. These intimate he was also her lover. For seven years she was an almost inexhaustable source of bounty, making largely possible the prodigal life he led during that period. The full amount he extracted from her is not known, but Casanova quotes her nephew as reproaching him in 1767 for his mulcting her of as much as a million francs.

On their first meeting she discoursed to him on chemistry, magic, and the occult, claiming to be in possession of the philosophers' stone. She showed him her renowned library, begun by Claude d'Urfé in the sixteenth century, and added to extensively by herself. It included numerous manuscripts on the occult, among them one by the famous Raymond Lull, some of which were to pass eventually to the National and Arsenal Libraries in Paris and the National Library of Vienna. Her chemical laboratory amazed him; he was particularly impressed by a powder for the transmutation of metals, one of the problems of alchemy absorbing an astonishing number of persons in the eighteenth century, who dreamed of converting base metals into gold through a powder of projection or the philosophers' stone. It is evident that she was as well versed in the occult as he, with one fundamental difference: While Casanova made use of the paraphernalia of magic and the occult to mystify others, both for his pecuniary advantage and to give himself importance, he was aware of their absurdities; she, on the contrary, was convinced of their efficacy. In writing from Vienna in 1779, N.W. Wraxall stated that there were no less than 3,000 persons then engaged in that city in search for the philosophers' stone, adding that those so interested were provided with "charcoal, utensils, crucibles and every requisite at the Empress Maria Theresa's expense."[5]

Such independent testimony tends to make more plausible

Casanova's circumstantial account of Mme. d'Urfé's alchemic activities, and a single detail enables us to bring precise verification to bear on them. In the course of their conversation, the marquise informed Casanova she had received "in 1743 from M. Vood in person a keg of platine del Pinto." This Mr. Vood, who remained a mystery to previous commentators, was none other than Charles Wood, master assayer in Jamaica, who, in 1741, was the first to bring to Europe specimens of platinum, found in the Rio Pinto de Choco. His brother-in-law, Dr. William Brownrigg, was the first to publish an account of experiments with platinum in a communication of December 5, 1750, to a fellow member of the Royal Society, William Watson. As printed in the *Philosophical Transactions* of that Society, the metal is denominated as "Platina di Pinto," and explicit reference is made to the efforts of contemporary alchemists to transmute it into gold.[6] We are presented here with one further striking example of the confidence that may be accorded Casanova. According to Dr. L.B. Hunt of Johnson Mathey & Co. Ltd. of London, the details recorded by the Venetian in his *Histoire* on the chemistry of platinum "are perfectly correct."

Mme. d'Urfé, whose wealth permitted her the most costly fantasies, may have been of amazing credulity, but it is evident that she was also markedly versed in the latest developments about metallic substances, so much so that her activities are not to be neglected by the historian of science or of the occult. The division between these two, it must be remembered, was slender in the eighteenth century.

In the early relations between Mme. d'Urfé and Casanova, what particularly impressed her about him was his success not only in reading an enciphered manuscript but also in deciphering the key, consisting of an arbitrary series of letters. As she knew far less about cryptography than Casanova, his application of the principles of this science bewildered her and reinforced her conviction that he possessed magical powers. Casanova's thorough familiarity with cryptanalysis is evident not only from what he tells us of his decipherment of the d'Urfé manuscript, but also from his enciphered signature to one of his pamphlets, published in 1785, *Lettre à Messieurs Jean et Étienne L.*[7] Mme. d'Urfé's credulous character persuaded her that Casanova possessed the philosophers' stone as well as the power to communicate with the elementary spirits. This power she herself coveted. But, as it was her belief it was only given to men, she conceived the fantastic project of having Casanova effect the transmigration of her soul into the body of a male infant, born from the union of an ordinary man with a woman of divine origin. We shall find Casanova engaged in 1762 and again in 1763 in such an operation with her. In extenuation of his conduct he offers much the same explanation as that for his abuse of Bragadin's confidence:

> If I had spoken out like an honest man and told her that her theories were nonsensical, she would not have believed me. I therefore let matters take their course. Moreover, my self-love could only be flattered in seeing myself treated as the most profound of the Rosicrucians, as the most powerful of mortals by a lady related to the first families of France and who, above all, had an income of 80,000 francs, a splendid estate and several magnificent homes in Paris. I was quite sure that she would refuse me nothing, and although I had no definite plan of profiting from her wealth, either in whole or in part, I did not have the strength to renounce this power.

Specious reasoning, certainly, but it cannot be said that he was lacking in candor, nor can he be charged with hypocrisy. "I do not pretend," he once said, "to be among the number of upright men."

It was at the home of Mme. d'Urfé that Casanova made the acquaintance of one of the most extraordinary and mysterious figures of his century, the Count de Saint-Germain, given to the occult with far greater pretensions than Casanova, claiming to have been born several centuries previously and to have the power of making diamonds and of arresting old age. No biographer or historian has ever penetrated the secret of his birthplace or his parentage. Most generally accepted is the belief that he was born at Bayonne about 1706, son of a Queen of Spain, Princess Marie de Neubourg (wife of Charles II), and of a Portuguese Jew. Such a hypothesis would explain the source of his mysterious wealth, his possession of a veritable art gallery of paintings, his facility in many languages, and his breadth of culture, including his ability as a painter and a violinist. It explains also the welcome given him in various courts, and not least that of Louis XV, who employed him for a time as a secret agent.

Casanova gives us a striking portrait of him at their first meeting:

This man, instead of eating, spoke from the beginning to the end of the dinner, and I listened to him with the greatest attention for no one spoke better than he. He represented himself as prodigious in everything, he wished to astonish and, in truth, he did so. He had a decisive manner which, however, was not displeasing for he was a savant, speaking well in all languages, a great musician, great chemist, of an agreeable appearance and with the ability to make friends of all women, for at the same time that he gave them paints with which to embellish their skins, he flattered them, not to make them younger, for that, he said, was impossible, but to preserve and keep them in the state in which he found them by means of a water that costs much but of which he made them a present. This very singular man, born to be the most barefaced of all imposters, declared with impunity, with a casual air, that he was three hundred years old, that he possessed the universal medicine, that he made anything he liked from nature, that he created diamonds, and that from ten to twelve little ones he made a large one with no diminution of the weight and of the purest water. For him, these were trifles. I did not find him unpleasant, but neither did I find him respectable. I found him astonishing in spite of myself, for he amazed me.

This picture of Saint-Germain offers concisely that recorded in a more extended form in many contemporary accounts. He was given every aid in his alchemic researches by Louis XV, and Casanova tells us that the monarch provided Saint-Germain with an apartment at Chambord and with funds for a laboratory, after he had interested that blasé king in chemical experiments, and after he had gained the favor of the Marquise de Pompadour by encouraging her to use his water of youth. Count Dufort de Cheverny, who was in a position to be well-informed through his post as introducer of ambassadors at the court of Louis XV at this time, refers to Saint-Germain as a "Rosicrucian, a wandering Jew, who made precious stones and diamonds at Chambord." On September 4, 1756, the Marquis de Marigny, brother of the Pompadour, wrote that the King had assigned quarters to Saint-Germain at Chambord, and two days later, the majordomo of that Chateau reported Saint-Germain's arrival there.[8] A curious detail, corroborative of the attachment Mme. d'Urfé had for Saint-Germain, is that his best-known portrait is one executed of him at her instance.[9]

Casanova was to meet him again in Holland early in 1760 and claims to have seen him in Paris in June 1761, but of this we have no confirmation from any other source. Their last meeting took place at Tournai in March 1764 where Saint-Germain, under the name of M. de Surmont, had been charged by Cobenzl, Austrian minister in Brussels, to organize a manufactory for the dyeing of silks and the production of hats.[10]

Though Casanova makes no further mention of Saint-Germain in the *Memoirs*, he devotes a page to him in his *Soliloque d'un penseur*, along with Cagliostro, whom he treats with disdain while not withholding a certain admiration for his more distinguished fellow adventurer. He notes Saint-Germain's death in Schleswig, where he did, indeed, die on February 27, 1784.

In 1758, when Casanova met Mme. d'Urfé and was introduced to Saint-Germain, French finances were in a critical state, because of the prodigality of Louis XV, as well as the drain of the Seven Years' War. Holland was then the financial center of Europe. A banker suggested to Casanova that he should propose to M. de Boulogne, in order to ease the French financial situation, the sale of French bonds at Amsterdam, the purchase there of securities of countries with a better credit than that of France, and the negotiation of these for cash at more advantageous terms than obtainable if French securities were disposed of directly. Casanova explored the suggestion with de Bernis, who advised him to take it before the Controller General. De Boulogne, finding the idea excellent, proposed to forward bills in the amount of twenty million to Count d'Affry, French ambassador at the Hague, with whom Casanova was to take counsel.

Casanova has confused his two visits of 1758 and 1759 to Holland when he states that he had on the first a letter of recommendation from the Duke de Choiseul to d'Affry, which was actually given him on his second visit. In 1758 Choiseul had not yet become foreign minister as de Bernis did not relinquish this post until October 9. It was a common practice to employ men other than regular diplomatic agents for various tasks abroad, so that Casanova's service in such a capacity was not unusual. As in his Dunkirk mission, he could be disavowed if he failed, and rewarded in the measure of his success.

A letter of Count d'Affry to the Duke de Choiseul of October 15, 1759, refers to Casanova's visit in 1758, thus:

> I asked him the object of his voyage and he informed me he came here for business affairs and to negotiate securities, as French ones lost too much value when sold [in France]. I replied that I hoped he had not come to Holland to give them discredit.[11]

Leaving Paris about October 14, 1758, Casanova arrived in Holland a few days later, where he remained until the first days of January 1759, occupying himself with the disposition of the twenty millions. The first offer he received was one of ten million in liquid funds and seven in paper. Having been instructed to make no commitment involving more than eight percent loss, he referred the offer to Paris, to M. de Courteil of the finance department, who ordered him to return to Paris in the absence of more advantageous conditions. Another offer was obtained involving only a nine percent loss but with no commission for himself. Transmitting this, with an urgent recommendation for its acceptance, he expressed the hope that he would be at least reimbursed for his expenses and accorded an indemnity. He was authorized to conclude the deal, but was left unremunerated on his return on the grounds that he had profited amply enough, as evidenced by the letter of exchange for 100,000 florins which he had brought back with him.

That Casanova had profited substantially, he leaves us in no doubt, but these profits, according to his account, were derived from sources other than the transaction on behalf of the French treasury. Mme. d'Urfé had asked him to dispose of securities of the Gothenbourg India Company which she was unable to negotiate in Paris because of the penury of liquid funds. Although we have only d'Affry's letter to support Casanova's word of his semiofficial French financial mission, his statement of the transaction entrusted to him by Mme. d'Urfé is corroborated by letters of Amsterdam bankers, showing the sale by them of such securities on his behalf described as belonging to "Madame la Marquise." When Casanova realized 12,000 francs more than she had paid for these, she made him a present of this sum. With corroborative testimony of this transaction it is reasonable to conclude that he succeeded equally, as he claims, in disposing of the French securities.

In Amsterdam he had made the acquaintance and gained the confidence of Thomas Hope (M. d'O of the *Memoirs*), head of one of the most important trading establishments in Holland. Hope was a Freemason, and this tie no doubt served to facilitate their understanding. According to Casanova, Hope had a daughter, Esther, of whom he became enamoured. For a long time, Esther was thought to be Hope's daughter—a hypothesis that was never satisfactory because Hope had no legitimate daughter. But recently the director of the National Archives of Holland, the late Mr. Hardenberg, identified Esther as Hester Hooft. She was the daughter of Hendrik Hooft (1716-94), who lived in Amsterdam, at Herengracht No. 507, and became mayor of that city in 1769. At age seventeen, Hester married a George Clifford, and after his death in 1776, she married a Jan H. van Kinsbergen.[12] She died in 1795.

When the Venetian sought to amuse Esther with his cabalistic pyramid, the father proposed to Casanova that he consult his oracle as to the fate of a Dutch vessel two months overdue, the owner of which was desirous of disposing of it for ten percent of its value. Unaware of Hope's intentions, Casanova obtained a reply that the vessel had not been lost, as reported, but that news would be had of it shortly. Hope thereupon confided, to Casanova's consternation, that he proposed to purchase the vessel, and no arguments on Casanova's part that the oracle was not infallible could dissuade him. Casanova's cabalistic powers, fortunately for him, were sustained when the vessel turned up. It was a lucrative deal for him, as Hope insisted on giving him a bill of exchange for 100,000 florins and authorized him to draw on him at any time for the remaining 200,000 florins, or ten percent of Hope's profit.

That Casanova brilliantly succeeded in his first mission to Holland, both to his own pecuniary advantage, as well as to that of the French government, would seem fairly evident. On his return to Paris the Farmer-General, M. de la Popelinière, was profuse in his compliments on what Casanova had accomplished for the French State, advising him that he would do well to consider adopting French nationality.[13] According to Casanova, the Duke de Choiseul informed him that in the event he succeeded in negotiating in the future a loan of a hundred million florins in Holland he would see that he obtained a befitting dignity. When Casanova called on M. de Boulogne, on his round of visits after his return, and informed him that he had an infallible project to augment the King's revenues by twenty million, the controller general of French finances remarked:

> Put it into execution and I will have the King grant you a pension of a hundred thousand and letters of nobility if you wish to become French.

These remarks assume added significance when we learn from the original text of the *Memoirs* that, in Casanova's account of his audience at the court of St. James in London in 1763, the initial version of his conversation with the Queen contained two references to his French naturalization, while in another passage there is mention of a letter of introduction from M. de Chauvelin, describing him as French by naturalization. These were subsequently stricken out of the manuscript by him. In the absence of fuller evidence, we are left to the hazardous realm of conjecture. It is possible that the reference in 1763 may have had to do with the French naturalization suggested to him in 1759; there is certainly no record or other intimation that steps were ever taken by him to consummate the design proposed to him after his successful Holland mission.[14]

# CHAPTER 6

# *Mlle. X.C.V. and Secret Machinations*

Casanova left Holland about January 3, 1759, and was in Paris a few days later. The approximate date is established beyond question by a letter of January 8, 1759, from Justinienne Wynne (Mlle. X.C.V.) in Paris to her Venetian lover, Andrea Memmo, friend of Casanova. An author of some repute in the eighteenth century—admired as such by Charles Nodier—Justinienne was the daughter of a Venetian woman and Richard Wynne, a member of the British gentry. At the end of 1758, she and her family left Venice for England, where they were to claim the parental estate. Their voyage was interrupted in Paris, where Justinienne was to give birth to a child whom most commentators have heretofore attributed to Memmo, but who may well have been by another.[1] Casanova had flirted with her in Padua in 1753, when she was a girl of eighteen. She was later to make a brilliant marriage, on November 5, 1761, with Count Philippe Orsini-Rosenberg, Austrian ambassador to Venice. Brunelli found in Padua two of three manuscript volumes of her letters to Memmo, which were the basis of Brunelli's *Amica del Casanova* in 1924.[2]

Through the aid of Signorina C. dalle Fusine, I found in 1955 in
Venice the missing manuscript volume, comprising fifty-four
letters, several of capital importance in substantiating in minute
detail some of Casanova's particulars. Thus, in Justinienne's letter
from Paris of January 8, 1759, to Memmo, we read:

> I have seen at the Comédie Italienne the amiable and most beautiful
> comédienne known as Catinon who dresses as a man to represent a
> fop. I assure you she is a prodigy. This same evening in a loge near
> me was Casanova, whom you know, making a magnificent ap-
> pearance. He came to greet us and now is with us every day,
> although his company does not please me and he thinks this does
> not matter to us. He has a carriage, lackeys, and is attired resplen-
> dently. He has two beautiful diamond rings, two different snuff-
> boxes of excellent taste, set in gold, and he is bedecked with lace. He
> has gained admittance, I do not know how, to the best Parisian
> society. He says he is interested in a lottery in Paris and brags that
> this gives him a large revenue, although I am told that he is
> supported by a very rich old lady [Mme. d'Urfé]. He is quite full of
> himself and is foolishly proud; in brief, he is insupportable except
> when he speaks of his escape [from the Leads], which he recounts
> admirably. I talk with him about you very often . . .

Justinienne gives herself away in the last line. It is the dust a
woman would throw in a man's eyes to beguile him. If we turn to
the *Memoirs*, we shall find that her account of the meeting with
Casanova confirms in every detail that given by him.

There is more. In the same letter she tells of her acceptance of an
invitation from the Sardinian ambassador to attend a ball on
January 13th at the Opera with Farsetti, whom Casanova himself
mentions. She chose as her costume for that occasion a very
gallant black domino. They arrived at two in the morning and did
not leave until six. "The room, although not large, was well
lighted" but "so many whores were present we could not take off
our masks or dance," with the result that she "remained a great
while in a loge to look on" and "was very much bored." Let us
compare this with Casanova's account. He was invited to dinner
by Camille, an actress, with a number of girls and their lovers.
They went to the Opera ball, where Casanova lost himself in the
crowd.

I had no mask on, and I soon found myself attacked by a black domino whom I knew to be a woman, and, as she told me a hundred truths about myself in a falsetto voice, I was intrigued and determined to find out who she was. At last I succeeded in persuading her to come with me into a loge, and as soon as we were inside and I had removed her mask, I was astonished to find she was Mlle. X.C.V.

She had written Memmo she would wear a black domino and, recalling the event thirty years later, Casanova described her costume with astonishing fidelity. And yet the myth persists that Casanova was a consummate liar! In her account of the ball, she makes no mention of Casanova, which is understandable if she felt any inclination for him, as the sequel was to prove. She had no scruples about discussing in her letters Farsetti and the prominent M. de la Popelinière, who were both paying court to her, but in whom she had no interest, as she made clear to Memmo. With all her astuteness as a woman, she no doubt feared she might involuntarily betray her feelings in further references to Casanova whose insinuating ways with women were well known to Memmo. Casanova tells us they had a tender tête-à-tête in which they discussed M. de la Popelinière's suit for her hand in much the terms with which she refers to him in her letters to Memmo. The inestimable importance of Justinienne's letter is the interpretation given by one of Casanova's heroines of two events recorded in the *Memoirs*.

Although Casanova's name is absent from the other unpublished letters of Justinienne Wynne to Memmo, they are nonetheless of importance as confirming other facts recounted by Casanova. Thus, he tells us that after dining one day with the Wynnes:

> We all went to Passy to a concert given by La Popelinière and remained to supper . . . The man who entertained everyone at table and who ate nothing was the adept St. Germain. All that he said was bragging but was noble and full of wit. I have never in my life known an abler and a more seductive impostor.

The occasion was doubtless one of the two concerts to which Justinienne refers in letters to Memmo of January 15, 22, and 29, 1959. In the first she wrote:

Finally that evening it was arranged by Farsetti that I would go with the other members of the family to La Popelinière . . . He is the richest financier of Paris, he is magnificent, is very able, spends treasures, and, with it all, is considered most avaricious in certain things. He gave a concert especially for us, and I had to be in evening dress and amiable, while in the most melancholy humor.

In the next letter she wrote:

I went on Monday to M. de la Popelinière, as I wrote you. There were many people, and the master of the house was most agreeable to me. The concert was given expressly for us, and, in fact, I found it the best orchestra in the world. The violoncello was better than any I had ever heard, the hautboys also, while the forest hautboys and the clarinettes and wind instruments, which are not heard with us, are admirable . . . He invited us very graciously to the regular concert given every Saturday.

On the 29th she wrote:

I went out only to attend Saturday the great concert of La Popelinière where there was a large crowd of men and women. Unmannerly with everyone, he was particularly polite to me and invited me to dine on Wednesday.[3]

In addition to the confirmation they bring to the *Memoirs*, the letters are of importance for the details given of one of the most talked of Parisian figures of his time. Farmer-General of the public revenues, M. de la Popelinière was distinguished for the concerts that he organized and of which Justinienne Wynne gives us these intimate glimpses. His home was situated on what is now the rue Raynouard in Passy where he had at his disposition a spacious theater, the finest singers and dancers of the Opera, and an orchestra directed by Gassac, one of the great artists of his day, or by Gâffre, an incomparable harpist.[4] The fact that Casanova left us few details of these concerts, such as offered by Justinienne Wynne, can doubtless be explained through his admitted lack of enthusiasm for music. Casanova's purpose in attending the concerts was less the entertainment available than to see and be seen.

Late in January or early in February, when Justinienne confided to Casanova that she was pregnant, he arranged to take advantage of another Opera ball to conduct her to a midwife, who has been identified from contemporary records as Reine Demay Castres. According to Casanova she offered to perform an abortion for fifty louis. After some inconclusive discussion they took their departure, leaving her two louis. On emerging, Justinienne suggested that Casanova take her for a moment to see the country house he had engaged nearby on returning from Holland the previous month. Known as "Petite Pologne" ("Little Poland"), it was situated in what was then the country but is now in the vicinity of the Gare St. Lazare. It had two gardens, one of which was terraced, a stable for twenty horses, three imposing apartments; and Casanova rented it for a hundred louis annually from Marin Le Roy, whose popular title, bestowed on him by Louis XV, was that of the "Roi de beurre", "butter king." A coachman, two carriages, five horses, and two liveried lackeys were acquired by Casanova at the same time. It was a measure of his changed fortune after his return from Holland. On his arrival in 1757, he had lodged with Mario Balletti and his family in the rue Petit-Lion near the Italian Comedy; upon returning from Holland, he had "attractive quarters in the rue Comtesse-d'Artois" although not for long as he is shown in February as being back again in his former domicile. Petite Pologne appears to have been acquired for purposes of relaxation, supplemental to his town quarters, where he would be able to entertain on the scale that his newly found prosperity warranted.

Justinienne's unexpected suggestion that they look in on his country estate persuaded Casanova that the happy moment for which he had longed was now to be realized. He had already made overtures to her, but he was never one to press matters. Some few days previous, when he had offered her 50,000 écus, she had shown her appreciation by unwonted tenderness, "enfolding me in her arms and pressing her mouth to mine. It would have been unworthy on my part to seek more in such a moment," he had reflected. Accordingly, he had abstained from pressing his advantage.

Now, at the Petite Pologne, a bottle of champagne was opened and an omelette served. When the bottle had been emptied, they rose and:

> . . . employing gentle force, I fell on the bed, holding her between
> my arms, but she opposed my purpose, first with sugary words,
> then by more serious remonstrances, and, finally, by defending
> herself.

For Casanova it was enough. The very idea of violence revolted
him. "The play is ended" was his philosophical comment; he
added that "renewing the assault entered my mind only to be
disdainfully rejected."

Nothing is more characteristic of him in his relations with
women of refinement than this scene, however far removed it may
be from the popular misconception of him. He was attentive,
considerate, quick to proffer assistance, financial and otherwise, to
those women who appealed to him, and seldom brutally de-
manding. Is it any wonder women generally were devoted to him?

Having dissuaded Justinienne from resorting to an abortion,
termed by him "a criminal" procedure and as likely to imperil her
life, he assured her he would bring about her relief by an "aroph,"
which had been suggested to him by Mme. d'Urfé whom he had
consulted. Casanova states she had found a description of it in the
works of Paracelsus and Boerhaave where, in fact, it is mentioned.
Composed of saffron, myrrh, and other ingredients, and mixed
with wild honey, it was represented as menstruation-inducing.
The manner of its internal administration, as suggested by Casanova, to achieve the most efficacious results, involved circumstances so delicate they are best left to the imagination. At length
she overcame her scruples, and the experiments were undertaken
in a garret room of her hotel. When they failed, as Casanova had
almost expected, nothing remained to her but to await the child's
birth in some refuge to which she might have access without the
knowledge of her family. Casanova addressed himself for that
purpose to his ever-faithful friend, the Countess du Rumain, who
arranged for an abbess of her acquaintance, of noble birth, to
receive Justinienne in a convent outside Paris, where Casanova
assisted in spiriting her. Such devotion to a woman about to have
a child by another man was not exceptional for him; there is
another instance in 1760 and still a third in 1767, under much
more tragic and trying circumstances for him. Nothing could have

been more to his credit than either the first or the last instance. He had many faults, but it is extremely doubtful that any woman of his acquaintance would ever have called him a cad.

Casanova, suspected by Mme. Wynne of kidnapping her daughter, was recognized in the street by the midwife and identified by a certain Marquis de Castelbajac, accompanying her. A criminal charge was made against him, from which he extricated himself only after the Countess du Rumain had revealed the true facts in confidence to M. de Sartines, the police commissioner. The suggestion has been made, and it seems a plausible one, that Castelbajac, of doubtful reputation despite his noble birth, was either employed by members of La Popelinière's family, interested in blackening the reputation of Mlle. Wynne, whose hand he was seeking, or that Castelbajac was bent on blackmailing the famous financier by revealing the pregnancy of his beloved. Whatever the circumstances, Charles Henry and Gaston Capon have published documents from the Paris archives that confirm in their essentials Casanova's recital.[5]

The most important is a deposition dated March 16, 1759, of the midwife Reine Demay Castres. According to her declaration, she had been approached by an intermediary about February 8 or 10, a rendezvous was arranged for a gentleman and lady to call on an affair of mutual interest, and:

> . . . towards three o'clock in the morning, he arrived with the young lady, young and beautiful, enveloped in a long cape of gray silk, lined with marten, her face very white, her hair and eyebrows brown, neither tall nor small, and very thin, speaking French with difficulty; that the man, putting his word in, said to her: "There is the young lady of whom I spoke." The said young lady said to her: "Madame, you must render a service to Monsieur and to me." Upon which her companion, having resumed, said: "Madame, Mademoiselle is already in an advanced state of pregnancy. She has a violent mother capable of dishonoring her if she learns the state in which she finds herself, and as she has a very favorable marriage prospect, we would very much like her to be disembarrassed. You must give us the pleasure of preparing a potion that will cause an abortion." That she had manifested her surprise at such a proposal and had persistently refused to hear in any way of it, and that to

persuade her no doubt and bring her around, he had counted out fifty louis on the mantelpiece of the chimney, and having said to him that were he to give her ten times as much, she would not undertake so dark a deed, they went away.

The midwife added that she had been given two louis for her trouble and that having inquired, during their conversation, whether he did not fear to venture out in the streets of Paris with the young lady, he had told her:

They had taken every precaution not only to escape attention, but to protect themselves otherwise from all insults that could be offered them; that he had thereupon exhibited two pistols, which he said could each be discharged three times, that having wished to show them to the young lady, she had said to him: "Put away the arms, I am frightened." To which he had answered: "Even should you wish to fire them, you cannot as they are secret and with springs."

It is evident that the midwife had turned the account to her own advantage and that the facts presented by Casanova have more the ring of truth than hers. The police must have been so convinced, for she was arrested on April 20, 1759, and imprisoned, as Casanova reported and as it seems from the judicial archives.[6] While, understandably, none of these details are found in Justinienne's letters to Memmo, we do know from these that she attended balls at the Opera, not only on January 13, 21, and 28, but again in February, remaining until six in the morning on each occasion. It was probably at a ball in February, some days after the 8th, that Justinienne slipped away, in the company of Casanova, to consult the midwife. Justinienne's letters reveal also that the convent where she immured herself from April 4 to May 27 was a priory of benedictines at Conflans-Saint-Maur. The abbess, Mme. de Mérin-ville, in religion Sister Eustachia, delivered her a good conduct certificate, as the *Memoirs* affirm. Drafted as a letter to Mme. Wynne, who had it registered before a notary, it forms by no means the least curious document concerned with a scandal with which a great part of Paris was for a time occupied:

Mlle. Justinienne Wynne has finally opened herself to me yesterday evening . . . I do not think you can have any grief against me for having received her. I would not indeed have exposed a young person of her age and appearance to have gone alone in search of other religious communities, considering that she was ripe for reclamation. No one moreover has come here to inform themselves about her. She has received no one whatsoever, nor any letter from anyone, and conducted herself here with much piety. She appeared to me to have a charming character. I love her with all my heart and only give her up with the greatest regret for her greater happiness.[7]

In the face of all these concordant facts, we have every reason to credit the entire recital of Casanova, even in its most intimate details, which, obviously, will never be proved by documentary evidence. Almost a quarter of a century later, there was a ceremonious exchange of letters between them when she was a great lady and Casanova was eking out a modest existence in 1782 in Venice. He wrote, praising one of her books and sending her one of his own. Zottoli seized upon the formal style of the letters as proof that their relations never had the intimate character the *Memoirs* represent. This conclusion ignores both the effect of time on human relationships, as well as the highly stilted style that characterized correspondence even between husbands and wives in the eighteenth century.

The lavish scale of living that Casanova had assumed on his return from Holland in January 1759 suggests considerable financial resources. That he had realized important profits from his operations in Holland is clear. He could count also on considerable revenue from the French lottery, and important subsidies from Mme. d'Urfé. In a summary of his life written for a friend on November 17, 1797, he estimated that in 1759 he was a millionaire. However, he coveted still greater wealth to satisfy the prodigal tastes to which he had become habituated. With his fertile imagination, he embraced a suggestion made to him that he set up an establishment for painting patterns on silk after the manner of Chinese fabrics, which then had great vogue, at a cost of one third less than those imported. With the concurrence of the Prince de Conti, who had jurisdiction over the Temple area in Paris, enjoying a special regime, Casanova set up his enterprise there in anticipation of an annual revenue of 200,000 francs. Twenty pretty girls, who became successively his mistresses, were employed, and upon each he settled furnished quarters, although he retained none as favorite for more than a week. Louis XV could afford to maintain a comparable Parc-au-Cerfs, but such prodigality on the part of a private individual could not endure indefinitely, especially when the enterprise failed to yield the returns anticipated. A crisis occurred when, three days after Casanova had sold to Jean Garnier 50,000 francs worth of shares in the undertaking, a trusted employee absconded with the liquid assets. Garnier, foreseeing bankruptcy, demanded reimbursement. Upon Casanova's refusal, a suit was brought against him for annulment of the contract. He tells us the suit might have been compounded but for the service on him at the same time of two other warrants brought by creditors with indirect claims against him.

Casanova does not offer details of these two additional claims, but Charles Samaran found certain incomplete information about them in the judicial archives.[8] One was concerned with a letter of exchange for 2,400 livres drawn on Casanova on April 11, 1759, by his brother, Francesco, in favor of Carlo Genovini and endorsed by Charles Henry Oberti. Both Jacques and Francesco were sued by Oberti in May for payment. On August 3, 1759, upon expiry of the postponement allowed, Casanova in turn sued Oberti for payment of a bill, dated March 23, 1759, for 3,000 livres, drawn by one Châtellereau in favor of Casanova and ostensibly accepted by Oberti. Oberti pleaded that his signature had been forged, notwithstanding a letter purportedly written by him recognizing its validity.

The other warrant involved a letter of exchange for 2,400 livres drawn on November 20, 1758, by Henry de la Haye in favor of Genovini, accepted by Casanova, transferred by Genovini to Mercier & Sandrin and by them to Louis Petitain. Upon Casanova's refusal to pay when condemned judicially, he was arrested on demand of Petitain on August 23 and imprisoned in Fort-l'Evêque, from which he was released on the 25th after reimbursing Petitain. On that same day, Casanova lodged a complaint that the letter of exchange had never been accepted by him. On September 4, Petitain was presented with a letter of exchange for 11,890 livres, ostensibly signed by him, but which he claimed was a forgery of Casanova.

Much has been made of these various legal proceedings, first brought to light by Charles Samaran in 1914. Particular emphasis has been given, by those quick to impute criminal intentions to Casanova, to the complaint made by Oberti on August 22, that the bill of exchange purportedly signed by him on March 23 was a forgery. Notwithstanding Charles Samaran's researches, he was unable to pierce the mystery surrounding the final termination of any of these legal proceedings. He did discover that on December 22, several months after Casanova's departure from Paris, and after experts had examined Oberti's complaint, an order was issued for Casanova's arrest and his incarceration in the Conciergerie pending his examination on that criminal charge.

There are echoes of these difficulties in a letter from Justinienne Wynne to Memmo from London on November 3:

> Casanova (but you will have already heard) has been arrested for fraud and, when on the point of being hanged, has escaped from prison.

It was doubtless on the basis of this same report that Gradenigo recorded in his journal in Venice on December 4:

> It is rumored that in Paris, Jacques Casanova, Venetian, is going to be hanged as guilty of crimes he has committed.

Both reports were exaggerated and they have continued to be from that day to this. Charles Samaran has cited a letter from the Countess du Rumain to Casanova in June 1760 in which she remarks that he had had to do with a rascal, that no proof had been adduced against him and that "the examination that was made of your papers, establishing your innocence, should put your mind to rest."

Countess Rumain was not alone in her estimate of Oberti as a rascal. Writing to Casanova twelve years later, the Marquis de Prié, himself involved with Oberti, refers on October 27, 1771, to a certificate he sought from Francesco Casanova that would establish "clearly the knavery of Oberti." In a further letter of November 16, 1771, Prié observed that "the knavery and rascality of Oberti are as clear as Roche water."[9]

That Casanova consorted with knaves and adventurers of dubious character is abundantly clear from his *Memoirs*; that he was bound in consequence to have been involved with doubtful letters of exchange is equally manifest. However, no evidence has ever been brought to light attesting his own culpability. The offense was so serious that, in the eighteenth century, if he had been guilty, it is unlikely that he would have escaped the galleys or the gallows, or have retained the friendship of prominent bankers as well as many other distinguished Europeans. There is an even more persuasive argument against assuming him guilty of any malpractice on this occasion. Hardly more than a month later, on September 29, 1759, the Duke de Choiseul, minister of foreign affairs, wrote the French ambassador at the Hague, Count d'Affry:

> Monsieur de Casanova, Venetian, who is already known to you, sir, proposed to return to Holland where he has already enjoyed your kindness on the first trip he made there. You know that he is a man of letters, whose purpose is to extend his acquaintances, particularly in the field of commerce, and I am satisfied that you will accord him your good offices at such times as he may have occasion to have recourse to them. I shall be obliged to you on my side for the favorable reception that you may wish to give him.

Casanova tells us that one of his purposes in returning to Holland was to negotiate a loan at five percent on behalf of the French government with the States General or a private company. From Choiseul's letter it may be inferentially concluded that Casanova's mission had the blessings of the French authorities. It is possible but improbable that he would have received Choiseul's letter of recommendation if he had been guilty of malfeasance.

He left Paris about September 20, 1759, and arrived in Holland near the end of that month. He did not call immediately on Count d'Affry who, when acknowledging Choiseul's letter on October 15, had not yet seen Casanova, but referred only to his earlier visit.

This man has indeed come here some fifteen or eighteen months ago. The young Count de Brühl, nephew of the prime minister [Count Henri de Brühl, famous prime minister of Augustus III of Saxony] had given him a letter from M. Kauderbach [Saxon Minister in Holland] who presented him to me . . . He appeared most indiscreet in his purposes, and as he wished to extend these much beyond the territories of Venice, I was obliged to give him my advice. He remained still some time here, went afterwards to Amsterdam, where I understand he lost heavily at play. He returned to Paris, and I have had no further news from him.

Some three weeks ago, two Venetians passed here. They said he was still in Paris, where the part he way playing was hardly becoming, but they may have exaggerated and, as he spoke ill of his compatriots, it is quite possible that they felt entitled to do the same for him.[10]

Casanova tells us he dined with d'Affry on his first visit in the company of Kauderbach. One of the two Venetians mentioned in d'Affry's letter was M. Cornet, representative in Holland of the Electors of Bavaria and Cologne, who had "declared publicly in my residence that M. de Casanova was the son of a comédienne." That was enough for the French ambassador, whose snobbishness was a trait not unusual with diplomats, particularly of the old school. D'Affry's grievance, however, went much deeper. As the official representative of the French government in Holland, he felt slighted by the presence of Casanova as its special envoy. Diplomats generally resent special representatives, who do not have to abide by ordinary diplomatic rules and who lessen the role of the regular ambassador. From Casanova's account of his reception by d'Affry it is obvious that this skilled diplomat knew how to conceal his anger. The difference between Casanova's report and the ambassador's letter should not lead to the wrong conclusion that Casanova's account is unreliable. Also, we should not be misled by the Duke de Choiseul's reply to d'Affry in which he states not to know Casanova personally and recommends not to socialize with him. (Casanova probably had received his letter of introduction from a *Viscount* de Choiseul.) Casanova informs us of such numerous details of his conversations with the Duke de Choiseul that there can be no doubt that Choiseul knew him personally. This situation would not be the first in which a politician deems it advantageous to deny personal knowledge of someone whom in reality he knows quite well.

In Holland Casanova renewed his friendship with Esther and Thomas Hope, but also with several characters of doubtful reputation, including the Chevalier de Talvis, also known as de la Perina, with whom Casanova had dueled in Paris in 1752. At a faro game, in which Count Piccolomini held the bank, Casanova unwittingly accepted a false letter of exchange. To cash it, he had to turn to the authorities, and Piccolomini was compelled to reveal that the false letter was made out by Talvis and a Baron Wiedau. These two forced Casanova, at the point of a pistol, to give them money with which to escape from Holland. It was not the last of his misadventures with them.

Another acquaintance whom Casanova met in Holland was the Count de Saint-Germain. Saint-Germain had also been charged by the French court with a mission to raise a loan as well as with instructions to sound out the possibility of the conclusion of peace between France and England for the ending of the Seven Years' War. The exact date of his arrival in Holland has never been determined. Casanova is our sole authority for indicating his presence there before his own departure at the beginning of February 1760. The earliest other mention of him is by the French consul at Amsterdam who reported his arrival there on February 16. In the bitter rivalries at the French court over Saint-Germain's activities, Choiseul was finally able to obtain the King's authority to have d'Affry seek from the Dutch government Saint-Germain's arrest and return to France. Casanova reports how Saint-Germain was given warning by the Dutch of the French purposes, and how he was assisted by them in escaping to England on April 16, 1760.

The account given by Casanova of Saint-Germain's activities in Holland, supported in part by contemporary records, has historical interest. His report errs in one particular in representing Calkoen as the Dutch intermediary instead of Count Willem Bentinck. A more serious error is Casanova's claim to have been confided the facts orally by Thomas Hope. As Casanova left Holland in February, he could only have learned them from Hope in correspondence, as was probably the case. Casanova may have chosen the more dramatic form of dialogue to present the circumstances in sharper relief. There are other examples in the *Memoirs* of the presentation of confirmable facts in settings occasionally other than the true ones. Thus, Casanova leads us to believe it was in Holland at the end of 1759 that he learned of Manon Balletti's marriage, which did not occur until six months later. In this instance his confusion may have been due to a faulty memory.

# CHAPTER 7

# Cologne, Stuttgart, and Switzerland

Unsuccessful in raising a loan for the French government, Casanova decided on a tour of Germany. He went first to Cologne, where he arrived about February 7, 1760, and was cordially received by those in authority, including Count de Torcy, commanding the French troops. It had been his intention to continue on to Bonn the next day, but a beautiful woman, to whom he was introduced at the theater the evening of his arrival, so far excited his curiosity that he needed little urging from her to postpone his departure. There followed, during a stay of some weeks, trysts with her in a chapel by which access was obtained to her home. The mention of her age as twenty-five, and the presence in her household of a widowed sister-in-law with children, of whom her husband, "bourgomaster X," was guardian, have made possible her identification as Marie (Mimi), born in 1734, wife of Franz van Groote, Cologne mayor, whose brother died in 1756, leaving a widow and children. The charming Mimi van Groote already had a suitor, General Kettler, Austrian Military attaché, of whom Casanova was to fall inevitably afoul.

About February 13, he attended with his new love a small costume ball given by the Elector at Bonn. Avidly interested in all things Venetian, the Elector invited Casanova to dine with him the next day and presented him a gold snuffbox with his portrait. At the ball everyone was in peasant costumes, provided from the Elector's wardrobe. Such festivities, known as "Wirtschaft," dated from as early as the sixteenth century at German courts, differing from French and Italian masked balls in that the German participants wore disguises prescribed by the princely host, rather than choosing their own costumes. Casanova tells us that the Elector spoke to him in Venetian, with which he is known to have been familiar. Such was his predilection for Venice that at Brühl he employed Venetian gondoliers on the lake of his chateau and, in his entourage, Italian pages. At this period, Italy and particularly Venice were considered as incomparable models of culture and good taste. Far from questioning the authenticity of Casanova's account of Clement August's Court, as Ennen and Gugitz have done, F.W. Ilges, in his masterly study, *Casanova in Köln*, has presented a wealth of detail substantiating Casanova's historical accuracy, and has noted the remarkable exactitude of his portrait of the Elector.

At the conclusion of the festivities at Bonn, the wife of the mayor, supposedly Mimi van Groote, suggested to Casanova that he invite the Cologne ladies and their escorts to breakfast at Brühl, a chateau of the Elector situated between Bonn and Cologne. Delighted to comply with her request, and at the same time to shine as prodigal host, Casanova arranged with Count Verita, an Italian in the Elector's service, to make use of the chateau. When Verita inquired how much of an outlay he wished to make, Casanova mentioned 200 ducats, and was informed that the Duke des Deux-Ponts had not spent more for a similar entertainment, two years previous. This was in Casanova's usual style, conceived with an idea of impressing his guests, so much so that Kettler, who was present, expressed the opinion that Casanova must have been commissioned by the Elector to organize it on his behalf.

The last day of the carnival, which fell in 1760 on February 19, Kettler gave a supper ball, and when Mimi van Groote learned that Casanova had not been invited, she insisted that he should

nonetheless attend. At first, he objected to the impropriety of such
an act, but his hesitation was overcome when she informed him
that he could not give her a greater mark of his attachment. He
pointed out, however, that her proposal exposed him to the risk of
his life, as he would be unable to accept a rude reception from
Kettler.

Proceeding to the general's after the theater, Casanova attached
himself to a canoness, fond of Italian poetry. It may appear
incongruous to us that a canoness should assist at so worldly an
entertainment and should later even participate in the dancing,
but in the eighteenth century women of noble birth who had
chosen a monastic life not uncommonly availed themselves of the
privilege given them to attend balls.

Kettler, who was the last to arrive in the company of Mme. van
Groote, failed to perceive his uninvited guest until everyone was
seated and the person Casanova had displaced was left standing.
While Casanova maintained an animated conversation with the
canoness, the general, passing in review those at table, observed
him at length, and remarked, "Sir, I have not invitd you." In no
respect discountenanced, Casanova replied in a firm but respectful
tone, "That is true, General, but, being sure that it could only be
an oversight, I came all the same to pay my respects to Your
Excellency."

His handling of so delicate a situation was in every respect
characteristic of him: adroit, bold, but at the same time respectful,
and preserving a perfect sangfroid. It called forth all his qualities
as an actor, and he rose to the occasion with all the more merit
since his lines had to be improvised. While all those present
preserved a dead silence, Casanova resumed his conversation with
the canoness, as if oblivious to the tension that had supervened.
Finally the others, taking the lead from him, entered in turn in
conversation.

The general, making no further overt move, lapsed into sulking.
Casanova, awaiting his opportunity, seized it when one of the
guests, referring to Count Biron who had become in 1737 Duke de
Courland, succeeding the last Duke Kettler, declared that his one
merit had been his attachment to the Empress Anna of Russia.
Interrupting the speaker, Casanova remarked that:

His great merit was that of having faithfully served the last Duke Kettler . . . It was Duke Kettler himself who, by an heroic act worthy of history, sent him to the Petersburg court, Biron never soliciting the duchy. He wished only to assure himself of the County of Württemberg, while recognizing the rights of the youngest branch of the House of Kettler which would rule today but for the caprice of the Czarina who insisted on making her lover a duke.

Kettler, dumbfounded by Casanova's extensive genealogical knowledge (similar to that of Louis XV), declared with evident satisfaction that he had never found anyone better informed than Casanova, adding that, in the absence of the Empress Anna's caprice, he would have inherited the Duchy that had fallen to Biron. In expression of his satisfaction, he immediately ordered that a bottle of wine, bearing the label 1748, be passed to his uninvited guest. While ostensibly making his peace with Casanova, he was not, however, in the end, to lose his rancour for the Venetian who had displaced him in the heart of Mme. van Groote, his love.

Casanova's Amsterdam antagonist, Baron Wiedau, who had been forced to flee from Holland, had apparently preceded him at Cologne. On February 25 nursing the grievance he had against him, he caused his arrest, of which Casanova tells us nothing, but which was reported to Choiseul by Laugier, French chargé d'affaires at Bonn, on March 9, 1760:

An unknown one calling himself Baron de Wiedau demanded the arrest of Casanova of a judge at Cologne, claiming he owed him 5,000 florins. Casanova was arrested as he left the home of Count de Torcy, where he was dining. He denied the debt, but to avoid imprisonment, he deposited a ring, snuffbox, gold watch, 25 louis, and a letter of exchange for 3,800 florins. The judge has turned this over to Baron von Wiedau who came here, deposited the letter of exchange with an attorney for its redemption and has left at once for Mayence.

Yesterday a young Frenchman arrived here from Cologne . . . This unknown one maintains that Casanova was imprisoned in Fort-l'Évêque at Paris . . . that recently in Amsterdam, where he saw him, Casanova had engaged in such misdemeanors that the principal officer of that city ordered his arrest, together with the Baron de Wiedau, his associate, that they escaped just in time, that they have been at Utrecht and Cologne, and that their quarrel in this last city was only a pretense habitual to them to pursue their cheating ways.[1]

The Frenchman who had given this evidence was identified by Laugier as Talvis, adding that he had the air of an adventurer. Mr. H. Hardenberg, director of archives at the Hague, caused an extensive search to be made of the Amsterdam archives without finding anything corroborative of Talvis's statements nor, for that matter, of Casanova's statements that Talvis and Wiedau had been obliged to flee Holland. Abbé Marc-Antoine Laugier, a Jesuit and tyro in diplomacy, obviously was not aware, as we are by Casanova's testimony, that Talvis and Wiedau were birds of a feather who had evidently fallen out since their escape from Holland, and that Talvis was clearly endeavoring to besmear his former companion and Casanova as well.

On April 13, Laugier wrote again to Choiseul:

M. de Casanova is no longer here, and I do not know where he has gone. It has been confirmed that he was at Amsterdam, that the principal officer of the city sought to arrest him on account of his rascalities, but that he fought with the police and made his escape. It is known from Venice that he is of low extraction and that he deserved in his country worse than imprisonment. His departure has anticipated the receipt of letters that would have unmasked him.[2]

All that may be said in defense of the naive Laugier is that he was as deceived as the Cologne authorities. Ilges found documents establishing that when those authorities discovered how they had been imposed upon by Wiedau, they undertook, in June 1760, to bring a suit against him, with the complete exculpation of Casanova. Of course we learn nothing of this from Laugier's reports; no one has ever heard of a diplomat contradicting his own dispatches.

In paying homage to the mayor's wife, Casanova had made a mortal enemy of Kettler. The latter had left for Paris and, on the day after his arrival, on March 23, 1760, encountered M. de Bausset, French Resident at Bonn, on leave. He made him so remarkable a communication that de Bausset conveyed the details in writing the following day to the Duke de Choiseul:

> M. de Kettler has spoken to me of a certain Casanova about whom my secretary [Laugier] has already had the honor to inform you. M. de Kettler claims that he should be watched closely and that for some time he has kept him under strict surveillance. He suspects him to be a most dangerous spy, capable of the greatest crimes . . . He believes him to be linked with a spy ring and with badly disposed Dutch officers. M. de Kettler has obtained information of a terrible conspiracy through certain papers found in his baggage. He considers that he is in a position to take appropriate action if that is necessary and you order it . . . The seriousness and importance given by M. de Kettler to this subject of Casanova have incited me to inform you without delay. I am ready, sir, to execute your orders, whether they be that M. de Kettler should have the honor of informing you in person as to what he knows about the matter, or that I continue my investigations.

Ilges, the first to bring this important document from the French archives to light, remarked that, astonishingly enough, the report made little impression on Choiseul. Replying on his behalf, the head of the Paris police, Berryer, informed Bausset coldly and briefly that any further investigation was unnecessary. To Ilges, such an indifference could be interpreted only in one of two ways: Either Choiseul was fully acquainted with Casanova's secret activities or he had instructions, while professing to ignore these, to extend him covert protection.

The question has often been raised, in the light of Casanova's extensive journeys over the greater part of Europe, whether they may not have had some hidden purpose. It has been suggested that he was an agent of the Jesuits or the Freemasons, or perhaps a spy. This last appears much more the reasonable hypothesis. It is given weight by Kettler's testimony as well as by the reserve displayed on the part of Choiseul towards it. There is an intimation, however, slight, in the *Memoirs* themselves that Casanova was a secret agent. In 1760 at Soleure he cautioned Mme. Dubois: "for the future do not read or so much as touch any of my papers, as I am the depository of secrets of which I am not free to dispose."

From the court of the Elector of Cologne he made his way about March 20, 1760, to that of the Duke of Württemberg, at Stuttgart, In the eighteenth century, Germany was no less divided than Italy, which was separated into numerous Papal States, the Republics of Venice and Genoa, the Kingdom of the Two Sicilies, the Kingdom of Naples, that of Sardinia and Savoy at Turin, the Duchies of Florence, Milan, Mantua, and Modena. In Germany, the one tie binding its many principalities was that of the Holy Roman Empire, the Emperor of which was elected by the various heads included within its confines.

At the time of Casanova's visit to Stuttgart, Duke Charles Eugene maintained, as Casanova has observed, one of the most brilliant of these petty courts. He was given over to dissipation and lavish display, and though his infidelities had been numerous, his consort had left him, not so much for these, but, according to Casanova, for some outrageous offense, which he does not specify. For all his own dissipation, the duke had made of Stuttgart one of the cultural centers of Germany, where he had attracted Jean Georges Noverre, creator of the world famous ballets, as well as Niccoló Jomelli, known as the Italian Gluck, one of the greatest opera composers of the century. With Casanova's widespread acquaintances in the theatrical world, many of the members of the duke's court were already known to him, including in particular the Gardella, prima ballerina, wife of Michael del Agata who, with the famous choreographer Sauveterre, had organized in 1758 the Opera and the Comedy ballet at Stuttgart. At the duke's request, according to Casanova, Agata had ceded his wife to him as mistress, and she had become the Pompadour of the court, with the title of "Madame," employing her talents when the duke tired of her, as her more famous prototype, in passing the dancers successively into the arms of the duke. The picture that Casanova gives us is typical of the depraved atmosphere that prevailed at this time not only in Stuttgart but at other German princely courts as well.[3] It is a striking one, and Casanova, with his customary verve and attention to detail has portrayed it well.

At Stuttgart he had the ill fortune to fall in with three Württemberg officers who, with the promise of play and women, persuaded him to accompany them to a house of prostitution, where he encountered his old acquaintance Pocchini and the latter's two "nieces" whom he had previously met in Holland. In a game of cards into which he was enticed, and under the influence of drugs introduced in his drink, he lost 4,000 louis in pledges. In the end he found himself in so helpless a condition that he had to be transported to his inn in a sedan chair where, upon undressing, he discovered he had been stripped of his watches and a gold snuffbox. Casanova was never a heavy drinker; the loss of his wits on this occasion was due not to inebriation but to the drugs administered to him.

After vainly seeking justice of the duke, he was confined to house arrest and threatened with impressment in the army unless he paid up. While temporizing with his three creditors, he succeeded in transferring his jewels and all his effects, concealed on the persons of his theatrical friends, from his quarters to those of the Binetti, mistress of the Austrian ambassador who was lodged in a residence overlooking the city walls. Effecting his escape by a clever stratagem under circumstances as ingenious, if not as difficult, as from the Leads, he was lowered, with his belongings, from the room of the Binetti to a coach awaiting him beneath the city walls, and was off on April 2, 1760. Ilges found in 1926 at Stuttgart in the archives a document signed "De Julliers," apparently the real name of the servant, Le Duc, that confirms in part Casanova's report. He himself tells us that when escaping from the quarters guarded by a sentinel, he had been obliged to leave Le Duc behind to checkmate the guard, with orders to rejoin him at Furstemberg, which he did some days later after temporary incarceration by the infuriated authorities. The document discovered by Ilges, dated April 9, 1760, was a request by the signatory "De Julliers" that he be released. In it he describes himself as a former hairdresser in Paris; it may be recalled that Casanova gave high praise to Le Duc's ability in that regard. This record is significant in that it confirms indirectly Casanova's troubles at Stuttgart, and also assists us in establishing the chronology of this period.

Once Le Duc had rejoined him, Casanova headed for Zurich,

where he could not have arrived much before April 12. There, the fancy took him to pay an impromptu visit on foot, a march of six hours, to the celebrated Benedictine Abbey of Einsiedeln, where he momentarily gave thought to adopting a monastic life. The prince-abbé, Nicholas II Imfeld, with considerable insight into Casanova's character, counseled him to give two weeks reflection to his decision. On his return to Zurich, a beautiful woman who came to lodge with her two companions at his inn, awakened him from his spiritual dreams. He assumed the garb of a waiter to obtain access to her, but all the knowledge he gained was that she was newly married to a man considerably older than herself, that she had come on a pilgrimage with friends to Einsiedeln, and was from Soleure.

All thought of a monastic career was dispelled as he determined to proceed eventually to Soleure in her pursuit. He masked her identity discreetly under the name of "Mme. de . . . ," but the pains he took were in vain. We know that she was the Baroness de Roll whom Boswell was later to meet at Soleure on November 28, 1764, that she was twenty-two when Casanova first saw her, and she had been married a little more than a year to Baron Victor Joseph de Roll, twenty-seven years older than she. Her marriage act shows the date of July 29, 1750, but P. Grellet, an authority, is of the opinion that the date was perhaps incorrectly entered in the register.[4]

Much has been made by critics scornful of Casanova's veracity of the finding among his papers of a document dated April 24, 1760, establishing that on that date he pledged certain of his effects with a Zurich merchant, J. Escher, for the sum of eighty gold louis, notwithstanding the statement in his *Memoirs* that at Zurich he estimated he was the possessor of a fortune of 100,000 écus. This is as if one were to impute poverty to any wealthy man who borrowed money. When Casanova computed his possessions at 100,000 écus he was referring to his material ones and not necessarily to liquid funds. As a lavish spender and inveterate gambler he was constantly at loose ends financially. To obtain cash, while awaiting funds from Mme. d'Urfé or Bragadin, it was his common practice to pledge his effects. From his letters, we know he raised cash in this manner at Turin late in 1762, again at

Milan a little later, and there is record of his raising 50 sequins on his jewels in April 1763 at Genoa.

At Soleure he found a letter from Mme. d'Urfé awaiting him, enclosing one from the Duke de Choiseul, foreign minister, to M. de Chavigny, French ambassador. Casanova states that Chavigny had been ambassador at Venice thirty years before; what he intended to convey was, no doubt, that while enjoying the rank of ambassador he had made a visit to Venice. In this, as in a few other instances, Casanova errs not because of faulty memory, but because of mistakes made in the use of a language with which he was not altogether familiar.

The account Casanova gives us of Soleure, during his stay there from the end of April to the end of May 1760, affords us an intimate and charming picture of life in that town at this period. It was here that the French ambassador had his residence, as there was then no central capital for all the Swiss cantons. Berne, for example, had its own diplomatic representation abroad, while the papal nuncio resided not at Soleure, but at Lucerne. In passing from Zurich to Soleure, Casanova had gone out of his way to pay him a visit. He does not give his name, but we know that he was Niccolò Oddi and that he had assumed his functions only the December previous. There is a curious passage in the *Memoirs* in which Casanova states that he wrote to a woman in Soleure, Mme. F, advising her that when she went to Lucerne, and should she see the papal nuncio, "speak to him of me, and you will learn what reputation I have in Europe." There is no other reference in the *Memoirs* to this acquaintanceship with Oddi, who later became a cardinal. There is no question that Casanova enjoyed a reputation throughout Europe, if for no other reason than his escape from the Leads.

For distraction in Soleure there were amateur theatricals, piquet, exchanges of visits, and continual rounds of entertainment. Chavigny, who took Casanova under his wing, suggested that he rent a country place, perhaps the nearby Château de Waldeck, the better to accomplish his design on Baroness de Roll. The ambassador, after a most distinguished diplomatic career, was then about seventy years of age, and as interested in Casanova's intrigue as if it had been his own.

It proved to be one of the greatest deceptions in his life. When he arranged for the de Rolls to pay him a visit, another woman who had been attracted to him. Mme. F., invited herself for a stay. On the night of his tryst with the Baroness, Mme. F. succeeded in replacing her. It was not until the next day that Casanova was made aware of the ruse, when the baroness asked what had prevented him from keeping his rendezvous with her. He had even greater case for concern when Mme. F., after the revenge she had so melevolently wreaked upon him for his previous indifference, left him a note taunting him for having fallen into her trap. She added that she had probably bestowed on him an unwelcome present; he had better look to his health. In his double misfortune, Casanova took his attractive housekeeper, Mme. Dubois, into his confidence. When his servant, Le Duc, fell ill with the same disease with which Casanova soon was afflicted, it was Mme. Dubois who suggested he revenge himself on Mme. F. by representing to her that it was Le Duc rather than himself who had enjoyed her favors in the dark. The incident was finally turned to Casanova's satisfaction as well as to that of Le Duc, who was handsomely recompensed pecuniarily by the humiliated Mme. F. when she was convinced that it was indeed Casanova's servant to whom she had given her favors and her affliction.

As may be gathered, Mme. Dubois was a woman of superior intelligence. Casanova conceived for her a stronger affection, at least temporarily, than that which he commonly extended his loves. She quoted Locke to him and, after he had recovered his health, satisfied his carnal desires. Her identity has never been revealed; the little we know of her is what she told Casanova. Born about 1733 or 1734, she passed from the service of Baroness Louise d'Hermanche, of Lausanne, about 1751 into that of Elizabeth Montagu, famous British bluestocking, and married a Montagu valet de chambre about 1754. When he died at Windsor about 1757, she returned to her mother at Lausanne.[5]

When Casanova left Soleure, he took Mme. Dubois with him to Berne. While there, she received a letter from Lebel, majordomo of Chavigny, proposing marriage and offering her a marriage settlement of 100,000 francs. Although she wrote at once rejecting the offer, Casanova was disturbed by the thought that he could not

give her advantages comparable to those Lebel offered. To resolve
his perplexity he wrote to Chavigny requesting:

> enlightenment in the matter without concealing that I was in love
> but that, being at the same time an honorable man, it would be no
> less painful for me to give her up than to place an obstacle in the
> way of the permanent happiness of the Dubois.

Here we see the better side of Casanova. Conscious of his inconstant nature and indisposed to bind himself by marriage, he
never demanded that a woman sacrifice the opportunity of a
permanent establishment with another. Chavigny wrote him that
the honorable course would be to cede Mme. Dubois. After she and
Casanova had given some further reflection to the decision she
should take, it was at length resolved, after they had reached
Lausanne, that they should separate to permit her marriage.

What is most striking about the extraordinary assemblage of
women whom Casanova passes in review is the manner in which
he brings out their distinct personalities. Far from resembling one
another, they are as varied as portraits painted on canvas from life.
It is rare that, outside Shakespeare and Balzac, such a gallery of
portraits is given us; those who see in them an assembly of the
same types are singularly insensitive to the nuances of Casanova's
deft characterizations, which he presents less in descriptions than
through actions and in speech.

While in Berne, Casanova paid a visit to public baths known as
the Matte, of which other travelers have left description, but none
so detailed as his. From Greek and Roman times and perhaps even
earlier, public baths had been a center of prostitution; this was so
much the case in Switzerland that as early as the fifteenth century
they had been stigmatized as centers of debauchery. On his first
visit Casanova was accompanied into the bath by a woman he had
chosen from a number available. Although she was pretty and
young, he was not tempted by her charms; it was all too facile to
suit him, without the charm of coquetry, and, since she was
without clothing, without any element of mystery. After dressing
and paying for the bath, he offered her a tip of six francs, which
she indignantly refused. He perceived that her *amour-propre* had

been offended by his failure to yield to her attractions, and he departed mortified and in a bad humor.

When he told the story to Mme. Dubois, she expressed a desire to assume the attire of a man and to accompany him the next day to see the establishment for herself. There they chose two girls and spent two hours in the bath together, where, for all her modesty, she became there and then his mistress. It is noteworthy that far from dilating upon the circumstances in objectionable detail, he recounts them with the same clinical detachment as a doctor discussing a case history.

At Berne Casanova had made the acquaintance of a "M. de M.F." whose name he conceals because of the disclosures made concerning his daughter. M. de M.F. was, in reality, Louis de Muralt-Favre, and, as Casanova says, his eldest daughter was then thirteen years of age. But she was not, as he says, named Sara, that being the name of the youngest daughter, then aged nine. Casanova switched names as he did in 1744 when he reversed the names of the sisters Angelica and Lucrezia. After Muralt-Favre and his wife and eldest daughter supped with Casanova and Mme. Dubois, "Sara" took a strong fancy for the latter, and began to call on her and Casanova before they got out of bed. Excited by the caresses "Sara" bestowed on Mme. Dubois, Casanova was moved to caress Mme. Dubois in turn in "Sara's" presence. Eventually "Sara" invited Casanova to intimacy with her, further proof, if any is needed, of the slight importance attached to sexual acts in the eighteenth century, the more particularly as the invitation was seconded by Mme. Dubois. The episode was initially questioned by Pierre Grellet, who has given the most studious examination to Casanova's sojourn in Switzerland, until he discovered correspondence of 1771 according to which Louis de Muralt-Favre, financially ruined, did not hesitate to profit from the exploitation of his daughter's charms.[6]

Before leaving Soleure, Casanova had asked Chavigny to give him a letter of introduction to a cousin of Louis de Muralt-Favre, Bernard de Muralt, distinguished Swiss magistrate at Berne. The latter welcomed him cordially, and was asked by Casanova to introduce him in turn to Albert Haller, residing at Roche, who enjoyed a European reputation. It is noteworthy that Casanova never neglected an opportunity to make the acquaintance of men of outstanding intellectual gifts such as Haller. The Berne library possesses a letter of June 21, 1760, from Muralt to Haller relevatory of our subject:

> We have here [in Switzerland] for a couple of months, lodging at the Couronne, a foreigner named the Chevalier de Seingalt who was strongly recommended to me by the Marquis de Gentils at the instance of a prominent lady of Paris. He left here day before yesterday for Lausanne, where he will remain some time, and from where he proposes to visit you, being anxious: 1. to see you and 2. to see the salt establishment. This foreigner is worthy of being received by you and will be for you certainly a curiosity, for he is an enigma we have been unable to resolve here, nor discover who he is.
>
> He does not know so much as you, but he knows much. He speaks of everything with much fire, appearing to have seen and read prodigiously. It is said that he knows all the oriental languages. He wrote directly no letter of recommendation here for anyone. It appears that he does not wish to be known. He receives each day an abundant number of letters by post, writes every morning . . . He speaks French in an Italian manner, having been reared in Italy. He told me his history, too long to be recounted here. He will tell it to you if you wish. He tells me he is a free man, a citizen of the world, that he observes the laws of all sovereigns under whom he lives. He has led here a strictly regulated life. His dominant taste is natural history and chemistry; my cousin Louis de Muralt . . . who was strongly attached to him and who has given him also a letter for you imagines he is the Count de Saint-Germain. He has given me proofs of his knowledge of the cabala which are astonishing if true and make him something of a sorcerer . . . in sum, he is a very singular personage. He could not be better dressed and equipped. After you, he intends to go and see Voltaire to tell him, as well, how many faults there are in his books. I do not know whether so charitable a man will be to Voltaire's taste . . .

The sequel proved Muralt correct because, if we have no positive evidence of Voltaire's reaction to Casanova's visit, it is apparent from the distaste that the latter showed thereafter for the philosopher that Voltaire had not taken him as seriously as he doubtless felt he deserved. Casanova's habitual brashness and readiness to challenge Voltaire's views must inevitably have been ill received by a figure of such commanding reputation, unaccustomed to have his pronouncements disputed by one still unknown in the world of letters. The opening gambits in the first meeting between the two historic figures, the one at the height of his power and the other with no literary reputation, merits quotation:

> "This," I said to him, "is the happiest moment of my life. I have a sight finally of my master; it is for twenty years, sir, that I have been your pupil."
> "Honor me with another twenty, but promise me also to come and bring my fees at the end of that time."
> "I promise it, but promise me also to wait for me."
> "I give you my word and shall die rather than fail to keep it."

The Voltairian sally was applauded by the numerous visitors, as usual, in attendance. The scene was Les Délices, then Voltaire's residence near Geneva, and the date about July 5, 1760. The exchange of views between Casanova and Voltaire, which continued over a period of four days, during which Casanova was invited to dine each day at Les Délices, ranged over a wide variety of subjects, principally literary, and was concerned for the most part with Italian authors. It is possible to bring verification to bear upon some of their remarks. When Voltaire questioned Casanova about Count Algarotti, he told his visitor that if he saw him at Bologna he should ask him to send him his *Lettres sur la Russie* through the Milanese banker Bianchi. There is a letter of Voltaire extant of September 1760 to Algarotti in which this request is repeated with specific mention of Bianchi.

Questioned by Voltaire as to the branch of literature to which he devoted himself, Casanova replied "to none" for the moment, adding:

> that will come, perhaps. Meanwhile I read as much as I can and take pleasure in studying mankind while traveling.

Voltaire observed that his objective would be better attained through reading history. Casanova objected that history lied and was tiresome, while the study of the world when voyaging was more amusing. Horace, he added, was his itinerary, and he found him everywhere. He acknowledged also, in response to a question from Voltaire, that poetry was his passion, that he had written a dozen sonnets that pleased him, and two or three thousand he had never reread. Asked which Italian poet he admired most, he named Ariosto, adding that he could not say that he was fonder of Ariosto than others as he loved only that poet, although he had read all.

When Voltaire was reproached with the critical remarks he had made about Ariosto fifteen years previous, he offered in justification that he had read Ariosto as a youth at a time when he had an imperfect appreciation of the Italian tongue and had been influenced by the Italian judgment that at that time had placed Tasso above Ariosto. He added that he had subsequently retracted his evaluation. These remarks are perfectly in keeping with what we know from other sources. Between 1730 and 1750, in both his correspondence and in his published works, it is always Tasso whom he exalts, but about 1756, with the publication of *Essai sur les moeurs*, he appears to have revised his opinion when he places Ariosto's *Orlando furioso* above even the *Odyssey*.

Voltaire proceeded to recite two extended extracts from Ariosto and, when he had finished, observed: "All Europe will be informed by myself of the very humble reparation I owe to the greatest genius Italy has produced." When Voltaire published four years later in 1764 his *Dictionnaire philosophique*, he made specific reference to the change in his judgment for which he offered "humble reparation," in words identical with those attributed to him by Casanova, devoting a lengthy eulogy to Ariosto and only a few lines to Tasso. So striking are the similarities between Voltaire's views in these published writings with those reported by Casanova that a number of skeptical critics contend that he went to Voltaire's published works for the fabrication of his account.

Casanova, requested in turn to recite what he considered the most sublime stanzas of Ariosto, chose the last twenty-six of the twenty-third canto, in which the poet described the madness with which Roland became possessed, adding that since the age of sixteen he had read Ariosto two or three times every year until the lines had become linked in his memory. We even know the edition

Casanova must have used. As he refers to fifty-one cantos, it must have been one published in Venice in 1609, containing that number instead of the usual forty-six.

During the evening interludes between Casanova's visits to Voltaire he passed his times far removed from intellectual concerns. The first day at Les Délices he had been accosted by a councilman of Geneva, who has been identified as probably Michel Lullin de Châteauvieux, aged sixty-five in 1760, and known as a great libertine. He volunteered to present Casanova to three girls, two sisters and a cousin, who entertained them both in a highly unconventional manner during at least three evenings of Casanova's stay. The councilman assured Casanova that he had brought them up and that Casanova was the first other than himself to have enjoyed their favors. They are believed to have been the two sisters Fernette Elisabeth de Fernex and Marie de Fernex and their cousin Jeanne Christine de Fernex, then twenty-four, twenty-seven, and twenty-nine years, respectively.[7]

The second day of Casanova's visit to Voltaire, there was a discussion of Homer, Dante, and Petrarch. Of Dante and Petrarch Voltaire had expressed small opinion in his writings, and Casanova considered it wise to let him talk about those authors without directly challenging him. In his own account of the conversation, he noted that Voltaire had done himself wrong in passing such judgments when it would have been better for his critical reputation to have kept silent on the subject. Casanova contented himself with observing to Voltaire that "if those authors had not merited the esteem of those who had studied them, they would not have been placed in the high rank they occupied." These were not the only foreign classics for which Voltaire had little taste; he had none for Shakespeare, but that genius was not discussed, although we know from an occasional reference in the *Memoirs* that Casanova was acquainted with his works. Voltaire reminded him that Petrarch had been severely criticized by Tassoni. Casanova retorted that he had thus dishonored his good taste. "You must agree that his erudition is immense," Voltaire remarked, when speaking of Muratori. Not to be silenced, Casanova riposted with a quotation from Horace, *"Est ubi peccat"* (it is thus that he sins).

Voltaire conducted his visitor to his bedroom and showed him some 50,000 letters to which he had replied, remarking that he had kept copies of most of his answers. When Casanova let drop an Italian quotation with which Voltaire was not familiar, he asked from whom it was taken, and when Casanova answered that the source was Merlino Coccai, a Mantuan burlesque poet, Voltaire expressed a desire to examine a poem, described by Casanova as celebrated, with which he was not familiar.[8] The next day Voltaire thanked him for sending the poem, and the following and last day renewed his thanks for the good intention Casanova had shown, but not for the praise he had bestowed on the work, which had made him "lose four hours in reading nonsense." It was with the greatest difficulty that Casanova preserved his temper at the slighting references to a poem he held in such high esteem. It was one that had notably inspired Rabelais, anathema to Voltaire, who was far from sharing Casanova's broad-minded tastes in literature. It is this prejudice of the sage of Ferney against any author transgressing the strict classical tradition that explains Voltaire's antipathy to the Mantuan poet.

In the *Scrutinio*, written by Casanova some ten years before his *Memoirs*, the account is given in slightly different manner. In the former he stated:

> The next day I sent him at Les Délices a copy of the macaronic poem on which I had written comments. He accepted it but never said another word about it. I recounted this fact one day to one of his friends at Geneva, who wrote at once to Voltaire that I was curious to know if the history of Baldo had pleased him. Voltaire answered him: *One must have a strange taste to appreciate Merlino Coccai. I am sorry that M. de Casanova had thought to make me a nice present! I would gladly return it to him for it is nonsense.* Cut to the quick, I wrote him a letter in Italian to tell him: *I think that all things that please you are good, but I am not convinced that all those that displease you are bad.*[9]

It was an exchange characteristic of the two men, both excessively vain, the one accustomed to delivering judgments that were respected, and the other no less assured of his own, and not disposed to be intimidated by even one so Olympian as Voltaire. The sparks were bound to fly before they parted.

In the end the conversation shifted away from literature to religion and to politics. The exchange of their views on the latter is of particular appositeness to us today. "Loving humanity," Voltaire observed, "I wish to see it happy, as I am, and free; superstition is not reconcilable with liberty. Where do you find that servitude can bring about the happiness of a people?"

CASANOVA: "You would like to see, then, sovereignty vested in the people?"

VOLTAIRE: "God forbid. There must be one alone who governs."

CASANOVA: "Superstition is then necessary, for without it the people will never obey the monarch."

VOLTAIRE: "By no means a monarch, for the name suggests despotism, which I must hate as I do servitude."

CASANOVA: "What do you mean? If you wish but one to govern, I can only visualize a monarch."

VOLTAIRE: "I would have him command a free people, and for that he would be its chief, and one would not be able to call him monarch, for he could never arbitrate."

CASANOVA: "Addison tells you that this monarch, this chief, is not among existing possibilities. I am for Hobbes. Between two evils, one must choose the least. A people without superstition would be philosophers, and philosophers have never wished to obey. The people can never be happy unless crushed, oppressed, and held by chains . . . Your first passion is the love of humanity. *Et ubi peccas.* This love blinds you. Love humanity, but you should love it such as it is. It is not capable of absorbing the benefits you would bestow upon it, and in doing so you render it unhappy and more evil. Leave it the beast that devours it. This beast is dear to it. I have never laughed so much as when I saw Don Quixote embarrassed at having to defend himself against the galley slaves whom, on account of his great soul, he had just freed."

Despite the four days spent by Casanova with Voltaire from about July 5 to July 8, the name of the former is nowhere found in the latter's correspondence. In a letter of July 7, 1760, to M. Thiriot he does remark, in an allusion that seems most certainly to refer to Casanova:

> We have here an amusing fellow, quite capable of fashioning a kind of *Secchia rapita*, and of describing the enemies of reason with all the intemperance of their impertinence. Perhaps my droll one will make a gay and amusing poem on a subject that hardly so appears.

Reinforcing the conclusion that Voltaire was undoubtedly referring here to Casanova is specific mention by the latter of having observed, on the second day of his visit, in Voltaire's bedroom, a copy of Tassoni's *Secchia rapita*, and of Voltaire's describing it as the only tragicomic poem Italy could claim.

There is another possible reference to Casanova by Voltaire. Writing to Albergati on September 15, 1760, Voltaire stated: "It is true that you have afforded me just now pleasure by your translation and by your good answer to this Ca . . . " Theodore Besterman, of the Voltaire Institute, is of the opinion that there "is certainly little doubt that the reference here is to Casanova."

The account of Casanova's visit to Voltaire as recorded in the *Memoirs* is but an abridgment of one he spent a part of a night and a day recording. Unhappily this longer version has never come to light, but he may have incorporated parts of it in his *Confutazione*, *Scrutinio*, and *À Leonard Snetlage*. In the last is found this reflection:

> I have all my life dreaded the charge of plagiarism. The only means of safeguarding me from it has been to quote. Voltaire made light of it. He said that what he had written was his despite Philippe de Comines having written two hundred years before him. But a Voltaire could speak in this fashion.

That these are not idle words is indicated by a letter Casanova addressed from Dux on April 13, 1791, to Count Lamberg. The *Gazette de Brünn* had published in March 1791 a note on Giovanni Casanova stating that Jacques Casanova, brother of the artist, was the author of the latin couplet decorating Giovanni's portrait of Raphael Mengs. To this Casanova replied that the attribution did him too great honor, that it was from the pen of Giovanni, "excellent Latin poet," and that the writer, although versed in such poetry, "did not consider himself sufficiently capable to produce two verses worthy of the century of Augustus."[10]

Early-nineteenth-century critics, other than German, paid scant attention to Casanova's revealing portrait of Voltaire. More recently, Georg Brandes has drawn upon it in his biography of that writer. Zottoli, in his study of Casanova, considers the chapter on Voltaire the most important in the *Memoirs*. Maynial, who has given it the most detailed and searching examination, has concluded that "altogether the picture is exact, and nothing can alter its historical and documentary importance."

# CHAPTER 8

# Mlle. Roman, Avignon, Marseilles, Nice, Genoa, Florence, and Rome

From Geneva, Casanova headed south toward Rome and Naples. His first stop was at Aix-en-Savoie, now Aix-les-Bains, filled in July, then as now, with a crowd of visitors, taking the waters and gambling. At that time it formed a part of the Kingdom of Sardinia and consequently attracted many Italians with a passion for cards. Casanova was not averse to tarrying overnight, unable to resist the plea of a pretty woman, Mme. Z., who made up to him on his arrival. What persuaded him, however, to defer his departure for several days was a chance encounter with a nun whom he at first mistook for M.M. and who, it turned out, bore that same name in religion. She had come from Chambéry to Aix, alleging the waters were necessary for her health but, in reality, to disburden herself of a child. With customary gallantry, Casanova was quick to aid her; his reflections on doing so offer an admirable insight into the philosophy that so largely governed him:

> In the light of my character it was impossible that I abandon her, but I had no longer any merit in so doing; I had become amorous of

this new M.M. with black eyes. I was determined to do all for her, and certainly not to allow her to return to the convent in the state in which she was. It seemed to me that in saving her I was executing the will of God. God had willed that I mistake her for M.M. God had made me win much money [in play at Aix]. God had furnished Mme. Z. so that the curious might not learn the true cause of my deferred departure. What have I not attributed to God throughout my life! In spite of that, the lowest of those judging me have always accused me of atheism.

His assistance to this second M.M. extended to the administration of opium to the nun chaperoning her so that she would ignore in her sleep the birth of the child. When the dose proved too strong, M.M., fearful of a scandal that might result, informed Casanova that she had decided not to summon a doctor, but to let nature take its course. When Casanova acquiesced and the chaperone failed to awaken, it is plain from his report that he was an accessory before the fact to an unwitting murder. It is almost superfluous to add that he became the new M.M.'s lover.

When M.M. returned to Chambéry, Casanova continued to Grenoble where, for a week, he entered into the social life of that town, thanks to a letter of introduction from the Marquise d'Urfé. At a concert he was taken with a Mlle. Roman-Coupier, of good family in modest circumstances. He laid determined siege to her unsuccessfully; she was willing to marry him but would not yield to him short of a consecration of their union.

The idea came to him to draw her horoscope, which he did in eight pages after cannily gathering details of her previous life. To these he added the prediction that fortune awaited her in Paris as mistress of the King, provided she was seen by him before her next birthday. In December, while in Florence, he tells us that he received a letter announcing that Mlle. Roman, beliving her horoscope would never be realized unless she went to Paris, had gone there. Five months later, in May 1761, he was informed by her aunt that Mlle. Roman had become the mistress of Louis XV, had a beautiful home in Passy and was five months pregnant. She gave him a letter to Mlle. Roman's sister in Paris, Mme. Varnier, on whom he called the following month, and through whom a meeting was arranged in her home with Mlle. Roman. The description she was to give him of her situation, including the contrast she drew between her melancholy state of luxury with that of her happiness at Grenoble when she had nothing, is one of the most interesting passages of the *Memoirs.*

French historians have debated as to how much truth may be attributed to Casanova's account. While it is not to be expected that his own role would appear in contemporary chronicles (Mlle. Roman informed him that she had thought of confiding it to the King but feared calumny), there is nothing in them in any way contradictory to Casanova's report. Barbier, writing in December 1761, stated that Mlle. Roman had been the King's mistress for about a year, while Du Gast de Bois de Saint-Just confirms she was introduced to the King by Mme. Varnier and that he gave her a beautiful home in Passy.[1] Moreover, Charles Samaran has noted that the autobiographical pages of April 8, 1775, left by her, reflect precisely that melancholy described by Casanova. We know also that a child was born to her of the King on January 13, 1762, Louis-Aimé de Bourbon. As Cucuel remarked:

> For once our man had bent destiny to his caprice, and one does not know what is most to be admired in this adventure: the audacity with which he has forged predictions of this kind, or the course of events that undertook to transform into reality the product of his imagination.[2]

From Grenoble Casanova passed, aboard a "commodious boat" by the Isère to Avignon, where he arrived about the middle of August, according to a letter establishing that date. It is the only record we have of the transport of passengers as well as merchandise by that means in the eighteenth century. His principal objective was a visit to the shrine of Petrarch at Vaucluse, and to that end he lingered a few days. At the time of his visit, Avignon, which had been for a brief period, beginning in 1309, seat of the papacy, was still under the dominion of the Pope, ruled in his absence at Rome by a papal vice legate, Gregorio Salviati, whom Casanova names and who had arrived on April 9, 1760. It was not until 1791, with the French Revolution, that Avignon passed finally under French authority.

Casanova's visit receives particular authentication by his mention of a young man-about-town named Dolci, described by him as "son of the captain of the vice legate guard." Records show that there was a captain of the Swiss guards at the vice legate palace of that name. He met also there an actress, Marguerite Astrodi, whose sister Rosalie, better known and more talented, he had already frequented in Paris some eight years previous. With Marguerite's hunch-backed companion, with whom she was playing at the local theater, Casanova spent an evening of debauch. He also met at his hotel, and generously assisted in their plight, the Stuards, an adventurer and his so-called wife, who were about to be ejected from the inn for lack of funds.

The compassion he manifested so often towards pretty women in distress was revealed in the horror with which he looked upon the possibility of her being put in the street with no other resources than her own person, which she had refused to exploit. He had ceded, he states, to a movement of pity with no thought of self-interest. Casanova's opinion of the putative husband as a contemptible ne'er-do-well was reinforced when he sought later to thrust Casanova in her arms to raise funds. One of Casanova's most marked characteristics was a fear of being duped, and, suspecting that the two might be in connivance, he decided to accept Stuard's offer of Mme. Stuard for the sum of twenty-five louis. When he entered her room, where she was in bed, she informed him that although she was ready to pay with her person for the sum her husband had specified, he should feel more humiliated than she, forced as she was by necessity. Apostrophizing her conduct, he told her that he was not a brute, that he would pay over the twenty-five louis without exacting anything from her and solely moved by pity. He added that, whatever the sum she accepted from a man, she was a lost woman as long as she did not share, or appear to share, the sentiment of the man to whom she gave herself. The account Casanova gives of the two, including her profound melancholy which oppressed him, sensitive as he was to the least expression of sadness in women, received unexpected illumination when we discover, as we shall see shortly, the true identity of the woman and her companion, the one of good bourgeois family, and her seducer, a thorough-paced rascal.

In Marseilles, Casanova met Rosalie, a maid in the home of a prostitute. Rosalie had but recently left home when scolded by her mother for flirting with a Genoese merchant who wished to marry her. Casanova had only to hear her tale of distress to take her under his wing. Equipping her with a suitable outfit, he persuaded her to accompany him to Genoa, to which they set out by the usual route, first overland to Antibes and then by felucca, leaving his carriage, which he would reclaim three years later. Obliged to put in at Villefranche because of rough weather, they proceeded to Nice, where they spent three days and where Casanova made the acquaintance of the commandant, an elderly officer whose name he misspells "Peterson." He was a fairly notable personage of his time, born in 1692, son of Sir Hugh Paterson of Bannockburn, second baronet and one of the many Scottish Jacobites in the eighteenth century who had emigrated and taken service with foreign governments. Now lieutenant general in the army of the Kingdom of Sardinia, which exercised jurisdiction over Nice until 1860, James Paterson had entered the Sardinian service in June 1716 and on June 17, 1752, had been named governor of the city and province of Nice, a post he held until April 16, 1763, when he returned to England. He died at Bath in 1765. An excellent administrator, he was of considerable aid in keeping the British informed of French naval movements in the Mediterranean at a time when Villefranche was a virtually British naval base and Sardinia was neutral in the struggle that divided Europe during the Seven Years' War.[3]

Attentive to all that went on within his province, Paterson interrogated Casanova about a number of recent travelers, including a certain Charles Iwanoff, who had preceded Casanova from Grenoble, and M. and Mme. Stuard, whom he had met at Avignon. Dr. F.L. Mars, intrigued by these references, investigated the Sardinian archives at Turin and found there a letter from Paterson of May 19, 1760, some four months before Casanova's visit in September. This letter, confirming Casanova's report, stated that a young man calling himself Baron de Neisen, with a young woman whom he represented as his wife, had arrived in Nice, and that the grand vicar, exercising the usual strict surveillance as an ecclesiastical authority, had demanded their marriage certificate, which they had been unable to supply. When they were ejected from their inn for nonpayment of their board, they were reexamined by the authorities and told a different story. They now claimed to be Baron Stuart of Frisot and Countess de Loo, both of the province of Liège, who had run away together, unbound by marriage, eighteen months earlier in order that the countess might escape the marriage tie her father wished to force upon her with a man considerably her elder. According to Paterson, the grand vicar was convinced of the truth of their tale, especially since the girl's education appeared above the common, and since she refused pecuniary aid despite her misery, for fear of risking her honor. Paterson announced that she had been placed in "an honest home" awaiting clarification of their circumstances from the grand vicar at Liège.

Through happy coincidence, Dr. Mars found next in the archives of Aix-la-Chapelle a letter of June 16, 1760, from the Bourgomasters of the city to the vicar general of Nice, stating that the so-called Baron Stuart was in reality a Tuard of Aix-la-Chapelle, while his companion was Marie Anne Constance Louise des Grafs, daughter of a lawyer of the same city. She had escaped from her home with the "adventurer."[4]

Reembarking on a felucca, Casanova and Rosalie arrived in Genoa the following morning. From another source, we are given details of their arrival omitted in the *Memoirs*.[5]

Disembarking one day at the Ponte Reale of Genoa, arriving from Antibes in a splendid equipage and in company of another traveler, he saw running towards him with open arms, a certain Gritti, who played the part of Brighella, and was one of his intimate friends. The adventurer assumed a grave air, and darting a stern eye at him, he said "You are mistaken, I am the Chevalier de Saint-Galle." Brighella was astonished, but before he could recover from his surprise, the pseudo chevalier gave him a wink as much as to say: "Listen, look, keep quiet." And Gritti let him pass and only recounted it after his departure.

The presence in Genoa in 1760 of Luigi Gritti, a Venetian who played the parts both of Brighella and Pantalon in the troupe of

Pietro Rossi, is supported by a reference a little later to Pietro Rossi in Casanova's own account. He was in Genoa "manager of a troupe of comedians," and Casanova gave him a translation he had made of Voltaire's *Écossaise*, which Rossi offered to produce.[6] As in Soleure a few months earlier, Casanova took himself a part in the play, that of Murray.

In Genoa, where he was to remain for some two months, Casanova received the visit of Marquis Gian Giacomo Grimaldi,[7] whom he had met previously at Avignon, and with whom he was to continue to maintain friendly relations for several years. He had been succeeded only two years before as Doge of Genoa. He was as captivated as Casanova by a pretty face, and immediately cast a covetous eye on Rosalie and interested himself in finding a suitable companion for her, moved no doubt by the consideration that if she could be displaced by another in Casanova's affections, he himself might succeed in stepping into the breach. He appears to have been extremely shrewd and skillful in playing his cards, more so perhaps than Casanova suspected. He not only introduced Veronique, an attractive young Genoese, to serve Rosalie, but upon learning that her Genoese intended was none other than his godson, the young merchant Paretti, he arranged a luncheon with the inclusion of Paretti, his uncle and aunt, Casanova, and Rosalie, with no previous intimation to these last of his plans. Casanova was outraged by the trick played on him by the cunning marquis. However, upon reflection, and on the proposal of Paretti that Rosalie enter a convent until she could be assured to which of the two she owed her pregnancy, following which he was still prepared to marry her, Rosalie, looking obviously to the main chance, accepted. With the departure of Rosalie, Veronique's mother had placed with her as chaperone her daughter's sister, Annette, but she was so far from being able to fill that role that she yielded to Casanova's blandishments when Veronique held out on him. In the end Veronique was also willing to surrender, but it was too late. The several characters in this drama will reappear with Casanova's passage through Genoa again in 1763.[8]

He set out about the middle of November for Florence, Rome, and Naples, and after passing through Leghorn and Pisa, arrived towards the end of the month in Florence, where he remained

until about December 19. At the Opera there, he was dumbfounded
to see as prima donna the Thérèse Lanti he had left in Rimini
sixteen years previous. She recognized Casanova from the stage
and, at the end of the act, beckoned to him with a fan. He joined
her in the wings, and after the exchange of a few hurried words she
gave him a rendezvous at her quarters the following morning.
Upon returning to his seat, he realized that in his excitement over
their meeting he had failed to inquire as to her present name or
address. He asked a young man seated next to him the name of the
principal singer and learned, to his astonishment, that she was his
wife and bore the name of Palesi. Thérèse, as we now know, was
none other than the famous singer Angiola Calori. She showed
Casanova a son she represented as his. He claims that she, her
husband, and himself were guests of Sir Horace Mann, who had
resided in Florence since 1737 as British minister, and as such had
a very distinguished position there. Although there is no verification of this in the letters of Mann, now at the Yale University
Library, there can be no question that Casanova knew the British
diplomat. He is found under the name of "Nobil Cavaliere Orazio
Mann, Inviato Straordinario di S.M. Brit. alla Corti di Toscane,"
among the earliest subscribers in 1775 to Casanova's partial translation of Homer's *Iliad*. The description he has left of Mann, the
garden of his home, and his art gallery of paintings, sculptures,
mosaics, and engraved stones, conforms in every respect with what
is known of the British representative and of his hospitable life in
Florence.[9]

Another important acquaintanceship Casanova renewed in
Florence was that with Abbé Gama, a Portuguese whom he had
known in Rome in 1744 and who, as secretary of the Portuguese
embassy to the Vatican, now proposed that Casanova represent
Portugal at the Augsburg Congress, scheduled to convene in the
summer of 1761 to bring about European peace. Through
Thérèse, Casanova met Marianne Corticelli, a Bolognese dancer.
It was an unlucky turn of fate, as events were to prove both for her
and for him, when he chose her as an instrument in the regeneration of Mme. d'Urfé in 1762.[10]

We have to rely solely on Casanova's word about these encounters, but there is another person he mentions, Charles Iwanoff,

whose presence is confirmed by the Florence archives. This shadowy adventurer, who may have been a native of Dantzig and who represented himself as a Russian nobleman, had been the author of a false letter of exchange some months earlier according to the *Gazette de Schaffhouse* of March 19, 1760. Casanova met him first in Grenoble, then in Avignon, and once more in Genoa, In each instance, he avoided Iwanoff's overtures. In Florence, Iwanoff wrote him from the Hôla Poste in Pistoia, enclosing a bill of exchange, and asking that Casanova arrange for its negotiation. Suspecting it to be false, he returned the bill in person at once, and advised Iwanoff to solicit the aid of his landlord for its cashing. When the bill was later found false, Casanova was invited to make it good on the grounds that Iwanoff had received it from him. When he refused, he was summoned by the chief of police of Florence who tried to induce him to reimburse the innkeeper. Casanova replied that to do so would be to acknowledge that he had been a party to the cheating. The following day he received word from the chief of police that while he could not force him to pay, he would have to leave town in three days.

Through a search in the Florence archives, three letters have been found for us, dated December 2, 4, and 12, 1760, from the chief of police to the judge of Pistoia, which not only in part support Casanova's account, but add some interesting details. The first acknowledges receipt of information about the young foreigner (Iwanoff) who had been "for some weeks in Pistoia" and adds "that information is being sought about the person (Casanova) who moved from the Hotel Vannini in Florence to the Nuova Osteria in Pistoia." In the second letter the chief of police states that contrary to his first information, the chevalier residing at the Hotel Vannini is not Portuguese but Venetian, "a man of letters, smart and cunning, representing himself as capable of various activities." The judge was asked to ascertain, if possible, the character of the intrigues between the two individuals and to ensure that the former should not impose on those who might too readily loan him money. It was added:

> The person who lodged at the Hotel Vannini lives decently but not lavishly and has no debts whatsoever. He is accompanied by two

persons, one of whom serves him as secretary [Costa], the other as valet [Le Duc], and there is besides a local servitor ["laquais de place"].[11]

This same person passed in the beginning as the Chevalier Sangalli [Seingalt], now in the hotel register he is inscribed under the name of Chevalier Santacrux, of Portuguese nationality. He is supposed to remain until the 17th of this month, having the intention to go to Rome and then to proceed to Naples, where he knows the Duke de Matalone.

Casanova had adopted in 1759 the title Chevalier de Seingalt, why or under what circumstances we do not know. We first hear of its use in Grenoble in July 1760. At Augsburg, the next year, when taxed by a magistrate as to why he used a false name, Casanova denied it to be such, adding that he should:

". . .inquire of the banker Carli through whom I cashed 50,000 gulden."

"But I know that your name is Casanova, so why do you call yourself Seingalt?"

"Because that name is mine and belongs rightly to me as I added it myself. No one can claim it, and besides, everyone is free to call me Casanova if he so desires."

"Either one or the other must be your name; a man cannot have two names. And now tell me, by what right can one add another name?"

"That is clear: everyone has the right to use the alphabet as he likes. I have chosen eight letters and have combined them in such a way as to produce the word Seingalt. I have chosen to add this to my name and, as it alone belongs to me, I maintain that no one can have any pretensions to it."

"That is a strange argument; your name ought to be none other than your father's."

"You are mistaken. The name that you bear you have had from your forefathers and from an ancestor who did not inherit it from his father. It is even true that under these circumstances you were once called Adam. Don't you admit this, Mr. Magistrate?"

"I admit it, but the thing is new to me."

"There you are again mistaken. Far from being a novelty, it is very old, and I shall make it my duty to bring you tomorrow a whole litany of names that have been invented by very honorable men who are living today, and enjoy them peacefully without being cited to appear at the city hall to render an account to anyone unless their signature is repudiated to the detriment of society."

"But you must admit that false names are forbidden by the law."

"I wish to repeat to you that nothing can be more genuine than my name. Even your name could not be any more genuine as it is possible that you are not the son of the one whom you perhaps consider your father."

He smiled, arose, accompanied me to the door, and said: "I am going to inform myself about you from M. Carli."[12]

Besides the name of Chevalier de Seingalt, Casanova occasionally used that of Count de Farussi after the maiden name of his mother, but "Chevalier Santacrux" presents something of an enigma. One explanation is that Abbé Gama had counseled him to use this Portuguese name in anticipation of the Augsburg mission proposed to him.

In the third and final letter of the chief of police of December 12, 1760, we learn that Iwanoff, described as "vagabond," had fled from Pistoia and that the chief was considering the measures to be taken against his "companion," Casanova, of the Hotel Vannini in Florence. It must have been a few days later that, as we learn from the *Memoirs*, Casanova was given orders to leave Florence within three days. While we do not have the entire file of letters exchanged between the chief of police and the Pistoia judge, it is clear from the evidence available that no malfeasance could be established against Casanova over the Iwanoff bill of exchange or else he would not have been permitted to leave. Gugitz maintained that Iwanoff was a figment of Casanova's imagination; these letters should dispose finally of that hypothesis.[13]

Although Casanova remained only ten days in Rome on his way to Naples and another ten days on his return, it was sufficient for him to make important new acquaintances and have a new love affair. With striking facility, he could turn from serious affairs of the mind to the satisfaction of his senses. We have already observed a notable instance of this when, during his stay in Geneva, after passing the day with Voltaire, he spent his nights with three girls of good family but of easy virtue. Many men have done likewise, but none have so frankly revealed this side of his life. Thus the portraits Casanova presents of himself and others have an extraordinary vitality, a lifelikeness that makes other memoirs stale and flat by comparison. One must go to imaginative writers such as Shakespeare and Chekhov to find comparable life in the raw, not idealized and romanticized, but as it is in all its dimensions, sublime and ridiculous, tawdry and noble. It is noteworthy that even in the freest passages of Casanova's *Memoirs*, forming not ten percent of the whole, there is no suggestion of pornography. He gives erotic details, when he does, to add the essential element of truth to the narrative, and to round out the characters. If such details have appeared or have been represented, otherwise, the fault lies not so much with Casanova, as with Jean Laforgue, whose version of the *Memoirs* in French is that on which the judgment of posterity has been largely based. It is now evident, with the publication of Casanova's original text in 1960, that Laforgue, rather than pruning away Casanova's licentiousness, as his task was commonly considered to have been when his text first appeared in 1826-38, often gratuitously accentuated Casanova's narrative when it dealt with erotic situations, and in many instances transformed unadorned descriptions with prurient details foreign to Casanova's pen.

In Rome Casanova lodged on the Piazza di Spagna at the Ville de Londres which he misnames Ville de Paris, the proprietor of which, Charles Roland, had a daughter, Thérèse, who was to marry Casanova's brother Giovanni in 1764. In 1760 Giovanni was a pupil of the celebrated painter Raphael Mengs, with whom he lodged. We not only know the exact address, Via Vittoria No. 54, but the name of the boardinghouse keeper, Francesco de Rossi, who had premises in the same building, and from whom Mengs and Giovanni Casanova took their meals.[14]

After fifteen years' absence, Casanova was anxious to have news of Cecilia Monti, mother of the two sisters, Lucrezia and Angelica, whom he had known in Rome in 1744, but when he went to the Minerva in search of her, he learned that she had died a year earlier. This further substantiates the supposition that Cecilia Monti was, in reality, Cecilia d'Antoni. The records of Minerva parish in Rome reveal that Cecilia d'Antoni moved from that parish in 1754, and there is no further mention of her. She would have been sixty-eight in 1760. Through Giovanni Casanova and Mengs, then head of the Academy of Painting in Rome, Casanova was introduced to the artistic world of that city. He gives us a description of his visit to Countess Cheruffini, mistress of Cardinal Alexander Albani, where he met the renowned archaeologist and art historian Johann Winckelmann who, two years earlier, had been named librarian and keeper of the extensive collection of antiquities of the cardinal. Giovanni Casanova was working at this time in close collaboration with Winckelmann, to whose *Monumenti inediti* he contributed certain designs. Casanova tells us that Winckelmann escorted him to the Villa Albani to see the celebrated ceiling that Mengs was painting there, which he is known to have begun in July 1760 and to have completed in March of the year following. Casanova's amazement at the richness of the Villa and the remarkable collection of antiquities it contained is understandable as it was even then one of the most renowned in the world. After being pillaged later by the troops of Napoleon, the collection was eventually dispersed.

In his dedication to letters, Casanova also called on Cardinal Passionei, librarian of the Vatican, to whom he decided to make a personal gift of a valuable book, a *Pandectorum liber unicus* for the cardinal's own important collection. In this Casanova was doubtless prompted by a certain pique in having been left standing initially during the audience. The cardinal, presumably to make amends for what, in his touchiness, Casanova had interpreted as demeaning him, had presented him with a copy of a funeral oration he had published in Latin on the death of Prince Eugene. In offering him in return a much more valuable book, Casanova's thought must have been: He has not treated me with the consideration to which I feel I am entitled; I shall show him that I am capable of a nobler gesture than he. Casanova, however, had not sufficiently calculated on the cardinal's astuteness.

Later Casanova was received in audience by Pope Clement XIII, whom he had known as a bishop at Padua, and he drew from the Holy Father hearty laughs with the account of his reception by Cardinal Passionei. But the Pope predicted that the cardinal would return Casanova's gift unless Casanova was willing to accept payment for it. The latter remarked that in such a case he would return the cardinal's funeral oration as he was not a bookdealer. He was obliged to do so: The cardinal, declaring the book was too valuable a present, did proffer payment, and Casanova immediately returned the less valuable book the cardinal had sent him. He made a present of the *Pandectorum* to the Vatican Library. It may have been as a return for this gift that he received shortly thereafter the Papal Order of the Eperon d'Or (the Golden Spur). So proud was he of this distinction that he had it mounted with precious stones. Five years later he gave up wearing it when, in Warsaw, Prince Czartoryski ridiculed his possession of a decoration described as "a drug on the market worn only by charlatans." The Order had one virtue: it gave him the right to bear the title of "Chevalier," one, however, which he had already assumed the previous year.

# CHAPTER 9

## Naples, Portuguese Mission, Geneva, and Turin

In Florence, Casanova had told Thérèse of his intention to visit the Duke de Matalone, whom he had first met as a child in Naples in 1744, and whom he had seen in Paris in 1752, at which time the duke had made him a pressing offer of hospitality. Before making his presence in Naples known to the duke, Casanova made inquiries of his other Neapolitan friends, including in particular Lucrezia and her husband the lawyer, Giacomo Castelli, whom we have previously identified as Anna Maria and Alessio Vallati. The latter had died some years before, and his widow, Casanova was told, was living some twenty miles from the city, as a paying guest with the distinguished family of the Marquis Berardo de Galiani at Saint Agata.

When Casanova called on the duke at his palace, the latter insisted that Casanova should lodge with him. But his wife, the daughter of the Duke de Bovino, far from sharing her young husband's friendship for Casanova, treated him with great haughtiness. Since de Matalone was generally credited with impotence, there was great surprise when, in 1758, his wife gave birth to a son, the last of this distinguished line. When shown the son, Casanova remarked that he had been unwilling to believe the news of the birth when first apprised of it. Glancing toward the duchess and, in an effort to ingratiate himself with her, he observed that it was now possible for him to make honorable amends for his incredulity when perceiving "the angel" who had accomplished the miracle.

The duke conducted Casanova to the San Carlo theater, habitual rendezvous of Neapolitan society, where the young King, Ferdinand I, to whom he gives the age of nine years, was present for the celebration of an anniversary, the character of which Casanova was unable to recall when writing his *Memoirs*. It is possible for us to supply the detail and to fix the date. It was the anniversary of the King's own birth, ten years previous, on January 12, 1751. King of Naples under the title of Ferdinand IV, he had succeeded two years earlier, as Ferdinand I, to the Kingdom of the Two Sicilies when his father had assumed the throne of Spain as Charles III. The performance witnessed by Casanova, although he does not name it, was the *Attilio Regolo* of Metastasio, set to music by Jomelli. Another spectacle he attended lasted four hours, of which we have like testimony from a contemporary traveler who noted also, as had Casanova, that the opera was more a social gathering than an event of musical interest, as was the case indeed at this time throughout Italy.[1] An example of contemporary manners that Casanova remarked upon with his customary attention to detail, was the use by the Neapolitan aristocracy of the second person singular in conversation with strangers, as a mark of hospitality and of particular esteem. The duke had employed it when welcoming him. At the theater, when he presented Casanova to the beautiful mistress, Leonilda, whom he had taken, as he stated, "for form's sake," she in turn made use of the second person singular when speaking to him. This form of intimacy was reserved elsewhere for use by husbands, wives, and sweethearts, by adults addressing children, or by superiors to inferiors.[2] Casanova's remark that Leonilda had been taken as a mistress by the duke for the sake of form, virtually impotent as he was reputed to be and as Leonilda herself subsequently confirmed to Casanova, was one that correctly characterized prevailing customs of the aristocracy, both in Naples and throughout Europe; the keeping of a mistress was the essential mark of a *grand seigneur*.

Casanova conceived such a passion for Leonilda that he informed the duke he would be obliged to cease to see her unless he was willing to cede her to him in marriage. When the duke assured him that he had only to obtain her consent, and that was forthcoming, arrangements were made to send for Leonilda's mother, who was residing "not far removed," in order to sign the marriage contract. The duke stated that Leonilda's mother had made him the girl's guardian seven years previous, presumably on the death of the father, with the promise that he would have her educated and prepared for an advantageous marriage. The scene was now set for one of the most dramatic denouements in Casanova's colorful life.

On the day Leonilda's mother was expected, he went to call on his banker. Upon returning at eight o'clock for supper, he found the three protagonists of the drama standing before a fire. On Casanova's appearance, the mother uttered a cry and fell, almost fainting, into a chair. It was Anna Maria Vallati, or rather Donna Lucrezia, as he called her, with whom he had been intimate in Rome in 1744, seventeen years ago. Casanova, suspecting the worst, asked her to accompany him alone to an adjoining room. There she recalled the letter she had written her mother, Donna Cecilia, which had been communicated by her to Casanova in January 1745 announcing Lucrezia's pregnancy. She added that Leonilda would be seventeen years of age in six months and that there could be no least doubt that he was her father.[3]

All thought of marriage was at once abandoned, and Casanova, to find solace, informed the duke that he intended to spend the night with the mother and daughter. He had previously assured Lucrezia, in reply to her anxious inquiries, that he had left Leonilda as intact as had the duke, and so she remained even after the night spent in the arms of the two. If the scene is shocking to us, let us not forget that we are dealing with the eighteenth century, one of the most frivolous and corrupt ages in history, when one of the highest dignitaries of France and in the Church of Rome, Cardinal de Tencin, was guilty of incest with his sister.[4] Few works lay bare so starkly the degree of decay marking that century as Casanova's *Memoirs*. He has revealed, as a surgeon dissecting a corpse, both the superficial and hidden aspects of an organism, the pus from which would burst in 1789. To employ a

Marxian phrase, it was a society that carried within itself the seeds of its own destruction. What is remarkable about Casanova's depiction of this aspect of the age in which he lived is that he never passes judgment or appears conscious of the unstable foundations of the society he was mirroring.

Casanova offered to marry Lucrezia and take her with him on his travels, but, as Henriette before her, Lucrezia, fearing doubtless his inconstant character, would only agree if he consented to establish himself in Naples. A sedentary life offered no appeal to him, and there was doubtless another consideration to which he makes no reference. Lucrezia, or in reality Anna Maria Vallati, was not approximately his own age, as he states, but was forty-six, ten years older than he. After making a present of 5,000 ducats to Leonilda for her eventual marriage portion, he was off again on his interminable wanderings.

He made his way back to Rome and paused there for only a few days. His brother Giovanni gave him an onyx cameo bearing the name of the sculptor, Sostratus, which Casanova states he later sold to Dr. Maty of the British Museum for three hundred pounds sterling. The description given by him of the cameo as that of Venus in her bath does not correspond with that of an onyx cameo, now in the British Museum, of a satyr clutching the robe of a bacchante, inscribed with the name of Sostratus. As, in the opinion of authorities of that Museum, the cameo in question was engraved in modern times, it is possible that the gem given Casanova by his brother was one of the fabrications to which he lent himself so unscrupulously, to the great despair of Winckelmann. Giovanni's unscrupulousness eventually led to his rupture with that eminent German art historian when he sold him two paintings as ancient works of art, which proved to be fabrications of his own. Appointed director of the Academy of Beaux-Arts in Dresden in 1764, Giovanni suffered the further ignominy of being condemned in 1767 in Rome by default to ten years in the galleys for an alleged false letter of exchange. This did not, however, alter his status as director in Dresden, where he died in 1795.

As was his custom, Casanova provided himself before leaving Rome with a letter of recommendation from Cardinal Giovanni Francesco Albani for the Papal nuncio, Monsignor Borromei at

Vienna.[5] Cardinal Albani's letter enables us to judge the reputation Casanova enjoyed in high ecclesiastical circles:

> The gentleman, Giacomo Casanova de Seingalt, will present this letter to Your Excellency. I love and esteem him much, for I have known him here as a man both honorable and versed in letters, as well as in the affairs of the court and of commerce. Accordingly I hasten to recommend him to Your Excellency and beg you to assure him a friendly welcome and such useful protection everywhere he shall present himself.

The letter was, in reality, a form of passport most useful to Casanova when traveling in northern Italy, parts of which were under the dominion of Austria.

Coincidentally, Casanova sought a letter from Mengs to Sir Horace Mann, which did not reach him, however, until after he had passed Florence. In the *Memoirs* he tells us that upon his arrival there one of his first visits was to Mann. That cautious diplomat expressed astonishment that Casanova, before returning, had not settled his affair with the police. With what to us appears to be some effrontery on Casanova's part, he solicited the hospitality of Mann's home. The British representative with whom, so far as we know, Casanova was not intimate, rejected the request on the grounds that he might compromise himself in sheltering the visitor. It is possible Casanova may have been prompted to impose on Mann by their common tie of Freemasonry. That he did indeed call on Mann is established through a letter of Mengs to Casanova of February 28, 1761, stating that he had heard from Mann of Casanova's passage through Florence and expressing regret that his letter of recommendation had not been received in time for its presentation to the British diplomat.

When he returned to his inn after his interview with Mann, Casanova found an agent of the police who informed him that his superior desired him to call. Taking umbrage at the message, he determined to leave for Bologna without ceremony, accompanied by a Bolognese dancer, the Corticelli, whom he had met in Florence two months earlier. He remained in Bologna with her for some ten days, until she set out for Prague where she had been engaged for a year as second dancer.[6] Casanova had been nursing for some time the project of using her for the regeneration of Mme. d'Urfé, and it was agreed that they would meet the following year. After the Corticelli had taken leave of him, he set out for Modena and Parma and finally Turin, where he was awaited by the Abbé Gama, and where he remained from March to May 1761. Gama promised that he would have in May letters of credence and full instructions for his Portuguese mission to the Augsburg Congress from Francisco de Almada, Portuguese ambassador to the Vatican from 1759 to 1760, of whom Gama was the secretary. In 1760 the Portuguese mission to the Holy See had been compelled to leave Rome after the offense offered the Pope's representative at Lisbon by the Marquis de Pombal, incident to the campaign initiated by him against the Jesuits in Portugal. As a result Gama had sought temporary refuge in Turin. Before Casanova left that city, Gama had given him a letter to Lord Stormont, British representative at the Congress, who had been named such on April 26, 1761, and with whom Casanova was to concert in the fulfillment of his task. With this he set out for Augsburg by the roundabout way of Chambéry, Lyons, Paris, and Munich, his purpose being to obtain financial assistance from Mme. d'Urfé.

During his stay in Turin, in addition to occupying himself with affairs of the heart, he formed a number of acquaintances and friendships of some permanence with officers in the government of the Kingdom of Sardinia, of which Turin was the capital, as well as with a number of other residents of distinction. They included the Chevalier Joseph Ossario, foreign minister, and his deputy, Chevalier Carlo Adalberto Flaminio Raiberti, a native of Nice who, after appointment as secretary of state in 1732, had been made on July 3, 1745, principal assistant in the foreign ministry, in which capacity he served until 1771. A number of letters from him to Casanova, written between 1765 and 1769, reflect the cordiality of their relations. According to the *Memoirs* Raiberti had as mistress a former dancer, Mazzoli, whom Casanova saw much of both in 1761 and on his return to Turin in 1762 and 1763. Another source describes her as a singer, gives her full name as Anna Maria Teresa Mazzola, a sister of Carlo, chief pastry cook of the Prince de Carignano, and states that Raiberti was secretly married to her. It was only on his deathbed that he publicly recognized the marriage.[7] Both Ossario and Raiberti were to be of assistance to Casanova in 1762 when he was expelled from Turin in November and through their influence was enabled to return two months later.[8]

Other friends he made during this visit to Turin included Paolo Baretti, brother of the distinguished writer Giuseppe Baretti, Count Cocana de Trana, and the Chevalier Brézé whose partiality was more particularly horses, rather than women, as attested not alone by Casanova but also by contemporary testimony. It was to Brézé that he resold horses he had purchased for a Jewish woman, Lia, for whom he conceived a temporary passion. He was to meet Brézé again in 1769 at Lugano, where the latter had gone to buy horses.[9] The most lasting friendship Casanova formed at Turin was that with Count Gian Giacomo Marcello Gamba della Perosa (1738-1817), the de la Perouse of the *Memoirs*, whose deep attachment to the Venetian was terminated only by Casanova's death. Most of his friends at Turin were libertines as he, as their correspondence shows, with the additional common interest of literature. It is possible that they were also Freemasons; we know that Perouse was.

In Turin Casanova had renewed acquaintance with an adventurer representing himself as the son of the Marquis Désarmoises, whom he had originally met at Aix-en-Savoie the year previous. At the hotel where Casanova lodged at Chambéry he met Désarmoises' daughter who stated that she had been obliged to run away from her home in Lyons to escape the incestuous designs of her father. He had not only opposed her marriage to the young man with whom Casanova found her, but had attempted to assassinate him in his fury in finding him a rival. Désarmoises had written to Casanova from Lyons, pleading with him to persuade his daughter to return. Instead, Casanova assured the couple that he would stop at Lyons en route to Paris and persuade the father to give his consent to their marriage. Faithful to this promise, he saw Désarmoises upon arriving in Lyons and extracted from him his agreement in writing, signed by two witnesses, which Casanova forwarded by express the same day to Chambéry.

At Chambéry Casanova lingered to see M.M., the nun of that

town whom he met in 1760 at Aix-en-Savoie when she was delivered of a child. Casanova had met her relative at Grenoble, a Mme. Morin,[10] and, communicating with the latter, he had persuaded her to come from Grenoble and accompany him to the convent in which M.M. was confined. After breakfast at the convent, he proposed to give a dinner for twelve at the same table at which half the guests would be within the convent proper and the other half in the parlor, separated only by a thin grill, used in convent parlors at that time to permit guests to have access to the inmates. The dinner was a great success. The guests were eight nuns, including M.M., a ravishing young boarder, and six of their companions, Mme. Morin, her daughter, Casanova, Mlle. Désarmoises, all of whom were thoroughly intoxicated before the repast was over. Casanova returned the next day to have a better look at the young boarder. M.M. brought her to the grill, and M.M., herself refusing with obstinacy the renewal of Casanova's caresses, placed no obstacle to his addressing himself with considerable license to her companion. The picture he has left us of the relative freedom permitted at this time in some convents could not be more revealing.

When he arrived in Paris, Casanova informed Mme. d'Urfé, his prodigal benefactor, that he had need of a liberal letter of credit and watches and snuffboxes to distribute as presents at Augsburg. To spur her generosity, he represented that the operation for her regeneration would take place as soon as Querilinth, "one of the three chiefs of the Rosicrucians," was freed from captivity by the Inquisition at Lisbon. One of the purposes for his Augsburg mission, he announced, was to arrange for this with Lord Stormont. Unfortunately, Casanova used bad judgment in leaving Costa, the secretary engaged the previous year at Avignon, with orders to await the presents Mme. d'Urfé was assembling and bring these to Augsburg, Costa absconded with the loot, and it was not until 1784 in Vienna that Casanova saw him again. Happily, Mme. d'Urfé's letter of credit for 50,000 francs was sent to him directly.

Casanova states that he presented his letter to Stormont in Munich, and there is, in fact, an announcement in the *Augsburger Zeitung* of July 22, 1761, of his presence at the hotel Zum Goldenen

Hirschen in Munich. He states also that he called on M. de Folard, the French minister, of which Charles Samaran has found confirmation in the archives of the Quai d'Orsay, in a dispatch of Folard dated August 12, 1761. During the month Casanova remained in Munich, he lost heavily at play, and, what was even worse, contracted venereal disease from the Renaud, a dancer of his acquaintance. She was to have a small niche in history as the wife of Charles Auguste Boehmer, one of the two jewelers involved in the diamond-necklace scandal with Cardinal de Rohan, which precipitated in 1785 the ruin of Marie Antoinette and the French monarchy. By September, Casanova, who had gone on to Augsburg, learned that the Congress would not convene. Peace negotiations between Frederick the Great and Britain had been broken off on September 20, 1761, thus compromising the Congress's purpose of achieving a general European peace.

While no official documents have been found confirming Casanova's role in the Congress,[11] his account conforms with what we know of the preparations made for it. It is probable that the Portuguese ambassador, de Almada, was authorized to send a representative, that he confided the task to Gama who saw in Casanova a highly gifted negotiator. It may appear incongruous today that a foreigner would be entrusted with a diplomatic mission, but in the eighteenth century there was not that strict sense of nationality that was to prove the curse of Europe after the Napoleonic Wars. Religious faith was the touchstone, not nationality.

With the nonrealization of the Augsburg Congress and the recovery of his health, Casanova returned to Paris to set in motion the regeneration of Mme. d'Urfé. Three weeks were spent at the beginning of 1762 in the necessary occult preparations, after which

> . . .it was decided that I should seek a maiden in a place the spirits would indicate to me, whom I was to impregnate with a male child in a manner known only to the Rosicrucian fraternity. The boy, born alive, will have received no soul from nature. Immediately after his birth, he will be presented to Mme. d'Urfé, and she will hide him for seven days in her bed. On the termination of these

seven days, Madame will die with her lips on the lips of the child, who will receive her soul. From this moment, it will become my obligation to watch over the boy in collaboration with a secret Chief of the Order. As soon as my son will attain three years of age, Mme. d'Urfé will recover consciousness in his body.[12]

The operation had to take place at the full moon of April, May, or June. Arrangements were made by him for his accessory, Marianne Corticelli, to be conducted by her mother and an escort from Prague to Metz, where Casanova would meet her while Mme. d'Urfé awaited the two at her family chateau of Pontcarré. The Corticelli had been represented as the last survivor of that Lascaris family which had reigned at Constantinople, allied to that of Mme. d'Urfé. In consequence, upon Casanova's arrival with his protégé on April 5, they were welcomed by the marquise with feudal ceremony. The operation was fixed for the full moon of April 8, at which time Mme. d'Urfé solemnly assisted with Casanova's efforts to impregnate the Corticelli with that male child into whose soul that of the marquise would pass. Fearful that she might test a virginity Casanova had attributed to the Corticelli, he prudently forbade her this on pain of impairing the operation. When, on its conclusion, he interrogated the oracle to ascertain whether it had been successful, he was careful to obtain a negative reply. The second trial was fixed for Aix-la-Chapelle.

They arrived there at the beginning of May. The list of visitors at Aix, in the *Cologne Gazette* of May 21, 1762, shows the arrival of "the Chevalier de Seingalt, Venetian, with Madame, his wife," at the Bains de S. Corneille, then one of the principal resorts of foreigners at this popular watering place. Aside from our knowledge that these lists were published some days after the arrival of the persons named, Casanova's presence at Aix early in May is evident from his account of the sequence of events. Thus he witnessed the death in a duel of a "French officer" to whom he gives the name of "d'Aché," who was survived by a charming widow, and an even more attractive daughter, Mimi. He informs us that when the duel occurred it was full moon, which dates it as May 8.

When Ilges examined the records at Aix, he found notice of the burial on May 11 of a certain Alexandre Theodore Lambertz, "captaine du régiment Royal Piémont." This led us to an examination of the French war archives at Vincennes, which revealed the file of a François Theodore Lambert, born in 1717 at Mussy Levesque, who served as a "cavalier" in the St. Simon regiment in 1734, adjutant-major in 1746, transferred to the "régiment de Royal Piémont" in January 1762, and thereafter disappears from the records. Once again there emerges from beyond the grave the true name of a mistress of good family which Casanova was at pains to conceal. The lovely Mimi d'Aché could have been in all likelihood none other than Mlle. Lambert.

Aside from the love affair at Aix, Casanova was also occupied with the regeneration of his credulous older companion. Before a second operation could be undertaken, the Corticelli showed herself to be less tractable than Casanova had anticipated. When he appropriated the presents bestowed upon her by Mme. d'Urfé, she threatened to expose him. Turning the tables on her with his habitual astuteness, he informed the marquise that they must search for another virgin as the Corticelli had been bewitched by a black spirit and had become quite mad. The credulous Mme. d'Urfé readily accepted the explanation, and only laughed at the charges brought against Casanova by the Corticelli.

After consulting his oracle, Casanova informed Mme. d'Urfé that she must write to the moon at its forthcoming phase for guidance as to the next step to be taken in her regeneration. On that date, June 22, Casanova undressed, by a bath, with Mme. d'Urfé. He pronounced cabalistic words which she repeated after him as she handed him a letter to the moon which he solemnly burned. They then entered the bath together, Casanova concealing in his hand a letter he had prepared as a reply from the moon. Written in silver characters on green glazed paper, it appeared ten minutes later on the surface of the water. According to the moon's message, the regeneration was to be deferred until the spring of the following year at Marseilles, with the appearance there of Quirilinth, the Rosicrucian chosen for the magic operation. Casanova tells us that this ceremony at Aix took place at one o'clock after midnight. The relative accuracy of his calculations may be judged from the fact that, according to astronomical reckonings, the first phase of the new moon was on June 22, 1762, at precisely one hour and twenty-seven minutes after midnight.

From Aix-la-Chapelle the party proceeded by easy stages to Besançon. There Mme. d'Urfé took leave to continue on to Lyons, while Casanova headed for Geneva from where he packed the Corticelli and her mother off to Turin to await him there. At Geneva he made no effort to see Voltaire again, fearful probably of a cool reception, but he did renew acquaintance with one of the more remarkable women of the *Memoirs*, Hedwige, niece of a Protestant pastor.

It has been suggested that she was probably Anne Marie May, born in 1731 and left an orphan in 1743 when she was taken into the home of the husband of her mother's sister, a pastor who appears himself to have been a widower in 1762. Casanova had met her cousin, Helen, at the home of the Fernex sisters, with whom he had renewed acquaintance, in the company of his libertine councilman of Geneva. Helen's widowed mother, probably a sister of Hedwige's mother, as well as of the pastor's deceased wife, was on tender terms with the pastor. Profiting from this, and smitten with Helen, Casanova invited her, the pastor, Hedwige, and Helen's mother, to dinner at a lakeside house ceded to him for the purpose by his banker. It was probably Mon Repos, since 1898 the property of the city of Geneva. After subtle theological discussions with Hedwige, who had a masterly knowledge of the Bible, he exchanged lessons of a different character with her and Helen, when he made women of them both in scenes which for their voluptuousness match those involving M.M. and C.C. in Venice.[13] Since this chapter of the *Memoirs* is one of four lost while Laforgue was working on the text, we have no means of knowing how far this particular episode may have been embroidered by him with that license which he has taken everywhere with Casanova's own generally restrained love descriptions.

From Geneva Casanova headed for Turin, stopping for some days at Lyons to replenish his purse at the generous hands of Mme. d'Urfé. She was informed that he was proceeding to Turin to meet Frederic Gualdo, "chief of the Rosicrucians," known also as "Querilinth," whom he had chosen to effect her regeneration the following spring at Marseilles. As Gualdo was a well-known

Rosicrucian adept, who had disappeared mysteriously during the previous century, Casanova's obvious reason was to mystify Mme. d'Urfé in leading her to believe that the operation on her would be performed by a legendary personage. Casanova's continual postponements of this rite on which she set such store were to ensure the continuance of the presents she plentifully bestowed upon him in her grateful credulity.

The person Casanova had in view to fill the role of Gualdo was Giacomo Passano, born about 1700, adventurer, poet, and painter of erotic miniatures, whom Casanova had first met the previous November at Leghorn. Passano, known also as Ascano Pogomas, was destined to become Casanova's outstanding evil genius among the several disreputable characters at whose hands he suffered. He would have disappeared into dust, leaving no trace, but for the few details given of his career by Casanova.[14] A letter of December 3, 1762, from Joseph Bono of Lyons refers to a formal agreement, drawn up a little earlier, outlining the conditions of employment of Passano as Casanova's secretary, Casanova so engaged him presumably the better to exercise a hold over him for the occult activities he was intended to perform as "Querilinth" with the marquise.

If Passano remains, even in the role of a villain, at best a shadowy figure, we are somewhat better informed about Bono who here enters Casanova's life for the first time. From records in Lyons it is learned that Bono had been established there as early as 1755. From then until his death on November 8, 1780, he was a leading silk merchant and banker.[15] It is possible, although no proof can be adduced, that Bono's acquaintanceship may have been first formed by Casanova during his silk-printing activities in 1759 in Paris. It is equally possible, again without evidence, that Bono may have been a Rosicrucian or Freemason, in common with so many of Casanova's more intimate contacts. It is noteworthy that it is Bono to whom he invariably turned from 1762 to 1769 in moments of embarrassment. Bono's unalterable devotion to the adventurer, whose many failings often taxed his patience, is amply attested in fifteen letters from him to Casanova. While these letters are concerned largely with Casanova's business dealings, Bono does not hesitate to offer friendly advice indicative of his deep esteem for his correspondent, and to plead with him on more than one occasion that he mend his prodigal ways.[16]

Taking leave of Bono and Mme. d'Urfé at Lyons in September 1762, Casanova proceeded by way of Chambéry to Turin, where he arrived the same month and not, as he states, at the beginning of December. During his stay he made a brief visit to nearby Alessandria, as it seems from a letter of October 20, 1762, written to him there by Count Trana.

One of the great hostesses at Turin at this period was the Countess de Saint-Giles, who appears to have taken an interest in the Corticelli. Casanova had found the latter awaiting him on his return, but he dismissed her when he discovered her in *flagrant délit*. Mme. de Saint-Giles attempted to persuade Casanova to forget the incident, and when he refused, she threatened to publish a story she had read that did not do him honor. Impervious as he was to threats, Casanova ignored her. A few days later, a manuscript containing the history of Mme. d'Urfé, the Corticelli, and himself, was published. But it was so badly written that no one could read it to the end.

As Mme. de Saint-Giles enjoyed great prestige at Turin, it may well have been that it was through her influence with the chief of police, Count d'Aglié, that Casanova was expelled from Turin early in November. He gives no explanation himself, and none has ever come to light. The only document bearing on it is the draft of an undated letter addressed by him to d'Aglié, which is interesting not only for its suggestion that Casanova himself was not aware of the reason for the order, but also for the light it throws on certain disputed aspects of his life. It reads in part:

> After you pronounced the frightful sentence for my departure from this city next Monday, I have complained to no one . . . What are my crimes? In what way have I violated the laws, in what respect am I thought prejudicial to society? . . . Is it my disgrace at Venice, sir, which has made me feel the force of your Glory? Permit me to state to you that the sovereigns and ministers of other states have considered that the anger of my native land, excluding me from my country, was a reason for them to extend me their protection. Protection of the unfortunate, is it not one of your maxims, sir?

The Elector of Bavaria in 1750 [1756], a month after my escape, found me at his feet requesting asylum, introduced by Count de Valvason, Venetian employed at his Court. Mme. the Countess de Coronini opened her home to me and, honored by the protection of the Cardinal of Bavaria, it only depended on me on look on Munich as my land. In Paris, the Cardinal de Bernis, then abbé and minister for foreign affairs, who was French ambassador during the time of my fatal imprisonment, welcomed me and offered me employment, and M. d'Argenson did the same. Our ambassador in Paris did not receive me, but Count de Cantillana, Neapolitan minister, and Count de Starhemberg, minister of Vienna, did not disdain to receive me at their table. Prince Charles de Lorraine informed me that I might remain permanently at Brussels, while the late Elector of Cologne was pleased to hear me read my poems in Venetian dialect which that Prince loved. His reigning Holiness received me two years ago with the kindness of a father, told me that the time of my penitence was not yet ended and, having learned that I was doubly a doctor in law, sent me a diploma of Apostolic Protonotary which I can show you. M. the Cardinal Passionei recommended me to H.E. the Cardinal de la Lanza, and Cardinal Alessandro Albani gave me a very full passport. Cardinal Giovanni Francesco Albani gave me a letter from the Papal nuncio resident in Vienna that I can show you, sir . . .[17]

When d'Aglié failed to be moved by Casanova's appeal, the latter left for Geneva, where he remained until about December 12, awaiting the results of the intercession of his friends in Turin to remove the ban on his presence. This is clear from correspondence to him, as well as his passage through Chambéry on returning to Turin early in January 1763. The only reference to this in the *Memoirs* is an indirect one when he remarks, apropos of a promise to Helen and Hedwige on taking leave of them in August 1762, that he would see them again before two years had passed, adding that, in fact, they had not so long to wait.

While still awaiting permission to return to Turin, Casanova was contemplating how he might confound his enemies upon his reappearance. Such an inference is warranted by a letter of Bono to him at Geneva on December 3, 1762. Bono's suggestion was that he should arm himself with a letter of recommendation for a person of distinction in Turin, obtained from someone of weight. It is possible that he did indeed act on this recommendation, for there is mention in the *Memoirs* of a letter from the Countess du Rumain, enclosing one from the Duke de Choiseul, minister for foreign affairs, to the French ambassador at Turin, M. de Chauvelin. Casanova recalled that he had already met Chauvelin at Soleure but desired to be known to him "under a weightier title."

With his position at Turin once again assured, Casanova, fond as he was of the dramatic and of drawing attention to himself, hired a house outside the city for a ball. To it he invited not only the diplomatic corps, including M. de Chauvelin and his wife, but also all the dancers who had converged upon Turin for the carnival. Among these was Agathe, of whom he became enamored. He let her want for nothing, and presented her with a resplendent pair of diamond earrings. Hugh, Lord Percy, smitten with her, offered to exchange with Casanova his own mistress for the latter's with, as additional inducement, whatever sum he might fix. Although he spurned this, Casanova at length agreed in view of the advantageous settlement Percy offered Agathe, including the sum of 2,000 guineas when and if they separated. Casanova was to find her later, in 1770, in Naples.

Heir of an immense fortune, Lord Percy was himself so grateful to Casanova that, learning of the latter's intention to visit England, and in reply to his request for a letter of introduction to his mother, the Duchess of Northumberland, he drew from his pocket a portrait of her encircled with diamonds. "It is the best letter of recommendation I can give you," he assured him, adding that he would write his mother that it would be returned to her by Casanova unless she decided to let him retain it. As Casanova observed, the gesture was one that would only have occurred to an Englishman; suggestive as it was of the theater, he could well appreciate it.[18]

# CHAPTER 10

# *The Marquise's Regeneration and Death*

Casanova spent three weeks in Milan during the carnival of February 1763, gambling and indulging in a round of festivities. Contrary to his usual habit of lodging at a hotel, he had accepted the hospitality of Count Giuseppe Attendoli-Bolognini, whose acquaintance he had made in Turin. The latter's Spanish wife coveted a superb poppy-colored dress of Tours silk, richly ornamented with sable, given Casanova by Mme. d'Urfé for the Corticelli. When the countess's titular lover offered to buy it for a thousand sequins, Casanova proposed to give it to her for a night's favors. When she protested that he did not love her any more than she did him, he informed her brutally that if he sought to sleep with her, it was to mortify her insupportable pride. It is one of the rare instances in which Casanova's usual delicacy in relations with women was subordinated to a stronger impulse: that of revenge. He himself admitted more than once that vengeance was a dominant trait in his character, as is revealed very strikingly here. Eventually, Casanova sold the gown to the countess's lover, and turned the money over to her husband, who complaisantly arranged for his guest to enjoy his wife. Casanova's subsequent further humiliation of her, in his remark that it was not his fault if her charms had no power of awakening his senses, is one of the most cynical passages in the *Memoirs*. The most that can be said in his extenuation is that he reproached himself for his behavior. The incident may explain why so many women have no taste for his work. He himself, with characteristic candor, observes that his female readers will doubtless detest him and that when they do he can only approve. To Opiz on July 27, 1792, in the course of writing his *Memoirs*, he remarked:

> I am a detestable creature, but I am not anxious that it should be known, and I do not covet the honor of being detested by posterity.

That he was not detested even by Countess Attendoli-Bolognini is indicated by a friendly letter, found among his papers, that she wrote him a few weeks after his leavetaking. She may have been carried away by his frankness; few men and fewer women have so stripped themselves before the world as he.

Another incident reveals what psychologists would call the exhibitionist side of his character, as well as his inventiveness. Having offered to provide for five of his friends costumes certain to protect their incognito at a masked ball, Casanova purchased the richest costumes available from the most expensive second-hand clothier in Milan. With a stiletto he then slashed numerous holes in each, and ordered a tailor to repair them with the finest materials, which would accentuate not only their richness but their damaged state as well. When Casanova displayed to his two male and three female companions their costumes as beggars in rags, but of astonishing richness, they were enraptured by the novelty of his conception. Upon their appearance at the ball, they were, as he had anticipated, the sensation of the evening, and his immense vanity was gratified.

The stay in Milan was interrupted by a visit of some three weeks to the castle, or Gothic palace, of the Attendoli-Bolognini family, near Milan at the village of San Angelo. It was inhabited by Count Pàolo Attendoli-Bolognini, to whom Casanova gives the name of Count Ambroise. All his pains to conceal the identities of the count and his wife's charming sisters, Clementine and Eleanore, have proven vain. It has been established that Clementine was Angela Gandini and that Eleanore was her sister Fulvia. After Casanova's departure, the former married Don Bassano Nipoti, and Fulvia became a nun.

It was inevitable that Casanova would pay court to one of the two sisters; that he did not involve himself with both was indicative of his genuine attachment to Clementine. As she was versed in mythology, he gave her the name of Hebe, and to her he was Iolas. They shared a love of literature[1] including in particular Ariosto, which sent Casanova to Lodi to purchase books that he thought would please her. He was surprised to find so many available in that town, particularly translations into the Italian, the only language she knew. He brought her back a sack full, containing about a hundred volumes of "poets, historians, geographers, physicians, and philosophers," as well as a few good romances translated from Spanish and French. When he learned that neither she nor her sister had ever visited Milan despite the fact that it was only fifteen miles distant, he proposed to give them the surprise of a day's excursion to a destination he would not disclose until their departure. With his Milanese friends he arranged an elaborate dinner to await the entire family on the day appointed. To give climactic effect to the whole, he had provided that three sumptuous dresses await the three sisters with servants to assist them. His passion was to astonish others; consequently when the girls learned that they would visit a city they had never seen, and when, once there, they found resplendent robes awaiting them, their delight could not have pleased him more.

Few men have divined so thoroughly as Casanova the secrets of winning women. He never spared expense or begrudged the time spent in devising schemes to minister to their slightest caprice. Forced to disclose the destination to the two sisters the night before their departure, he was given his reward by Clementine. Upon their return from Milan, he spent the last nights of his stay in her arms, while her sister slept, or so pretended, according to Casanova, alongside them. It is another curious insight into the manners of those days. Wholly aside from these intimate bedroom details, which, unlike most chroniclers, he neither conceals nor overemphasizes, the picture he has left us of the pastoral life of the Italian nobility in the eighteenth century has the delicate charm of a painting of Fragonard or Greuze with all the nostalgia they convey of a bygone age. The castle of San Angelo, which Casanova tells us was at least 800 years old when he visited it, has disappeared, together with the inmates whose memory he has immortalized.[2]

Before leaving Milan, he met his former Venetian gambling associate, Antonio Croce, traveling with a Mlle. Crosin, a Marseilles girl of good family whom he had seduced. When Croce disappeared, she appealed in her distress to Casanova, who was generous enough to offer to conduct her to Marseilles, where he had arranged to meet Mme. d'Urfé. "I was proud to find myself capable of living with a very pretty girl with no other motive than the commendable one of guaranteeing her from opprobrium." We may believe him, as this is not the only instance of its kind. Let us avoid the inconsistency of certain critics, quick to credit his unfavorable aspects while questioning those circumstances in which he portrays himself in an advantageous light. If he was a compound of the base and the noble, he did not differ in this respect from the mass of humanity.

Proceeding to Genoa with Mlle. Crosin, he found awaiting him Giacomo Passano, his secretary. A visit to Marquis Gian Giacomo Grimaldi, who had contrived to take Rosalie out of his hands, disclosed that he was in Venice, but a servant indicated her residence. She had become Mme. Paretti six months after he left Genoa in November 1760. With her he found Veronique, now her chambermaid, and when he expressed a desire to engage her sister Annette to serve his niece, as he designated Mlle. Crosin, Rosalie laughingly observed that he seemed to have numerous relatives, recalling that it was in that capacity she had traveled with him three years previous.

While in Genoa, Casanova had an unexpected call from his youngest brother, a ne'er-do-well, Abbé Gaetano Casanova, always a source of annoyance to him, who later died a priest in Rome in 1783. He had run off from Venice with an attractive girl, Marcolina, whom he proposed to take to Switzerland and marry. Casanova conceived a fancy for her and took her unceremoniously out of his brother's hands. A few days later, with Gaetano, Marcolina, Mlle.

Crosin, and Passano, he embarked for Antibes on a fellucca, the usual mode of travel, in the absence of suitable roads, for those journeying to France.

When the sea became overly rough, they put in at Menton, then part of Monaco. An extended description is given of Casanova's visit to Prince Honoré III and the Princess, daughter of the Marquise de Brignole, who had been the prince's mistress before his marriage to her daughter. The account of this visit has been accepted unquestioningly, even by so captious a critic as Gugitz. Dr. Francis Mars, in an examination of Monacan archives, has established that the prince and princess could not have been in their principality on April 9, 1763, when Casanova visited Monaco.[3] Dr. Mars has, however, found such striking verisimilitude in Casanova's portraits of the princely couple that we cannot but conclude that the memorialist probably met them in Paris and, either intentionally or involuntarily, set the episode, written many years later, in Monaco. The acuteness and veracity of his observations in general is nowhere better illustrated than a few pages later in the *Memoirs*, where he notes that the commandant at Antibes was one-armed. In Mars' investigation of the archives of the French war ministry, he discovered that the commandant, Baron Prosper-Marie de Lesrat, had lost his left arm in 1744.

At Marseilles, Casanova's first call was on Mme. Audibert, whom he had earlier met on his journey through that city in 1760. She remained a mythical character until recently, when a notice indicating that she had maintained a gambling salon was discovered in the Marseilles municipal archives.[4] Casanova appears to have had considerable esteem for her, and it was to her that he entrusted Mlle. Crosin, and with Mme. Audibert's cooperation he at length reconciled the girl with her parents.

Casanova's primary interest, however, was the regeneration of Mme. d'Urfé, whom he found awaiting him impatiently at the Hôtel des Treize-Cantons. She was enthusiastic at the news that he was accompanied by Querilinth (Passano) and exhibited to Casanova seven presents intended for her regenerator, including seven precious stones of the finest consistency: a diamond, ruby, sapphire, emerald, opal, oriental topaz, and yellow chrysolite, each weighing seven carats. Determined that the presents should not fall into

Passano's hands, he proposed that they be enclosed in a box and that each be consecrated on seven successive days to the seven planets. When these rites had been observed, Casanova conducted Mme. d'Urfé to the seashore. There the box, weighing fifty pounds, was cast into the sea, to the great satisfaction of the marquise, and still more to that of Casanova, who had substituted an identical box containing fifty pounds of lead for the box with the precious stones, of which he had taken possession.

It had been Casanova's original intention to employ Passano for Mme. d'Urfé's regeneration, but he was now even more embarrassed by Passano's demands than he had been with those of the Corticelli. Passano threatened to reveal Casanova's dupery unless he were given 50,000 écus as his part of the spoils, of an estimated value of twice that sum. Not to be intimidated, Casanova consulted his oracle in Mme. d'Urfé's presence and drew from it the message that seven salamanders had transported the true Querilinth to the milky way and that Passano was in reality the evil genius Saint-Germain, who had been transformed by a female gnome to do away with Semiramis (Mme. d'Urfé). She was counseled to leave to Paralis (Casanova) the task of getting rid of Passano, while entertaining no doubt about her regeneration. This she was assured would be undertaken by him, three days after the end of the consecrations and after a water sprite had purified the two by bathing them together.

In consequence of Casanova's oracular message, Mme. d'Urfé ignored a letter Passano wrote her, in which he revealed that Casanova had brought two girls with him to Marseilles and that he was shamefully deceiving her. Having to admit at least temporary defeat, Passano agreed to leave for Lyons with an order drawn on Bono there for a hundred louis payable to him if presented on April 30, 1763. In similar fashion, Casanova rid himself of his brother who had been a source of annoyance to Marcolina.

The stage was now set for one of the most extraordinary episodes in the history of human credulity. Marcolina, far more amenable than the Corticelli, was chosen as the water sprite who would bathe Casanova and Mme. d'Urfé and otherwise contribute to the success of the magical undertaking. From the description given by Casanova of the rising of the moon we can fix the exact time and date of Mme. d'Urfé's regeneration as between five and five-thirty in the afternoon of April 26, 1763. Afterward, Mme. d'Urfé preceded Casanova to Lyons, where she was to pour two bottles of sea water into the Rhône and the Saône. Casanova lingered to attend the marriage of Mlle. Crosin to a merchant she had met in Genoa, into whose arms she passed from Casanova's with the facility that characterized love in the eighteenth century, when mistresses enjoyed the same honor as did wives.

The carriage transporting Casanova and Marcolina to Lyons broke down a little beyond the Croix d'Or near Aix. Hospitality was offered them in a nearby château, which Charles Samaran has identified as most probably Luynes, property then of the Margalet family. The following day, upon arriving at Avignon, Marcolina disclosed that one of their hostesses, who had taken pains to keep her face concealed, had given her a letter for Casanova. It was addressed to "The most honest man of my acquaintance" and bore only the word "Henriette." He recalled that she had written him in the same laconic style from Pontarlier after parting from him at Geneva in 1749. He had then received from her the single word "Adieu."[5] No woman ever touched his heart so deeply as this member of the "nobility" of Aix.

On the paths opened by Charles Samaran's researches, information has been uncovered indicating that Henriette may well have been Jeanne Marie d'Albert de St. Hippolyte, daughter of Jeanne Marie de Margalet, sister of the seigneur of Luynes. Born at Aix on March 22, 1718, she was married on February 4, 1744, to Jean Baptiste Laurent Boyer de Fonscolombe, "avocat en Parlement," son of the "noble Honoré Boyer, Seigneur de Fonscolombe, Ecuyer, Conseiller secrétaire du Roi, maison couronnée de France en la chancellerie de Provence." The father-in-law answers the description of "Vieil officier" from whom Henriette escaped at Civitavecchia in 1749, when he, then aged 66, was presumably taking her to be placed in a convent. If she were Henriette, she was seven years older than Casanova, but the description of her as only twenty-two in her marriage act in 1744 proves that she appeared younger than her years, for she was then actually twenty-six.

What is highly significant is that she had only two children, a son born in 1744, and a daughter in 1746, which leads to the reasonable conclusion that there may have been a rupture with her husband shortly after 1746, and the cessation of marital relations before Casanova's meeting with her in 1749. Although her husband did not die until 1788, and in 1763 she could not therefore have been a widow, as described by Casanova, she may have represented herself as such. Casanova stated that she was living when he was writing his *Memoirs* (1790-98), and we know that Jeanne Marie Boyer de Fonscolombe survived, in fact, until October 8, 1795. We know also that two of her brothers, Esprit and Joseph-François Auguste-Jules de St. Hippolyte, were Chevaliers de Malte in 1763, when Casanova remarked the presence of a "chevalier de Malte" at the château, the seigneur of which in that year would have been her first cousin.

What gives further plausibility to the proposed identification of one of the most fascinating figures in the *Memoirs* is that curious reserve displayed by Henriette when she failed to make herself known to Casanova in 1763, and again in 1769. There was, of course, a natural disinclination to revive a buried romantic imprudence. But there were motives that went even deeper. In 1763, at the age of forty-five, every feminine instinct in her would have rebelled against Casanova's discovery of how she had been marked by the ravages of time. It also explains Casanova's failure to recognize her in 1769 when he encountered her, then aged fifty-one, at a social gathering in Aix. While the identification of Henriette with Jeanne Marie Boyer de Fonscolombe cannot be accepted as incontestable in the absence of supporting evidence, it offers the most tempting hypothesis available.

When Casanova arrived in Lyons about May 15, 1763, one of the first persons with whom he put himself in touch was Joseph Bono, the Lyons silk merchant and banker, with whom he enjoyed a close attachment. With the blunt frankness reflected in his correspondence, Bono now informed Casanova, as recorded by him in the *Memoirs*, that Passano, who had preceded him to Lyons, desired:

> . . .that the public should know that you are the greatest villain alive, that you are ruining Mme. d'Urfé by impious lies, that you are a sorcerer, a forger, a thief, a spy, a clipper of coins, a traitor, a cheater at cards, a slanderer, an utterer of false letters of exchange, a

counterfeiter of handwritings, in short the most abominable of men.

It is a measure of Casanova's extraordinary candor that it is he who records for us this indictment of himself. When he threatened to take legal measures counter to those instituted against him by Passano, the latter, thus intimidated, offered to withdraw his charges for a hundred louis, which Bono paid, without Casanova's knowledge, so he tells us, obtaining a complete retraction and the departure of Passano from Lyons. From Bono's letters to Casanova, found in his papers, it appears that the indemnity was a thousand Piedmontese livres, about fifty louis, paid to Passano with Casanova's knowledge, but only in September 1763. This is confirmed by a receipt from Passano to Bono acknowledging the sum received for the account of Casanova and declaring that it had been accorded by "pure good will and generosity." Bono's letters to Casanova in London indicate that early in the summer of 1763 he was giving thought to winning Passano over by providing a refuge for him in Venice, perhaps with Bragadin. The plan must have been abandoned after Passano effectively poisoned Mme. d'Urfé's mind against Casanova. He was informed by Bono in a letter of July 7, 1763, that he knew it for a fact that "the marquise is discontented with you." So were her relatives, who must have been alarmed at the manner in which she was being exploited. It was Passano's hope that he might succeed Casanova in the marquise's confidence. When this expectation was not fulfilled, he left Lyons in September. Five years later, his shadow fell across Casanova's path in Barcelona. It was doubtless with particular reference to Passano that Bono wrote bitterly to Casanova on July 7 that "you have the knack of making enemies of those you befriend."

Casanova saw Mme. d'Urfé for the last time in Paris in June 1763 on his way to London. He had sent her on ahead of him from Lyons in May to await her regeneration at the hands of an Englishman whom he had promised to send her from England. It was the final act in a comedy that had lasted seven years. The rupture between them, no doubt already simmering, must have followed shortly after this last meeting. Disinclined, as he obviously must have been, to disclose the circumstances, he tells us that in August 1763 he received in London a letter from Paris announcing her death. Actually, she did not die until November 12, 1775. What he probably received in London that August was a letter notifying him of the withdrawal of her confidence; she was thenceforth dead for him.

If there are minor inexactitudes in Casanova's account of his relations with Passano, and striking omissions in regard to those with Mme. d'Urfé, there is an even graver fault to be noted. The *Memoirs* record the passage through Lyons at the time of Casanova's sojourn there, in May 1763, of a Venetian embassy, headed by Ambassador Querini, returning from London after congratulating George III on his accession to the throne. We know that the mission was in France the first days of June, and in Lyons only in July, from the 11th to the 14th. The anachronism in Casanova's account admits of two possible explanations. He may have met in Lyons in May subordinate members of the mission, returning in advance of the main party and, to import a greater aura to the occasion, substituted these for the former; or he saw Querini in Paris at the beginning of June (because Casanova arrived in London on June 13 coming from Paris) and then placed this encounter to Lyons.

# CHAPTER 11

## *England*

A rriving at Calais, Casanova engaged a packet boat for the crossing to Dover for six guineas, the identical amount paid by Smollett, who made the journey the same year. Casanova might have traveled by the public packet boat for six francs, but this would not have conformed with his style. Nor would it, of course, have been becoming for the Duke of Bedford, British ambassador to France who, appearing shortly thereafter, was chagrined to find that the only boat available had been engaged. Pressed to cede it to the duke, Casanova informed him that he could dispose of it except for the small space necessary for himself. The duke accepted and insisted on reimbursing Casanova for the six guineas, but, when he declined, a compromise was effected by which each paid half.

Many commentators have testified to the prime interest of Casanova's account of his nine-month sojourn in England, so highly illuminative of English peculiarities, and the more astonishing since he never learned the language. His salty description of the country on arrival is strongly suggestive of certain pages of

*The History of English Literature* by Taine, who is known to have been an avid reader of Casanova in his youth.

In London Casanova's first call was on one of his oldest acquaintances, Thérèse Imer, on whose account he had been dismissed from the home of Senator Malipiero in Venice. She was born about 1722, daughter of Joseph Imer, who had been the lover of Casanova's mother. He had seen Thérèse again in Venice in 1753 when she had come to visit her parents with her children, Joseph, born in Vienna on December 8, 1746, and Wilhelmine Friederike, born February 15, 1753, at Bayreuth. Thérèse had married the dancer Pompeati and, after parting from him, had become mistress of the Markgrave of Bayreuth. Passing thence into the arms of Prince Charles de Lorraine, she had been for a time directress of theaters at Brussels. She was later forced to flee to Holland to escape imprisonment because of debts, and Casanova had found her there late in 1758, singing under the name of Mme. Trenti. She had then taken the name of Cornelys, from that of a Dutch lover whom Casanova refers to as Rigerboos, in reality Jean Rijgerbos Cornelis.[1] Since Casanova's last parting with her in the first days of 1759, her fortunes had once again radically changed. As Mme. Cornelys she had become a fashionable figure in London with the assemblies she conducted at Carlisle House on the east side of Soho Square, described by a contemporary as "by far the most magnificent place of public entertainment in Europe." The highest aristocracy, including members of the royal family, were her patrons. Such was the repute of her establishment that when the Duke of Brunswick was married on January 24, 1764, to the Princess Augusta, sister of George III, the subscription ball on that occasion was held at the Carlisle House, and attended by Casanova. Mme. Cornelys' name looms prominently in important chronicles of the time, and is immortalized in Smollett's *Humphry Clinker* of 1771.[2]

Mme. Cornelys had arrived in London about 1759, and after renting Carlisle House, she had ordered the construction of a large building, of two great rooms, one above the other, for balls and concerts. From a copper plate found in the cornerstone when the building was pulled down, it appears that the first stone was laid on June 19, 1761, and that her first protrectress was none other than the famous Elizabeth Chudleigh. Of extraordinary talents, as Archenholz and others have testified, Mme. Cornelys gave annually twelve balls and suppers to the nobility and twelve to the middle classes at two guineas a head, for which no extravagance was spared; and once a year a fancy-dress ball was given on the anniversary of the establishment.

Casanova had brought with him from France Joseph Pompeati, her son, whom he had escorted from Holland to Paris in January 1759, when Mme. d'Urfé had placed him in a Parisian boarding school with her nephews. Casanova now found Sophie Imer, Mme. Cornelys' daughter, of whom he claimed to be the father.[3] He tells us that when he met her in London she played both the harp and the guitar and sang with admirable taste, facts that are explicitly confirmed by John Taylor, who knew her well later in life. Because of the position Mme. Cornelys had acquired in English society, and perhaps concerned that she might be compromised, she received Casanova with what he regarded as undue reserve for so old a friend. His pride was touched to the quick, and he thereafter showed her the same indifference, and by the acquaintances he rapidly formed he proved that he could make his way on his own. That Mme. Cornelys nevertheless entertained high esteem for Casanova is proved by a letter she wrote to Passano when the latter was endeavoring to collect unfavorable evidence against Casanova in order to destroy Mme. d'Urfé's confidence in him. The letter, written after Casanova's arrival in London, informed Passano that:

You must know that M. de Casanova has been known to my family before I came into this world and was by it well received and loved . . . At the age of four or five years, I came by degrees to know him, at the age of eleven I lost sight of him, having begun to travel. In the year '45 [February 2], I was married in Vienna in the church of St. C. [St. Etienne]. In '54 I saw him again at my father's . . . In '59 I encountered him in Holland, where he honored me with a thousand offers of friendship and service. I was then on the point of sending my son to Paris, and on this occasion he had the kindness to accompany him to London, I asked him to bring him with him . . .

You see then, sir, that I have known only kindness from M. de Casanova, as well as graciousness and friendship, due to so long an acquaintance, and I repeat that I know him only as a man of honor and probity whose actions toward me (as I do not doubt with all the world) have been those of an honest man.

It is true that all men are guilty of ill-considered acts in their life, and those who do not commit them in their youth do so in their old age, with the bad result that when one is old these follies are looked upon with malice, but in youth they are regarded as the caprices of such age.[4]

About this time, George Fermor, second Earl of Pomfret, erroneously referred to in the *Memoirs* as Sir Frederick Fermer, was one of Mme. Cornelys' protectors. Some years later, young Joseph became a tutor of the earl's son. Joseph Pompeati appears to have been highly regarded generally in later life, and showed far greater solicitude for his mother when she fell into distress than did his sister Sophie. The sister later entered the employment of Lady Harrington, became a companion of the Dowager Lady Spencer, was employed by Princess Augusta to distribute her charities, spent the last days of her life with the Dowager Viscountess Sydney, and died on June 25, 1823, as "Mrs. Sophia Wilhelmina Williams." Despite her extravagance and constant difficulty in making both ends meet, Mme. Cornelys continued her assemblies for some twenty years after Casanova saw her in London at the height of her glory. After falling on evil days, she died in Fleet Prison on August 19, 1797, in her seventy-fifth year.[5]

Casanova had been given an introduction to Lady Harrington, one of the leading hostesses in London, by Francesco II Lorenzo Morosini, whom he had met in the suite of the Venetian embassy, returning from London to Venice. Casanova described her as notorious for her gallantries and she, in fact, had been known at one time as the "Stable Yard Messalina." As her residence was within the precincts of the court, it was described as immune from the prohibition governing card playing or music on the Sabbath (i.e., Sunday). According to Casanova, spies lurking in the streets or hearing or suspecting such activities, would take advantage of the opening of a door to seize those so employed. Accustomed as he was to the Continental attitude towards Sunday observance, he found it especially incongruous that, while amusements deemed innocent in other countries were suppressed, no comparable restraints were imposed on houses of prostitution. This testimony of Casanova's has been challenged by Bleackley, but there is evidence given by another contemporary traveler that on Sunday in London theaters and public houses were closed, every form of play was forbidden, including dancing, and that it was forbidden to sing or play a musical instrument in one's home.[6]

While playing whist at Lady Harrington's, Casanova was guilty of the faux pas of settling his losses of fifteen guineas in gold rather than in banknotes. When Lady Harrington took him aside to acquaint him with the breach of a British social custom, he was particularly perplexed when informed that the winner whom he had offended had profited to the extent of fifteen shillings. As he had occasion more than once to remark, there was never any accounting for the English.

On this occasion he was introduced to the Duchess of Northumberland and was able to present her at once with her portrait that her son Hugh, Lord Percy, had given him as a letter of introduction, five months previous in Turin. Another notable acquaintance he made at Lady Harrington's was Sir John Augustus Hervey, later Earl of Bristol, described by David Erskine, editor of his *Journal*, as "the English Casanova." In 1744, Hervey had married the madcap Elizabeth Chudleigh, who had abandoned him to live with the Duke of Kingston. In what Erskine terms a "manifestly collusive suit in the Ecclesiastical Court," she obtained a ruling that she had never been Hervey's wife, thereby permitting her to marry in 1769 the Duke of Kingston. Later, a charge of bigamy was brought against her by an interested member of the duke's family; she was convicted by the House of Lords in 1776 but was saved from the penalties of her felony, including branding on her hand, by her husband's peerage. As Erskine has noted, it was "the most notorious matrimonial scandal" of the eighteenth century in England. Casanova not only met two of the three parties involved, but, what is equally curious, the closest English friend he made during his stay, Henry, tenth Earl of Pembroke, was involved in an affair in 1762 with Kitty Hunter, Hervey's mistress.

When he met Hervey in St. James Park one day and asked him the name of the man with whom he had been conversing, Casanova was astonished to learn that Hervey's friend had been a brother of

Lord Ferrer's who had been hanged in 1760 after having been convicted by a unanimous decision of the House of Lords of the murder of his steward under particularly atrocious circumstances. Casanova considered that the brother had been dishonored by Lord Ferrer's crime, but Hervey was quick to disabuse him. Dr. Johnson expressed the identical statement to Boswell on April 6, 1772: "No man is thought worse of here, whose brother was hanged.[7] Casanova's reaction is more understandable in view of the fact that in France at this time the entire family of a man of rank convicted for a capital crime was disennobled and deprived of all public employment.[8]

Lord Pembroke, whom Casanova met shortly after his arrival, was at this time twenty-nine years of age and already known as one of the gayest blades in London. He had been Lord of the Bed-chamber of George II, and the year previous had published *Method of Breaking Horses*, which was adopted by the British cavalry and continued to be used until well into the nineteenth century.

As Pembroke was acquainted with the pick of the light ladies of the town, he was of great aid to Casanova until he had found a mistress. At Pembroke's suggestion he visited the "Star Tavern" in Piccadilly. Casanova appears to have been unaware that in London in the eighteenth century the emblem of a star at a tavern was as significant as a red light to mark a house of prostitution. Grosley, in a contemporary description of London, remarks that such taverns served as regular places of business for prostitutes, with rooms or boudoirs in the rear reserved for their purposes. Casanova was at first embarrassed to make known the purpose of his visit in the face of the gravity and decent manners of the landlord.[9] When he overcame his scruples and confided that Lord Pembroke had suggested he would find there the prettiest girls in London, the landlord, assuring him he had not been mistaken, called a waiter and ordered him to send for a girl in the same tone he might have used to command a bottle of champagne. A dozen were paraded successively in review, for which he had only to pay a shilling for the porters of their sedan chairs. Archenholz, who visited London at this time, confirms in every particular Casanova's description, stating that at certain bagnios the girls were fetched in chairs as required and that a girl who was sent for and who did not please received no gratuity but was only recompensed for the cost of her chair.[10]

The bagnio, or bathhouse serving as brothel, is said to date in England from the twelfth century. Such was its reputation that when, in 1649, a doctor petitioned Parliament to open bath establishments throughout England, the petition was rejected on the grounds of morality. With the Restoration they took on new life, and in time houses of prostitution came to have the generic name of bagnio, even when they were not bathing establishments. Of these Casanova has not left us so full a description as he has of the Matte in Berne. With his penchants, however, not a week had elapsed after his arrival before he had paid a call at a bagnio. Of this visit he wrote that it was a place where:

> . . . the rich go to sup, sleep, and bathe themselves with a high-class prostitute, a creature not rare in London. It is a magnificent debauch and costs only six guineas. One may economize and reduce the expense to a hundred francs, but an economy that detracts from pleasure is not for me.

He visited another bagnio with Pembroke, accompanied by the Garrick sisters, well known in the gallant world, being mentioned by Capt. Edward Thompson in *The Meritriciade* (1761) and in *The Courtesan* (1765).

To spare Casanova a disappointment, which he had experienced at the "Star Tavern," Pembroke provided him with the names and addresses of a number of girls at four and, six guineas and a single one marked twelve, who was the mistress of a duke. Disillusioned with two for whom he sent his servant, he decided to resort to his own initiative. In the vicinity of Covent Garden he found a French-speaking girl whom he invited to the theater and supper after they had agreed on a fee of three guineas. When she proved to be a Miss Kennedy in Pembroke's six-guinea category, Casanova concluded that he would do better thereafter on his own. He was to meet Miss Kennedy at least once again, at the bagnio of a Mrs. Welch at St. James in Cleveland Road.

It was at Mrs. Welch's that he was introduced to the famous Kitty Fisher, covered with diamonds to the value of 500,000 francs, and awaiting a duke who was to conduct her to a ball. Informed that he might have her for ten guineas, pending the duke's arrival, he declined because of his inability to converse with her. When she had left, Mrs. Welch told him that Kitty had swallowed a banknote of a thousand guineas given her by Sir Richard Atkins. However, Casanova probably distorted the real story in his memory. Archenholz, writing in 1787, stated that some twenty-five years earlier Kitty had passed the night with the Duke of York, who had no more than fifty guineas on his person to give her. In her indignation at receiving less than a hundred, the price then of her favors, Kitty sent the bill to a pastry shop to be put into a tart to be eaten.[11]

In the Prince of Orange Coffee-House, opposite the King's Theatre, at the bottom of the Haymarket, Casanova met, on the day of his arrival, one of the most prominent Italians residing in London, Vincenzo Martinelli. Casanova observed him correcting the proofs of the *Decameron* and immediately subscribed for four copies. The question has been raised as to how Casanova could have seen in 1763 proofs of a work whose title page bears the date of 1762. A possible explanation for this anachronism has been suggested by Mrs. E.H. Torne, who has made a study of Martinelli's sojourn in England.[12] It is quite probable that, although the edition bears the date of 1762, it did not actually appear until 1764. There is an edition bearing this date, and one dated 1766, which retains in the colophon the date of 1762. As further evidence supporting the hypothesis that the earliest edition was not actually published until 1764, Mrs. Thorne has observed that the edition dated 1762 contains a portrait of Martinelli engraved by Bartolozzi who did not arrive in London until 1764, and whom Martinelli probably could not have met before that date.

Martinelli at this time was one of the best known Italian men of letters in England. According to Boswell's *Life of Johnson*, Boswell, Johnson, and Oliver Goldsmith dined on April 15, 1773, with Martinelli at General Paoli's. It was through Martinelli that Casanova was introduced to Dr. Maty, head of the British Museum. Through Maty he was presented to Dr. Johnson with whom he had an extended conversation on the etymology of certain words. This "walking dictionary" as Casanova termed him was thoroughly proficient in the subject, as author of his recently published

*Dictionary* (1755). The details of this curious encounter are found not in the *Memoirs*, but in Casanova's own philological work, *À Leonard Snetlage*.[13] Casanova met Boswell also in the following year in Berlin, at "Rufin's," where Casanova was staying. Under date of September 1, 1764, there is this entry in Boswell's journal:

> I dined at Rufin's, where Neuhaus, an Italian, wanted to shine as a great philosopher, and accordingly doubted of his existence and of everything else. I thought him a blockhead . . .

There is extant a letter addressed to Casanova at Wesel thus: "M. le Comte de Nayhaus de Farussi," making the reference unmistakable *casa nuòva* [*nova*] meaning "new house" or, in German, "Neuhaus." It is impossible to imagine two less compatible persons than Boswell and Casanova, the one, at twenty-four very much of a prig, and the other, at thirty-nine, possessing the assurance of a mature man of recognized accomplishments. Casanova doubtless found Boswell insufferable, as many have before him and since, and, in his impatience with Boswell's pretensions, undertook to pull his leg with an abstract disquisition that hardly reflects his considered beliefs. If, as it appears, Boswell's "Nehaus" was indeed Casanova, we have too explicit evidence of Casanova's deeply religious convictions to attach importance to the inference Boswell makes of his skepticism. Not taking Boswell seriously, he no doubt let himself indulge in practice flights of imagination much as a virtuoso practicing scales on a musical instrument. Boswell, who was singularly lacking in any sense of humor, accepted all that Casanova said as serious. It is a pity we do not have Casanova's opinion of Boswell, which would, in all probability, have been mordant.[14]

Casanova nowhere discloses the purpose of his visit to England, but from Bono's letter of September 28, 1763, we learn that it was for the establishment of a lottery similar to that with which he had been associated from 1757 to 1759 in Paris. Two such lotteries were already in operation in England, and it was doubtless with a view either to participating in one of these or to establishing a new lottery that Casanova bore a letter of introduction to Lord Egremont, secretary of state. The latter died on August 21, before the letter could be presented, and the lottery project seems to have been abandoned. If he did not meet Egremont, Casanova did have access to King George III and the Queen, to whom he appears to have been presented, presumably on June 19, by the Chevalier d'Eon, French minister and private agent of Louis XV.

Casanova himself states that he was presented by the French ambassador, Count de Guerchy, but as the latter did not arrive until October 18, 1763, and was not himself received by the King until October 21, it seems more probable that it was d'Eon, a Freemason as Casanova, who was the introducer.[15] George III and Queen Charlotte were accustomed to hold court on Sunday morning after chapel, and it was on a Sunday that Casanova states the presentation occurred. The King spoke to him in a voice so low and indistinguishable that, not able to understand him, he could only respond with a bow. This description conforms with the King's known "indistinct and precipitate utterance."[16] The Queen, on the contrary, was quite animated in her conversation, and when she remarked that Casanova's compatriot, Querini, the Venetian ambassador who had recently visited the court, had called her a little devil, Casanova, quick to pay a compliment to the fair sex, suggested that what Querini had doubtless meant to say was that she had the wit of an angel.

Of the many curious figures of the eighteenth century, it is remarkable that there is hardly one with whom Casanova's path did not cross, and of whom he does not give us at least a profile, if not a full-length portrait. By no means the least intriguing of these was the Chevalier d'Eon, three years his junior. D'Eon, of effeminate appearance from an early age, had been fond of assuming the garb of a woman. As such, he had come to the particular attention of Louis XV, who had instituted in the middle of the century a system of personal diplomacy through his own special agents, independent of the minister of foreign affairs. Not only was the minister left in ignorance of their activities, but he was frequently hampered by policies counter to those of his cabinet, which the King pursued on his own. When the Duke de Nivernais was sent to London to negotiate a treaty concluding the Seven Years' War, d'Eon accompanied the duke as first secretary to his embassy. When the duke returned to France in April 1763, d'Eon was not only named minister plenipotentiary, while awaiting the appearance of Nivernais' successor, Ambassador Guerchy, but was charged by the King with preparing an invasion of England, and this but a few weeks after the signature of peace. Having received compromising documents, d'Eon was in a position to dictate his own terms even to the King when, with the arrival of Guerchy, his commission as minister was withdrawn. There were polemics in the press, suits and countersuits between d'Eon and Guerchy, to the great embarrassment of the King, who feared possible public exposure of his personal diplomacy.

Casanova touches only briefly on what became the most discussed diplomatic scandal of the century. While d'Eon did not reveal documents having to do with the secret mission entrusted to him by the King, he did publish on March 22, 1764, a volume, to which Casanova makes reference, reproducing correspondence with Guerchy and the French government. Casanova records also that a wager of 20,000 guineas was made in London on d'Eon's sex, and we know this was no exaggeration since one wager even became the subject of an action at law.[17] If Casanova was convinced that d'Eon was a woman, his deception was one shared by many others, including even a French emissary sent by the Count de Broglie, intermediary of Louis XV, with his secret agents to appease d'Eon and put an end to his extravagances. Writing to the King in May 1772 after the return of Drouet, the agent, Broglie assured the King that d'Eon was a woman.[18] After the successive failures of various intermediaries to bring d'Eon to reason, Beaumarchais at length succeeded in inducing him to sign an accord on October 5, 1775, embodying various financial advantages and the assurance that he would not be pursued on his return to France, one of the express conditions being that he was to assume a woman's garb for the rest of his life. This provision appears to have been introduced to ensure that he would not be challenged to a duel by the son of Guerchy who had, in the meanwhile, returned to France and died in chagrin over the dispute that had compromised his diplomatic mission. D'Eon himself eventually returned to London, where he died in 1810. An autopsy performed on his body gave final and conclusive evidence that he was a man.

Through Vincenzo Martinelli, whose acquaintance Casanova had made on the first day of his stay in London, he had found, on that same day, an elegantly furnished house of three stories in Pall

Mall, which he engaged with housekeeper for twenty guineas a week. After about three weeks, however, he lamented his lack of a companion, and to supply a need essential to him, he conceived the idea of displaying under one of his windows this announcement:

> Second or third floor to be let, furnished, at a moderate rental to a young lady alone and independent, speaking English and French, and who will receive no visitors by day or by night.

At the end of some days, after passing in review scores of applicants, he had the visit of a pretty and refined young Portuguese girl called "Pauline," stranded temporarily after a romantic flight from Lisbon. It is important to note that she later confided that she had read a notice about the flat in the *Advertiser*.

For years investigators have sought vainly the advertisement of which, Casanova claims, notice was taken by the London press. Convinced that it existed, we searched the files of all London newspapers of about the date of June 28, in the British Museum. Our search was rewarded with the finding of the notice in the *Gazetteer and London Daily Advertiser* of July 5, 1763:

> A small Family or a single Gentleman or Lady, with or without a Servant, may be immediately accommodated with a genteel and elegantly furnished first floor, with all conveniences; to which belong some peculiar Advantages; it is agreeably situated in Pall Mall, with boarding if required; it may be entered on immediately, and will be let on very reasonable Terms, as it is no common Lodging House, and more for the sake of Company than Profit. Please to enquire at Mrs. Redaw's, millener, exactly opposite Mr. Deard's Toy Shop in Pall Mall, near the Hay Market, St. James's.

Note first of all the subtlety and astuteness of this announcement as compared with the brazenness of the notice Casanova reconstructed in his mind after thirty years. He arranges with a millener, Mrs. Redaw, perhaps of French origin, as were most modistes of the time, to receive prospective tenants. Families and single gentlemen were to be rejected; the inclusion of these in the advertisement were decoys to conceal Casanova's real purpose: finding a mistress.

Mrs. Redaw no doubt had instructions to send for Casanova's inspection only young and attractive French-speaking applicants. While it is hardly conceivable that a young girl of Pauline's refinement would have responded to such an appeal as that quoted by Casanova in his *Memoirs*, it is entirely plausible that, in her reduced circumstances, while awaiting funds from Portugal, she would have been attracted by the discreet notice in the *Advertiser*. Every element justifies the conclusion that Casanova fathered the advertisement quoted: the date, the location of the house, and the name of the newspaper.

Pauline's history, as told by Casanova, is of such a romantic character that skeptics have dismissed it as fiction. A Portuguese writer, Teófilo Braga, less categorical, expressed in 1882 the opinion that confirmation might be found perhaps in unpublished Portuguese family archives.[19] Internal and other evidence gives Pauline's story a high degree of plausibility. Her father, to whom the name of X . . . mo is given, was said to have been imprisoned in connection with the conspiracy against the life of the King, as a result of which the Marquis de Pombal, Portuguese prime minister, had taken in 1758-59 ruthless action against many Portuguese notables. However, until now it has not been possible to identify Pauline's father with any of the many conspirators whom Pombal executed or imprisoned.[20] According to Pauline, Pombal was so uncertain of the degree of her father's guilt that he was neither brought to trial nor was his property confiscated. Immured in a convent, of which her mother's sister was the abbess, Pauline was later placed by a grandparent with the latter's sister-in-law, the Marquise X . . . mo apparently the wife of Pauline's great-uncle and a year later was presented to a protégé of the Princess of Brazil, Count Fl . . . , as the fiancé chosen for her. Pauline, to escape the match proposed, appealed to Pombal, who sent a messenger to her, Count Al . . . , directing her to temporize. She fell in love with the messenger, who was about to leave on a mission to London, and it was agreed that Pauline would disguise herself as a man and Count Al . . . as a woman and that they would leave together to escape the marriage that had become more and more difficult for her to avoid. All went well until the vessel on which the two lovers had embarked arrived at Plymouth. Pauline's disappearance had been discovered, and it was suspected that she had fled with Count Al . . . ; orders were sent by a faster vessel to arrest her and send her back to Lisbon. As it was Count Al . . . who was dressed as a woman, it was he who was taken into custody at Plymouth, while Pauline, purportedly Count Al . . . , was allowed to disembark and make her way to London. Arriving there in 1762 with only a few jewels, in her extremity she had seized on the opportunity offered by Casanova's advertisement to obtain living quarters at the least possible expense to her.

No tale could be more romanesque, and yet there are facts that give it verisimilitude. There is first the notice in the *Advertiser*. In addition to this, Casanova tells us that the night Pauline yielded to him there was a full moon, and it has been determined that there was such a full moon on July 24, 1763, at the period that conforms precisely with his narrative. What is more, in one of the few dates Casanova offers us for this period, August 10, 1763, he tells us that he accompanied Pauline to Calais to see her off on her return journey overland to Lisbon and that, leaving her at Calais on August 12, he returned to London by way of Dover and had a stormy voyage. Bleackley has reported that the press noted a violent storm in the Channel that very day. There remains one further supporting detail. Casanova had given Pauline his servant, Clairmont, to see her safely as far as Madrid. About the month of October, Casanova received a letter from her from that city announcing that she was taking Clairmont with her as far as Lisbon. He later learned that the shop on which Clairmont had embarked for England had been sunk. It has been determined that the *Hanover*, homeward bound from Lisbon, was lost on December 2, 1763, off Falmouth, with sixty passengers, and Clairmont may well have been among them. As we have already learned that the initials with which Casanova tries to protect the identities of certain personages in the *Memoirs* correspond in general to their true names, the clue to the mystery of Pauline may someday be found by a Portuguese genealogist in the identification of the Marquise X . . . mo, X . . . mo, her father, Count Fl . . . , and Count Al . . . whom she married upon her return to Lisbon in 1763. Casanova maintained a correspondence with her for some years, and it was not until his departure from Spain in 1768 that, in the absence of letters from her, he abandoned the plan he had nurtured, since her departure from England, of visiting Lisbon to see her again.

There followed an adventure with a young woman of quite a different character, Marianne Charpillon, whose mother and grandmother had been little better than prostitutes and who herself amply deserved that epithet. The police reports of Berne and Paris give eloquent testimony of their activities. The grandmother and her three sisters were the issue of a respectable Swiss pastor, David Brunner, but after his death they assumed a life of easy virtue. Catherine, the eldest sister, became the concubine of Michel Augsburgher and gave birth to the mother of the Charpillon, Rose Elizabeth Augsburgher, born about 1721, who settled in Paris about 1739 with her mother and aunts. There Marianne was born, and one and all continued their debauchery. Casanova had first met them in Paris in 1759 where, in the Palais Marchand, in one of his characteristic caprices, he had offered to the Charpillon, then aged about thirteen, a pair of earrings for which she had expressed a desire. In that same year, the mother and her two sisters had given Casanova two bills of exchange for 6,000 francs drawn on a Swiss jeweler who became bankrupt before they fell due, and when Casanova endeavored to obtain reimbursement, they had disappeared.[21] Casanova does not tell us how he made the acquaintance of the Charpillon's family after his chance encounter with her and her aunt in a shop. We can reconstruct the possible threads from police and other archives. Count de Rostaing, lover of the Charpillon's mother, whom Casanova later found with the family in London, was also the lover of Marguerite Brunet, known to have been a procuress for Casanova in Paris. The Augsburghers left Paris in 1759 for London, and it was at the beginning of September, 1763, that Casanova had the misfortune to encounter Marianne again at the home of a mutual friend. He recalled that he had been given a note of introduction to her under the name of Charpillon, which she had assumed in London, by Morosini, while the latter was en route to Venice from London and Casanova on his way to England. She lost no time in inviting herself to dine with him in the company of her aunt, on which occasion Pembroke was present also. That experienced roué warned him against her, but Casanova was destined to fall into her trap. He agreed to dine with her two days later, and we know that it was September 12 from the letter she wrote reminding him of the appointment.[22] Casanova notes that the family lived on Denmark Street, Soho. He was wrong only as to the parish; Bleackley found in the Holborn rate books that the Augsburgher family paid a rent of $24 annually for their house in Denmark Street, St. Giles-in-the-Fields.

Prostitute that the Charpillon was, she played a scheming cat-and-mouse game with him, costing him in the end no less than 2,000 guineas, while refusing him her favors, to his rage and humiliation. For once in his life the great lover had been brought to book by a cheap little whore; it was from this time that he dated his decline. Pierre Louÿs was inspired by the story to write *La femme et le pantin*; those who have read Casanova's version find it generally the more moving of the two. The Charpillon bears some resemblance to the Sara of Restif de la Bretonne's *Dernière aventure d'un homme de quarante-cinq ans*. Both were tarts with little to recommend them; if Restif was forty-five, Casanova was only thirty-eight, and his misery was the more poignant after successes never enjoyed by Restif.

Casanova's break with the Charpillon came in November. After she had held him on the hook and tantalized him unmercifully, he found her in the arms of a barber. In the extremity of his passion he was ready to forgive her for this. Remarking upon how he had been completely blinded and duped in a manner to render him ridiculous, he offered from the depth of his heart the explanation that the instinct of women teaches them greater secrets than all the philosophy and research of men. Upon returning to her home to renew his suit, he was informed that she was dying. He resolved to commit suicide and was on his way, burdened with lead, prepared to throw himself into the Thames, when an English friend he met dissuaded him from his purpose. After an evening's debauch, they went to Ranelagh where the Charpillon was seen in perfect health dancing the minuet. With the scales at last torn from his eyes, Casanova determined to prefer charges against the Charpillon's mother, Rose Elizabeth Augsburgher, and the latter's sisters for the bills of exchange they had never redeemed from 1759. He went before a magistrate, and after he had taken oath, a writ was issued on the basis of which the Charpillon's mother and aunts were arrested and taken to prison. Despite a diligent search, no record has been found of these proceedings. In explanation, a British authority on legal procedure has stated that in the eighteenth century it was a common practice to imprison without a hearing persons accused of nonpayment of debts, and that if the obligation was subsequently discharged or settled out of court, no judgment would have been recorded.

British commentators, notably Horace Bleackley, have remarked upon the interesting detail offered by Casanova incident to the arrest of Mme. Augsburgher, namely the insistence of the authorities that she and her sisters be unmistakably identified when the arrests were made. Such concern was due to the great indignation that had been aroused in April 1763 by the apprehension of John Wilkes and his printers on the charge of seditious libel under a general warrant that had not specified their names. Serious riots had followed, with prolonged debates in Parliament and the award of heavy damages to the victims in a court of law. In insisting that the constable making the arrest of the Augsburghers should be accompanied with someone capable of identifying them, the authorities were taking pains to avoid a comparable blunder.

According to the *Memoirs,* two weeks after Casanova had had the Augsburghers arrested, he was returning on a Sunday from an assembly at Mme. Cornelys' when he, in turn, was taken in hand, on complaint of the Charpillon, brought before Sir John Fielding, bound over in the sum of forty guineas to keep the peace, and released after the giving of sureties by Pegu, his tailor, and Maisonneuve, his wine merchant. Leslie-Melville, biographer of Fielding, has pronounced Casanova's narrative a "fair and interesting commentary" on that magistrate's administration of justice, and has added that it is from Casanova alone that we learn that Fielding spoke fluent Italian. Leslie-Melville suggests that he must have learned it from his mother, whose first husband was a native of Italy.[23]

No record has been found of Casanova's legal proceedings against the Augsburgher family, but full confirmation has been obtained of the Charpillon's action against him. According to the records of Clerkenwell Court, Middlesex County, "James Casanova of Pall Mall, Gentleman" appeared before Sir John Fielding on November 27, 1763, on complaints laid by Mary Ann Charpillon and Elizabeth Augbour [Augsburgher] Charpillon. He was bound over to:

> appear at the next General Sessions of the Peace to be held for the County at Hicks-Hall in St. John's Street then and there to answer what shall be objected against him, and in the meantime to keep the peace . . . and especially toward Mary Ann Charpillon and Elizabeth Augbour Charpillon.

The records show his two sureties to have been John Pagus [Pegu], tailor, of Church Street, St. Anne's, Soho, and Lewis Chateauneau, wine merchant, of Marylebone Lane.[24] Casanova's bail was fixed at £100 and the two sureties at £50 each. He was ordered to appear at Hicks-Hall on December 5, 1763, later adjourned to April 1764. It was then a common practice, as it is today in England, to bind over a person to keep the peace and, if there were no further cause for complaint, not to prosecute. That is what appears to have occurred in the present instance as there is no record of any further prosecution or judgment. By April 1764, Casanova had left England, so that he was never tried or even indicted.[25] The account Casanova gives of his hearing before Sir John Fielding with the latter's blindness concealed by a bandage, in which Fielding is quoted as first condemning him to perpetual detention, may have been due to Casanova's faulty recollection of the proceedings after thirty years, to a misunderstanding of Fielding's exact words, or to a desire to render the account more highly dramatic. What Fielding may have said was that *if convicted* Casanova rendered himself liable to imprisonment, but, as his own account of the proceedings shows, he was able to clear himself and to obtain his release after posting bond to keep the peace.

It was in keeping with Casanova's vengeful nature that he would seek some original means of holding the Charpillon and her family up to public scorn. He bought a parrot and set about repeating to it in French: "The Charpillon is a greater whore than

her mother." The purchase must have been made a few days after
his arrest, for there was an advertisement on December 9, 1763, in
the *Public Advertiser* announcing the availability of talking par-
rots "At the Parrott, in Oxford Road, near Charlotte Street, Soho
Square." A friend, hearing the words, which the bird had quickly
learned, suggested that it be offered for public sale. Casanova,
pleased with the proposal, fixed the price at 50 guineas. He adds
that the Charpillon found his method of vengeance amusing, but
that the mother and her aunts, in their anger, consulted legal
counsel who informed them that, while they could not bring suit
for libel against a parrot, an action was possible against Casanova
if it could be proved by two witnesses that the parrot had been
trained by him. A friend suggested that, in the light of this, he
would do well to maintain the greatest discretion as to his part in
the instruction of the bird. Casanova remarks that he was all the
more disposed to circumspection in view of the facility with which
false witness could be obtained in London. He cites having seen in
a window a large sign with the single word "Witness" which was
intended to convey the information that false testimony was
available for a fee. We know that it was similarly available at this
time in France.

According to Casanova, the *St. James Chronicle* published an
amusing commentary on the parrot. Neither this nor a number of
similar press notices to which he makes reference have been found.
However, we know from Ange Goudar's *Espion françois* that such
notices, with witty commentaries on the news of the day, were a
feature at this time of some of the dozen or more London newspapers of the period.[26] Most of these papers were ephemeral, and
few have survived. Those of which files remain, including the *St.
James Chronicle*, were not accustomed to print the notices Casanova attributes to them; it is evident that, failing to recall the name
of the newspaper that published this and other notices, he designated the *Chronicle*, the leading journal of the day, for want of a
better name.

Ange Goudar was an adventurer and pamphleteer of no mean
order, whom Casanova met first in Paris, probably about 1759. He
was born in 1708 at Montpellier, son of Simon Goudar, an
inspector general of Languedoc Manufactures. His first known

published work was *L'aventurier français* (Amsterdam, 1746) followed by *Pensées diverses*, which appeared in Paris, 1748. This was followed by a variety of pamphlets and books on political and economic subjects as well as on music and the dance, published anonymously, under his own name, or under that of his pretended wife, Sara Goudar, and of which a number were dedicated, curiously enough, to Casanova's friend Lord Pembroke. Casanova, who was intimately associated with Goudar in London and again in Naples in 1770, is one of the principal sources of our knowledge of a man who has never attracted the attention that his voluminous and generally solid output abundantly merits.[27]

Writing to Lamberg, July 28, 1787, Casanova remarks:

> Let us come to Goudar, and when you wish to know anything about all the adventures on the earth, our contemporaries, come to me, for I have known them all.

Casanova's characterization of Goudar as "intelligent, a pimp, a thief at cards, a police spy, a false witness, crafty, bold, and ugly," while perhaps in some measure just, was no doubt colored by a certain jealousy towards one whose literary reputation had so far exceeded his own.

Goudar had arrived in London from Paris about 1760, and had become intimately linked with the Augsburgher family, with whom he was Casanova's intermediary on more than one occasion. in particular with the Charpillon. It was Goudar who had offered to sell Casanova a specially contrived chair in order to subdue her. Equipped with springs, it seized and held immobile the person seated in it. That such chairs existed is evident from their mention in a number of eighteenth-century works.[28] The very idea of an instrument, which he termed "diabolical," was quite repugnant to Casanova, to whom a woman's voluntary submission was essential.

Goudar was engaged at this time in what was to become his most popular work, *L'espion chinois*, which first appeared in 1764 in six volumes, and went through half a dozen editions, including an English translation (London, 1765; Dublin, 1766). Casanova himself contributed a few letters to it. Goudar's *Histoire des Grecs*, published in 1757, an account of the wiles of professional gamblers with which he was thoroughly familiar, attracted sufficient attention to warrant five other editions. According to the Chevalier d'Eon, Goudar was employed by Guerchy to write three anonymous pamphlets against his subordinate, with whom he was at swords' points. The first, published in October 1763, was the opening salvo in Guerchy's campaign against d'Eon, who replied in a *Note*, published on November 30, to which Guerchy, through Goudar, made answer in December in a *Contre-note*. It was the publication of this last pamphlet that precipitated d'Eon's decision to print in March 1764 his *Lettres, mémoires et négotiations particulières*, to which reference has been previously made.[29] Guerchy not only brought suit for libel against d'Eon but caused Goudar to publish a third pamphlet for which the writer was paid twenty guineas. Goudar is said to have been arrested on the Strand subsequently on complaint of his printer, Becket, for having failed to discharge the expenses of publication. On Easter Day, 1764, the choleric d'Eon administered a public caning to Goudar in Green Park.[30] It is curious that Casanova, who was acquainted with both men, should make no reference to the Goudar pamphlets, but only to d'Eon's publication, which, of course, created by far the greater stir.

In the period after Casanova's rupture with the Charpillon, he met at the Marylebone Gardens, a popular place of public entertainment in London, acquaintances made in Berne three years previous. They included Louis de Muralt-Favre and his wife and two daughters; with the eldest, whom he calls Sara, Casanova had had intimate relations. Although her actual name was Marguerite, she is known to have gone by the name of Sara in her family, despite the fact that her younger sister was so christened.

On April 15, 1762, Muralt had been appointed Berne representative in London, but when Casanova had called on him shortly after his arrival in June 1763, Muralt had turned the cold shoulder to him. Muralt now again saluted him coldly, and Casanova inquired of his wife what the former had against him. She replied that Passano had written horrible things to her husband about him. Not only is there a letter of record of Passano of July 11, 1763, attesting this, but the details presented in general about Muralt's activities in London are substantiated by the Berne archives.[31] It was Casanova's misfortune to have put Passano in touch with Muralt in 1762 at the moment when Passano was entering his service as secretary, and with the break between the two in May 1763 Passano had enlisted Muralt's aid in destroying Mme. d'Urfé's confidence in the Venetian. That Muralt was in correspondence with Mme. d'Urfé is proved by a letter of Bono of November 10, 1763, in which reference is made to a letter from Muralt from London to the Marquise proposing a manuscript on the secret of long life for the sum of $12,000. When she received it, she must have reflected that in breaking with Casanova she had fallen between Scylla and Charybdis.

Bono's letter suggests that Muralt was still in London at the end of 1763 as Casanova says in his *Memoirs*, notwithstanding Grellet's contentions to the contrary. According to Grellet, Muralt had been relieved of his functions in London in July 1763 owing to various irregularities, and had been summoned to Berne where he had arrived on October 10, 1763, to answer the charges against him. What appears entirely probable is that he was permitted to return to London and settle his affairs. When Casanova met him at Marylebone Gardens, it was in December, on the eve of his definitive departure with his family.[32] Muralt was in such financial distress that Casanova's generous entertainment of the family at the Gardens softened him. Casanova found his old passion for "Sara" renewed to such degree that he resolved to follow the family to Switzerland.

Visiting the Muralts the next day to offer them a temporary lodging at his house, he learned that they could not withdraw their belongings until they had paid a rent of $40. Casanova immediately advanced the sum and later a further $50 to save Muralt from imprisonment for other debts, but his generosity did not move "Sara" to renew her intimacy with him, except on one fleeting occasion. Casanova's proposal to leave with the Muralts for Switzerland was interpreted by the mother as a proposal to marry her daughter; she discussed it with her husband, who declined on the grounds that she had been promised to M. de W., as well as by reason of their difference in religion. The decision was not in the end displeasing to Casanova, as the word "marriage" had frightened him out of his wits and brought him to his senses.

Sara de Muralt, the real Sara, finally did marry Frederic de Wattenwyl or Watteville or Vatteville in 1785.

When the Muralts departed about the beginning of 1764, Casanova was again at loose ends. Goudar, ever in the offing and at his elbow particularly for affairs of the heart, introduced him to five Hanoverian sisters who had come with their mother to London to recover damages done to their property by the British Army. The mother, about to be imprisoned for debt, appealed to Casanova for aid. Embittered by his experience with the Charpillon, and doubtless recalling the money he had vainly thrown after "Sara," he displayed a callousness not common to him. He observed to the mother:

"Madam, I am a libertine by profession . . . I have told your daughters how I feel, and if you are wise you must agree. I can well admire girls who wish to preserve their virtue, but in that case I shall never be their friend. If your daughters wish to remain virtuous, why let them, but then they must not tempt men. I leave and assure you I shall not see them again."

"Wait a moment, sir. The Count . . . was my husband; hence my daughters are entitled to respect also by reason of their birth."

"Very well! What greater sign of respect can I give you than in not seeing them again?"

"Have you no pity for our sad situation?"

"Very much, but I refuse to allow this to influence me inasmuch as they are pretty."

"What a reason!"

Casanova's better nature was at length moved by the mother's appeals.

"We are reduced today to a diet of bread."

"In that case I will gladly entertain all of you at dinner."

"You are an eccentric individual. They will be sad as I am going to prison. They will tire you. Give them rather the money you would spend for dinner."

"No Madam, I must have at least the pleasure of sight and sound for my money. I will stay your arrest until tomorrow and, in the meantime, Providence may possibly intervene in your behalf."

If his conduct in these circumstances reflects that of an un-principled roué, it was not exceptional. Two distinguished British noblemen, Lord Pembroke and Lord Baltimore, had shown them-selves no less heedless of the family's distress when appeal had been made of them for aid. They had even exceeded Casanova in their callousness in imposing the condition of payment after rather than before the yielding of the sisters to them. This is not to excuse Casanova but is evidence that his principles or lack thereof were shared by many of his contemporaries of the highest society.

When the mother was imprisoned after a day's delay, she overcame her scruples, moved into Casanova's home with the five girls, and shut her eyes to his successive affairs with each. On returning to Hanover, she parted with him on excellent terms, thanking him for the hundred and fifty guineas he had given her for her daughters. The names of four are specified: Victorine, Auguste, Hippolyte, and Gabrielle, and it is mentioned that the family was of Stöcken in Hanover.

Inquiry of the Director of Archives at Hanover has disclosed that the estate of Stöcken in 1789 was in possession of the Chevalier von Schwicheldt, who married Marianne Hippolyte von Fabrice in 1741. After his death in 1766, she cared for their five surviving children, of whom there were three daughters: Berthe Auguste, born in 1744, Louise Charlotte Sophie, born in 1749, and Amalie Oelgarde, born in 1755. It is significant that the name of Auguste given by Casanova to the third of the five daughters was born by the first of the Schwicheldt sisters and that the mother was christened Hippolyte, a name ascribed to another of the five daughters. This shifting nomenclature has already been found to be part of Casanova's procedure of redistributing given names in a family, as previously observed with Sara Muralt and the "Monte" sisters. According to Casanova the eldest Hanoverian girl, whom he does not name, eloped in 1764 with her love, the Marquis della Perina, to Naples, where he found her in 1770. Another of the sisters, Auguste, is stated by Casanova to have remained behind in London in 1764 as mistress of Lord Pembroke. This would account for two of the five daughters and would explain why these only numbered three when the family became a charge of the mother in 1766 on the death of the father. These facts, the provenance of Stöcken, the similarity of names and the respective ages of the sisters, except for the youngest, Amalie, all strongly suggest that, although the mother of the five Hanoverian sisters was not a widow in 1764 nor was her husband at this time a count but only of noble family, she was in all probability Marianne Hippolyte von Schwicheldt.[33]

When the Hanoverian sisters departed, Casanova was in desperate financial circumstances, having run through $12,000 since his arrival in England; he now had only eighty guineas in ready cash. To add to his misfortune, he encountered a Baron Stenau and, gambling with him, was offered in settlement of his winnings a bill of exchange for 520 guineas. Casanova negotiated it unsuspectingly with a banker who, when finding it false, summoned him to make it good, or face the possibility of being hanged for what was a capital offense in England. Stenau had fled in the meanwhile, and Casanova, finding himself ill with a disease contracted from the Baron's mistress, had no other recourse than to flee in turn.

In addition to the portraits Casanova has drawn for us from his London sojourn, of a number of historical personages and of others not so well known, he has left us a vivid picture of both the seamy and the surface life of England in the eighteenth century. He has left us also descriptions of Vauxhall, Ranelagh, and Richmond, so famous as pleasure resorts at this time, and has besides afforded us glimpses of long-forgotten manners. He was astonished at the slight consideration shown the royal family which, on this account, ventured out but rarely in public except for public ceremonies, at which time hundreds of constables assembled to protect them. He found it curious that the English ate so little bread and that, in taverns, no soup was available, while boiled beef was regarded as fit only for dogs.[34] Disquieting to him was the information communicated to him by his old theatrical friend, Mme. Binetti, that the lover of a married woman was liable to conviction for criminal conversation if even found seated on her bed. He was told that several rich Englishmen had suffered the loss of half their wealth to the complaining husband. In consequence they had become careful about frequenting married women, and in particular those of Italian origin. The inference is left that blackmail may have had something to do with the English caution in this respect. Apart from certain vagaries in the law, Casanova found it good, but too easily subject to abuse. It was more frequently interpreted according to the letter than in accordance with the legislators' intentions, and Casanova observed that the enactment of new legislation was constantly made necessary for stricter interpretation of the old.

He was puzzled by the emphasis placed on wealth. Asking a banker friend about the identity of a certain man, he was informed that he was worth a hundred thousand. Casanova objected that he had asked the man's name, not what he was worth. In reply he was informed that "Here the name is nothing, the value everything."

He records two incidents as a witness, which it seems fairly certain must have been recounted to him by others. One was concerned with a man knocked out after boxing, whom a surgeon had not been permitted to treat because of a bet that had been made that the man would die. It is strongly suggestive of an almost identical tale set down in a letter of September 1, 1750, by Horace Walpole to Sir Horace Mann. The other was of a riot, when spectators at the Drury Lane, angered at a change in the program, sacked that theater. This incident is known to have occurred on January 25, 1763, before Casanova's arrival in England.[35] It is probable that Casanova was so impressed by the two stories recounted to him by others that, in writing his *Memoirs*, he fancied he had himself witnessed the incidents or, again, as a master storyteller he preferred to place them in the first person.

# CHAPTER 12

## Germany, Russia, and Poland

Casanova left London about March 13, 1764, and crossed the Channel to Calais, more dead than alive. After pausing in Brussels to await funds from Bragadin, he proceeded to Wesel, where he had the good fortune to meet Major General John Beckwith, whose acquaintance he had made some months previous at the country home of Lord Pembroke. Beckwith persuaded him to put himself in the hands of a Dr. Peipers who, in accordance with the frequent practice of the times in the treatment of venereal diseases,[1] gave him lodging in his home and kept him under his care for five weeks. Casanova was traveling with a godson, Daturi, whom he had met unexpectedly in London. Daturi had need of hospital care, and Casanova applied for a passport for him to Beckwith, who directed him to seek it from Major General Salamon, commander of the Prussian troops at Wesel. We are not obliged to accept Casanova's report for the truth of these statements. Not only has a letter survived from Dr. Peipers to him but, what is more, one from Beckwith of April 15, 1764, counseling Casanova to apply to Salamon, as the only authority authorized to issue such documents.

En route to Berlin he paused at Brunswick and spent a week in study at the nearby library of the Duke of Wolfenbüttel, rich particularly in ancient manuscripts. Of his stay he wrote:

> I lived in the most perfect tranquillity with never a thought of the past or future, my work preventing me from taking into account the existence of the present. I see today that only a few trifling circumstances were wanting to make of me in life a real sage, for virtue has always had for me more attractions than vice. On those occasions when I was a sinner it was only through heedlessness.

It was at Wolfenbüttel that he began work on his translation of Homer's *Iliad*, which he was to publish in Venice in 1775-78. Here he found hints not to be found in any commentator of that work, not even in Pope, whose rhymed version he admired, but whose notes he found deficient.[2]

Casanova had met the Duke of Brunswick in London on the occasion of the subscription ball given at Mme. Cornelys' on January 24, 1764, eight days after the Duke's marriage to Princess Augusta, elder sister of George III. At the time Casanova had noted that the Duchess de Grafton wore no powder in her hair, to the disapproval of other women present, although within six months the style had been accepted on the Continent. These details are one of many examples of his importance as a historian of manners. While no other source, so far as is known, attributes this innovation to the Dutchess of Grafton, it has been suggested that "the rational change of wearing the natural hair instead of wigs" with powder and pomatum, was instituted in 1763.[3]

At Brunswick, attending a review of troops by the Duke of Brunswick, he encountered, in the elegant society assembled to view the ceremony, Elizabeth Chudleigh, who, he states, inquired when he had left London. She is described as wearing a robe of muslin with only an underslip of batiste underneath. In the pouring rain her light garments so attached themselves to her body that she appeared naked, without being in any way embarrassed, heedless of the rain and refusing to take shelter under the elegant tents provided for the occasion. The description he gives could not conform more with her known character. A portrait of her exists as she appeared at a ball at the Venetian ambassador's in London on May 1, 1749, with her breasts exposed and, as Mrs. Elizabeth Montagu wrote to a correspondent, in a muslin dress "or undress, as if she were Iphigenia for the sacrifice, but so naked the high priest might easily inspect the entrails of the victim."

In Berlin, where Casanova arrived at the end of June, and where he was to remain until the middle of September, he lodged at an inn kept by Mme. Rufin, a Frenchwoman, whose hotel, situated on the Poststrasse, was known as Zu den Drei Lilien. It was here that Boswell dined on September 1, 1764. Casanova states that he lodged with Mme. Rufin but gives the name of her inn as the "Hotel Ville-de-Paris." He has evidently confused it with a hotel where he stopped in later years, situated in the Bruderstrasse; the landlord was a French refugee, Quien, but his hotel was not opened until about 1767.[4]

The first call he paid in Berlin was on his former Parisian lottery associate Jean Calzabigi who, after leaving Paris, had introduced a lottery in Brussels, had suffered a bankruptcy, and had come with a mistress to Berlin, where he had been charged by Frederick the Great with the introduction of a lottery. Thiebault, who spent twenty years in Frederick's service, and who arrived in Berlin in 1765, confirms in part Casanova's account. According to Thiebault, Calzabigi was employed at a salary of 15,000 francs and arrived in Berlin with both a mistress and a carriage. In Berlin, Calzabigi appears to have been the technical counselor for the lottery rather than directly interested, as Thiebault states that once the project drawn up by Calzabigi had been approved by the King, he entrusted the direction of it to Counts de Reuss and de Reichstadt.[5] By 1768 the lottery had passed under the direction of Baron Krohn according to a letter of June 8 of that year from Baron Bodissoni to Casanova. In one of Casanova's subsequent audiences with Frederick the Great he expressed his distrust of the lottery, which he termed "the lottery of Genoa," and it was thus that the lottery was commonly referred to in the eighteenth century. The Genoese lottery, archetype of those that spread within and outside Italy, originated from the drawing by lot of the names of senators to serve as governors. In Venice, such a lottery with five numbers instead of names and with nine drawings annually, was instituted as early as 1590. It was taken over by the Republic in 1715, suspended in 1726, but reestablished in 1734.[6]

In Berlin Casanova found another old acquaintance, George Keith, tenth Earl Marischal of Scotland (1686-1778). Keith was a typical representative of the many international figures of the eighteenth century, of whom we have already seen examples in Bonneval Pasha in Turkey and General James Paterson in Nice who had found service with governments other than their own. Compelled to leave Scotland for his Jacobite sympathies, Keith had fled to Spain and from there to Russia, where his brother was a general in the Russian service. Casanova had first met him, not, as he mistakenly states, as Prussian Minister at Constantinople, but when Keith was returning in 1745 through Constantinople from Russia to Venice. He had seen him again in Paris in 1751, where he was then Prussian minister, remaining, except for a brief return to Scotland, in the Prussian service until his death. High in the confidence of Frederick the Great, Keith suggested to Casanova that he would do well to seek an audience of the King. Casanova was quite taken aback at the proposal and questioned whether Frederick would take any notice of such a request. When Keith assured him that the Prussian sovereign replied to everyone, the Venetian ventured to frame a respectful letter asking for an audience. We have further testimony as to Frederick's accessibility, and the part Keith played in introducing distinguished foreigners to the King. Five years later, Louis Dutens was presented to Frederick through the intermediary of Keith, while de Langle, who visited Berlin about this time, has recorded:

> . . . there is no sovereign more accessible. Write to Frederick and he replies at once; a request once received is recorded the same day.[7]

Casanova's first audience took place about July 7 in the gardens of Sans-Souci. We can determine the approximate date by particulars he gives of the court, controllable by contemporary chronicles. He states that the Duchess of Brunswick visited her brother at this time, which necessitated the removal of Frederick from Sans-Souci to Berlin. On that occasion an Italian opera was presented at the Charlottenburg theater, where the celebrated Denis, an old flame of Casanova, native of Venice, and godchild of his mother, danced at the representation, at which Casanova also assisted. We know that the duchess arrived on July 9, that the opera given was *I portentosi effetti della natura*, and that, in fact, Mme. Denis, principal dancer of the Court, appeared in it on July 19. A portrait of her, which Frederick caused to be painted, is, or was, at Sans-Souci.

While Frederick was with his royal guests at Berlin, Mme. Denis conducted Casanova to Potsdam to visit, in the King's absence, about July 23, the royal apartments at Sans-Souci. In the King's room, on his working table, Casanova observed half-burned papers, which comprised, as a valet informed him, Frederick's *History of the Seven Years' War*, which had caught fire through an accident. Casanova's account is entirely correct, as we know that a part of the monarch's manuscript was charred through the negligence of a lackey in November 1763. The King had left the room for a short time when drip from a candle ignited the manuscript, and when he returned, he was able to save only a part. Casanova was informed that Frederick had been so vexed that he had renounced the continuance of the work. This would explain why the damaged papers still remained on the sovereign's desk. Casanova added that he must have reconsidered his decision as the history was published after the King's death. Casanova was not only an accurate observer, but well-informed. The manuscript was eventually published in 1788, with certain changes introduced by Count Hertzberg.

Through Keith, Casanova was informed that the King was prepared to appoint him one of five governors of a newly created corps of Pomeranian cadets of the nobility at a salary of 600 écus. Far from flattered by the offer, he refused it when he saw the miserable lodgings destined for the governors, and their abject situation.

Revisiting Potsdam early in September with a Venetian friend, Baron Bodissoni, desirous of selling Frederick a painting of Andrea del Sarto (perhaps that now in the Berlin Museum), Casanova attended a military parade being reviewed by the monarch. When the King perceived Casanova, he approached him, inquiring when he intended to leave for Petersburg and whether he had been recommended to Empress Catherine. When Casanova replied that he was leaving shortly and had only a recommendation to a banker, Frederick remarked that this was even better, and expressed the hope that if Casanova returned to Berlin he would be glad to have news of Russia from him.

There can be no doubt that Casanova had two interviews with Frederick and that their conversation followed substantially the form reported, with perhaps some difference of detail. A memorandum left by Casanova supplements and, in a few particulars, departs slightly from the account recorded in the *Memoirs*. In the former we find:

> The day when questioned by him, the late King of Prussia, as to who in my opinion was the greatest of Romans, I replied that it was Attilius Regulus. His Majesty said that for him it was Sylla. I found this neither extraordinary nor reckless; the King did not tell me that Sylla was the greatest of Romans, but that he was *to his way of thinking*. A way of thinking is the younger brother of good taste; one must defer to everyone.
>
> The late King of Prussia was, besides a great king, a man of wit, a man of letters also, but I did not notice that he pretended to be wiser than another. He considered himself well enough informed and sufficiently far-seeing to speak in a decisive tone, but he listened, and his way of yielding was that of changing the subject by interrupting the interlocutor with a question that was overwhelming as it came out of the blue. That is why in my *Memoirs*, and in my *Confutazione*, I call him an intrepid interrogator. When he said to me when walking in the garden of Sans-Souci that Sylla was his hero in preference to Attilius, he avoided all that I could have said to the contrary by asking me how many line vessels the Venetian Republic could launch in case of war. I told him the truth of what I knew, and the King said to me that I was mistaken; but when he saw that I was going to enter into details, he asked me what I thought in general of taxation. I was undertaking to reply when, my opinion having displeased him, he spoke of a peristyle to his right, and of the fountains of Versailles, and told me that his beautiful garden could not have access to the waters of either the Spree or the Oder, but when he perceived that I wished to enter into the subject of hydraulic architecture, he interrupted me and, dismissing me, told me to go and see Marshal Keith.

I went away, congratulating myself that I had gained an estimate of him but not he of me; in this I considered myself sharper than he. I was displeased with myself for not suspecting that Sylla must be his favorite hero, the more particularly as I had been present at the opera *The Triumph of Sylla,* of which he was the author; that Sylla had made himself master of his own land and had freed it by his own will, an achievement the Great Frederick was obliged to admire, since he felt himself unique among all monarchs capable of imitating him, or because he knew that he was not capable of this. The retirement of Sylla will always represent a true triumph and the greatest a man can accomplish as he triumphed over himself. A thing admired is not always to be proven by the wise admirer, but he is not obliged to render an accounting of his thought to anyone.

Casanova left Berlin in the middle of September 1764, with letters of introduction for M. de Keyserling, grand chancelor of Mittau, and his sister, the Duchess of Courland. He arrived with only three ducats in his pocket. After taking chocolate with Mme. de Keyserling, he was spurred by one of those capricious impulses that he confesses he could never resist, and left his last three ducats for the pretty Polish girl serving him. When he returned to his inn, a Jew approached him, offering to change his Prussian money. When Casanova replied that he had only ducats, and therefore no occasion to utilize his services, the Jew offered to advance him funds in return for a bill of exchange on a Petersburg banker. Casanova was at a loss to understand the Jew's confidence in him until he learned that he had gained credit as a man of great means because of the liberal tip he had given. News of it had spread through the town.

Next he went to Riga, and remained there until December 15; he was well received by Charles Ernest de Biron, Prince de Courland, a bon viveur of Casanova's ilk, and also a fellow Freemason. In reporting of his visit to Riga, he commits one anachronism for which it is difficult to account, namely that during that period, from about October 20 to December 15, 1764, he saw Catherine the Great on a visit she paid to that city. Actually, Catherine is known to have made this visit some months earlier, from July 10 to August 5. It is not the first occasion on which he claims to have been an eye-witness to events he could not possibly have seen: Two have already been cited incident to his visit to England. In each instance, the details he gives, aside from her personal presence, are true. Since there was no palpable reason for misrepresentation on his part, the most reasonable explanation would appear to be that, as in England, the event was recounted to him and made such a powerful impression on his memory that some thirty years later, when he was writing his *Memoirs*, it had been transformed in his mind as one at which he himself had been present. That Casanova left Riga about December 15 is established by a customs document issued him there on the 10th for the passage of Count de Farussi, the name under which he was traveling, together with his secretary, baggage, and carriage.

He arrived at St. Petersburg about December 21 and found a lodging in a street known as the Million. The principal inconvenience he encountered was the general use by the merchant class of German, a language that eluded him to the end of his life. To supply certain deficiencies in the furniture of his hotel room, he was obliged to purchase drawers and a table, to serve him in writing and where he might place his papers and books.

On the day of his arrival, his landlord informed him that in the evening there was to be a masked ball for 5,000 persons at the Imperial Palace, open to the public and free of charge on the presentation of a ticket. That the information given by Casanova is exact is established by a letter of the British ambassador, Sir George Macartney, who, writing in February 1766, noted that masked balls at the palace, for which no charge was made, were open to all those who were able to obtain tickets, which were easily available for the five or six thousand who generally attended them.[8] Such a ticket was provided Casanova by his landlord, and it was there that he saw Catherine the Great for the first time, in the company of the then ruling favorite, Gregory Orloff. Two years earlier, Gregory and his four brothers—John, Alexis, Theodore, and Vladimir—had organized the coup d'état which, through the murder of Catherine's husband, Peter III, had brought her to the throne as Empress. On the occasion of the masked ball, both Gregory Orloff and Catherine were wearing, the better to disguise themselves, cheap dominoes, and Casanova observed Catherine seat herself among those speaking Russian to overhear their conversation in the expectation, as he suggests, that the subject might be concerned with herself.

While wandering about the extensive rooms Casanova was attracted by the voice of a masked woman surrounded by a number of admirers. Her Parisian manner of speaking persuaded him that she was an old acquaintance, and when she finally lifted her mask, he was astonished to find that she was Mme. Baret, a silk-stocking seller of the rue des Prouvaires, whom he had known in Paris in 1759, and with whom, when she was only sixteen, he had had more than one tender tête-à-tête at his country place, the Petite Pologne. She informed Casanova that after his departure from Paris she had attached herself to a M. d'Anglade and, leaving him, had joined the director of a French comic opera, who had brought her to Russia as an actress under the name of Langlade. At present she was being kept by Count Rzewuski, Polish ambassador. After Rzewuski's departure, Casanova renewed his liaison with her, until she took on a more advantageous lover, Count George Brown, an Irishman who had risen high in the Russian service. Casanova tells us that she died soon afterwards of scarlet fever. His account could not be better documented by contemporary records. J. von Stählin, confirming her arrival in Russia in 1764, describes her as an excellent comedian, despite the modest disclaimer she made to Casanova that she could neither sing nor dance. It was the following year in Warsaw that he learned of her sudden death in a letter of April 11, 1766, from one of the cousins of the Orloffs, Stepan Stepanovich Zinovieff.[9]

Casanova's ability to gain the lasting friendship of men of distinction in many countries was evidenced in the case of Zinovieff, later Russian ambassador to Spain; ten years afterwards, Zinovieff, with whom he had continued correspondence after his departure, was a subscriber to his *Iliade*. It was through Zinovieff that, soon after his arrival, and after Mlle. Langlade had taken on another lover, Casanova found a mistress to whom he remained relatively constant until leaving Russia. Unlike most of his other attachments, she was a simple peasant girl named Zara whose astonishing beauty had attracted him, when he was dining at Catherinhoff with Zinovieff and a party of friends. The latter arranged for Casanova to purchase Zara from her family for 100 roubles. He taught her Italian and, with the concern he habitually displayed for women who attached themselves to him, he arranged for her transfer to the famous Italian architect Antonio Rinaldi, a resident of St. Petersburg, when he himself left Russia.

Other Russians of distinction with whom Casanova formed something more than casual ties were Semion Kirillovitch Naryshkin, Adam Vassilievitch Olsuvieff, and Peter Ivanovitch Melissino. Olsuvieff was one of the intimate collaborators of the Empress. Casanova terms him with perhaps some injustice as the only lettered man he met in Russia. Melissino, founder of the Russian artillery, was reputed for his varied gifts; what the three had in common with Casanova was not only, in the case of the last two, their intellectual gifts, but also an addiction to the pleasures of the senses, Melissino being particularly given to debauch. Casanova made the acquaintance also of two of the most notable figures in Russia, Princess Dashkov, who had played a part in the conspiracy against Peter III, and Count Nikita Panin, Freemason and leading statesman. With his customary acumen he picked up the report that Panin was the father rather than the lover of Princess Dashkov. It was faithful as far as it went; historians have been debating ever since whether he may not have been both.

His account of his visit to Russia is not in strict chronological order. Thus we know that the description he gives us of the benediction of the waters of the Neva on Epiphany occurred on January 17, 1765. In a large hole made in the ice a priest was plunging babies for baptism. As he let one fall out of his hands and disappear beneath the ice, he called out *Drugoi*, or "pass me another," with no attention paid to the missing child. Casanova could not contain his astonishment when he observed the parents of the infant overcome with joy, certain that their infant child had ascended to heaven. The Russian clergy he found extremely ignorant, and he thought the Muscovites the most superstitious Christians on earth. Aside from Kronstadt, Tsarskoye-Selo, and Peterhoff, the only visit he made during his nine months' stay in Petersburg was one by way of Novgorod to Moscow. As he aptly stated, those who have not seen Moscow have not seen Russia.

The description he gives of Russian manners and customs

reveals how little these have changed in two centuries. To question an order of the government, a ukase, was a crime of lèse-majesté; the heavy drinking and toasts that were inevitable accompaniment of meals, with one toast drawing forth another, are suggestive of contemporary Soviet practices. At a dinner of twenty-four covers offered by General Alexis Orloff, from which the secretary of the French embassy had to be transported bodily to bed, Melissino offered to his host the toast: "May you die the day you become rich," an illusion to the prodigal generosity of Orloff. Casanova found Orloff's response, while equally typical of the Tartar temperament, more to be admired. "May you only die by my hands," he proposed in reply. The occasion was a great review outside of St. Petersburg, which, although it appears toward the end of Casanova's story of his Russian experiences, is known to have taken place on January 25, 1765, shortly after his arrival. Not to be outdone, Casanova before his departure gave a farewell dinner and ball for thirty persons to repay the courtesies extended to him, including fireworks, supplied to him gratis by Melissino.

The highlights, of course, of Casanova's Russian sojourn were the three interviews he had with Catherine the Great, arranged for him by Panin in the summer garden on the Neva. The first conversation was concerned with Casanova's comments on the observations he had made about Russia, ending with a reference on his part to Frederick the Great and to his insufferable habit of not permitting his interlocutor to complete the development of his thought. When questioned by Catherine as to why he had not attended the instrumental concerts given at her palace on Sunday afternoons, Casanova answered that he had been present at one, but that he had the misfortune not to like music. Smiling, Catherine turned to Panin and remarked that she knew another of like mind.[10] Casanova adds that he had heard her express her indifference to music when leaving an opera. Thus he was playing the role of an artful courtier in profiting from his knowledge of her tastes to cultivate her good graces. In the hope that another meeting might open the way to employment in Russia, Casanova did not fail to frequent the summer garden at the instance of Panin, who informed him the Empress had twice inquired of him. On his second meeting with her he seized an opportunity she gave him, in speaking of the eleven days difference between the Russian calendar and that in use in most of Europe, to suggest the advisability of adopting the Gregorian calendar. It was a subject to which he had given much thought. One of the manuscripts that he bequeathed to his nephew-in-law at his death, and which was acquired by Brockhaus along with the text of the *Memoirs*, was called "Rêveries sur la mesure moyenne de notre [temps] selon la réformation Grégorienne," written in 1793.[11] Casanova recalled that Peter the Great had desired to adopt this calendar and had only been dissuaded from doing so by its failure in England, with which Russia was closely allied commercially. When Catherine observed that Peter was not a savant, Casanova was bold enough to take issue with her and declare that he was a genius of the first degree. Casanova had drawn her into a discussion of the calendar, which she did not feel herself sufficiently well informed to pursue, for she interrupted it by saying that she would be pleased to resume the subject another time.

A week later the opportunity presented itself when Casanova was summoned to her side in the garden he had sedulously frequented in the hope of seeing her again. She entered at once into a discussion of the calendar, taxing his own country, Venice, with beginning the year on March 1, and with a different computation of the hours of the day from that of other countries. The disadvantage she saw in the adoption of the Gregorian calendar was that it would abridge the lives of all her subjects by eleven days and would change the observance of their birthdays and that of the Saints of the Church. Casanova was convinced that she must have been briefed on the subject in the interval between their last conversation, and this was later confirmed by him by Olsuvieff. In her affability and graciousness, which contrasted with the brusqueness of Frederick the Great, Casanova found her much the superior. While the King of Prussia, in Casanova's opinion, owed his success in large measure to the favor fortune had bestowed upon him, Catherine's success, on the contrary, was due to her own superior merit. The Prince de Ligne, who knew the Empress intimately, commenting on Casanova's judgment of her, remarked that he had "never seen one so profound, so brilliant."

In accordance with the regulations of that time, he was obliged to announce his intention to leave Russia in the newspapers at least fifteen days in advance of his projected departure. With a passport delivered to him by Count Alexander Galitzin, in the name of "Graf [Count] Jacob Casanov de Farussi" and dated September 1, 1765, he set out for Warsaw about the 15th, and arrived there on October 10, 1765, accompanied by a French actress, Valville, who was returning to Paris. Equipped with useful letters of introduction, including one from the influential Anglican minister at St. Petersburg to Prince Adam Czartoryski, he was received with favor by the leading Polish families, as well as by King Stanislas Poniatowski. Had he not aroused the enmity of a powerful Polish nobleman, he might well have found employment at the court and that security for which he was searching in view of his declining fortunes. These expectations were not to be realized. On March 4, 1766, five months after his arrival, while dining with the King, he was invited to accompany him to the theater. Two Italian dancers, Anna Binetti (an old friend) and Teresa Casacci, had divided Polish society in their bitter rivalry. As Casanova's more intimate friends were in the camp of the latter, he had, out of loyalty for these, espoused her cause. In her pique, the Binetti incited her lover, Count Xavier Branicki, to humiliate publicly her old friend. During an intermission, Casanova paused briefly at the loge of the Binetti to greet her, and found her with Branicki. When he passed on to the loge of the Casacci, Branacki followed and informed him that he was in love with her and was not in a humor to tolerate a rival. Judiciously Casanova answered that he would cede his rights with pleasure to such a nobleman. Branicki, determined to provoke a quarrel, replied that a man who yielded was a coward. "The term is rather strong," Casanova observed, touching the hilt of his sword as he left the loge. "Venetian poltroon," Branicki shouted. Casanova turned and remarked with sangfroid that a Venetian poltroon was capable of killing a brave Pole.

As he had proved on many occasions, Casanova was anything but a coward. He was never one to seek a quarrel, but had more than once held his own in the several duels to which he had been provoked. He does not tell us when he had acquired his superior ability as a swordsman, perhaps at an early age when a student at

Padua. His first duel was in 1749 with Count Celi, whom he put to flight; in other duels he speaks of his use of *une botte droite*, or right thrust, infallible in vanquishing his opponents. However, when he summoned Branicki the next day to give him satisfaction, Casanova was obliged to agree to the use of pistols rather than swords. As Branicki was a renowned marksman, Casanova would most likely have met his death had he not, with great astuteness, thrown his adversary off balance at the moment of firing by announcing his determination to shoot him in the head. Losing his stance, Branicki inflicted only a light wound in Casanova's left arm, and himself suffered a perforation of the intestines. Pursued by Biszewski, one of Branicki's friends, Casanova escaped assassination by taking refuge in a monastery. In his blind fury, Biszewski made his way to the home of Casanova's friend Tomatis and fired a pistol point blank at that gentleman's head. When he missed and Count August Moszynski intervened, the latter was slashed with a sabre by the infuriated Pole. Almost immediately after the incident, Moszynski, who was a minister of the crown, rendered a report to the King in a letter that corroborates in minute detail the account given by Casanova.[12]

Although Branicki subsequently made honorable amends and Casanova was received on his recovery for a time with the same favor, the duel marked a turn in the tide of his fortunes at Warsaw. To give the tempers of Branicki's friends time to cool, Casanova decided to absent himself for some weeks in a tour of the provinces. This offered the further advantage to him of opening the way to a more intimate insight into the conflicting cross currents of Polish political intrigues, revolving about the Russophobes, better known as "patriots," and the Russophiles centering around the King and the powerful Czartoryski family. The seeds were already being sown for the eventual partition of the country between Russia and Prussia. Casanova was fascinated by the eddies that were already stirring; his Polish sojourn was to bear fruit eight years later in one of the most serious of his studies, *Istoria delle turbolenze della Polonia* (History of Polish Troubles), published in three volumes in 1774 at Gorizia on the eve of his return from exile to Venice.

He has left a brief account of his tour of the provinces, which it has been possible to supplement from other sources than his memoirs. He was first a guest for a week of the famous "castellane" and Russophobe Catherine Kossakowska at Leopold (Lemberg). From there he passed to her Russophobe neighbor Count Venceslas Rzewuski and thereafter to Count Franciszewski Potocki in Christianpol of the same "patriot" party. He tells us that he was the bearer of a letter of introduction to the last-named from the influential Count A. de Brühl of Dresden, which is confirmed by the survival of the original letter.[13]

Upon his return to Warsaw in late June, after an absence of about six weeks, Casanova discovered that opinion had hardened rather than softened against him in the interval. He was received, he tells us, not only coldly but positively badly. In his absence Mme. Geoffrin, intimate friend of the King, had arrived on June 6 from Paris. While Casanova does not charge her with responsibility, it is fairly obvious that she was the inspirer of unfavorable tales about him to the King. Casanova tells us of the receipt by him shortly after his return of an anonymous letter informing him that the King had been told that he had been hanged in effigy in Paris after having absconded with funds belonging to the French lottery and that he had exercised in Italy the shameful profession of a strolling player. What is striking about his account is the complete candor with which he reproduces this gossip about himself without any attempt to refute or deny it.

In the light of these reports the King charged Count Moszynski with an investigation of Casanova's background. His choice was seemingly dictated by Moszynski's acquaintanceship with the Venetian, whose part he had taken after the latter's duel, perhaps on the strength of their common Masonic tie. In any case, an undated letter has been found in the Polish archives addressed to the King by Moszynski submitting a report on Casanova. It begins with a reference to his origin. His mother is stated to have been an actress, almost a bar sinister in the eighteenth century. He was described as an intriguer and a first class gambler. Mention is made of his statements to numerous persons of the "discoveries" he had made during his trip. This caused Moszynski to observe that a man capable of making "reports" might turn to other occupations. The inference would seem that Casanova may have been a spy. However, his straitened financial situation was hardly in keeping with such a status. Moszynski himself emphasizes Casanova's slender financial resources and expresses the fear, with admirable prescience, that his debts would fall on His Majesty to discharge.

Casanova himself reveals that he would have left Poland forthwith but for the debts he had contracted. To raise funds, he wrote to Venice, and it was while awaiting a reply that he received the visit of an emissary of the King ordering him to leave Warsaw within one week. In his indignation he drafted a letter to the King stating that his creditors would no doubt forgive him when they learned of the circumstances under which he had been obliged to depart. While ruminating on how he might convey his letter, he received a visit from Moszynski who offered to act as his intermediary.[14]

Professor Jan Reychman, a Polish scholar, has found in the correspondence of King Stanislas August in the Warsaw State Archives an undated letter signed by Casanova, apparently addressed to Moszynski, comprising a detailed account of the former's debts, an expression of his intention to leave within twenty-four hours after they had been discharged, and a statement that, in the meanwhile, he did not dare leave his room, presumably for fear of being waylaid and slain. With the letter there was found a separate sheet with the heading, "It is thus Ariosto speaks to Cardinal d'Esté," and these verses in Italian from Ariosto's *Orlando furioso*:

> Most Worthie Prince your virtues high and rare
> With tongue and penne I praise, and ever shall,
> Although my words and verse inferiour are,
> In number and in worth to match them all:
> But all above this one I do compare,
> And far prefer, and pure divinest call,
> That giving gracious eare to those are greeved,
> Yet ev'rie tale is not by you beleeved.
> Oft have I heard your highness hath refused,
> Although the same most earnestly were sought
> To heare the guiltlesse absent man accused,
> (And when a great complaint to you was brought)
> You have the matter and the man excused:

Suspending still your judgement and your thought,
And keeping till the truth were truly tride,
Ever one eare for the contrarie side.[15]

Nothing could have been more apposite to Casanova's situation in relation to the King than these verses from the Venetian's favorite Italian poet. From their presence in the King's correspondence it may be reasonably surmised that, in all probability, these stanzas of Ariosto represented the "letter" Casanova says he drafted to the King, which Moszynski offered to bring to Stanislas August's attention. At the same time, Moszynski very likely suggested to Casanova that he outline, in a communication addressed to him, the precise state of his indebtedness. On the strength of this statement, and of the verses intended for the King, that sovereign thereupon sent Casanova 1,000 ducats, as stated in the *Memoirs*, and as confirmed by an undated note found in his papers:

For M. Casanova. You are a man of your word. I have found you as such; may a better fate await you in the countries to which you are going, and remember that you have in me a friend. A. Moszynsky.

To this was appended the following notation by Casanova:

Having received a thousand ducats from the King of Poland when he ordered me to leave Warsaw three months after my duel, I sent his minister the bills of my creditors. He wrote me this letter and I left the same day with Count Clari, June 8 [July], 1766.

Casanova tells us that he discharged his debts of 200 ducats the day after his receipt of the 1,000 ducats and that he left the next day for Breslau.

The importance of these archival discoveries is the general confirmation they furnish of Casanova's own account of his visit to Warsaw.[16]

That he remained on excellent terms with Branicki, and with other distinguished Polish acquaintances, including in particular Princess Lubomirska, is clear not only from the *Memoirs* but as well from surviving correspondence, and by the dedication of his

*Nè amori, nè donne* to Branicki in 1782. His duel with the latter
was to remain one of the greatest prides of his life; in publishing
an account of it in 1780, he offered the first intimation that he
might eventually recount the history of his life in its entirety.

There is a curious passage in the *Memoirs* in which Casanova
reports an exchange he had with King Stanislas shortly after the
duel before falling into that sovereign's disfavor. The King asked
him if, suffering from an insult from a patrician in Venice, he
would have challenged him to a duel. Casanova replied that he
would not, as the patrician's pride would have stood in the way of
his consenting so to honor him, adding that he would have abided
his time and, once in a foreign country, he would have demanded
satisfaction.

No doubt it was partly because the duel had involved so high a
dignitary as Branicki and a commoner such as Casanova that it
attracted such extended notice in the European press, including a
paper so far afield as the *London Public Advertiser*, of September
3, 1766.[17]

It is difficult for us today to visualize the deep class differences
that existed in the eighteenth century. Something of this, in regard
to Casanova's duel, is reflected in a letter of the Abbé Taruffi from
Warsaw on March 19, 1766, to Francesco Albergati in Bologna
recounting the duel in very much the same terms as those in the
*Memoirs*. What Taruffi found so astonishing was that a Polish
nobleman of Branicki's rank should have consented to a duel with
an "Italian traveler whose only distinction was his honor and his
sensibility." Melchiore Cesarotti, Paduan poet who evidently entertained animosity to Casanova, apparently saw the letter and
wrote to Taruffi:

> It is pleasant for a Venetian to see Casanova transformed into a
> hero; he is a worm who has been suddenly changed into a butterfly.

To this Taruffi replied on June 25, 1766, when Casanova was on
the point of leaving Warsaw:

> It is a pity that the illustrious Casanova, formerly a hero and
> fictitious nobleman, and above all a so-called wit, has not had the

ability to sustain his great role . . . Shortly after his brilliant feat, some unfortunate anecdotes, well authenticated, faded his laurels; wonder was replaced by contempt, and the stick reclaimed its rights . . . There in consequence is our glorious butterfly, transformed suddenly into the state of a worm.[18]

A worm he may have been for Cesarotti and Taruffi, but he has long ago risen above them as a butterfly.

# CHAPTER 13

## Dresden, Vienna, Spa, and Spain

At Dresden, where his mother resided, he found peace for a time, from July to the end of December 1766. On a visit to Leipzig in September he had the unexpected call of a beautiful Frenchwoman to whom he gives the name of Mme. Blasin, whom he had met two years earlier in England. At the country home of Lord Pembroke, Casanova had met the Marquis de Castelbajac, the adventurer who had sought to undo him in 1759 in Paris by inspiring a charge against him of seeking to bring about an abortion for Justinienne Wynne and of kidnapping her. Castelbajac had been accompanied by Mme. Blasin, who he then pretended was his wife. Also present were General Beckwith, whom Casanova later met at Wesel in 1764, and a certain Count de Schwerin, nephew of the field marshall of that name, one of the most famous generals of Frederick the Great.

On this occasion, Casanova tells us, Schwerin had withdrawn from his pocket the ribbon of the Order of the Black Eagle, stained with the blood of his uncle when killed in combat in 1757; Schwerin explained that he had been ordered by Frederick to conserve it. Remarkably, this story is corroborated by Thiebault, contemporary French biographer of Frederick, in a slightly different form. In his account, Schwerin is stated to have been imprisoned at Spandau for gambling debts of more than 60,000 livres and to have traveled thereafter to England "exhibiting for money a bloody shirt" belonging to his dead uncle. In common with Casanova and all memorialists, Thiebault has confused the sequence of events. Schwerin was not imprisoned at Spandau until May 12, 1767; he spent twenty years there and was released only after Frederick's death.[1] As a confirmed gambler and a roué he was imprisoned on more than one occasion. When Mme. Blasin called on Casanova at Leipzig, she informed him that she had left Castelbajac for Schwerin, with whom she had been living for the past three years, and that, with his arrest for a false letter of exchange, she was now on the street and penniless.[2] Whether through forgetfulness or by express intent, Casanova has omitted to mention in the report of his meeting with Mme. Blasin that he was not only aware of the presence of Schwerin in Leipzig, but that it was at the express invitation of Schwerin that he had made the journey from Dresden. This is established through an undated draft letter, found in Casanova's papers, addressed to "M. the Count de Schwerin at the fair in Leipzig in the autumn of 1766," in which he stated that:

At your urging, Sir, I have left Dresden to come here as you hoped that I might aid you in undertaking good business. Having seen that I was unable to serve you, and fearing even that I would become a burden to you, you have seized on the biribi dispute to quarrel.

If it is for this reason, you are wrong, for Casanova has never been a charge on anyone . . .

The beautiful woman, who lives with you, merits your esteem and is undeserving that you should be jealous of her, the more particularly as she has given you no occasion to be. If my gay spirits have given you umbrage, you should have told me. I am a man who listens to reason, I am capable of appreciating men with their faults, and the more churlish their faults, the more I pity them . . .

You owe me thirty-seven florins, and it is perhaps because you fear I shall reclaim them that you no longer care for me, that you are reduced to seeking pretexts. You are wrong, Sir, as I despise thirty-seven florins and, far from imposing on the purses of my friends, I am ready to replenish them with my own.[3]

It seems entirely probable that subsequent to the writing of this letter Schwerin was arrested for a false letter of exchange, and that Mme. Blasin, deprived of a protector, had addressed herself to Casanova. He, of course, took immediate pity on Mme. Blasin, conducting her with him back to Dresden—a fact tending to support Schwerin's arrest—and thence to Prague and Vienna. In Vienna Mme. Blasin represented herself as a modiste, and Casanova defrayed her return expenses to her husband, a pharmacist at Montpellier. After her departure, Casanova lodged with a certain François Schrotter, and there is a letter of February 5, 1767, addressed by him to Casanova after the latter left Vienna, in which reference is made to his having found in the effects left behind by Casanova a letter to "Mme. La Tour, a modiste." Gugitz has drawn the inference that this may well be the real name of Mme. Blasin, and there was, in fact, a Latour at Montpellier at this time who was an officer (beadle) of the master pharmacists.

In Vienna, Casanova had the misfortune to run afoul of Antonio Pocchini, gambler and fellow adventurer, whom he had first met in 1741. He was enticed to Pocchini's quarters by his nine-year-old daughter whose precociously erotic conversation in Latin appears to have been accompanied by acts in keeping with her speech. Casanova was there set upon and robbed of his purse. However extraordinary Casanova's story of this Adelaide Pocchini may appear, we know from the *Wiener Diarium* of November 29, 1766, that her accomplishments were all those attributed to her by the Venetian. Thus, we read:

> November 24, 1766, the little daughter of a noble Paduan, arrived here recently, M. Antonio Pocchini, was present in the house of Count Colalto; she was about nine years. She was interogated in French on ethics and on physical science in Latin. What is extraordinary is that the said young girl who had had but four lessons in German, responded intelligibly in that language to all questions put to her. All those present rendered homage to this child by their applause.

She died on August 31, 1767, at the age of nine years and eight months in Vienna.[4]

Before Casanova could report his misadventure with Pocchini, he was summoned before the Statthalter, Count Schrattenbach, shown his half-empty wallet and a pack of cards, accused of breaking the law by gambling, and ordered to leave Vienna. When Casanova protested he was the offended party, and submitted a memorandum describing the occurrence of the evening before, Schrattenbach declared it was nothing but a tissue of lies, that, in Casanova's words, "it was known who I was and why I had been sent away from Warsaw." That Empress Maria Theresa interested herself personally in the affair is proven by a letter of January 26, 1767, found by Gugitz at Linz, from Schrattenbach to the governor, stating he had received a note in the handwriting of the Empress directing the expulsion of Casanova and that he had notified him on the 23rd that he must leave by the 27th. Through an appeal to the powerful Kaunitz, Casanova obtained a respite of three days. That prince was to become the patron of Francesco Casanova, and there is record of a friendly letter written by him in 1789 to Jacques indicating that he was far from sharing the Empress's ill will towards Casanova.

The personal interest taken by the Empress in Casanova may at first glance appear curious on the part of a sovereign occupied with important affairs of state. However, she is known to have concerned herself with all that went on in Vienna. Wraxall tells us:

> With a view to obtain information, she set apart particular hours, when the lowest and meanest of her subjects are not only admitted to see her, but permitted to speak to her confidentially and freely . . . Very secret and curious facts reach her through these channels . . . Unfortunately, she is much too inclined to listen to such narratives, and to credit stories often partial, mistaken, or malignant. It is one of her prevailing weaknesses.[5]

One of the most curious circumstances in Casanova's life is that his recurrent difficulties with the authorities in many cities— Rome in 1745, Paris in 1759, Cologne, Stuttgart and Florence in 1760, Turin in 1762, Warsaw in 1766, Vienna and Paris in 1767, Madrid and Barcelona in 1768, and Florence in 1771—did not affect the friendship and esteem of those in high places, as attested by their correspondence with him. Through the many disreputable acquaintances he also formed, it was perhaps inevitable that he should have been repeatedly involved with the police. If he did not forfeit the regard of those in a position to be informed of the circumstances, his fault may have been the consequences of indiscretions rather than studied misdemeanors. He left Rome in 1745 with a letter of recommendation from Cardinal Acquaviva, and Paris in 1759 with one from the Duke de Choiseul. Expelled from Turin, he was able to return after a few weeks through intervention of powerful friends. His unceremonious expulsion from Vienna was probably due to the Empress's implacable hostility to gamblers and those of loose morals.

At Augsburg he tarried for four months, spending much of his time with Count Maximilian Lamberg, whom he had met in Paris in 1757 and who remained one of his most devoted friends until Lamberg's death in 1792. Casanova tells us he was attracted particularly to Lamberg for his literary talent and erudition. Lamberg in turn paid tribute to Casanova in his *Mémorial d'un mondain* (1774), writing of him as "a man known in the world of letters, a man of profound knowledge," and remarking upon the numerous friends he had among the nobility. Yet neither Casanova's talents nor Lamberg's intervention succeeded in getting Casanova the post to which he aspired with the Elector of Mannheim.

While at Augsburg, being in need of funds, he wrote requesting a hundred sequins of Prince Charles de Courland, with whom he had contracted a friendship at Riga, and who was then in Venice. In exchange, he set forth in his letter the formula for the philosophers' stone. The prince sent him the funds but failed to burn the letter as he had been asked to do, attaching more efficacy to the formula and, in consequence, to the letter than Casanova did. A few months later the prince was arrested in Paris and imprisoned in the Bastille for three months for forging bills of exchange and the signatures of a number of bankers. On this occasion his papers were seized and, among them, Casanova's letter. By a strange turn of fate, with the fall of the Bastille, the letter, with other documents taken from prisoners, was found and published in 1789. The publication determined Casanova to include the text and an explanation about it in his *Memoirs*. Carra, who published the Bastille documents, and had access to files that have since disappeared, noted that the Prince de Courland had learned from Casanova "the secret of a form of ink that vanishes on paper in such a way that it cannot be imagined that it ever bore any writing."[6] That Casanova was familiar with such a procedure we have already observed in connection with the regeneration of Mme. d'Urfé at Aix-la-Chapelle on June 22, 1762.

When passing through Cologne, Casanova stopped to call to account the editor of the *Gazette de Cologne* for an article dated Warsaw, July 30, 1766: "Le Sieur Casa-Nuova, assés connu dans les Feuilles, aiant voulu reparoitre icy, ces jours derniers, la Cour lui a ordonné d'en sortir au plutot" ("Mr. Casa-Nuova, well known in this publication, wanted to return here recently, but the Court ordered him to leave immediately"), the text as it appeared in the *Gazette* No. 6 of 1766 differing slightly from that of the Memoirs. Casanova's memory was at fault in identifying the editor as Jacquet; he was in reality Abbé Jeaurinvilliers, successor in 1765 of Gaspard Jacquemotte.

Proceeding to Aix-la-Chapelle, Casanova found a number of Poles and other Warsaw acquaintances, including Count Tomatis and his wife, with whom he traveled to Spa, arriving there on August 1, 1767. As the season, a little later than that at Aix, was at its height, Casanova stated he had to seek accommodations with a merchant. After his face had been slapped by the niece of his host when he made advances to her, he moved to quarters, in the same street opposite, which had been vacated the previous day by the Duchess of Richmond. A card found among Casanova's effects of a shop, Au Cordon Rouge, of M. Durieux in the rue de l'Assemblée, enabled Ilges to identify Casanova's first lodging at Spa as situated at number 45 in that street where a M. Durieux had in fact his place of business. Ilges also found Casanova registered on August 1 at number 11 in the rue de l'Assemblée at the Fontaine d'Or. As the names of visitors to Spa were entered in published lists generally some days after their arrival, and as Casanova had only spent a few days with Durieux, this initial sojourn would seem to have been ignored when his stay was recorded.

In offering these precise details supplementary to Casanova's

more general account, Ilges confirmed likewise from the records
the presence in Spa of many people named by Casanova in the
*Memoirs*. Thus the Princess Lubomirska, General Roniker, and
the "grand notaire" Rzewuski, whom Casanova mentions, are
found registered, the princess on July 6, 1767, at the Hôtel de
Flandre, Roniker on July 18 at the Pigeon Blanc, and the two
Rzewuski brothers, presumably Count Franz and General Joseph,
on August 9 at the Hôtel Cour de Mannheim, while the Marquis
de Caraccioli, whom Casanova had last seen as Neapolitan ambassador at London, was registered in that capacity on August 9,
1767, at the Hôtel La Cour de Prusse.[7]

A curious and rare little guidebook, *Tableau de Spa*, published
anonymously five years later, supplements details that Ilges found
in substantiation of Casanova's report. We shall cite from it only
those parts that confirm his narrative. Of the estimated two or
three thousand foreign visitors to Spa annually, hardly two hundred came for the waters, but at least a hundred rascals came in
search of victims at the gambling tables. The men were so excited
by play they had no time to give to women. The local merchants
engaged not only in their commerce, but acted as moneylenders on
objects of value, as did M. Durieux, Casanova's landlord. A good
meal was to be had for an écu, better than in Paris and at the same
price. The garden of the Capucins was a particular rendezvous of
gallant encounters. It is noteworthy that Casanova, inveterate
theatergoer, makes no mention of any theater at Spa. There was
one, but the Spa guidebook tells us it was of disgraceful mediocrity,
owing to its lack of financial support, with the result that a score
of directors who had sought to promote it had become bankrupt.

Spa was then under the Prince-Bishop at Liège, whose sovereignty disappeared only with the French invasion of 1792 after an
intermittent rule of centuries. The author of the *Tableau de Spa*,
in remarking, as Casanova, that a portion of the gambling profits
passed into the coffers of the Prince-Bishop of Liège, exclaimed
indignantly:

How is it that he soils his hands with gold so vile as that which Spa
provides! What: the revered pastor of a holy religion whose divine
moral inspires that horror which every good Christian should have

for gambling the Chief, the Pontiff of a Church which counts more than one saint among its founders allows the spread in the center even of that same Church, of the devouring and deplorable passion for play, encouraging it even by the granting of exclusive privileges.

To Casanova it was not unusual to frequent gaming tables of which the patrons were high in the Church of Rome, and it is not to be expected, therefore, that he would draw any lessons of the morality involved, even if such should have been in keeping with his character. For him it sufficed to record matter-of-factly that a part of the profits from gambling at Spa passed to the Prince-Bishop, one part to the unauthorized gamblers, and a third, which he estimated at half a million annually, to the dozen professionals, authorized by the sovereign and his associates. The anonymous author of the *Tableau de Spa* states that in 1782 these last numbered eight and enjoyed one-fifth of the profits, which amounted annually to about eighteen or twenty-four thousand louis, or approximately the half million of Casanova.[8]

Among the Spa visitors whom Casanova found some days after his arrival in his second lodging was the "Marquis Don Antonio della Croce," whom he had last seen in Milan in 1763 when Croce had abandoned Mlle. Crosin to his care. Croce was now with a young Brussels woman of excellent family, whom he had seduced and to whom Casanova gives the name of Charlotte L. It is a fact the marquis, as he called himself, was registered "with a young girl" on September 1, 1767, but at the Grand Monarque and not at the Fontaine d'Or where Casanova was staying, while his so-called secretary was registered as "M. Conti, captain in the service of the Duke of Würtemberg" on the same date at the Prince de Stavelot. It is evident that Casanova placed Croce at the Fontaine d'Or, his own lodging, probably through a lapse of memory.

Casanova would have left Spa in the middle of September but for the attachment he had conceived for Charlotte. Acquainted as he was with the unstable character of Croce, he foresaw a catastrophe attending her, and he did not have the courage to abandon so interesting a person. His premonition of impending disaster was realized sooner than he anticipated. Croce, after losing all his money at cards, and after having pawned all of Charlotte's jewels, announced to Casanova that he had no other alternative than to make his way to Warsaw on foot and abandon to him the task of informing Charlotte of his flight, and of looking after her when he was gone.[9] It is clear that Croce, familiar with Casanova's compassionate disposition towards women in distress, was counting on him to care for Charlotte in her pregnancy and approaching confinement.

With a disinterested devotion, which renders his account of the circumstances among the most moving of the *Memoirs*, Casanova accompanied her to Paris and cared for her until her death in October in childbirth. More than a hundred years later, Dr. Guède found in the Paris archives full confirmation, including her identification as Charlotte Lamotte. Returning from Charlotte's funeral, Casanova had news of a second affliction: a letter from Dandolo, announcing the death on October 14 of the faithful Bragadin, who had sent Casanova 1,000 écus from his deathbed.

His troubles were not yet ended. Presumably at the instigation of Mme. d'Urfé or her family after an encounter with her nephew, who had bitterly upbraided him for his despoliation of his aunt, he was handed a letter of cachet ordering him to leave Paris within forty-eight hours, and France in three weeks. From Princess Lubomirska, in Paris, he obtained a letter of introduction to Count d'Aranda, head of the Spanish government, and from the Marquis de Caraccioli, another faithful friend, letters to Prince de la Catolica, Neapolitan minister at Madrid, to the Duke de Lossada, and to the Marquis de Mora-Pignatelli. These were to open Spanish doors for him, and it was for Spain that he set out on November 19, 1767, with a passport dated November 15, signed by the Duke de Choiseul, assuring him specifically, as he states, post horses. The passport was conserved, as he notes, and was found among his papers. Morel-Fatio in 1906 in his *Études sur l'Espagne* has remarked upon the precision of Casanova's comments on those Spanish affairs within the range of his observation; more recently Professor Sarrailh has done the same.[10]

From Bordeaux Casanova crossed the Pyrenees to Pamplona by muleback. In one of his rare observations on the beauties of nature, to which the eighteenth century was singularly insensitive, he remarked that the Pyrenees were more agreeable, varied, and picturesque than the Alps. When he arrived at the Alcala gate of Madrid, particular attention was paid to the books in his possession, which were taken from him and only returned some days later at the lodgings he found in the Calle de la Cruz, a street still existing in the neighborhood of the Puerta del Sol. Another traveler making the same journey about the same time remarked that the Inquisition was particularly concerned with books forbidden by the religious authorities. At Madrid, upon finding that the brasiers that served for heating were insufficient, he caused to be constructed a stovepipe for the stove he acquired, with the pipe running out of the window. In many of these forgotten domestic details, his veracity can be established. The Italian traveler Gorani has recorded that at this period chimneys were virtually unknown in Spain.[11]

Casanova's first call was on the head of the Spanish government, Count d'Aranda, to whom he bore a letter of introduction. The reception was distant and formal. The count inquired coldly of Casanova his purpose in visiting Spain, to which he replied that it was to study the manners of a people not known to him, and at the same time, to put his slender talents, if possible, at the disposal of the government. D'Aranda observed that Casanova had no need of him for his first objective and that he should address himself to his ambassador for support in the second. When Casanova states that he was not sure whether he would be received by the Venetian ambassador, the minister remarked that without that ambassador's support he could expect nothing.

Advised by the Duke de Lossada in the same sense; and in order to obtain access to the Venetian ambassador, Mocenigo, Casanova called on his secretary, Gaspar Soderini, who expressed astonishment that he should have had the effrontery to present himself at the embassy. Casanova's response could hardly have been excelled. After remarking that he would have been more subject to criticism for not paying his respects to the ambassador, he added that the latter was not in Madrid as the representative of the Venetian Inquisitors, with whom he had been involved, but of the Venetian Republic, of which he was a national. As it was his duty to respect in the ambassador the representative of the Venetian state, it was the ambassador's duty to extend to him protection as a Venetian.

The following day, Casanova received the visit of Count Manuzzi, son of the Manuzzi whose reports had contributed to Casanova's imprisonment in the Leads. Manuzzi, aware that Casanova was acquainted with the reputation of the ambassador as a pederast, informed him laughingly and unashamedly that he was Mocenigo's minion, and that he was prepared to be of every assistance to him. Mocenigo was later arrested, in 1773, by the Venetian Republic for sodomy and imprisoned for seven years, as Casanova states and as confirmed by contemporary chronicles.

The favor Casanova subsequently enjoyed at the hands of the ambassador was facilitated not alone by Manuzzi, but also by the intercession of Casanova's Venetian protector, Marco Dandolo, as well as that of Girolamo Zulian. This member of the Venetian Great Council wrote the ambassador on behalf of the Inquisitor Mula that as the Tribunal had no complaint against Casanova touching his honor, he might be extended every protection. There is a letter of April 16, 1768, from Zulian to Casanova stating that the ambassador had written that it would give him great pleasure to extend to him such attentions as might be appropriate. Zulian added that he was happy to know that Casanova was satisfied with the ambassador's conduct towards him.[12] Thereafter he was received, and entered on terms of relative intimacy with some of the greatest grandees of Spain.

Soon after his arrival, in seeking distraction, as was his wont, he began to frequent the theater, and, during carnival, the masked balls held in what was known as Los Cañons del Paral, permission for which had been authorized in 1763 by d'Aranda.[13] Such was the authority of the Inquisition and the repression exercised against the commission of any possible improprieties by the public that Casanova found the boxes of the theater open to the view of the pit so that one might have a full view of the legs of the men and the skirts of the women. When a neighbor expressed astonishment that the Italian police did not insist upon the same form for theater boxes in Italy to prevent lewd acts in the audience, Casanova replied that neither the French nor the Italians thought of taking umbrage at this. In one of the boxes he observed members of the Inquisition scanning both the actors and the spectators to observe any irregularities. Whenever the viaticum passed in the street outside, the sentinel posted at the door shouted "Dios," at which spectators and actors alike fell to their knees until the procession had passed. For him the religion of the Spanish existed entirely in its outward observance. As an example, he mentioned the practice of Spanish women who, before giving themselves to their lovers, began by covering with a veil any sacred image in the room.

He found it difficult to express himself in Spanish, and at one of the first masked balls he attended, he was asked by a neighbor, who later proved to be the Duke of Medina-Celi, why he was alone. When Casanova explained that he knew no women to invite, he was told that, as a foreigner, he had only to approach the parents of a suitable girl, request the honor of her company and, upon her acceptance, send her a domino, mask, and gloves and fetch her in a carriage. The duke was accompanied by a lady who invited Casanova to call, but when he did, he found her in mourning for the duke, whom we know to have died on January 16, 1768.

On St. Anthony's Day, January 17, 1768, Casanova, thinking to execute the suggestion of the duke, entered the Church of the Soledad. There were two in Madrid, but it is possible to identify the one to which he refers as that in the Calle de Fuencarral from the description he gives of a miraculous Virgin above the altar, which is still to be seen there. Observing a tall and beautiful girl as she left a confessional box and fell to the ground on her knees to make her devotions, he sized her up as one ideally formed to dance the fandango, which had so captivated him at the balls. He followed her to her home in the Calle des Desingano, existing today under that name, and presented himself to her father, a bootmaker but at the same time an hidalgo. As an example of Spanish pride, Casanova noted that Don Diego, as he calls him, would make his boots but would not take his measure for them. Casanova was able to persuade Don Diego to allow his daughter, Donna Ignazia, to accompany him to a masked ball, chaperoned by her mother. He found Ignazia, as most Spanish women, a mixture of voluptuousness and of religious bigotry. He was finally able to overcome the latter by persuading her not to go to confession so long as he remained in Madrid, since her confessor had frightened her into believing she would be damning herself if she yielded to the Venetian. The entire episode of his love affair with Donna Ignazia could not possibly be more Spanish, impregnated as it is with passion and religious devotion.

In Madrid he had, as elsewhere, his perennial difficulties with the authorities. Warned that the police were on his trail for the illegal possession of arms, he took refuge in the home of Raphael Mengs, the illustrious painter whom he had met in Rome seven years earlier. Mengs had been invited to Madrid in 1761 by Charles III, and was now a painter of the court. The many details given us of the personal characteristics of Mengs make Casanova's word portrait of him one of the most animated and lifelike of those we have of that distinguished artist, many of whose works hang today at the Prado in Madrid.

Tracked down at Mengs' residence, Casanova was arrested on February 20, 1768, imprisoned in Buen Retiro and released after two days with the most ample amends, as he claims, on the part of Count d'Aranda. It is certain that the imprisonment did not in any way affect his standing. According to the Busoni text of the Memoirs, his arrest was due not so much to the illegal possession of arms, but for disposing, under the most dramatic circumstances, of the body of a Spanish girl's lover whom she had assassinated in her home opposite his. The episode inspired Zola to write *Pour une nuit d'amour*, but its historical accuracy has never been established.

A temporary breach between Mengs and Casanova occurred at Easter that year. Fifteen days before, when the King departed for Aranjuez, accompanied by the diplomatic corps, the Venetian ambassador had invited Casanova to lodge with him there. Stricken with fever on the eve of his projected departure, while still a guest of Mengs, Casanova was unable to go to Aranjuez until the Saturday of Easter week, and even there was obliged to keep to his bed for some days. It was while he was still in his enfeebled state that he received a letter from Mengs announcing that his name had been posted by the priest of the parish as among those parishoners who, not believing in God, had failed to perform the Easter rites, and that, in consequence, upon Casanova's return to Madrid, he should seek lodging elsewhere. With rage in his heart,

Casanova called for a sedan chair, had himself transported to the church in Aranjuez, made a general confession, received communion the following morning at six o'clock, and obtained a letter from the priest certifying that he had observed Easter as a good Christian. He sent the letter to the priest in Madrid, and wrote to Mengs at the same time. He informed the latter that as a good Christian who had complied with the duties of the Church, he pardoned him his brutal and ill-considered behavior, counseling him to give heed to a Latin verse, known to all honest men, but which he ignored, that it was more shameful to reject a guest than not to accept him. Two years later, he met Mengs again in Rome, and the painter sought to make amends for his conduct, of which, he stated, he was better able to explain now that they were in a country of greater religious freedom. In Madrid he had been suspected of being a Protestant, and for that reason he had been obliged to endeavor to clear himself of any such imputation that might have been aggravated by his failure to take notice of Casanova's omission of a religious rite, as publicly proclaimed while the Venetian was a guest in his home. It was a measure of that religious intolerance reigning in Spain, of which Casanova gives more than one striking example. The people were the prey of bigotry and superstitions, slumbering in a seemingly ineradicable lethargy, of which he has left this penetrating analysis:

> Poor Spaniards! The beauty of your country, its fertility and richness are the causes of your lethargy, and the mines of Peru and of Potosí are the sources of your poverty, your pride and all your prejudices. This is paradoxical, but the reader knows that what I say is true. To become the most flourishing of all kingdoms on this earth, Spain needs to be conquered, overturned, and almost destroyed: it will be reborn to become the sojourn of the elect.

The letters Casanova had succeeded in obtaining from Venice, inviting Ambassador Mocenigo's favor, had arrived at the moment of his release from Buen Retiro. As evidence of the ambassador's friendly disposition towards him, Casanova was invited to dine with him and Mengs, the French Consul Abbé Beliardi, Count Pedro Rodriguez de Compomanes, and Pablo Olivades.[14] After leaving Spain, Casanova remained in correspondence with Compomanes, esteemed for his erudition and his works on public administration. Olivades had been charged with a scheme of colonization of Swiss and Germans at Sierra Morena, and in the discussion of that project on this occasion, Casanova, with his customary aplomb and readiness to express himself with authority on any question, so far impressed his auditors that he was asked to set forth his reflections in writing.

Upon his return from Aranjuez, Casanova was presented by Ambassador Mocenigo to the Spanish minister for foreign affairs, Marquis Paolo Girolamo Grimaldi, to whom he communicated his views on the Sierra Morena colony. Although he now gave himself with industry to the continued study of that project, and remained constantly in contact with the foreign minister on the subject, so that there was even question of his visiting Sierra Morena to examine the project on the spot, finally he came no nearer to the realization of his objective than he had with the many other schemes that had germinated within him.

While in London, he had proposed to the Venetian Republic a detailed scheme for the establishment in Venice of a manufactory of cotton fabrics dyed red in the Indian style. When he was at Mittau, on his way to Russia, dining with the Duke de Courland, the conversation had turned to the natural resources of the region, particularly minerals, and quite characteristically he had found himself engaged in the subject "as if I had made it my principal study." The Duke, imagining that Casanova had a much more expert knowledge than, as he confesses, he actually had, invited him to make a survey of the establishments of the duchy. The consequence was that he spent two weeks in a tour that took him to five copper and iron mines. With the same brashness he had exhibited when discussing the lottery in Paris in 1757, he proposed reforms that seemed to him useful, suggesting at one mine the construction of a small canal emptying into a rivulet which, by means of a dam employing three wheels, permitted an economy of twenty workers. The Duke was so satisfied with the report Casanova made on his return that he offered the Venetian his choice of a jewel or money. In his reduced circumstances he had no hesitation in indicating his preference for the latter, a sum of four hundred albert thalers.[15] While in Russia, he submitted a project for the introduction of mulberry trees in that country for the establishment of a silk industry, and in Warsaw he suggested a project for a Polish soap factory. In Spain, in addition to the studies he made for the Sierra Morena colonization, he proposed a tobacco manufactory in Madrid, which the government rejected, according to a letter to him from the Duke of Lossada, dated July 24, 1768.[16] His fertile imagination was forever elaborating imposing plans, but they were conceived without a solid foundation of knowledge and lacked that stability essential for their execution; they were deficient in fundamentally the same ways as his character. He could bluff his way through the conception of a lottery project whose execution remained in the technical hands of others, but he was never again so successful except in the one minor instance with the Duke de Courland.

In Spain he occupied himself particularly with economic questions, with a view to his material advancement. But he did not neglect the world of letters. While in Madrid he was approached by the chapel master of the Court, a Venetian protégé of Ambassador Mocenigo, and asked to suggest a subject to be put to music for a new opera. As the time was too short to send to Italy for a libretto, Casanova offered to write one of the three acts. It was subsequently performed at the court, and while the chapel master was rewarded handsomely, Casanova was disappointed that, as he was considered to be above working for money, his only compensation was in "compliments." He gives us neither the title nor the name of the chapel master who composed the music, and no known copy has survived.

Through Dominique Varnier, valet de chambre of Charles III, whom he met through Mengs, an acquaintance was made that enabled him to obtain intimate details of that monarch. Casanova offers a striking portrait of Charles, including many curious details of his personal life that are corroborated by those of another contemporary traveler, Joseph Gorani, who visited Spain in 1764, and 1765.[17]

The heedlessness of which Casanova was so often guilty was the cause of his eventual embroilment with Count Manuzzi, secretary of the Venetian embassy. When Manuzzi learned that Casanova had stated to one of their common acquaintances that the former's title was an assumed one, the doors of the embassy, as well as those of Spaniards close to the ambassador, were closed to him. It was, he noted, the first time in his life:

> . . . that I had to confess myself guilty of a monstrous indiscretion, committed without reason, of a frightful ingratitude such as I did not recognize in my character.

Having thus made himself *persona non grata* in Madrid, he left shortly afterwards in September for Valencia. There he committed a second indiscretion in accepting the favors of Nina Bergonzi, mistress of Count Ricla, captain general of Catalonia. In one of the frequent visits he later paid her in Barcelona, he encountered his old enemy, Giacomo Passano, who was seeking to dispose of his lewd miniatures to Nina. The next evening, as Casanova was leaving Nina's home, he was set upon by two men, from whom he finally escaped after thrusting his sword through the body of one. The next day, he was arrested and imprisoned for forty-two days. The circumstances contributing to his incarceration and subsequent release have heretofore never been elucidated. As a result of a discovery in the Lyons archives, we are now in a position to clear up at least part of the mystery.

Imprisoned on November 16, 1768, Casanova communicated with his friend Joseph Bono in Lyons. We do not have the letter, but we do know from Bono's acknowledgment of January 10, 1769, that Casanova's communication was dated November 26, or ten days after his arrest. In his letter, Bono wrote:

> You are in error to attribute to any other than to Passano the disaster you incurred in Barcelona; of this I have more than ample proof. As soon as I learned of your detention, I replied to your letter of November 26. I wrote to a merchant forwarding an attestation executed before a notary, which destroyed the accusations of your enemy. I sought even to calm him, and reproached him severely. Nor was this all: I charged M. Marquisio, minister plenipotentiary of His Serene Highness the Duke of Modena, who was here and who took the road to Barcelona on his way to Madrid, to employ

his offices with the captain general to obtain your release, and as soon as he arrived, he wrote me that you had been set at liberty.[18]

Casanova had evidently acquainted Bono with his plight and, in his letter, had presumably mentioned his encounter with Passano at the home of Nina, Ricla's mistress. Casanova, while not imputing principal responsibility for his arrest to Passano, must no doubt have mentioned charges that his adversary had repeated against him. Bono was no sooner in possession of Casanova's letter than he hastened to a Lyons notary, Bonteloupt, before whom he executed the following document, translated *in extenso* because of its exceptional importance:

> Today, December 9, 1768, before midday in the presence of the counselors of the King, notaries at Lyons, the undersigned in the study of Bonteloupt, situated in the rue de Lafont, parish of St. Pierre and St. Saturnin, appeared Sieur Joseph Bono, banker at Lyons, residing in the said rue Lafont and parish of St. Pierre and St. Saturnin, who, to testify as to the truth, has stated, certified, and attested upon his faith and conscience to have known Sieur Casanova de St. Gall, against whom he has no obligation to reclaim, although he has loaned him sometimes money, of which the said Sieur Casanova de St. Gall has made entire reimbursement, so that nothing is due him at present by this last. There is added by the said Sieur Bono that it has never come to his knowledge that the said Casanova de St. Gall has circulated in any place whatsoever false letters of exchange, nor that he has made any attempt, directly or indirectly, on the life of another person, of which appearance and attestation the said Sieur Bono affirms in the hands of the under-signed notaries, as sincere and truthful, with offer to repeat it before such judge as may be competent, requesting the act of said notaries who have executed it to serve and assist the said Sieur to whom he consents that expedition be made as is right.

>       Pourra       Joseph Bono       Bonteloupt

> Controlled at Lyons, December 10, 1768
> Received thirteen sols
> Morin[19]

There is no intimation of these facts in the *Memoirs*. What we do learn from them is that Abbé Marquisio, envoy of the Duke of

Modena, with whom Bono interceded in Lyons, spoke to Ricla about Casanova on December 26 and that two days later Casanova was freed. While Ricla may well have desired to put Casanova out of the way of Nina, it is evident from Bono's letter and from his notarial act that Passano, in a spirit of vengeance, had represented Casanova as indebted to Bono, as a circulator of false bills of exchange, and with attempts on Passano's life, of which Casanova had been previously accused by Passano in 1763 at Lyons.

We do know from the *Memoirs* that Passano had written to the Marquis Augustino Grimaldi della Pietra at Genoa in an effort to induce him to bring charges against Casanova for his failure to honor a gambling debt contracted in 1763. In that year, Casanova had lost 3,000 sequins to the marquis and, after paying him a third, had given him two letters of exchange for the balance, which he had been obliged to dishonor upon their presentation in England when he was in financial difficulties. In a letter of November 30, 1768, Grimaldi informed Casanova, who was then in prison, that he had refused to heed Passano's request, and returned the bills to Casanova to convince him that he was not disposed to add to the distress of those who were the victims of misfortune. It was out of a sense of shame at his inability to discharge his debt to Grimaldi that, some months later, Casanova chose the more difficult route from Marseilles to Turin by way of Nice and Tende, rather than by Genoa.[20]

In the light of Spanish bigotry, it may appear unlikely that Ricla, captain general of Barcelona, should have dared flout the power exercised by the Inquisition in Spain in the eighteenth century by living in sin with an actress such as Nina. However, for this we are not limited to Casanova's testimony. About 1771, a French traveler witnessed a masquerade on the Ramblas in Barcelona, of which he wrote some twenty years later:

> I shall remember always a group of masks that parodied an adventure that happened to Count de Ricla, then captain general of Catalonia. Contrary to the custom of his country and the pretended decent manners that prevailed there, he had dared to keep publicly a very pretty Italian singer. The Bishop of Barcelona, hypocritical as all Iberian bishops, was scandalized and ordered him to send

away the courtesan. The count, who had lived in Paris, and was accustomed to keep women, irrespective of the opinions of bishops, paid no attention to the reprimand nor to the counsel of his priest. This last wrote to the confessor of the King who was the Grand Inquisitor and, in response to the letter, the singer was taken at midnight from the arms of His Excellency, the captain general, and conducted to a foreign territory, even before she realized what was happening. It was this kidnapping of the Inquisition that the masks represented with lifelikeness and unusual audacity.[21]

Casanova later met Nina's mother at Marseilles, who confided to him that Nina was a daughter she had had by her own father and that Nina was therefore both her sister and her daughter. Casanova was in Bologna in 1771, where Nina had taken refuge after having been compelled to leave Barcelona. He states that she died the following year in misery of her life of debauchery and that Ricla, called to be minister of war, died a year later. He is known, in fact, to have received such an appointment in February 1772, but the date of his death was actually 1780.

Before leaving Barcelona, Casanova remarked upon the difficulties he had experienced in Madrid in August in obtaining a Spanish passport, denied to him until he was in possession of one from Mocenigo's successor, Querini. He tells us that through the intervention of highly placed Spanish friends, Querini was at length prevailed upon to issue him one but that, upon its receipt, he found to his indignation it was without the inclusion of any title, not even that of "Monsieur." Two letters to him of August 23 and September 3, 1768, from Dominique Varnier substantiate these curious circumstances.[22]

What is of special interest in Casanova's account is the evidence given that travelers in the eighteenth century were in need of a passport from their own country as well as one from the country in which they were traveling. When Casanova left Russia, he was issued a Russian passport, and he had also a French passport when he left Paris for Spain. There is frequent mention of this practice in the *Memoirs*, beginning with the issuance to him in 1745 of a passport by Cardinal Acquaviva in Rome. It survived until the middle of the last century, at least in British practice as late as 1858. Prior to that date, passports were issued in Britain not only to British subjects but also to persons of other nationalities, while British subjects traveling abroad might obtain not only a British passport but one issued by the government of the country to which they were traveling. Comparable examples occur frequently in the *Memoirs*.[23] The more closely these are scrutinized the more they yield of forgotten eighteenth century practices and customs, rendering the *Memoirs* a veritable social museum of the life of that era.[24]

# CHAPTER 14

# Wanderings That Bring Him to Trieste

Casanova now passed from Barcelona through Perpignan, Narbonne, and Beziers to Montpellier, where he began to think of Mme. Blasin, whom he had befriended in Leipzig and Vienna. Desirous of seeing her, he conceived an ingenious plan, illustrative of his inventiveness, in order to achieve that end without compromising her. In successive pharmacies he entered into discussion of the differences between pharmaceutical practices in France and those of the countries he had visited, confident that his remarks would reach the ears of the pharmacist's wife. His ruse paid off in the end with an invitation from Mme. Blasin that he might call on her.

From Montpellier he continued to Aix-en-Provence, where he remained four months, spending much time in the company of the Marquis d'Argens, friend of Frederick the Great and eminent man of letters, of whose last days Casanova offers us the only account. D'Argens, who bitterly repented having written his *Memoirs*, counseled his visitor against falling into the same error. Casanova assured d'Argens he:

. . . would never be guilty of such a folly, but in spite of that I have
been doing so every day for the past seven years . . . I continue to
write in nourishing the hope that my *Memoirs* will never see the
light of day . . . If that should not be the case, I count on the
indulgence of my readers, who should remember that I have only
written my story to prevent my going mad or dying of chagrin in
the midst of all the petty insults and disagreements I have had to
bear from the rascals with me in the Castle of Waldstein at Dux.

The four months spent by Casanova at Aix were marked by a
grave illness, in the course of which he was rendered devoted
service by a nurse. Seeking her after his recovery to recompense
her, he was assured by both the innkeeper and the doctor that
neither knew whence she had come nor where she had gone.

During his stay, his thoughts had naturally turned to Henriette,
that captivating creature who had made the deepest impression on
him of all the countless women he had known, whom he had first
met at Cesena in 1749, and whose path had crossed his again in
1763, near the Croix d'Or outside Aix. Now the third and final act
in the greatest romance of his life was about to take place.

I had often heard in various gatherings mention of her name, but I
had carefully refrained from inquiring about her in order not to
raise any suspicions that I knew her. Besides, I had thought she was
in the country. I waited during the six weeks after my great illness
in order to look for her and see her again while in perfect health. I
left Aix, therefore, with a letter in my pocket, expressive of my
intention, which I planned to convey to her, stopping in front of
her chateau and not leaving my coach until she might invite me in.

Whatever Casanova's other failings, we must grant him a full
measure of praise for the extreme delicacy he manifested, from
beginning to end, in his relations with Henriette.

On his departure for Marseilles in May, he halted near the Croix
d'Or where, six years previous, he had spent the night in Henriette's home without suspecting her identity, of which he had
learned only after his departure. A servant to whom he presented
his letter informed him that Madame was in Aix and would not
come to the country for another three weeks. When he was given
permission to enter in order to draft another message, he saw, to

his great astonishment, the nurse who had attended him during his illness. From her he learned that it was her mistress Henriette who had charged her with caring for him. To this domestic he confided his second note to Henriette, in which he informed her of his address in Marseilles. There, shortly after his arrival, he received word from her:

Nothing is more romantic, my friend, than the history of our remeeting six years ago in my country house, and now our present one twenty-two [twenty] years after our separation in Geneva. We have both aged; but will you believe me that while I still love you I am happy that you did not recognize me? It is not that I have become ugly, but plumpness has altered my physiognomy. I am a widow, happy and sufficiently at ease to be able to tell you that you will find in Henriette's purse the money lacking to you if you should need it. Do not return to Aix as this would provoke gossip . . . Now that you have given me such great proof of your discretion, I promise to tell you the whole story that was the cause of bringing us together in Cesena and the adventures of my return to my country. The first is a secret from all the world, and M. d'Antoine alone knows a part of it.

According to Casanova, he subsequently received some forty letters from her during the twenty or more years from that time to the writing of the *Memoirs*. It was his expressed intention to add these to his recital should she die before him. We know that Jeanne Marie Boyer de Fonscolombe, who we have suggested was Henriette, was, in fact, living at the time Casanova completed the first draft of the *Memoirs* in 1792. As no letters from Henriette have survived among the great mass of papers left by him, he doubtless destroyed these before his death in 1798, in ignorance of her demise in 1795, and under the presumption that she was still alive. It was a final and supreme act of delicacy to her, justifying her estimate of him as the most honorable man she had ever known.

It was at Aix that Casanova had his one and only encounter with Cagliostro, who, with Saint-Germain, enjoyed in the eighteenth century a renown as an adventurer exceeding that of Casanova. Remarkably gifted in the reproduction of paintings, engravings, and handwriting, Cagliostro exhibited to Casanova a

Rembrandt he had copied, which Casanova found more attractive than the original. Cagliostro's wife asked Casanova for a letter of recommendation, which he wrote. It was returned to him several hours later, with the request that he examine it carefully and note whether it was the letter he had written. When Casanova replied that he had no least doubt that it was, the Cagliostros smilingly produced the original, of which the one they had shown him was so skillful a forgery that it had completely deceived the writer. Astonished, but also disturbed by the implications of Cagliostro's amazing adroitness, Casanova remarked that such a gift should lead the imitator far and, if he were not careful, to the gallows. Cagliostro was counseled never to set foot in Rome if he were to escape great misfortune. As is known, it was in Rome that Joseph Balsamo, so-called Count Cagliostro, fell into the hands of the Inquisition.

In Marseilles, Casanova called on Mme. Audibert and with her made a visit to Mlle. Crosin, at whose marriage he had assisted six years before. As Mme. N.N. she was now the mother of three children. Casanova was mortified when she informed him he had aged, an observation repeated to him by his friends in Turin, the Chevalier Raiberti and Count de la Perouse. His constant traveling, the vicissitudes to which he had been subject, and particularly his imprisonment at Barcelona and subsequent long illness at Aix were beginning to take their toll. Now he was also increasingly preoccupied with his future and concerned over his depleted fortunes; at Marseilles he could count as liquid resources only fifty louis.

Disillusioned by his vain efforts to find employment that might have provided him with a stable situation, he now saw before him in 1769 but one recourse: a return to Venice. To gain favor with the Venetian authorities to that end, he conceived the idea of refuting Amelot de la Houssaie's *Histoire du gouvernement de Venise*, which had given great offense to the Venetian Republic upon its publication in 1676. Casanova had begun to assemble notes for the work at Augsburg in 1767, and he had occupied himself with it during his imprisonment in Spain. He was encouraged in his purpose by de la Perouse who had become one of his devoted friends. A native of Piedmont and of a distinguished family, whose brother-in-law was at this time Sardinian minister to Genoa, Perouse shared with Casanova a keen love of letters. The attachment of the former to his fellow Freemason is proved by a correspondence they entered into between 1769 and 1795, and by a visit Perouse subsequently paid him in 1773 when Casanova was on a visit to Count Torres outside Gorizia.[1] De la Perouse not only subscribed in advance for fifty copies of Casanova's projected work but was subsequently a subscriber both to the *Iliad* and *Icosameron*. It may have been through him that Casanova made an intimate acquaintance of the British minister at Turin, Sir William Lynch, designated in the *Memoirs* as the Chevalier L.[2]

From Turin he determined to settle at Lugano, where facilities existed for the printing of Italian books without censorship. It was there, where he remained from July to December 1769, that he oversaw the production of his *Confutazione*, the most ambitious work he had undertaken. The edition, in three volumes, was sold out within a year. His objective, however, had been less that of pecuniary gain than of having his exile lifted; to his keen disappointment, he had to wait another five years for this. At Lugano he found his old Soleure love, Baroness de Roll, and her husband, who was governor from 1768 to 1770. At Soleure she had been designated by Casanova as "Mme. de . . . "; here he called her "Mme. de R."

To prepare the ground for his return to Venice, Casanova communicated on August 1 with Berlendis, the Venetian minister at Turin, concerning the publication on which he was working. Berlendis replied to him on the 19th:

> I hope that the reception by the public will correspond to the talent of the author and that this publication will be an efficacious means of attaining the end you have in view . . . In all that I have written in your favor I cannot have been better rewarded than in the knowledge that my attention has been fully justified when writing of your arrival here and of your honorable conduct.[3]

When Casanova returned to Turin at the end of December, he called on Berlendis to give him a copy of the newly published *Confutazione* for transmittal to the Venetian Inquisitors. This is confirmed by a letter of December 30, 1769, from Berlendis, forwarding the copy.[4] There is likewise on record a letter from

Berlendis of July 8, 1769, to Venice reporting Casanova's earlier passage through Turin en route to Lugano in which he remarks that "he is the friend of several gentlemen of distinction and is frequently with the Chevalier Raiberti who is said to have a great predeliction for his talent and his intelligence."[5] In addition to Raiberti, Perouse, Lynch, Count Ricla, and de Quarsol, Casanova also frequented on his return to Turin Abbé Caisotti de Rubion, son of Count de Rubion, then ambassador to Spain and later viceroy of Sardinia, as indicated not only by Casanova's reference in his *Memoirs*, but also by surviving letters written to him by them.

With a letter of introduction provided him by Sir William Lynch to the British consul at Leghorn, Sir John Dick, Casanova set out from Turin in the hope of being engaged by his former Russian acquaintance Count Alexis Orloff with the Russian fleet he was assembling there to attack Turkey. Casanova states that Orloff was lodging at Leghorn with Sir John Dick; it is known from other sources that the two were intimately associated.[6] Orloff expressed his readiness to have Casanova accompany him on his expedition, but as a friend and without fixed employment. This hardly suited him. The time of carefree adventure had passed; he was now obliged to look for something that would ensure him at least a modest income, after the loss in 1763 of Mme. d'Urfé's financial support, and in 1767 that of Bragadin.

So it was that he resumed his errant life, passing through Parma and Bologna to Florence. Although he claims he did not touch there, this notice appeared in the *Gazzetta Toscana* on April 21, 1770:

> There remains in Florence that gentleman whom we described in the last Gazzetta as Sig. Giacomo Casanova di S. Gallo, a Venetian nobleman. We must state the person mentioned has come in person to tell us that he is . . . a Venetian but not noble, declaring that he had never attributed this quality to himself which greatly exceeds his qualifications and that he is restricted to being a good subject of that nation, but not a noble of that country.

Casanova's anxiety obviously sprang from a desire not to prejudice the Venetian authorities against him at a time when he was seeking to regain their favor.

From Florence, Casanova proceeded to Sienna, where he was persuaded to stop for a week by Bishop Gian Domenico Stratico, at that time a professor of Greek at the University of Pisa, whom Casanova had met through a letter of introduction from the bishop's brother, Count Simeon Stratico. Seven years younger than Casanova, the bishop was a thorough libertine and a man of great erudition, thus possessing two titles to the Venetian's affections. Their friendship is attested by a number of letters, certain of which have been published, both from the bishop and from his brother.[7] The Bishop gave Casanova letters of introduction to the intellectual society of Sienna, including the Marquise Violanta Chigi, at one time Stratico's mistress, and Abbé Chiaccheri, librarian of the university at Sienna, himself a libertine and scholar of no mean order.

The rage in eighteenth century Italy was the improvisation of verse. Chiaccheri introduced Casanova to two sisters, one of whom, Maria Fortuna, at this time only twenty, was already celebrated for her ability in this regard, amazing Casanova with her skill. She was later to publish two dramas, as well as other literary works. Casanova was so occupied by this cultivated society that he apparently had no time for any affairs of the heart during his brief stay. It is known that Maria Fortuna was the mistress both of Bishop Stratico and the Abbé Chiaccheri; the visitor may have been loath to poach on the preserves of his friends.

On the eve of his departure, he was solicited by the driver whom he had engaged to conduct him to Rome, to permit another passenger to accompany him. After an initial hesitation, he agreed when he learned that she was young and pretty and, from her pretended husband, who was traveling on horseback, that she was English. The denouement is not difficult to anticipate. On the journey Casanova found that the so-called husband was a French strolling player who had induced his companion Betty to run off from Sir B.M., her British lover at Leghorn. Betty's eyes were opened to the character of her seducer when he sought to thrust her into Casanova's arms in order to raise the funds he sorely needed; she appealed to her new-found friend to save her from the folly she had committed. Casanova proposed that they return to Leghorn; while they were on their way, after Casanova had been suitably recompensed, they were met by Sir B.M. seeking his lost mistress. What is of particular interest in the story is that Betty had been in the same school at Hammersmith with Sophie Cornelys, and with Nancy Stein, a friend of Sophie, to whom Casanova had taken a strong fancy in London. Betty told him that Nancy had run away with a young man, and it was to be presumed her fate had been an unhappy one.

Naples had always been favorable to Casanova. Accordingly, when it was suggested by Lord Baltimore, whom they had met, with Sir B.M. who had accompanied them to Rome, that they continue on to Naples, Casanova was happy to accede. In London he had already made the acquaintance of the eccentric Baltimore, one of the numerous lovers of the Charpillon whose favors Casanova had sought in vain. Baltimore had most probably met her through one of her pimps, Ange Goudar; it was he who was one of the first to call on Baltimore upon the arrival of the party in June 1770 at Naples.

Goudar had left London about 1764 with Sara, an Irish barmaid, who was destined to attain some celebrity both for her gallantries as well as for a number of works on music and the dance, published under her name, but more probably the productions of her husband. After expulsion from Vienna, they had spent the next two years in Venice, and in 1767 had settled in Naples, where they had taken a sumptuous villa to entertain the Neapolitan nobility and live on the product of Goudar's facile pen and the gambling dupes attracted to their home. In addition to his *L'espion chinois*, so well received that it had been translated into English, Goudar enjoyed considerable acclaim in Naples for a work he had published in 1769, *Naples, ce qu'il faut faire pour rendre ce royaume florissant* (Naples, what should be done to make this Kingdom flourish).

Casanova was astonished at Sara's transformation when he was received in her luxurious establishment, where she was surrounded by the nobility of many nations. Goudar had taught her to play the harpsichord and to sing. Count de Buturlin, brother-in-law of Princess Dashkov, and notorious for his debauchery, was present at the assembly. Buturlin conceived such a passion for Sara that he eventually induced Goudar to cede her to him for five hundred louis. Some months after Casanova's departure, Buturlin and the Goudars traveled through northern Italy together, with Buturlin defraying all expenses. Casanova errs in representing the Goudar's expulsion as the cause of their departure. On this occasion they left voluntarily. They returned to Naples at the end of 1773 and were expelled the following year. Except for the incorrect date, Casanova's account of the circumstances of the expulsion is well authenticated. Queen Caroline, consort of Ferdinand, who was King both of Naples and of the Two Sicilies, discovered a note he had received from Sara Goudar that left no least doubt of their adulterous relations. It read: "I shall await you in the same place and at the same hour with the same impatience as that of a cow for the approach of a bull."[8] Upon the insistence of the Queen, the Goudars were ordered from the Kingdom. A letter that Abbé Galiani wrote on September 17, 1774, to Mme. d'Epinay that "we have exiled the beautiful Mme. Goudar" confirms the approximate date.

Settling in Florence, Goudar was first imprisoned and then expelled, along with Sara in 1776 for publication of a reply to a pamphlet, *Discorso all'orecchio di Monsieur Louis Goudar*, in which he termed the anonymous author an "assassin." In a further pamphlet, written in 1777 after leaving Florence, Goudar returned to the attack and intimated that the writer of the original libel against him, Antonio Piazza, a well-known Venetian journalist, had had the collaboration of three others who, from the descriptions given of them, have been identified as including Casanova and Vincenzo Martinelli. There can be little doubt that Casanova collaborated in the pamphlet in view of its circumstantial references to Goudar's life in London and in Naples, with which Casanova was thoroughly familiar.[9] The Goudars left Italy perhaps for Holland, where they may have separated. Early in 1778 Goudar was back in London, to which he was to pay periodic visits. With the outbreak of the French Revolution he applied his gifts to pamphlet writing and died about 1791. Sara survived him until about 1800.

Queen Caroline, responsible for the expulsion of the Goudars, was not one who might with grace have reproached her husband for infidelity. She was the daughter of Empress Maria Theresa and the sister of Marie Antoinette, and there was no greater Messalina on any European throne. It has been suggested, and indeed it seems most probable, that she served as a model for the Marquis de Sade in some of the scenes of utter depravity which he depicts of Naples in his *Juliette*. Gorani has left an appalling account of the license and corruption of the Neapolitan court. Strangely enough, Casanova does not touch upon it; perhaps he did not see in it the immorality that impressed Gorani. It must be said also that there is singularly little gossip in the *Memoirs*; Casanova writes almost exclusively of events in which he was himself involved, at least according to his account; it is only on the rarest occasions that he presents details or stories merely related to him. At Naples he does remark upon the weakness of the King and his preoccupation at the age of nineteen with childish sports. The tossing of his subjects in a blanket was one of those to which he was principally addicted as if, Casanova remarks, he were a Sancho Panza. When he assisted at such a spectacle, his one regret was to observe the courtiers present slipping away to avoid the humiliation of being so tossed. He would have particularly enjoyed seeing Paul Nicandre, who had purposely brought up the King in such a way as to curb the natural expression of his innate gifts, given the tossing Casanova felt that he richly deserved. Gorani has commented also on the disastrous manner in which the King was raised by Nicandre:

> Saint Nicandre had the impurest soul that ever vegetated in the mud of Naples. Ignorant, given to the most shameless vices, having read nothing in his lifetime other than a prayer book of the Virgin, for which he had a devotion which did not keep him from plunging into the most debased debauchery, such was the man to whom was confided the important task of educating the King.[10]

Another adventurer whom Casanova met at Naples was Count Tomasso Medini, an inveterate gambler whose career merits some notice, both for his frequent appearance in the *Memoirs* and the once high literary reputation he enjoyed. He was banished from Venice in 1756 to Dalmatia, his birthplace, then Venetian territory;

later, he so far gained the favor of the Austrian authorities that he was given a post at Mantua, then under Austrian domination. He was "Capitaine de Justice" when Lalande found him there in 1765. Having been permitted to return to Venice in 1766 he was again expelled and went to Vienna where, as a fellow poet, he enjoyed the high esteem and protection of the great Metastasio. Casanova, who had had a severe altercation over cards with Medini in Venice, peremptorily declined to play with him in Naples, and their animosity eventually culminated in a duel at which Medini was worsted. Casanova was to meet him again in Rome and in Florence, where Medini was traveling with a mistress he had summoned from Mantua with her mother and sister, and whose charms he did not hesitate to exploit to raise sorely needed funds for his gambling debts. A letter from Count de la Perouse to Casanova of October 25, 1773, supplements details of Medini's life not hitherto revealed by his biographers. Arrested for debts at Vienna, he was twice imprisoned, the second time at Romaner Haus. On his release he sought an appointment as chamberlain from the Elector of Bavaria whose favor he so far gained as to be assisted in the printing in 1774 of an excellent translation of Voltaire's *Henriade*. The work was shown in manuscript to Casanova at Florence in 1771; he pronounced it equal to Tasso. Casanova's judgment was sustained by Metastasio who, according to Burney, expressed the opinion that Medini's verse was far superior to that of all living writers, while Lalande compared him to Virgil. Casanova states that for all Medini's acknowledged talents, his end came in a debtor's prison in 1788 in London. Casanova claims that he had warned him against going to England, predicting that he would end badly. A friend who visited him in prison later informed Casanova that Medini had avowed that his only purpose in ignoring Casanova's warning had been to prove him wrong. Medini, distinguished poet and gambler, is one of the many adventurers of the eighteenth century about whom we owe most of our information to Casanova.

One of the leading families in Naples at the time of Casanova's stay there was the Prince de Montena et Francaville, grandee of Spain, who lived in a style of the greatest magnificence. The King of Spain, Casanova tells us, had encouraged Francaville to reside in Naples in order that he not corrupt the Spanish Court with his homosexuality. As an example of the sumptuous entertainment the prince offered to distinguished visitors at his palace at Portici, Casanova gives us a description of a party he attended there where the guests included Sir William Hamilton, British ambassador, and Casanova's old acquaintance, the Duchess of Kingston. As a distraction, the prince ordered his young pages, his minions, to swim naked before the guests in a basin on the estate. The next day, when young girls were substituted for the young boys, Casanova remarks that the Duchess of Kingston was much less pleased. It was at the home of this same Francaville, "the richest gentleman of Naples and the greatest blackguard, where the luxury and magnificence were unequaled in Italy," that de Sade places a scene in *Juliette*. Although the orgy therein described is quite different from the aquatic display mentioned by Casanova, it is possible that the latter may have veiled certain details of it.[11] In a more scientific vein, Casanova presents an account of a priest who plunged naked into the same basin and remained on the surface of the water without the least movement. Casanova does not name him, but we know him to have been Dom Paolo Moccia de Fruttamaggiore from the investigation made by scientists of his unusual powers.[12]

Casanova himself is known to have taken a plunge, perhaps in the same basin of the prince. The incident is not mentioned in the *Memoirs*, but in a letter Casanova states that, in Naples, he found:

> the ugly Englishman Lee, who was at Warsaw during my time as adjutant general to the King, who challenged me to swim with him. I accepted the invitation, but he beat me, and I contracted an illness that almost killed me.

The Englishman in question was none other than Charles Lee who, after an adventurous life on the Continent, rose to the rank of major general in the American Revolution and died in 1781 in Philadelphia. His printed *Memoirs*, however, make no mention of Casanova.[13]

One day in Naples Casanova received a call from the eldest of the Hanoverian sisters he had known in London; she had married a Neapolitan, the Marquis della Pettina, and fled with him to

Naples. Pettina had been imprisoned for forgery seven years earlier, and his wife now appealed to Casanova to persuade the Duchess of Kingston to take her in her service that she might regain her home in Hanover. The duchess agreed, and the arrangement was made; thus terminated Casanova's final contact with the Hanoverian family which had beguiled his last days in London.

Casanova found also in Naples his former Turin mistress Agathe, now married to a lawyer, who welcomed Casanova heartily and who thoroughly approved his wife's action in restoring to her former lover, reduced in resources, the jewels he had given her in 1763. To Casanova it was another example of the mysterious ways of Providence. It is possible that Aniello Orcivolo, described as an advocate at Naples, who was a subscriber to Casanova's *Iliad* five years later, may have been the husband of Agathe.

The first news Casanova received on his arrival in Naples was that the Duke de Matalone had died since his last visit. We know that the duke had indeed died on December 10, 1765. As his widow had never been in sympathy with her husband's friendship for the Venetian, he could turn to none of the acquaintances he had made on his last visit, and was thus obliged to make new ones. Agathe had introduced him to a fourteen-year-old girl, Callimene, who took his fancy. She was the sister of a Mme. Sclopis, mistress of an Englishman named Acton whom Casanova had met at Turin on his way to Naples. Acton had made the acquaintance of Mme. Sclopis in Venice, and had concluded a deal with her husband according permission to his wife to travel with the Englishman for three years against payment of a thousand guineas. The period expired, the husband wrote reclaiming his wife who refused to return. The husband thereupon appealed to the British minister in Venice and even sought to have the affair taken up officially by the Venetian Republic. So important a diplomatic question was settled in the end unofficially by renewal of the original contract for a period of two years at the same price. There is every reason to believe that Callimene, with whom Casanova entered into a liaison during his sojourn, was Agata Carrara who later became a professional singer and whom he saw again in Venice after his return there.[14]

Through the Abbé Galiani, whom Casanova met when he was

about to leave for Rome, he learned that "Lucrezia Castelli," who had been residing at the home of the Abbé's brother Berardo when Casanova had last been in Naples, was now living at Salerno with the Marquise de C., her daughter. Determined to visit them, Casanova set out for Salerno and, after taking rooms in an inn, dispatched a note to "Lucrezia" informing her of his arrival. He accepted her subsequent invitation to be a guest of the Marquise de C. at a property not far distant. "Leonilda" had married the Marquis in 1765 and welcomed Casanova with something more than filial affection. At the time of the visit in 1770 the Marquis was aged sixty and was himself the son of a Marquis de C. born about 1675, who had died five years earlier. "Leonilda's" husband was impotent, but Casanova set to work to provide him an heir despite the fact that "Lucrezia" had given him every reason to believe that "Leonilda" was his daughter. The year after his departure she gave birth to a son whom he saw in Prague in September 1791 as a member of the suite sent by the King of Naples to the coronation of his brother-in-law. This third Marquis de C. married in 1792 at about the time of the death of his legal father. Despite these precise particulars it has so far not been possible to discover the family name of the Marquis de C. At one time Croce suggested that it was Cammarota but Zottoli has questioned this ascription. The clearing up of the mystery demands the knowledge of one versed in the genealogy of Salerno families in the eighteenth century.

Before Casanova took leave for the last time of "Lucrezia" or Anna Maria Vallati as her name appears to have been, and of "Leonilda," his daughter, he was persuaded to accept from the marquis 5,000 ducats that he had left with the Duke de Matalone nine years earlier as a dowry for "Leonilda." His acceptance of this, and of the jewels he had once given to Agathe, was a measure of his depleted fortune.

Casanova left Naples after a stay of about two weeks with the Marquis de C. at Salerno; this is established by a receipt he conserved dated September 11, 1770, from the innkeepers Giovanni Grasso and Lehman. He tells us that on his return journey to Rome he met at Montecassino Prince Xavier de Saxonia. This is one of a number of examples of his confusion of memory, as the

prince is known to have visited Montecassino on June 9, 1770, so
that the encounter must have taken place on Casanova's journey
from Rome to Naples and not vice versa. His memory, however,
was far from being at fault when he wrote that the day after his
arrival in Rome he took attractive lodgings in the home of a cook
opposite the Spanish embassy on the Piazza di Spagna. Through
the researches of Valeri it is known that the cook was Francesco
Poletti, that the house was number 290 (today number 32), the
quarters were on the second floor, and that the daughter with
whom Casanova promptly engaged in an affair was indeed named
Marguerite and was, as he states, sixteen years of age. Valeri also
confirmed that Casanova's neighbor was Abbé Giacinto Ceruti.[15]
Notwithstanding the difficulties that developed between the two
over Marguerite's affections, they remained on cordial terms
according to their subsequent correspondence.

Marguerite had a glass eye of a color that did not match her
natural one. Casanova quickly gained her good graces when he
had an English oculist, John Taylor, make her an eye of enamel
that was a perfect counterpart of her good eye. Chevalier Taylor, as
he was more commonly known, had been oculist to King George
II and subsequently to many European monarchs. Casanova could
not have chosen a man more competent.[16]

In Rome Casanova's old friend de Bernis, now cardinal and
French ambassador at Rome since 1769, had become the greatest
figure in that city next to the Pope. Sir Horace Mann wrote to
Walpole in 1772 that no one since Cardinal Acquaviva had lived
in Rome with such magnificence, expending annually, it was
estimated, no less than twenty thousand pounds.[17] De Bernis had
at this time as titular mistress Princess Santa Croce. Nothing
perhaps gives greater verisimilitude to Casanova's account of de
Bernis' relations with the princess than his mention of the ambassador's importation from Lyons of materials for his mistress free of
papal customs duties. He was neither the first nor the last ambassador to abuse his diplomatic privileges for a woman's favors.

It was perhaps Casanova's modest circumstances, as compared
with his former affluence, that made him at first hesitate to
approach the cardinal-ambassador. When de Bernis heard of his
presence, he sent for him and gave him news of their old mutual

love, M.M., with whom he still maintained correspondence, characteristic of his constancy to his friends. Too old for extraordinary adventures, he took a keen interest in facilitating Casanova's intrigue with two boarders in a Roman convent, obtaining for him not only access to the girls, but permission to take them to theaters and dances. Thus Casanova easily organized after theater parties in the private room of an inn, and attained his ends by one of his classic devices of working on two at a time, and employing his oyster game, which consisted of passing oysters from the girl's lips to his.

The picture he has left of Rome at this time, including ecclesiastic no less than laical intrigues, is a highly faithful one. Pope Clement XIII, who had died in 1769, permitted gambling, but had forbidden dancing. As Casanova notes, with some satisfaction, his successor, Clement XIV, had reversed these regulations. Casanova enters extensively into the intrigues that had centered about Clement XIV for the supression of the Jesuits, as demanded by Charles III of Spain and other powers, and in which de Bernis took an active part. Although the bull for the suppression of the Jesuits was issued only on July 21, 1773, the question was already brewing during Casanova's stay between September 1770 and July 1771. According to Casanova the King of Spain had received letters from Clement when the latter was a cardinal, concerning the Jesuits, and Charles threatened to publish these letters, on the strength of which Clement had obtained the necessary support for his election as Pope.

The eighteenth century papal elections were dictated almost exclusively by dynastic considerations; at this time, the principal influences exerted were from the rulers of Spain, France, and Austria. It was they who pulled the strings and determined the votes of the cardinals under their suzerainty; this power was all the more possible since no cardinal could be appointed in the territory of these rulers without the approbation of the latter.

Historians are not in accord as to what previous assurances Cardinal Ganganelli, elected Pope in 1769, may have given about the Jesuits, or the role this may have played in ensuring his election. What we do know is that de Bernis, assisting in the conclave in 1769, took a part in the proceedings so pleasing to his government that it was largely on the strength of it that he was named ambassador in that same year. It is probable that Casanova absorbed much of the gossip circulating in Rome concerning the election, if not from de Bernis, from those close to him. In any case, Casanova's account is confirmed by Baron de Gleichen who, significantly, cites de Bernis as his source. According to Gleichen, Clement XIV was only induced to issue the bull against the Jesuits "by the positive menace to publish the promise in his own handwriting to abolish the Order of the Jesuits in order to obtain the tiara."[18] Casanova also goes at some length into the reports that circulated after Pope Clement's death in 1774 that he had been poisoned by the Jesuits. Sir Horace Mann echoes the view expressed by Casanova, and similar ones were conveyed by de Bernis on September 28, 1774, to Louis XVI. The subsequently accepted view of historians is against that commonly held immediately after the Pope's death. It is now considered most probable that he died a natural death. The suspicions that prevailed were a measure of the violent passions aroused over the Jesuit issue.

Casanova's stay in Rome would not have been complete without study. Two or three weeks after his arrival he was introduced by Prince Santa Croce to the library of the Jesuits where he was given special facilities, including the privilege of taking those books he needed to his home; he was also furnished with a key enabling him to enter by a side door so that he could come and go as he liked. Winckelmann's biographer, Justi, has noted that the illustrious German scholar was accorded like privileges by the librarian, Pietro Lazzero.

Casanova was also diligent in attendance at the famous Academy of Arcadians, founded in 1690, of which he was at this time made a member under the Arcadian name of d'Eupolemo Pantareno and to which the most famous men and women of letters of Italy and other European countries belonged. He states that he was admitted on Easter Friday under the patronage of Cardinal Domenico Orsini and that he read an ode on the passion of Jesus Christ on that occasion. The Roman newspaper *Cracas* of March 23, 1771, reported the meeting mentioned by Casanova, but it was held on Thursday, March, 21, in Passion week. The presence of "Signor Giacomo Casanova" is noted, and there is reference to a sonnet read by him, not an ode. He had already attended a session on February 21, at which time the same journal reported:

> Signor Giacomo Casanova, Venetian, recited an elegant and most erudite discourse in which he offered the most precise clarification of this passage of Horace: *Scribendi recte sapere est principium et finis.* He demonstrated thereafter that the most celebrated poets and, in particular, Homer, were true philosophers. The discourse was greatly applauded.

It seems clear that Casanova's memory has failed him here and that it was on February 21, or perhaps even earlier, that he was admitted to the Arcadians.[19] That he must have been a member before March 12, 1771, is apparent from a letter to him on that date from Simeon Stratico in which it was remarked that "the Academy of the Arcades gives you more work than I would have thought."

There is mention in the *Memoirs* of his having gone on one occasion to the Capitol to observe the distribution of prizes to young students of painting and design, where he met Raphael Mengs and Pompeo Battoni, as well as a number of other painters acting as judges. The ceremony, which took place on April 21, 1771, was the presentation of prizes of the Academy of Saint Luke, of which Mengs was a director, and Battoni one of the judges, as appears from a surviving published account in which there is included a sonnet by Casanova "of the Arcades."[20]

In addition to Mengs, who had returned to Rome from Madrid the previous year, Casanova met young Manuzzi who had been the indirect cause of his leaving Madrid. On Casanova's departure from Barcelona for France he had been warned by his driver, as they made their way towards the frontier, that they were being followed by three ruffians. The driver, suspecting that they had designs on Casanova's life, persuaded him to engage a guide to lead them to Perpignan by a different route than that commonly pursued. At Aix-en-Provence Casanova had received a letter from his brother Francesco in Paris, acknowledging one written by the former from Perpignan and expressing the utmost gratification in having this confirmation that he had escaped assassination on the Catalonian border. Francesco confided that the news of Jacques' death had been communicated to him in the most positive terms by Manuzzi when the latter arrived in Paris with Ambassador Mocenigo. For Casanova the mystery of the conspiracy against him was at once resolved. If Manuzzi had been so assured of his death, the plot against his life could only have been at his instigation. Nevertheless, when Manuzzi called on him in Rome, he accepted his overtures to bury the past. In explanation he observed:

> My heart betrayed my reason, as has often happened during my life.
> I accepted the peace he offered and requested so pressingly.

There was doubtless another motive: He no longer possessed the financial security that had in the past given him reassurance; nor was he now of an age to maintain the bravado that had inspired many of his actions. The spirit of vengeance that might once have caused him to seek satisfaction had been so tempered that he was now disposed to accept rather than to challenge what fate offered him.

Casanova states that he left Rome in June 1771, but this is another chronological error; it is clear from unpublished correspondence that he could not have departed until July. It is more than strange that one who was faithful to so many minute details of his existence should have been so careless about his dates. There is an additional inexactitude here, in his omission of mention of an unpleasantness he experienced before leaving. The only information we have of it is in a letter from Simeon Stratico from Naples of May 4, 1771:

> I am distressed at the lamentable accident that has happened to you. Mr. Resident has promised me that he will write the truth and, in consequence, in your favor. I still do not know what to say about this rascal from Piedmont. Listen to my advice; so far as may be possible, do not let the history of this event spread here. Rome is agitated, she is a silly woman, and badly recounted stories are detrimental; furthermore, even when they are well told, they do little good.

The references are so enigmatic that it is impossible to suggest of what minister resident Stratico is writing, unless it was the minister at Naples. And who is the Piedmont individual? One might assume that reference is made to Casanova's old enemy from Piedmont, Charles Henry Oberti (see *Casanova Gleanings*, I, 1958, p. 15). What is clear is that Casanova was the center of some unfavorable gossip on account of which he may have been persuaded to leave Rome.

In a letter he wrote to Prince Lubomirski on June 14, 1772, he stated that he went to Florence in the hope of finding employment with the Grand Duke de Tuscany, the future Emperor Leopold II. He did not succeed and, in fact, suffered expulsion at the end of five months. It was his misfortune to find in Florence Premislas Zannovich, a young adventurer on the threshold of a notorious career; Casanova had known him in Venice as a child. With a confederate, Zen of Venice, and aided by the enticements of a Venetian dancer, Marianne Lamberti, Zannovich succeeded in despoiling an English nobleman Lord Lincoln of 12,000 guineas at cards. That is an amount mentioned by Casanova in the *Memoirs*, and also mentioned in a pamphlet published in 1785 where a circumstantial account is given of the fleecing:

> . . . This fine person [Zannovich] left Naples to go to Florence, where he noticed Lord Lincoln in love with the Venetian dancer Lamberti. Zannovich determined to take in this rich Englishman, who was only nineteen. He dashes off to the dancer, catches her fancy, offers to go shares with her, charms the Lord, makes him laugh, then drink, then gamble, and wins from him twelve thousand guineas . . . [21]

Sir Horace Mann, in a letter to Horace Walpole, while not so clear as to the final sum involved, was fully aware, as British Resident at Florence, of the scandal when he wrote:

> What did the Duke of Newcastle say to his son's being so great a dupe to a proud prostitute and a set of sharpers? He had literally lost to them forty thousand zecchins but, after supper, he was let to win two cards, one of eighteen, the other sixteen thousand, and then thought himself happy to leave off with a debt of eleven hundred, for which he has given his Obligations, besides a thousand in presents to the Girl. [22]

Not only were Zannovich and Zen expelled, along with Marianne Lamberti, but so also were Casanova and Count Medini, likewise in Florence, for allegedly having shared in the fraud; both Casanova and Medini appear to have been wholly guiltless. A piquant aspect of the affair was that before expulsion Medini had paid Casanova a visit to complain at not having been offered a participation. Before Casanova's departure, Lincoln's tutor stated that the duke had advised his ward not to pay but that Lincoln had rejected this as dishonorable. The entire episode mirrors the prodigality and reckless living that marked the progress of many young British scions on the continent in the eighteenth century.

Casanova did not leave Florence before writing the duke a letter of indignation at the arbitrary procedure adopted towards him, concluding with a passage eminently Casanovian:

> The auditor, chief of your police, has informed me that I might go and speak to Your Royal Highness at Pisa, but I have feared that such a measure on my part might appear to be an act of temerity to a prince who, according to common law, should not speak to men after having condemned them but rather beforehand.

Casanova then proceeded to Bologna, and one of his first visits there was to the papal legate, Cardinal Branciforte whom he states he had known in Paris twenty years previous when the latter had been sent by the Pope with swaddling clothes for the newly born Duke of Burgundy. That Casanova's statement is exact is indicated by Dufort de Cheverny's own *Memoirs*, according to which:

> It is customary on the birth of an heir presumptive that the Pope send swaddling clothes, usually by a prelate who, as a reward, obtains from France the cardinal's hat. It was, on this occasion, the Nuncio Branciforte, former vice legate at Avignon, large, fat, plump, in the full maturity of his years, and who, through his attire, had the air of a bishop and, in physical appearance, that of a colonel of dragoons.

Casanova's own portrait of Branciforte is in complete conformity:

> We had been together in the Lodge of Freemasons. We had also had delightful suppers with pretty young girls . . . This cardinal was both a man of wit and what is known as a *bon vivant*.

He was not only that but he was also known as a pederast, and in another version of the *Memoirs*, that of Busoni, Casanova offers two examples of these tendencies, which to him appeared as "ignoble." That it was no uncommon vice, and also one repulsive to Casanova, is indicated by a reproach once addressed to Casanova, by his friend the Prince de Ligne, because of the unfavorable judgment Casanova entertained of it.

With another prelate, Abbé Severini, Casanova was introduced to the most attractive dancers and singers at Bologna with whom they indulged in a round of pleasures. Another ecclesiastical dignitary of whom mention is made was the Papal Vice Legate Ignazio Buoncompagni, who was engaged in a secret intrigue with a popular singer, Margherita Viscioletta, to whom Casanova also paid court. In need of funds, and having put up his carriage for sale, Casanova was deeply offended at the haughty manner in which Buoncompagni attempted to beat down the price. When Viscioletta pleaded with Casanova to let her love have it for the price offered as it was to be a present for her, he ceded when he was assured that his recompense would not be solely financial. What was especially pleasing to him was the satisfaction he obtained in avenging the affront to his pride. It was plain to him that Buoncompagni had been obliged to draw the conclusion that the agreement over price had only been obtained at the cost of the fidelity of the vice legate's mistress. Casanova is not alone in his imputation of loose morals to that prelate. Gorani has left a portrait of him, if anything severer than Casanova's, remarking that he loved women to excess and possessed an imperious and vindictive character.[23]

During his stay in Bologna, Casanova fell foul of still another dignitary, the Marquis Albergati Capacelli, friend and correspondent of Voltaire, who had been a subject of discussion between Casanova and Voltaire in Geneva in 1760. Albergati had but lately become the occasion of gossip for having requested a divorce from his wife on the grounds of impotency after having had two children by a dancer whom he was desirous of marrying. Under laws then in force in Italy, as well as in France, Albergati submitted himself to a test of his physical incapacity before four judges, and his "relative" impotency having been established, his marriage was annulled. Armed with a letter of introduction to Albergati, Casanova was bitterly offended by the casual manner with which he was received. Later Albergati returned the visit and, not finding Casanova in, left a calling card with the title of "general." Casanova concluded that this factitious honorific must have been assumed by Albergati with his appointment as chamberlain at the Polish court where chamberlains were assimilable to adjutants general. Delighted at being able to obtain vengeance, he had printed a pamphlet, of which every copy was sold in a few days, in which Albergati's pretentiousness was ridiculed in burlesque dialogue. The copies must have been quickly read and as quickly disposed of, for not one has survived.

An even more renowned figure whom Casanova encountered at Bologna was Carlo Broschi, known as Farinelli, one of the most famous singers of his day. In Spain he had so captivated Philippe V that Farinelli, paid a salary of 50,000 francs, loaded with honors and enjoying high political influence, had no other musical task than to sing, during ten years, to the King, a repertoire limited to four lyrics. So renowned was Farinelli that the Electress of Saxony, herself a talented musician, came especially to Bologna on April 6, 1772, to visit him there in his retirement, as Casanova testifies and as is proved by contemporary records. The Venetian has left us details about Farinelli that are found nowhere else, in particular about the passion he conceived in his declining years for the wife of his nephew.

At about this time, Casanova was toying with the idea of returning to Poland and Russia until a correspondence, inspired by his one remaining protector, Dandolo, with Pietro Zaguri, Venetian nobleman and senator, persuaded him to make for Trieste, where he would be as near as possible to the Venetian Republic. Dandolo had interested Zaguri in agitating for permission for Casanova's return to Venice. This prominent patrician was to remain one of his devoted friends, with whom he would exchange many letters until the eve of his death.

While Casanova was on his way to Trieste via Ancona, his presence there was reported to the Venetian Inquisitors on October

12, 1772, by G.M. Bandiera, Venetian agent, who has left us this
sharp portrait:

> . . . he goes and comes everywhere, a frank face and the head held
> high, well attired. He is received in a number of homes and spreads
> the news that he has the intention of leaving in some weeks for
> Trieste and from there to Germany. He is a man of forty years at
> most [forty-seven, in fact], of high stature, of good and vigorous
> aspect, very brown of skin, with a vivacious eye. He wears a short
> and chestnut-colored wig. From what I am told, he is of bold and
> disdainful character, but, especially, he is full of the gift of gab and,
> as such, witty and learned.[24]

Trieste, where he arrived on November 15, 1772, was to be his
haven for two years. Here he resumed work on his *Istoria delle
turbolenze della Polonia*, the notes for which he had accumulated
six years earlier in Warsaw, and on which he had been working
intermittantly ever since. Three of a projected seven volumes were
published in 1774 at Gorizia, but the remaining four did not
appear because of a dispute with the printer.[25] The work, of high
erudition and penetrating in its observations, reflects his absorption
with contemporary Polish history and a sympathy he always
manifested for the fate of that unhappy country. A Russian
historian, B. von Bilbassoff, has passed this approving judgment
of it, while not recognizing the identity of the author:[26]

> Of greatest interest is the internal history of Poland from 1764 to
> 1767. Especially well analyzed are the respective positions of the
> parties, although one must not forget the clerical tendencies of the
> writer. Of importance for us is the information about Polish
> opinion concerning the relationship of Russia with Poland, and
> the Polish Kings, as well as the policy of the Russian ambassador,
> Prince Repnin and Stanislas August.[27]

He had time also to collaborate in the drafting of a comedy, *La
forza della vera amicizia*, produced in Trieste on July 18, 1773, and
to write and publish a number of poems laudatory of several
prominent ladies and of successive Austrian governors. In honor
of one of these he wrote the libretto of a cantata, referred to by a
local newspaper as "the most brilliant part of the program" whose

composition was "due to the celebrated pen of M. Casanova."

With the facility displayed by him for making friends of those in authority, he had gained the confidence of Count Wagensberg, appointed governor in 1773. Aware of these close relations, the Venetian consul suggested that Casanova might ingratiate himself with the Republic by obtaining permission for the passage of the weekly diligence from Trieste to Mestre by way of Udine.[28] When Casanova succeeded in doing so, he was rewarded with 400 francs and invited to undertake the more difficult task of persuading the return of Armenian monks to Venice; they had left there and set up a printing establishment in Trieste to supply Armenian books to Armenian monasteries throughout Turkey. Count Wagensberg, who had been ready to assist his protégé in projects that did not prejudice Austrian interests, took umbrage at efforts to induce the return of the Armenians whose presence was advantageous to Austria. Casanova made his peace with the governor by assuring him that he would never have undertaken the mission had he not been certain it would prove abortive. Wagensberg was all the readier to accept the explanation as he had found Casanova a useful instrument for the communication of confidential information that the Austrian government desired to have passed to the Venetian Republic to induce those authorities to be more responsive in various frontier matters of mutual interest. Casanova's information continued to be found so valuable that he received a further emolument of a hundred ducats and promise of a monthly stipend of ten sequins. He was now not only less embarrassed financially, but, as he states:

> I was not displeased to be in the employ of that same tribunal that had deprived me of my liberty and whose power I had challenged. It seemed to me a triumph, and I felt in honor bound to be useful to it in every manner that did not violate natural laws or those of men.

Meanwhile, his friends in Venice, the procurator Lorenzo Morosini, Senator Pietro Zaguri, and his faithful patron, Marco Dandolo, were seconding his own efforts to obtain permission for him to return to his native land. That moment came at last when a safe-conduct was issued him on September 3, 1774, and he reentered Venice on the 14th of that month after an exile of eighteen years.

# CHAPTER 15

# Casanova as Gambler

Gambling played so important a role in Casaonva's life that it warrants detailed examination, particularly since the picture he has left of it is highly revealing of his era as well as of his own career. In the *Memoirs* Casanova gives an incomparable account of music and musicians, doctors and medicine, and the state of many of the arts; he has left us an equally inclusive portrayal of gambling, which occupied much of his time, as it did indeed that of many others. He mentions basset, piquet, biribi, primero, whist, quinze, and numerous other forms of eighteenth century gambling but, above all, faro, which was the rage at every court, casino, and place of public or private entertainment, including even that of prince-bishops of the Church.[1] If, as has been seen, gambling at Spa was only under the auspices of the prince-bishop of Liège, that at Presbourg in 1753 was under the personal direction of the prince-bishop of Gran who was also primate of Hungary, Nicolas Csoky. When Casanova's companion, Talvis, persuaded Csoky to wager his entire faro bank on a single card and Talvis won, the astonished ecclestiastic inquired:

"If your card had lost, sir, how would you have paid?"

"Your Highness, that is my affair."

"Sir, you are more fortunate than prudent."

If anything is to the credit of the bishop in this incident it is that he paid up without a whimper while pronounced a fool by those present.

From his early youth Casanova was an inveterate cardplayer, as were most Venetians. He admits he was ill-advised to follow this penchant:

> for I had neither prudence enough to leave off when fortune was adverse, nor sufficient control over myself when I had won.

He confesses that what impelled him to play:

> was a spirit of avarice. I loved prodigality, and my heart bled when I found myself compelled to spend any money that I had not won at the gaming table.

Whatever the popular conception, Cassanova was never a professional gambler who derived any substantial part of his resources from cards. He once contemplated taking up gambling as a profession, when he returned from Corfu early in 1746 and was at a loss what to do in Venice. At the end of eight days and after losing consistently, he abandoned all thought of such a career, although he never gave up cardplaying. Only occasionally is there reference to play to replenish his purse. At least twice he mentions that it was boredom that pushed him to gamble, as a distraction in an age when distractions were few. His opinion of the gambler who played to earn his living is one of scorn. He observes: "The Orloffs were aware that gamblers who are obliged to live by play must necessarily be rascals." In another passage he remarks: "Nothing could ever be adduced by professional gamblers that I was of their infernal clique and yet they persisted in believing me to be a Greek," that is, a professional cardsharper.

Casanova does not tell us where he gained his apprenticeship at cards; it must have been at a tender age. The earliest mentions of play in the *Memoirs* are at the home of his mother at Venice in

1736, and of himself as a student in Padua. His first admitted misadventure in gambling was in Chioggia in 1743 on his way to Rome. Two years later, playing basset and faro in Corfu, he again lost all his money. When he returned there after a brief abaence, the professional gambler with whom he had previously played, observing that Casanova had decided to be duped no longer, "judged me worthy of being instructed in those wise maxims without which games of chance ruin all those who participate in them." Once he was admitted as an associate, fortune so favored him that he became a local celebrity, his connection with a cardsharper in no way affecting his local standing.

Let's say it again: As we interpert Casanova and his century, nothing can do more to distort our perspective and impair our understanding of that epoch than to view it in terms of the standards of our own times. While today a cheat is barred from all casinos, the eighteenth century displayed an indulgent attitude towards "correctors of fortune," as cheaters were euphemistically known. In 1765 in Russia Baron Lefort informed Casanova that he knew:

> young men of the highest nobility who have learned to cheat and brag of it.

Cheating was accepted as a matter of course and was characteristic not only of the nobility in Russia, but throughout Europe. Ange Goudar, in his entertaining study of gamblers in the eighteenth century asserted:

> I do not say positively that there is no honest gambler; I say only that there are very few.[2]

Brandes has recounted how Mme. du Chatelet, after losing 80,000 livres at the Queen's table at Fontainbleau, was informed by Voltaire in the Queen's absence that she had failed to observe she was playing with scoundrels.[3] Similarly, Boswell, in a faro game at the Brandenburg court on September 28, 1764, was warned that "there are many people in Germany, even princes, who live by gaming; and they can play a thousand tricks.[4] There is ample corroborative evidence of this in the testimony left by Casanova. In 1746, when he lost 500 sequins, Bragadin laughed at his concern over a debt contracted by him with cheats and obtained not only the remission for it but the restitution of a sum he had lost in cash. In Vienna in 1753, when he saw a player after losing, and under the belief that he had been cheated, throw the cards in the face of tha banker, Casanova remarked that "the prudent Afflisio paid no attention to it," so accustomed was he, presumably, to such occurrences.

Nothing could be more illustrative of the temper of the eighteenth century in this regard than Marquis de Grimaldi's observation to Casanova in 1763 in Genoa after he had won a large sum at biribi from three professional gamblers. When Casanova objected that the charge that he had been in connivance with one of the three did him no honor, the marquis observed:

> Neither honor nor dishonor. One takes an interest in you, one is amused, and everyone admits that, in your place, he would have done the same.

Similarly, when Casanova denied to Cardinal Branciforte at Bologna in 1772 that he had profited from the fleecing of Lord Lincoln at cards, for which he had been expelled from Florence along with the real culprits, the papal legate replied "while laughing that he regretted that I was innocent." At almost the same time, the Marquis de Prié was writng to him from Milan on January 4, 1772, of the same report:

> I do not know why you make a secret of it . . . should you not have been a participant? I hope so at least with all my heart.[5]

Cheating was accepted in the eighteenth century, and it was for the prudent player to adopt such precautions as were available against being robbed. Playing at Aix-en-Savoie in 1760, despite the distinguished company present—or perhaps because of it—Casanova insisted on new cards at each deal and refused to play on one occasion when new packs were not at hand.

He himself never concealed the fact that he had resorted at times to sharp practices at cards. Having lost all his money at faro in Venice in 1763, he was approached by Croce, described as "a most skilful corrector of bad luck," who proposed that Casanova become his associate at faro to recuperate his funds. He avowed frankly:

> Certain that this well-known cunning fellow had not spread a snare for me and assured that he had the secret of winning, I was not so scrupulous as to refuse him my assistance and the profit of one half the gain.

There are frequent references to Casanova's ability to direct the play, particularly when he desired women to win, thereby showing his customary gallantry. Enjoying the hospitality of Count Attendoli-Bolognini in San Angelo, Casanova deliberately lost forty sequins at faro when undertaking to amuse the family, remarking that "otherwise I would not have been extolled as the finest player of all Europe." While the observation obviously reflects his vanity and embodies a certain exaggeration, it is clear that he possessed undoubted skill acquired by long application and shrewd observation. When Casanova was only twenty-one, Bragadin counseled him "never to punt, but deal, and you will always enjoy an advantage." That he accepted this advice is evident from his disappointment in 1754 that he could not hold the bank at the *ridotto* in Venice, where only patricians enjoyed this privilege.

His greatest assets as a gambler were his imperturbability, his cheerfulness when losing, and his failure to gloat over his winnings. "I was relaxed and smiling when I lost, and I won without covetousness." Illustrative of his exceptional sang-froid was the game of piquet he played at Sulzbach on a wager of fifty louis to be forfeited by the player who first withdrew. It was won, of course, by Casanova, after forty-two hours of uninterrupted play. At Aix-en-Savoie in 1760 when he was acting as banker at faro, a young Englishman proposed to stake a bill of exchange for an undisclosed amount on an ace. Casanova agreed when he was assured that the amount wagered did not exceed the bank. With only a dozen cards left in the pack, his offer to release the Englishman from the wager was declined. Casanova dealt twice more and, the ace not appearing, only eight cards remained. With four aces among these, and the bottom card not an ace, he repeated his proposal. "My Lord," he said, "it is two against one that the ace is here; I release you, give up." "No, you are too generous, draw," was the reply. Casanova drew, an ace appeared, but not a pair which would have halved his winnings. He pocketed the bill without so much as a glance at the sum, a gesture which, of course, greatly impressed the onlookers. When he examined it privately, he found it to represent the equivalent of some four hundred guineas.

For all his dexterity and knowledge of the tricks of gamesters, he was nonetheless frequently duped. When the cheating was too barefaced, he reacted violently. Thus in Venice, when "robbed in a palpable manner" by Count Medini, he obtained restitution at the point of a pistol. Similarly in Cesena in 1749 he compelled a cardsharper, Count Celi, to disgorge.

Like most amateur gamblers, Casanova apparently lost much more than he won. This is evident not only from the *Memoirs* but also from independent witnesses. Count d'Affry reported to Choiseul on October 15, 1759 that on Casanova's visit to Holland the previous year he had lost much at play. Bono, writing to him on March 18, 1763, from Lyons to Genoa, remarked: "I am sorry that gambling has been as unlucky for you at Milan as everywhere else."

For several years after his escape from the Leads in 1756, there was little mention of gambling. He was doubtless too preoccupied with the French lottery and may have felt that, as director, it was unbecoming of him to play. Such gambling as he indulged in until 1760 was intermittant and light. At Aix-en-Savoie in 1760 he seems to have profited substantially. We do not often hear of such large gains, but Aix was then an important resort of gamblers, particularly rich Englishman, and Italians, accustomed to play for high stakes. It was not until his arrival in Naples some months later that he referred to gambling on a comparable scale. While there, he estimated his winnings at about 60,000 francs after losses which had distracted his host but not him.

Casanova's introduction to cards in England in 1763 was at whist at Lady Harrington's. He does not seem to have been a good whist player, as he lost again when playing at the Charpillons'. When he departed from England with diminished resources in 1764, his great gambling days were approaching their end. At Magdeburg, en route to Berlin, he played moderately, thus "restricting myself to modest limits." Journeying from Berlin to St. Petersburg, he was considerably embarrassed to lose a hundred ducats in Dantzig. In Warsaw he did not have a purse "sufficiently well filled to engage with Polish players." At Spa, where gambling was the principle distraction, he continued to play with moderation. In Valencia he was persuaded to join at primero with Nina. He was careful at a game in which "the most prudent always wins," and pocketed several hundred doubloons, to which he was not indifferent in his straitened circumstances. In Naples the next year, when he shared a bank with Goudar:

> My purse was rapidly nearing exhaustion, and I had perhaps only this means of enabling me to continue to live as I had previously.

When the benefits of the partnership proved illusory, it was terminated forthwith.

Not only his great gambling days but his prodigal way of life had reached an end. Shortly afterwards in Rome he had to be content with the simple role of spectator. It was one of life's ironies that he was expelled from Florence for participation in the mulcting of Lord Lincoln in which he had no part; his innocence is established not only from a letter of Zannovich of January 15, 1772, but also from a plea he made at the same time to the Marquis de Prié for a loan. It was an incongruous finale to the gambling career of a man to whom cards had been a passion only little less than his love for women and for learning. It was during the lean years that followed that, in 1769, he included in his *Confutazione* a history of French playing cards. He could not indulge in gambling on the scale of his days of affluence, but found satisfaction in drawing on his encyclopaedic knowledge of one of the many subjects with which he was familiar, much as he sought later at Dux to revive the pleasures of another passion, women, when writing of his adventures after the old fires had become cold embers.

# CHAPTER 16

## Return from Exile

The *Memoirs* end with Casanova in Trieste in 1774 on the eve of his return to Venice. When writing them, he had been torn between an inclination to extend them to his last days and a desire to bring them to a close before entering into the painful events of his declining years. In the *Histoire de ma fuite*, printed in 1787, he specifically states that if he should ever undertake to write a full account of his life it would only be for the period 1756 to 1774. Writing to Opiz on July 20, 1793, after having completed in 1792 a first draft to the year 1772, he observed:

> I think I shall leave them there, for since the age of fifty I can only recount the sad, and that makes me sad. I write them only to amuse myself with my readers, actually I will pain them, and that is not worth while.

It is unmistakably clear from this and much other evidence that 1774 marked their terminal date.

For him as for Byron, the days of his youth were the days of his glory. He had drunk life to the lees, as few men before him or after, dissipating his extraordinary talents with that same reckless prodigality with which he wasted his material substance.

But his reception in Venice was most cordial. Even the Inquisitors invited him to their tables, eager to hear him personally tell of his escape from the Leads. Among the many friends he saw again were the brothers Memmo, Pietro Zaguri, Mme. Manzoni, Angela Toselli, Marcolina, Caterina Capretta (C.C.), and Christine and her husband, who helped Casanova financially. The friendship with M.M. does not seem to have been renewed. As Bragadin and Barbaro had died, only Dandolo among his three patrons was alive. Bragadin's debts had consumed all his assets, but Barbaro had bequeathed to Casanova a monthly stipend of six sequins, and he received the same amount from Dandolo. As this was not enough to live on, Casanova looked for other sources of income. He was offered to become an agent for the Landgrave of Hessen-Cassel, or to write contributions from Venice for Ceruti's *Éphèmérides romaines*, but these offers did not suit the Inquisitors. Since 1764, Casanova had intermittently worked on a translation of the *Iliad*—begun at the library of Wolfenbüttel and resumed in Florence in 1771. He published the first volume in 1775, the second in 1776, and a third in 1778, but then had to abandon the work for lack of funds. While he found only 339 subscribers, they included many prominent European figures, and the list reflected the number of his influential friends.

In 1776, when he found his pen inadequate for his subsistence, under the name of Antonio Pratolini he became secret agent of the Inquisitors. Some fifty of his reports survive in the archives, written with a certain eloquence, but of a banality in subject matter that contrasts strikingly with the spirited style of the *Memoirs*. His heart was obviously not in his work. At first he was paid for each report; as of October 7, 1780, he was employed regularly at a monthly salary of fifteen ducats. The relative financial security afforded him was not of long duration. At the end of 1781, in a letter to the Inquisitors, he refers to his failure in a task entrusted to him, requesting "aid to enable him to subsist to the end of employing himself vigorously in the future in the service in which he had been initiated." He was accorded a month's salary and continuance of payments in accordance with the values of his reports. The last he submitted was on October 31, 1782, on the eve of his final departure from Venice.

While taking the baths at Abano, near Padua, in the summer of 1779, he wrote *Scrutinio del libro "Eloges de M. de Voltaire,"* a polemic against that author, whom he had previously attacked in the *Confutazione*. Voltaire's criticism of his translation of the *Écossaise* and failure to acknowledge Casanova's letter when transmitting that translation to him in 1760 had touched his self-esteem to the quick and had made him:

> . . . enemy of this great man. I had subsequently criticized him in all the works which I have published, thinking to avenge myself in harming him. However, if those works should survive, these criticisms can hurt no one but me. I will be adjudged a Zoilus in daring to attack a great genius. His only faults were his attacks on religion. Had he been a proper philosopher, he would have kept silent on that subject for, even supposing that all he said was true, he ought to have known that the people need to live in ignorance for the general peace of the nation. *Vetabo, qui Cereris sacrum vulgavit arcanum, sub iisdem sit trahibus.*

Casanova's attack on Voltaire in the *Scrutinio*, as well as in his other works, was less a question of *amour-propre* than a fundamental difference in outlook on religion. It not only emerges in the above quotation but is found in his colloquy with Voltaire in 1760.

"Suppose," said Casanova, "that you succeed in destroying superstition. With what will you replace it?"

"I like that," Voltaire riposted. "When I deliver humanity from a ferocious beast which devours it, can I be asked what I shall put in its place?"

"It does not devour it," protested Casanova. "It is, on the contrary, necessary to its existence."

In 1766, attacking Soule's Voltairianism, Casanova wrote: "I like order and minds submissive to a belief."[1] It is a grave misunderstanding of his most profound convictions to treat lightly, as some critics have done, his report to the Inquisitors on December 28, 1781, on impious and licentious works. The keynote is his reflection that "these books, although their aim is not to mock religion, deserve burning." This attachment to religious faith was a fundamental trait in his character. It is one of the curious aspects of his psychology that, in the Age of Enlightenment, this man of such extraordinary intellectual gifts should have remained impervious to the French philosophers and encyclopaedists. Libertine he was, but only in the commonest interpretation of that word.

It was about 1779 that Casanova formed a liaison with an obscure seamstress, Francesca Buschini, renting a small house in Barbara delle Tole where he lived with her, her mother and brother. The thirty-two letters she wrote him, which he preserved, extended from July 1779 to October 1787 and are valuable not only for the sympathetic light they throw on her in her unreserved devotion for him, but also for the unique evidence they give of his life during these obscure years.

It was natural that Casanova, with his rich intellectual endowment, should pursue his writing. In January 1780 he instituted a monthly review, *Opuscoli miscellanei*, devoted exclusively to his own work, and including fragments of his history of Poland, various essays, a translation of Mme. Riccobini's *Lettres de Miladi Juliette Catesby* entitled *Lettere della nobil donna*, and *Il duello*, an account of his duel with Branicki. The publication was discontinued after July, presumably for lack of subscribers. Undaunted by this failure, he took the role of theatrical producer, drama critic, and publicist. In the light of his experience in Corfu and in Augsburg, it was not a role entirely unfamiliar to him. He engaged a troupe of French players, headed by Mme. Clairmonde, who was of some repute as an actress, and a first production was given at the S. Angelo theater on October 7, 1780. To stimulate patronage, he began to issue coincidentally a weekly journal of dramatic criticism, *Le Messager de Thalie*, of which eleven numbers appeared. If his activities as impressario ended in January 1781 through lack of support, it was through no lack of energy on his part as publicist. It has been observed that he was far ahead of the theatrical managers of his time in his adoption of double bills, issuance of alluring advance notices, and the stimulation of interest by promise of the unusual and esoteric.

Not long after his theatrical failure Casanova became secretary to Carlo Spinola, a Genoese diplomat to whom he had dedicated the first volume of the *Iliad* in 1775. Spinola, a wealthy and prodigal eccentric, who possessed a magnificent villa near Padua, had, some little time before, made a wager of 250 sequins with a certain Carletti that he would marry a daughter of Prince Esterhazy but, upon losing, had overlooked settling the debt. Casanova encountered Carletti, who was visiting Venice, in May 1782 at the home of Carlo Grimani. Casanova's service with Spinola suggested to Carletti:

> . . . the idea of addressing himself to Casanova and to ask him to recall to his employer the debt and to persuade him to settle it by a cash payment in installments. He assured Casanova that if he succeeded in having this arrangement accepted, he would be recompensed in a manner that his intervention merited. Casanova replied that at any other time he would have blushed at such a proposal being made to him, and still more at accepting it, but that the present state of his affairs not only compelled him to agree to it, but also to ask what sum he could count on in exchange for his assistance.
>
> "My delicacy," Carletti replied, "forbids me—" "No, no," interrupted Casanova with heat; "the delicacy should be on my side; I sacrifice it to necessity." Obliged to give an answer Carletti replied that it would be of an importance to merit the approval of a just man, such as Grimani, present at the conversation. "Then," Casanova replied, "I am satisfied, and I can trust myself blindly to the guarantee of this witness." Carletti turned over at once a paper recording the obligation Signor Spinola should sign.

Hastening to Spinola, Casanova obtained his signature and, returning to Grimani's, presented it to Carletti, declaring "I have fulfilled my duty; it is up to you now, M. Carletti, to fulfil yours."

The officer took the paper and found it in order. "It is all right," adding: "it is fair that I acquit myself of my debt." And withdrawing a letter from his wallet he hands it to Casanova, who opens it and finds it to be a receipt for a periodic payment pledged on Spinola's payments. Stupefied by this reading, Casanova protests

that this was not in the nature of his reward . . . Carletti argued
that he was fulfilling his obligation in this way and that he did not
consider that he was in any way recreant to his promise. "Yes,"
cried Casanova, irritated by such reasoning, "yes, in acting so one
breaks one's word." At this Carletti leaped up and far lost his
temper as to catch hold of Casanova and excoriate him, heaping
offensive and abject epithets on him, which put the latter beside
himself and caused him to leave. But he was prevented by Grimani
who, still present, had not uttered a single word. He broke his
silence to order Casanova to remain, while adding: "You are
wrong." He did not leave, and Carletti continued to mistreat him in
the most cruel and bloody manner. Finally the two separated, and
the affair became the talk of the town. Opinions were divided; some
defended Casanova, others Carletti, but everyone agreed in concluding that Casanova had been the most cowardly of men in
allowing himself to be insulted with impunity in the most outrageous manner in public view. The secretary of Spinola became
the object of general derision, and in those particular homes where
he was received the door was closed to him.[2]

An anonymous contemporary preserved the above account of
the occurrence. Overwhelmed by his humiliation and driven to
desperation, Casanova in his anger thought to take revenge in a
mordant satire, *Né amori, né donne*. Under the thin disguise of
mythological characters, Carletti was represented as a barking
dog; Grimani, under the name of Alcide, as an illegitimate son.
Blinded by his rancor, Casanova was so far deprived of his better
judgment as to portray himself, in the person of Econeon, as the
fruit of his mother's adulterous relations with Michele, father of
Carlo Grimani. It seems likely that the charge of being a bastard
was flung at him during the altercation. "Very well," Casanova
may have said to himself, "everyone says I am a bastard, but so is
Carlo Grimani. The difference is I have more right to the name of
Grimani than he."

It is unlikely that the censor would have approved publication
of the work had its significance been appreciated on first reading.
When its purport at length became known, indignation mounted
against the writer. Mature reflection convinced Casanova that he
had been guilty of one of the most egregious faux pas of his life. In

a justification, never published, he confesses he had been wrong in the belief that, by underlining the patience he had displayed, publication of the pamphlet would efface the stain cast on him or would open Grimani's eyes to the injustice done him in Grimani's own home when the latter constituted himself a protector of Casanova's rights. Nine years later, he even wrote Grimani asking forgiveness of his "audacious fault."

In the face of the storm unleashed against him, he took haven at Trieste in the hope that it would subside. It was not to be so. His influential friend, the procurator Lorenzo Morosini, wrote him counseling him to remove himself from the Venetian Republic as soon as possible. Casanova replied on September 22, 1782, that he would be obliged to defer his departure for a month until he could hear from his brothers, Francesco at Paris and Giovanni at Dresden, to whom he had turned in his distress. He added:

> I am fifty-eight, I cannot go on foot; winter approaches; and if I think of becoming again an adventurer, I begin to laugh when looking at myself in the mirror.

There was no other alternative. He returned briefly to Venice on January 17, 1783, to take leave of his faithful Francesca Buschini and head for Vienna. While there, nursing a still rankling bitterness, he surreptitiously introduced into the diplomatic bag of the Venetian ambassador an anonymous letter to the State Inquisitors stating that on May 25 an earthquake would raze Venice to the ground. According to the report of the French embassy in Venice the letter caused such a panic that many patricians fled the city. When Casanova returned from Vienna to Venice on June 16, 1783, presumably to recover a few of his belongings, he was prudent enough not to tarry. Without leaving his barge, he embraced Francesca, taking leave of her and of his native land for the last time.

# CHAPTER 17

## *Further Wanderings and Final Haven*

Casanova left Mestre on June 24 and proceeded by way of Bolzano, Innsbruck, Augsburg, and Frankfurt to Aix-la-Chapelle. There he met Catina, wife of that Pocchini who had been responsible for his expulsion from Vienna in 1767. Despite his grievances, he could not resist the tears provoked by her misery and the illness of her husband. But when she brought him to her home, the sight of his ancient enemy hardened his heart. Refusing Catina's plea for even a small coin, he took leave of Pocchini with the bitter words: "Adieu, I wish you a beautiful death." A spirit of vengeance had overcome his better nature, and when, shortly afterwards in Paris, Sara Goudar, abandoned by her husband, sent word to Casanova of her desire to see him, he ignored her appeal.

From Aix-la-Chapelle he passed to Spa, where he remained for a month. There an Englishwoman with a penchant for conversing in Latin engaged him to accompany her to Amsterdam. She proposed that they travel together for four years but:

> . . . at dinner in Saardam, tête-à-tête, she made me proposals that froze me with fear. I remained half an hour plunged in deep

thought. Recovering myself, I said to her: "Permit me, madam, as soon as you have returned to the hotel, that I leave you never to see you again and that I go where it pleases me." This strange woman merely answered me in Latin with these three words: *Sequere voluntatem tuam* [as you wish], and immediately handed me a bill addressed to her banker, in which she ordered payment to me of 25 guineas. Whereupon she left me alone.

In a letter of September 6, 1783, in which he told this story to Abbé della Lena, Casanova added that, while he would never reveal the proposal made to him, "a great event might, in time, enable you to find out."

After passing through the Hague, Rotterdam, and Antwerp, he reached Paris on September 20. Uncertain where to direct his next steps, he wrote Lena that by the end of that month he would have decided whether to go to Madagascar; if not, he would return to Italy, but not to remain there. In Paris he found asylum with his brother Francesco at the Louvre, and there he remained some three months, including a week's sojourn at Fontainebleau. Here he met a son of Marie-Louison O'Murphy by a French officer she had married after ceasing to be mistress to Louis XV, "of whose history he was completely ignorant and of which I did not consider that I should inform him." Casanova also met there a son he had had by Mme. Dubois, but he leaves us in the dark as to the circumstances. Few of his old friends remained in Paris, but he succeeded in making new ones, including one of the most distinguished foreign residents, the venerable Benjamin Franklin, diplomatic representative of the new American nation. In a letter of November 28, 1783, to Abbé Lena, Casanova wrote that he had been invited "by the celebrated American Franklin" to attend the opening session of the Academy of Science. More specific details are found in *À Leonard Snetlage*:

In the month of November 1783, I was at the Old Louvre, the room where the Academy of Inscriptions and Belles-Lettres was holding its session, a few days after the death of the illustrious d'Alembert. Seated by the side of the learned Franklin, I was somewhat surprised to hear Condorcet ask him if he thought it would be possible to give other directions to the aeronautic balloon. This was his reply: "This thing is still in its infancy, therefore we must wait." I was surprised.

It is unthinkable that the great doctor ignored that it was impossible to give to the machine a direction other than that depending directly on the wind that was blowing; but these people *nil tam verentur, quam ne dubitare aliqua de re videantur*. But Franklin would not have answered that way to a French questioner in a group of English.

Charles Samaran has found that the session was that of November 23, 1783, when a member of the Academy submitted a report on the ascension just made by the Montgolfier balloon. The experiments of the Montgolfier brothers had aroused enormous interest, including that of Franklin, whose opinion on the future of the balloon had already been the subject of discussion in the *Mercure de France* of September 1783.

Mr. Franklin has made an excellent reply to those who keep repeating: of what use will it be? What utility will be derived from it? "Gentlemen," the profound thinker replied, "it is a child that has just been born; perhaps it will turn out an idiot or a man of great talent. Let us wait until its education is complete before judging it."

Franklin was one of the signers of the report of the Academy of Science. While it is regretable that we are not offered Casanova's opinion of the future of aeronautics, we must be thankful to him for the precious details he has preserved of this historic meeting. We do know that he had sufficient confidence to comtemplate making a balloon ascent at Vienna the next year.

On receipt of a passport from the Venetian ambassador on November 13 while at Fontainebleau, Casanova set out about the 24th from Paris for Vienna with his brother Francesco. They passed by Dresden and reached Vienna about December 7. There Francesco was taken under the protection of Prince Kaunitz, while Jacques, undaunted by the cold, spent sixty-two days in travel to Dresden, Berlin, and Prague, presumably in search of employment. Finding none, he returned to Vienna in the middle of

February 1784, where he was happy to accept appointment as secretary to Sebastian Foscarini, Venetian ambassador, "to write his dispatches." Still other duties were entrusted to him by the ambassador in which Casanova was to demonstrate superior ability as a pamphleteer.

In 1773 the Zannovich brothers, one of whom, Premislas, was indirectly responsible for Casanova's expulsion from Florence in 1771, had duped the Dutch merchants Chomel and Jordan of a large sum in a fraudulent commercial transaction by imposing on the good faith of a Venetian diplomat, M. Cavalli. When the Venetian Republic, to which the Zannovich brothers owed allegiance, refused to compensate the Dutch merchants, Holland declared war on Venice on January 9, 1784. Venice proposed that Ambassador Foscarini concert with the Dutch minister at Vienna for a settlement, hostilities were suspended, and a conflict avoided by the intervention of Emperor Joseph II. It is most probable that Casanova's journey in March 1784 to meet the Emperor, returning from Italy, to which reference is made in a letter of March 20 to Francesca Buschini, had to do with the Emperor's good offices in the eventual settlement.

It is obvious from the knowledge Casanova was to display of the documents relating to the controversy that these had been placed at his disposal by Ambassador Foscarini. On their basis, Casanova published thereafter four pamphlets in which he effectively demasked the Zannovich brothers and offered a spirited defense of the Venetian thesis.[1] Casanova was moved not only by a rancor against Premislas Zannovich for having been the occasion of his troubles in Florence, but also by a desire to commend himself to Foscarini. In the end Holland renounced the indemnity of 400,000 florins it had sought, Cavalli was dismissed from the Venetian service, and the Zannovich brothers were perpetually banished from Venetian territory.

It is characteristic of many of the personages in Casanova's *Memoirs* that they enter and leave the scene at one juncture only to reappear at another. In numerous instances they are linked not only with Casanova, but with others of his dramatis personae. Goudar and d'Eon are one example; another is Stefano Zannovich, the other brother, whose fate was joined about 1786 with Elizabeth

Chudleigh. She was then sixty, widow of the Duke of Kingston. Although Stefano was only thirty-five, with her impulsive nature she accepted his proffer of marriage with no least inquiry into his shady background. After taking leave of her before concluding the ceremony, to exploit in Holland his assumed title of Prince of Albania, he was identified as the Stefano Zannovich who, with Premislas, had duped the Dutch merchants in 1773. He was cast into prison, where he committed suicide on May 25, 1786.[2] This reappearance of persons in the *Memoirs* and the manner in which their lives affect not only that of the principal actor, Casanova, but those of others as well, gives at times the impression that we are attending a play in which the world he represents for us is a stage. The impact is all the greater in that the drama is never underlined. The fact that he leaves many threads for us to assemble is one of the fascinating facets of his story. Many will remain forever unraveled, in themselves an incitement to the piercing of those mysteries that are left.

It was during the period of Casanova's residence in Vienna that he renewed contact with Lorenzo Da Ponte, celebrated librettist of Mozart, whose acquaintance Casanova had made in 1777 through Pietro Zaguri whom Da Ponte served for a time as secretary. In Da Ponte's own *Memoirs*, first published in full in New York in 1823-27, he tells us of the intimate talks he had with Casanova:

> . . . sometimes at Zaguri's and sometimes at Memmo's both of whom loved what was good in him and forgave what was ill, and taught me to do the same. And even now, after due consideration, I do not know to which side the balance leant. A little while before I left Venice, a trifling controversy over Latin prosody made him hostile to me. This singular man never liked to be in the wrong.

They met again in Vienna about 1783. There, in 1784, they were walking together on the Graben when Da Ponte witnessed Casanova's encounter with his former secretary, Costa, who, twenty-three years earlier, had made off with the presents Mme. d'Urfé had intended for Casanova's use at the Augsburg Congress. When Casanova hurled himself on Costa, Da Ponte intervened and almost by force got him out of the scuffle. While Casanova recounted the story of Costa's betrayal, the latter entered a café from whence he sent out to Casanova these verses:

Casanova, grow not heated, / You have stolen, I have cheated, / You the master, I the student, / In your art I am too prudent. / You gave me bread, I gave you cake, / Hold your tongue for heaven's sake.

These verses had a good effect. After a short silence, Casanova laughed and whispered in my ear, "The rascal is right." He entered the café and beckoned Costa to come out. They began walking peacefully together as though nothing had happened and on parting shook hands many times over, with every appearance of serenity and friendliness. Casanova returned to me with a cameo on his little finger which, by strange coincidence, represented Mercury, protecting god of thieves. That was its principal value. It was all that remained of that immense booty, but it actually befitted the character of the reconciled friends. I shall soon have occasion to speak again of this man who was such an extraordinary mixture of good and evil.[3]

In another passage Da Ponte has so confused and misrepresented the facts regarding Casanova's relations with Mme. d'Urfé that one is justified in treating the foregoing account with some reserve. It is noteworthy that Casanova himself presents a quite different version of his forgiveness of Costa. With no mention of Da Ponte's intercession, he states that it was a certain "Bertrand, living with the Sardinian minister" who "brought me to the heroic act" of pardoning Costa in Vienna in 1784.

What is of principal interest in the Da Ponte-Casanova relationship is Casanova's probable collaboration with Da Ponte in the libretto of Mozart's great opera *Don Giovanni*, which had its premiere on October 29, 1787 at Prague. Alfred Meissner in his *Rococobilder*, based on notes of his grandfather, G.A. Meissner, Prague professor and historian (1753-1807), presents a description of a meeting between Casanova and Mozart in Prague when, by a ruse, Mozart was locked in a room on October 27, 1787, to complete the overture of his work in time for the dress rehearsal that was to take place the following day. According to Meissner, Da Ponte was also present, but he could not have been as he had been called to Vienna. It has been suggested that, before leaving, Da Ponte has requested Casanova to aid with the finishing touches of the libretto. For the incident we have only Meissner's testimony. What we do know incontestably is that Casanova was in Prague as early as October 25, according to a letter of Count Lamberg to Opiz of November 4, 1787. Tending to substantiate Meissner's account are two manuscript sheets in Casanova's handwriting, found among his papers, representing a revision of the situation following the sextet in the second act in *Don Giovanni*. This text does not appear in the final Mozart score; so we are left to conjecture the part Casanova may have had in composing the text of a work that reflected, in certain aspects, his own life. Such authorities as Edward J. Dent, Paul Nettl, and Marcia Davenport agree that Casanova did take part in writing the libretto, but the precise extent of his participation cannot now be determined.[4]

After his marriage in 1792, Da Ponte called on Casanova at Dux in the hope of recovering a debt due him, but when he observed that Casanova's purse was the leaner of the two, he did not have the heart to dun him. When they were leaving, Casanova decided to accompany the couple to Teplitz, a few miles distant. There Da Ponte had to replace his carriage by another, and Casanova, who acted as broker, "in counting out the money kept two sequins for himself." Da Ponte's wife "had been dazed by the vivacity, the eloquence, the inexhaustible vein, and all the many ways, of that extraordinary man." A correspondence between the two, extending from 1791 to 1795, reflects a high esteem on Da Ponte's part and contrasts notably with the somewhat acidulous and frequently erroneous statements about Casanova in Da Ponte's *Memoirs*. In one of his letters in 1793 Da Ponte wrote:

> . . . in verse, drawing him a pathetic picture of my state and asking him for some money. But he paid no attention to me and replied wittily in excellent prose, beginning his letter thus: "When Cicero wrote to his friends, he never mentioned business!"

Some time in February 1784, Casanova attended a dinner given by Ambassador Foscarini. Among the guests was Count Joseph Charles de Waldstein, descendant of the great Wallenstein. Not yet thirty, chamberlain of the Emperor, seigneur of the Castle of Dux with a library of 40,000 volumes, addicted to racing and gambling, he had as ties that drew him to Casanova those of Freemasonry and the occult. His uncle, Prince Charles de Ligne, has thus described their first meeting:

> My nephew was attracted to him at the Venetian ambassador's where they dined together. As he pretended to believe in magic and to practice it, he spoke of the Clavicules of Solomon, of Agrippa, etc., and everything of that kind seemed to come easy to him.
> "To whom are you speaking of that?" exclaimed Casanova. "*O! che bella cosa, cospetto!* All that is familiar to me."
> "So," said Waldstein, "come to Bohemia with me. I am leaving tomorrow."

Casanova was hesitant, all the more since he had just entered Foscarini's service, and had on his hands a young girl, Caton M. whom "but for my guardian angel I would have foolishly married." She was not his only female attachment; there was also a certain Kaspar, later to become the mistress of the Emperor.

When Foscarini died on April 23, 1785, Casanova was once more adrift. After an old friend, Count Fabris, found him unacceptable as secretary, he considered for a moment becoming a monk. Instead, he decided to go to Berlin, in hope of finding a place in the Academy there. On July 30, he was at Brünn with a letter of introduction from Count Lamberg to J.F. Opiz, inspector of finance and mathematician at Czaslau. In a letter of August 5, Lamberg inquired of Opiz:

> Have you sounded out this extraordinary man? With the exception of the alchemist Saint-Germain, I know few persons who can equal him in the range of his knowledge and, in general, of his intelligence and imagination.

To which Opiz replied that Casanova had paused only briefly in his impatience to see Princess Lubomirska at Carlsbad, adding that he found him:

> a man worthy of our respect and affection, a benevolent philosopher for whom the great universe, our terrestial planet (apart from the Venetian State) is his country.

Reconciled at length to spending his last days at Dux, Casanova proceeded from Carlsbad to Teplitz where he found Count Waldstein. The offer made Casanova a year previous was apparently renewed, for he accompanied Waldstein to his castle at Dux to take up an appointment as the count's librarian at an annual salary of 1,000 florins, then about eighty guineas.

The ensuing thirteen years were of almost insupportable ennui and of increasing sadness over the old age stealing up on him. De Ligne has left us an inimitable portrait of those last days:

> There was not a day in which, whether for his coffee, his milk, the plate of macaroni he demanded, there was not a quarrel. The cook had failed to serve him his polenta, the stableman had given him a bad driver to come to see me, dogs had barked during the night; an unexpected number of guests had forced him to eat at a side table. A hunting horn had disturbed his ears by discordant notes not in key. The priest had annoyed him in endeavoring to convert him. The count had not been the first to greet him with a good morning. The soup had been intentionally served him overheated. A servant had made him wait for a drink. He had failed to be presented to a visitor of distinction who had come to see the lance that had pierced the great Wallenstein. The count had loaned a book without notifying him. A groom had not doffed his hat when passing him. He had become angry, they had laughed. He had shown his French verses, they had laughed. He had gesticulated declaiming Italian verses, they had laughed. He had made, on entering a room, the bow taught him by Marcel, the famous dancing master sixty years before, they had laughed. He had performed at every ball the grave step of his minuet, they had laughed. He had dressed up with his while plume, his suit of gold embroidered silk, his vest of black velvet, and his garters of rhinestone buckles on his silk stockings, they had laughed. "Cospetto," he exclaimed, "scum that you are, you are all Jacobins, you are disrespectful to the count, and the count is lacking in consideration for me in not punishing you."

His chagrin was enlivened only by an occasional visit of an old friend, such as Da Ponte or Croce, and by excursions to Prague in 1787, to Leipzig and Dresden in 1788, to Prague to attend the coronation of Leopold II on September 6, 1791, when he met

Leonilda's son, who perhaps was his own grandson, and in the autumn of 1795 to Thuringia for six weeks. According to de Ligne:

> God directed him to ask me for letters of introduction to the Duke of Weimar . . . and he departed secretly, leaving for Count Waldstein a letter at once tender, proud, honest, and irritating. Waldstein laughed and said he would return, Casanova waited in antechambers; no one would place him either as governor, librarian, or chamberlain . . . The excellent and very amiable Duke of Weimar welcomed him cordially; but he became at once jealous of Goethe and Wieland . . . At Berlin he declaims against the ignorance, the superstition, and the knavery of the Hebrews to whom I had introduced him, drawing meanwhile for the money they advanced him bills of exchange on the Count, who laughed, paid, and embraced him when he returned.

To escape the boredom he found so oppressive at Dux, he buried himself in his thoughts and in the expression of these in writing a succession of works. A few of these he published in Prague, but the great majority, comprising an immense range of literary, philosophical, historical, and mathematical subjects remained unedited among the mass of papers left at his death. The *Soliloque d'un penseur*, a polemic against adventurers in general and Cagliostro in particular, was published in 1786. This was followed by *Histoire de ma fuite* in 1787, an account of his escape from the Leads, and *Icosameron*, in five volumes, in 1788, concerned with an imaginary journey to the center of the earth. But for its prolixity it might have become far better known in view of its extraordinary imaginative power; it prefigures the motor car, telegraph, television, the airplane, and even asphyxiating gas—to make the scroll of future civilization complete. His failure to obtain more than 156 subscribers for a total of 350 copies was a bitter disappointment. His restless spirit was occupied also with a mathematical problem of the duplication of the cube on which he had been working since 1760. Three pamphlets on this subject, which had absorbed the attention of many scholars, from antiquity to Descartes and Newton, were published by Casanova in 1790. If he did not attain a perfect solution, he came closer to it than anyone previously, according to the testimony of Charles Henry, eminent French mathematician.

Despite such intensive mental activity he was able to engage also in a heavy correspondence and, in the spirit of gallantry that never forsook him, to occupy himself with placing advantageously with the Duke de Courland the orphan daughter of an old friend, Cecile de Roggendorf. The letters he exchanged with her reflect a morality and elevation of mind contrasting sharply with the cynicism that marks at times the *Memoirs*. Something of the nobility of feeling he entertained for a young girl he was never to meet is reflected in a letter of June 12, 1797, which he wrote to her brother:

> I have cultivated in your sister a love of the truth, moderation, submission, a noble pride which is not to be confounded with haughtiness and, finally, all those virtues suitable to her sex and befitting honor.

The idea of writing the history of his life had been in his mind since at least 1780. In 1789 or 1790 he set to work on the *Memoirs*, and he had virtually completed the first draft by July 27, 1792, according to a letter of that date to Opiz. From that time to the eve of his death, six years later, he was retouching and redrafting his work with the same care that he bestowed on all his literary productions. In the case of even so lengthy a work as the *Icosameron* he rewrote this no less than five times. During the composition of his *Memoirs*, he was constantly torn between an inclination to burn them and that of leaving them as the one last memorial of his passage on the earth. In the latter conviction he was fortified by the opinions of all those friends allowed to read the work in manuscript.

After vainly counting on fame for *Icosameron* and his mathematical works, he was at last to have his own judgment about one of his works ratified by posterity. Writing to Carlo Grimani on April 8, 1791, he confidently expressed the view that the *Memoirs* "will be translated perhaps into all languages," although to Opiz he wrote on July 27, 1792, that he thought the "cynicism" was "so outrageous" that their reading would be forbidden "in all countries where one loves decent manners."

He proved to be right on both counts: The *Memoirs* have been translated into some twenty-odd languages, including Arabic, Bengali, Hebrew, Japanese and Turkish, while they may still be forbidden in Eire, Spain, and Portugal. In what must be a circumstance without parallel in literary history, it was not until more than 160 years after his death that the text as he wrote the *Histoire de ma vie* in French was to be revealed to the world in 1960 by the German publishing firm of Brockhaus, into whose hands it had passed in 1821 for the derisory sum of 200 thalers. The manner in which the work had been published in adaptations or truncated editions belongs less to an account of Casanova's life than to a history of that text.

Early in February 1798, after publication the previous year of his final work, *À Leonard Snetlage*, comprising lexicographical notes and personal reminiscences, he fell ill of a grave bladder trouble. His friends, in their solicitude, sent him tempting dishes but, with the taste he had always manifested for highly seasoned and rich foods, he preferred even in his extremity crab soup. In one of his last letters, undated but obviously written on his deathbed to one of the friends most devoted to him during these days, the celebrated Elise von der Recke, he wrote:

> Friday morning. Through a painful malady nature has condemned me to a slow death but, through the grace of God, the end is not far off. As I can take no nourishment, my feebleness becomes more accentuated every day, so that I can no longer leave my bed.

It was at about the same time that his brother, Francesco, the member of his family to whom he had always been most devotedly attached, wrote him from Vienna:

> You say, my dear brother, that my letter has imparted balm in your blood; if that is so, I am well content, for I assure you that I would willingly give you mine if it might bring some relief to the desperate state in which you find yourself. Your letter has afflicted me beyond anything you may imagine, loving you sincerely, and if

I lose you, no one in this world can replace in my heart the place you occupy.

If he was without the immediate tender care of those most beloved, he had the consolation, if not of a human being, of a dog to which he had become deeply attached. In 1791 he had acquired a fox terrier to which he had given the name of Melampyge and over whose death three years later he had wept for hours. The little beast had inspired in Casanova a tender funeral oration in Latin. Princess Lobkowitz sent him from Berlin a replacement, to which he had given the name Finette. It may be supposed that Finette was by his side in his last hours and may have inspired in him a consideration of the relative faithfulness in life of man and beast.

If he had no blood relations at his bedside during these last days, there were present a nephew by marriage, Carlo Angiolini, who had married Marianne, daughter of Casanova's sister Maria Magdelena by her husband, Peter August, court musician at Dresden. It was to this nephew-in-law that Casanova bequeathed four of his many manuscripts: *Histoire de ma vie*, a study of the Gregorian calendar, an essay on customs, sciences and arts, and an essay on usury. In March 1789, he had sold to Count Waldstein ownership of all his papers, but since his memoirs and the three other manuscripts had been written after that date, he presumably considered himself free to dispose of these.[5]

The end came for him on June 4, 1798, at the age of seventy-three years, two months, and two days. According to de Ligne his last words were: "I have lived as a philosopher and die as a Christian." He was buried in the churchyard of St. Barbara at Dux, where a plaque outside the church walls reads:

Jakob / Casanova / Venedig 1725 / Dux 1798

In 1922 a stone bearing the inscription "Casanova— MDCCLXXXXIX" was turned up in the graveyard, perhaps a tombstone erected in 1799, but no signs were found of his remains.

He has no need of any monument of stone; his name has passed into almost every language, one of the few examples in history of the adoption of a proper name to represent a concept of which a patronymic has become the embodiment. He is, in fact, far more important than "a Casanova," representing as he does in so many ways the personification of that extraordinary century in which he lived. It is testimony to his genius that the *Memoirs*, forming one of the most complete panoramas ever depicted of an era, should have brought him, even in a form incomplete for 160 years, universal fame.

# *Chronology*

1725    Birth of Jacques (Giacomo Girolamo) Casanova on April 2. His parents are the actor Giuseppe Gaetano and his wife, the actress Zaneta Farussi. (It is possible that his real father is the Venetian patrician Michele Grimani.)

1733    Death of Giuseppe Gaetano. Jacques now lives with his grandmother.

1734-39    Student of law at Padua. But his main interests are medicine and chemistry.

1741-43    Leaves after Easter for Corfu and Constantinople. Returns to Venice before April 1742. Becomes doctor of laws 1742. Attends St. Cyprian Seminary March 1743. Incarcerated at Fort St. André, Venice, from end of March to end of July. Leaves Venice with Da Lezze about October 18. Quarantined at Ancona until end of November. Arrives in Rome in early December, in Naples about the 6th and in Martirano shortly thereafter. Returns to Naples about the 16th.

1744    From Naples to Ancona in January. Returns to Venice from Rimini and Bologna before the end of February. Leaves Venice for Naples after April 26. Leaves Naples, is at Marino May 31.

Enters service of Cardinal Acquaviva at Rome in June.

1745    Marriage of "Angelica" January 17. He is dismissed by Acquaviva some days later. Returns to Venice via Bologna. Leaves for Corfu in February, arriving in March. Leaves for Constantinople on July 1, arriving the middle of July. Leaves Constantinople October 12 for Corfu.

1746    Returns to Venice toward end of February, and earns a living as a violin player. Meets Bragadin April 21, who installs him in his palace. Works in the office of Leze, a lawyer.

1749    Leaves Venice early in the year for Milan and Mantua. In Mantua apparently from April to June. Meets Henriette at Cesena in July. Accompanies her to Parma and later to Geneva.

1750    Returns to Venice for two months, April and May. Leaves in June for Paris via Lyons, arriving middle of August.

1750-52    In Paris. Leaves middle of October 1752 for Dresden.

1753-55    Returns to Venice via Dresden, Prague, and Vienna, arriving late May. Meets de Bernis. Has affaires with C.C. and M.M. Is arrested, as the result of an intrigue, on July 25, 1755, and becomes a prisoner in the Leads.

1756-57    Escapes from the Leads November 1. Arrives in Paris January 5, 1757.

1757    In Paris he meets Calzabigi, with whom he organizes a state lottery, which makes him a rich man. August to September, goes on a secret mission for the French government, to report on the disposition of the French navy. At the same time, he begins his relationships with the Countess du Rumain and the Marquise d'Urfé. Meets the Count de Saint-Germain.

1758    In October, he goes to Holland on a quasi-official mission for the French government. Stays there to the beginning of January and meets Thomas Hope. Becomes richer as the result of the mission's success.

1759    Back in Paris, he now calls himself "Chevalier de Seingalt." Has an affaire with Justinienne Wynne (Mlle. X.C.V.). Tries to launch a silk industry (with Chinese motives), which, however, becomes bankrupt. Is incarcerated at Fort l'Évêque, falsely accused of passing bad checks. New trip to Holland in September to secure loans for the French government. This time, his mission fails.

1760    Therefore, he travels to Germany. In Cologne in February. Affaire with the mayor's wife, Mimi van Groote. Through Baron Wiedau's intrigues, he is arrested, but is rehabilitated. To

Stuttgart in March, where he is arrested for gambling debts, but manages to flee. Arrives in Zurich in April. Affaire with the Baroness de Roll. In Soleure (Mme. Dubois) from April to May, then to Berne (Sara). Conversations with A. Haller and Voltaire (July 5 to 8). Via Aix-les-Bains (M.M.), Grenoble, Avigon (mid-August), Marseille (Rosalie), Nice, and Genoa, to Florence by end November. Stays there till December 19. Meets Horace Mann and Abbé Gama. Is ordered from Florence and goes to Rome. There meets Winckelman and Pope Clement XIII, who makes him a Chevalier of the Golden Spur.

1761    Stays in Naples (Leonilda). Travels via Rome, Florence, Bologna, Modena, and Parma to Turin. There from March to May. Gama charges him with a mission representing the Portuguese government at the intended Augsburg Congress. Travels to Augsburg via Chambéry, Lyons, Paris, Châlons, Strasbourg, Munich (July). Learns in September that the Augsburg Congress did not become a reality. Leaves mid-December for Paris.

1762    Leaves Paris toward end of January to prepare the Marquise d'Ufé's "regeneration." His attempts "fail"in Pontcarré in April and in Aix-la-Chapelle inJuly. Via Besançon to Geneva (Hedwige). Via Lyons to Turin, arriving end September. Is forced to leave beginning of November. Goes to Geneva, where he stays to December 12.

1763    Return to Turin (Agathe) in January. Travels to Milan (February), where he meets Count Giuseppe Attendoli-Bolognini. Leaves March 20 for Genoa, Antibes (sees there the Marquise d'Urfé and on April 26 attempts another "regeneration"), Avignon, Lyons, Paris (end of May). Travels from Paris to London in June (meets there Thérèse Imer, alia Mme. Cornelys; Lady Harrington; Lord Pembroke; is presented to George III on June 19). The "Pauline" and "Charpillon" affairs.

1764    Flees from London on March 13 because of debts. Stays in Wesel April and May, then in Wolfenbüttel (library of the Duke of Brunswick). Begins translating the *Iliad*. In Berlin June to mid-September (audience with Frederick the Great on July 7, and again in September). Via Riga (October 20) to St. Petersburg (December 21). Conversations with Catherine the Great.

1765    Visit to Moscow. Leaves for Warsaw September 15, arriving October 10.

1766    Loses the Polish King's favor because of a duel with Count Branicki (March 5) and is forced to leave Warsaw on July 8.

Arrives in Dresden end of July, visits the Leipzig fair (Mme. Blasin), then travels to Vienna via Prague.

1767   Is banished from Vienna January 23. To Augsburg, Cologne, Aix-la-Chapelle, Spa (August-September), there an affaire with Charlotte L. Then to Paris (October). Banned through a *lettre de cachet* by Louis XV, he leaves for Madrid on November 19, via Bordeaux and Pamplona.

1768   In Madrid, meets Donna Ignazia (in the church de Soledad, January 17). Is accused of illegal possession of weapons, hides at the house of the painter Mengs, but is arrested on February 20 and is kept at Buen Retiro for two days. Leaves Madrid September 13, via Saragossa and Valencia to Barcelona. Has an affair with Nina Bergonzi, the governor's mistress, kills one of the attackers that the governor had sent for him, and is imprisoned for November 16 to December 28. To Perpignan, then to Narbonne.

1769   From Montpellier (Mme. Blasin ) to Aix-en-Provence (end of January to May 26). Meets here the Marquis d'Argens, Cagliostro, and Henriette, who conceals her identity. To Marseille, Antibes, Nice, Turin, and Lugano (there to December, printing the *Confutazione*). End of December back to Turin.

1770   Leaves Turin March 15; to Parma, Bologna, Florence (April), Sienna, Rome, Naples (June to mid-August; Callimene), Salerno (beginning of September; visits Lucrezia), then back to Naples, and to Rome on September 11 (Marguerite). Sees again de Bernis, who now is French ambassador and a cardinal at the Vatican.

1771   Is initiated as member of the Arcadian Academy on February 21, as "Eupolemo Pantareno." Leaves Rome for Florence in July. Is banished there end of December and goes to Bologna.

1772   Leaves Bologna end of September, arriving in Trieste November 15 (staying till 1774). Writes (till 1774) the *Istoria delle turbolenze della Polonia* and the comedy *La forza della vera amicizia*. Also carries out secret diplomatic missions for Venice, which on September 3 lead to the permission to return.

1774   Arrives in Venice September 14—after an exile of 18 years.

1776   Secret agent for the Inquisition (as "Antonio Pratolini"); regular salary 1780-81.

1779   Beginning of steady affaire with Francesca Buschini in July. Stays in Abano during the summer and writes here *Scrutinio del libro "Éloges de M. de Voltaire."*

1780 In January, founds the monthly *Opusculi miscellanei,* but ceases publication in July. Tries a career as impresario (the first performance with a French troupe at the San Angelo theater on October 7). Is editor of the weekly *Le messager de Thalie.*

1781 Declares bankruptcy in January. Is involved in a scandal with Carletti.

1782 Because of the latter and his pamphlet *Né amori, né donne* he is forced to flee to Trieste.

1783 Briefly in Venice (January 17), then to Vienna, and again briefly in Venice (June 24) to leave permanently (saying farewell to Francesca Buschini). To Bolzano, Innsburg, Augsburg, Frankfurt, Aix-la-Chapelle, Spa, the Hague, Rotterdam, Antwerp; in Paris September 20 (meeting with Benjamin Franklin). Leaves November 24, goes to Dresden, then Vienna, arriving December 7; then travels to Dresden, Berlin, and Prague, trying to find employment.

1784 Is unsuccessful in this, and returns to Vienna mid-February. Becomes secretary to Foscarini, the Venetian ambassador. Acquaintance with Lorenzo Da Ponte, with whom he collaborates (in all likelihood) on *Don Giovanni,* for Mozart. First meeting with Count Waldstein, who offers him a position in Dux.

1785 Loses his employment through the death of Ambassador Foscarini (April 23), travels to Brno and Teplitz, meets there Count Waldstein, and becomes his librarian. From now on, lives at the count's castle at Dux.

1786 Publication of *Soliloque d'un penseur.*

1787 Voyage to Prague. Publication of *Histoire de ma fuite.*

1788 Voyage to Dresden and Leipzig. Publication of *Icosameron.*

1790 Begins writing his *Memoirs.*

1791 Attends the coronation of Leopold II in Prague (September 6).

1792 Finishes the first version of the *Memoirs.*

1795 Voyage to Weimar, meeting with Goethe.

1798 Severe illness in February. Casanova dies in Dux on June 4.

# Notes

## INTRODUCTION

1. See *Histoire de ma vie*, III, p. 316, note 1, and IX, p. 380, note 1, as also "New Light on the Paulin-Busoni Edition," *Casanova Gleanings*, VII, 1964. The Paulin edition was reprinted in Brussels by Rozez and in Paris by Flammarion, but has never been translated into English.

## CHAPTER 1

1. Casanova was baptized Giacomo Girolamo, but the French transliteration of his name, Jacques, is one that he frequently employed, and that by which he has been most commonly known in the English-speaking world and in France.
2. G. Prezzolini, *The Legacy of Italy*, Vanni, New York, 1948, pp. 68-69.
3. Peruvian author, Luis Ulloa (*Christophe Colomb, Catalan*), has noted that a Juan Casanova was, indeed, with Columbus on a voyage.
4. Casanova, *Mémoires*, Sirène ed. I, p. 182, and R. Aloys Mooser, *Annales de la musique et des musiciens en Russie au XVIII siècle*, 1948, I, pp. 148-149, and the works mentioned in those studies.
5. *Lettres familières*, Lettre XIII, Paris, 1931, I, p. 155.
6. B. Brunelli, *Figurine padovane*, 1934; P. Molmenti, *Carteggi Casanoviani*, I, pp. 165-178.

7.  Moggi, "Casanova as Chemist," *Casanova Gleanings*, XIII, 1970.
8.  Its original title was *Satyra sotadica de arcanis amoris et Venus*, published at Lyons about 1660, a classic of the seventeenth century. Although the work was attributed to Luisa Sigea, the author was actually Nicolas Chorier. It was translated into French as early as 1730 as *l'Académie des dames de Meursius*, enjoying enormous vogue. More recently, it has been published as *Dialogues de Luisa Sigeia*.
9.  For the full text of the correspondence see *Casanova Gleanings*, V, 1962.
10. Sirène ed. II, pp. 298-299.
11. B. Brunelli, *op. cit.*, p. 24; De Ligne, *Mémoires*, Paris, 1828, IV, 6; and Sirène III, p. 287.
12. Moggi, *op. cit.*

## CHAPTER 2

1.  Burney, *The Present State of Music in France and Italy*, London, 1773, pp. 312-314; Lalande, *Voyage en Italie*, 1769, VI, p. 346.
2.  If any were needed, there is further confirmation of her presence in Piedmont in 1762 in two letters of the celebrated journalist Giuseppe Baretti of October 26 and November 17, 1762 (*Epistolario*, Bari, 1936, I, pp. 128-130) to his brother in Turin inquiring as to the impression made on him by Calori.
3.  *The Present State of Music in Germany*, London, 1775, II, pp. 29-30.
4.  *Histoire de ma vie*, XII, notes, pp. 290, 419.
5.  *Reminiscences*, London, 1826, I, pp. 103-104.
6.  *Casanova Gleanings*: "Identification of Certain Proper Names in Casanova's Memoirs," III, 1960; "Further Identifications," IV, 1962; "New Identifications," VII, 1964. The fictitious names given by Casanova to his loves were effective obstacles for years in the way of their identification. I was the first to advance and demonstrate the principles of his methods of concealment— probably my most important contribution to Casanova studies, unlocking as it has secrets concealed for more than a century.
7.  On returning to Rome in 1760, he tells us that she had married her lover, described as a doctor, and the son of a painter.
8.  Duclos, *Pièces intéressantes et peu connues pour servir à l'histoire* (Brussels, 1781, p. 103).
9.  The Prince de Ligne (1735-1814), born in what is now Belgium, was not only one of the most distinguished Europeans of his day, but also a writer of note. His works in thirty-three volumes were published in Vienna between 1795 and 1809, comprising "Fragment sur Casanova" and "Aventuros," two of the most searching and appreciative estimates we have of the Venetian. Casanova has no more admiring friend than this outstanding soldier and statesman of the Austrian Empire.
10. For Pocchini see B. Brunelli, *Figurine padovane*, 1934, pp. 22-30.
11. Extracts from the manuscript of Chevalier de Bauffremont, written in 1741, cited by S. Gorceix, *Bonneval Pasha*, Paris, 1953, pp. 200-203.

## CHAPTER 3

1. A Venetian sequin was the equivalent of ten shillings.
2. B. Marr and G. de Givry, "La Kabbale de Jacques Casanova," Sirène ed. III, p. ix-xxxi; *Patrizi e avventurieri*, Milan, 1930, p. 414.
3. N.W. Wraxall, *Memoirs of the Court of Berlin*, London, 1799, II, p. 252; L. Reau, *L'Europe française*, 1938, p. 54.
4. Doran, *"Mann" and Manners at the Court of Florence, 1740-1786*, London, 1876, I, p. 293.
5. Smollett, *Travels in France and Italy*, writing from Paris on October 12, 1763.
6. Dupaty, *Lettres sur l'Italie*, Rome 1789, I, p. 57.
7. Archenholz, *A Picture of England*, Dublin, 1791, p. 218.
8. Representing half the sum she is said to have received from her family. The amount is evidently either an exaggeration or an error of transcription.
9. The Duke of Clermont was Grand Master of all French lodges from 1743 to 1771.
10. L. de Gerin-Ricard, *Histoire de l'occultisme*, Paris, 1947; Alice Joly, *Un mystique lyonnais et les secrets de la Franc-Maçonnerie*, Macon, 1938; Gustave Bord, *La Franc-Maçonnerie en France*, Paris, 1908; Marius Lapage, *L'Ordre et les Obédiences*, Lyons, 1956, and his "Faits et legendes" in *Le symbolisme*, Laval, Sept.-Oct. 1958.
11. Ch. Samaran, *J. Casanova*, p. 34. The date of the report is given by error in Samaran's work as 1753 instead of the correct date, 1752.
12. Crébillon the elder, celebrated French poet and dramatist, was at this time seventy-six years of age, and survived for another fourteen years.
13. *The Israelites on Mount Horeb, an Oratorio in French and English, from Doctor de Geldern*, London 1773. (F. Heymann, *Der Chevalier von Geldern*, Amsterdam, 1937, pp. 294-295); Grimm, *Correspondence*, II, p. 326; Casanova, *Mémoires*, Sirène ed. V, p. 325; Voltaire, *Correspondence*, 1880, VIII, pp. 425-426; Samaran, *op. cit.* pp. 81-82.
14. It may be found also in Voisenon, *Oeuvres complètes*, 1781, III, pp. 217-222.
15. Parfait, *Dictionnaire des théâtres*, Paris, 1756, V, pp. 421-450; VIII, pp. 430-433.
16. Sara Goudar, *Supplé*ment aux remarques sur la musique et la danse, Venice, 1773, p. 71.
17. Burney, *The Present State of Music in France and Italy*, London, 1773, pp. 71 and 326; P. Nettl, *The Other Casanova*, pp. 41-58.
18. Soulavie, *Mémoires historiques*, Paris, 1802, pp. 219-228.
19. *Revue Française*, June 1957.
20. Jean Cailleux, in *Burlington Magazine*, Feb. 1966, presents persuasive reasons for concluding that Boucher's portrait of Louison O'Murphy, signed and dated 1751, is one now in a private collection in Paris.
21. *Les cannevas de la Paris ou mémoires pour servir à l'histoire de l'Hôtel du Roule, publiées par un étranger*, A la Porte de Chaillot, n.d. (1750).
22. Casanova left two separate accounts of his visit to the Hôtel du Roule, one

much more detailed than that published by Brockhaus in the *Histoire de ma vie* (1960-63). The extract here given is taken from the unpublished version, the French text of which appears in part in *Casanova Gleanings*, V, 1962.

23. Larchey, *Journal des inspecteurs de M. de Sartines*, Brussels, 1863, pp. 159-160, 202-203, and *passim*.
24. *Mémoires*, I, p. 140.
25. Hervey, *Journal*, London 1953, p. 91.
26. *Vie privée de Louis XV*, London, 1781, IV, p. 159.
27. Her history, one of the most charming in the *Memoirs*, is found in a variant chapter. For the text see *Casanova Gleanings*, VI, 1963.
28. *Memoirs of the Court of Berlin* . . . , London, 1799, II, p. 265; Cassanova, *Histoire de ma vie*, 1960, III, p. 337, Note (9). Temesvar is now Timisoara in Rumania.

# CHAPTER 4

1. The change to modern practice was made in Parma and Florence in 1749, in Venice only at the end of the century.
2. B. Brunelli, "Un mistero Casanoviano svelato," In *Atti e memorie della R. Accademia . . . in Padova*, 1937-38, vol. LIV.
3. B. Brunelli, *op. cit.*; Ravà, *Lettere di donne*, p. 189; J. Marsan, "Du nouveau sur C. C.," *Casanova Gleanings*, X, 1967, pp. 5-10.
4. Pierre Gruet, "M. M. et les anges de Murano," *Casanova Gleanings*, XVIII, Nouvelle Série 2, 1975, pp. 35-40.
5. P. Molmenti, *Venice*, Part III, *The Decadence*, II, pp. 81-82, offers many examples. See also Lalande (*Voyage en Itâlie*, 1769, VIII, p. 290): "It is not solely through devotion that a Venetian woman becomes a nun; formerly it was in order to gain greater freedom."
6. Unpublished correspondence of Justinienne Wynne in possession of the author.
7. Sir Marcus Cheke, *The Cardinal de Bernis*, London, 1958—an excellent study that credits Casanova's testimony in general. See also F. Drujon, "Notice sur la vie de Bernis" in De Bernis, *Poésies diverses*, Paris, 1882.
8. Casanova's etymological work, *À Leonard Snetlage*, 1797, pp. 82-83.
9. Casanova, *Histoire de ma fuite*, 1788, p. 14; Mola, *Rivista europea*, 1881, p. 866; Casanova, *Histoire de ma vie*, 1960, IV, p. 339.
10. He is referring to a house he had rented in March 1754 on the Brenta.
11. The letter, which I owe to Charles Samaran, was first published by De Barante in the *Annuaire-Bulletin* of the Société d'Histoire de France, 1911, and republished, with others, by A. Monglond in the *Revue d'Histoire Diplomatique*, 1938, pp. 22-24. It has escaped all commentators who have discussed the de Bernis-Casanova relationship.
12. Prince de Ligne, *Letters and Papers*, New York, 1899, I, p. 146.
13. *Memoires pour servir à l'histoire de la Marquise de Pompadour*, London, 1763, p. 38.

14. *Annotazioni degli Inquisitori di Stato,* March 29, 1775; E. Mola in *Fanfulla della Domenica,* August 18, 1912.
15. Montagu, *The Letters and Works,* London, 1893, II, p. 307.

## CHAPTER 5

1. Mouffle d'Angerville, *Vie privée de Louis XV,* London, 1781, III, p. 120.
2. Casanova, *Mémoires,* Sirène ed. V, p. 287, note 23 by Ch. Samaran.
3. For Casanova's connection with the lottery and the evidence confirming it, see Ch. Samaran, *Jacques Casanova, Vénitien,* Paris, 1914, p. 132.
4. Dr. Francis L. Mars has suggested that a mission that, on its face, appeared so senseless may have had a double purpose; one, to test Casanova's capacity, the other to impress British spies with the seriousness of the Channel preparations, while diverting attention from the more serious ones at Toulon with the assault on Minorca as their objective.
5. *Memoirs,* London, 1799, II, p. 269.
6. Donald McDonald, *A History of Platinum,* London, 1960, p. 23; J. Russell-Wood, "The First Experiments on Platinum," *Platinum Metals Review,* April 1961; Dr. L.B. Hunt, "Casanova on the Metallurgy of Platinum," *ibid.,* January 1962. When a great British industry finds Casanova's narrative worthy of attention, pause may be given to the caricatures drawn of him by the mythmakers: *Times Literary Supplement,* June 30, 1961; Nicolson, *The Age of Reason,* London, 1960.
7. Childs, "An Unknown Work of Casanova Identified," *Papers,* Bibliographical Society of America, 1956; W.F. Friedman, "Casanova Cryptologist," *Casanova Gleanings,* IV, 1961. The latter, a world authority, has pronounced Casanova's cryptographic knowledge as "more than noteworthy—it is quite remarkable, if not astonishing," seeing that the Venetian anticipated by more than a century the mathematical solution of ciphers of multialphabets, hitherto credited to Major Kasiski (1863).
8. Cheverny, *Mémoires,* Paris, 1886, p. 56; G. Voz, *Der Graf von Saint-Germain,* cited in P. Lhermier, *Le mystérieux comte de Saint-Germain,* Paris, 1943, pp. 69-70. See also, despite its errors, P. Chacornac, *Le Comte de Saint-Germain,* Paris, 1947; Gleichen, *Souvenirs,* Paris, 1868, pp. 120-134.
9. It was subsequently engraved by N. Thomas.
10. The facts have been confirmed by other sources, including P. Chacornac, *op. cit.,* pp. 121-136, with a wealth of detail. Working on the basis of a corrupt text of the *Memoirs,* he questions Casanova's account while citing documents that support it. Chacornac claims that the enterprise was liquidated in 1763, but, in the light of Casanova's veracity, which has now been confirmed in hundreds of details, it is reasonable to conclude that Saint-Germain was still at Tournai in March 1764 during the liquidation of the undertaking. For all Chacornac's industry, his study is to be accepted with extreme caution.
11. "Archives des Affaires Étrangères, série Hollande," 1959, published by A. Baschet in *Le Livre,* 1881, p. 22.

12. I owe this information to Marco Leeflang, a superb Dutch Casanovist.
13. Before the French Revolution, the collection of Revenue was farmed out in France to *Fermiers généraux* of whom La Popelinière was one of the most notable. The extortions and lavish living, made possible by the taxes wrung from the population, caused thirty-five of them to be tried before a revolutionary tribunal, with most of them summarily executed.
14. It is highly significant that Casanova himself states in the *Memoirs* that it was in 1759 that he began to use the title "Chevalier de Seingalt."

## CHAPTER 6

1. An unpublished letter, in the author's collection, from Justinienne to Memmo, warrants this conjecture.
2. Published in English as *Casanova Loved Her*, London, 1929.
3. From unpublished correspondence in possession of the author.
4. G. Cucuel, *La Popelinière et la musique de chambre*, Paris, 1913.
5. Charles Henry, *Revue Historique*, Paris, 1889, pp. 297-328; G. Capon, *Casanova à Paris*, Paris, 1913, pp. 381-392.
6. Samaran, *op. cit.*, p. 168.
7. Unpublished text, discovered by Ch. Samaran, published by F.L. Mars, "Pour le dossier de Miss X.C.V.," *Casanova Gleanings*, V, 1962.
8. Samaran, *op. cit.*, pp. 357-365.
9. *Casanova Gleanings*, I, 1958, p. 15.
10. "Archives des Affaires Étrangères, série Hollande," 1759, published by A. Baschet in *Le Livre*, 1881, p. 22.

## CHAPTER 7

1. "Archives des Affaires Étrangères, série Cologne," 1760. The first paragraph only was published by A. Baschet in *Le Livre*, 1881, p. 23.
2. "Archives des Affaires Étrangères, série Cologne," 1760.
3. P. Nettl, *The Other Casanova*, New York, pp. 101-108.
4. Grellet, *Les aventures de Casanova en Suisse*, p. 51. The marriage date was presumably July 29, 1759.
5. Mrs. Montagu's correspondence, consisting of 6,928 items, not all of which have been published, is in the Huntington Library at San Marino, California. An examination of it for the period 1751-57 has failed to disclose mention of the name of any foreign domestic who might have been Mme. Dubois. We do know that Mrs. Montagu was at Windsor in 1757.
6. Grellet, *op. cit.*, pp. 70-71; Sirène ed. VI, p. 321.
7. Haldenwang, *Casanova à Genève*, Paris, 1937, pp. 102-103. The initial F. with which Casanova designated them was happily preserved by Schütz in his translation of a chapter, subsequently lost, concerned with Casanova's

meeting with them again in 1762. This was one of the first four chapters of volume VIII of the autograph manuscript that were presumably never returned to Brockhaus by Laforgue upon the termination of the latter's work.

8. The *Macharonea*, printed under the name of Merlino Coccai, was by T. Folengo and appeared first in Venice in 1517. A French translation exists, Paris, 1601, reprinted as *Histoire maccaronique de Merlin Coccai*, Paris, 1859. See L. Messadaglia, "G. Casanova e Merlin Cocai" in *Nuovo Archivio Veneto*, 1938, pp. 1-85.

9. *Scrutinio*, Venice, 1779, p. 68.

10. C. ver Heyden de Lancey, *François J. de Casanova*, Paris, 1934, p. 35.

## CHAPTER 8

1. Paris, *Versailles*, III, 1817, p. 151.

2. Cucuel, *Revue du dix-huitième e siècle*, July-Dec. 1918, pp. 168-180.

3. Although he has no notice in the *Dictionary of National Biography*, he is mentioned in both Smollett's *Travels* and in Hervey's *Journal*.

4. F.L. Mars, "Casanova à Antibes, Nice et Menton" in *Casanova Gleanings*, II, 1959.

5. (Antonio Piazza), *Gazzetta Urbana Veneta*, May 31, 1788.

6. Bartoli (*Notizie istoriche de comici italiani*, Padua, 1782) is not only the authority for the details given of Gritti but notes that Rossi is known to have particularly distinguished himself in the Écossaise, which he states Goldoni imitated from the original French. According to Goldoni's *Mémoires*, his adaptation of the Écossaise was produced during carnival 1761 in Venice, and had recently been preceded there by two other versions, of which that at S. Samuele theater was a literal translation of Voltaire's play. It is possible that the script used in the last may have been that of Casanova, particularly if it were established that Rossi was playing in it.

7. Not to be confused with two other Grimaldis mentioned in the *Memoirs*: Giovanni Augustino, Marquis della Pietra, whom Casanova met at Genoa in 1763, and another Genoese, Marquis Paolo Girolamo Grimaldi, Spanish minister for foreign affairs from 1763 to 1777, whom Casanova met in Spain in 1768.

8. L.T. Belgrano (*Aneddoti e ritratti Casanoviani*, 1890, p. 20) proposed to identify Veronique with a Veronica Alizeri, born in 1734 near Genoa, daughter of a widow in distressed circumstances, of good family. The absence of any record of an Annette, or another daughter, together with Casanova's known discretion with his ladies' names, renders this ascription doubtful.

9. Doran's *"Mann" and Manners at the Court of Florence, 1740-1786* (London, 1876), including abstracts of Mann's letters to Horace Walpole, confirm in

many instances details of Casanova's own *Memoirs* where they touch upon the same subject.

10. Born September 27, 1747, daughter of Laura and Antonio Corticelli, she died in Paris probably in 1767 after tragic vicissitudes following Casanova's break with her early in 1763 at Turin. His last encounter with her was in Paris, not in 1763 as he mistakenly states, but in 1767. (L. Frati, *Resto del Carlino*, April 12, 1922; Sirène, ed., VII, p. 312; and *Casanova Gleanings*, III, 1959.)

11. A local valet, to whom Casanova makes frequent references in his voyages, was employed as a guide, as better acquainted with towns visited by a traveler than his personal servants. There is an excellent description of their usefulness in Smollett's *Travels*.

12. As the chapter of the original text has been lost, we have preferred to give a translation from the Schütz German text, more faithful than that of Laforgue.

13. For the full text of the letters of the Florence chief of police see *Casanova Gleanings*, III, 1960.

14. Casanova does not name him, but Valeri who, in his "Casanova a Roma" in the *Rivista d'Italia*, 1899, has verified many of the details of Casanova's several visits to Rome, found in the archives record of him and his activities.

## CHAPTER 9

1. Duclos, *Voyage en Italie, Oeuvres*, Paris, 1820, II, p. 665. Burney, *Present State of Music in France and Italy*, London, 1773, p. 326, noted that "music at the theatres and other public places in Italy seems but an excuse for people to assemble together, their attention being chiefly placed on play and conversation, even during the performance of a serious opera." For Casanova's several visits to Naples, see B. Croce, *Aneddoti e profili*, 1922, pp. 51-73; S. di Giacomo, "Casanova a Napoli," *Ars et Labor*, Milan, 1907.

2. In French this is called *tutoyer* (and in German it is called *duzen*), for which the only English translation would be the awkward "to thou."

3. The date given by Casanova is January 1744, which is evidently according to the Venetian calendar and should be therefore January 1745. The conversation between Casanova and Lucrezia took place in January 1761, so that Leonilda's birth date would be July 1744. As it has been established from a concurrence of numerous controllable facts that the first meeting between Casanova and Lucrezia took place in May 1744 and that he called on Lucrezia's mother in Rome in January 1745, Leonilda was born not in July 1744 but in July 1745.

4. The author is fully aware of the dangers of any comparison of the morals of one age with another. Unfortunately we are lacking a satisfactory history or comparative study of morals. The subject is vast, and the difficulties are great in the way of evaluation of moral concepts from one century to another.

5. As the letter to Borromei has not only survived but is mentioned specifically

nunication of Casanova in November 1762 to Count d'Aglié in
is obviously the one he had in mind when describing it incorrectly
essed to the Nuncio Onorati in Florence.

is record of her dancing at Prague in the autumn of 1761 in *Clemenza*
*ito* (O. Tauber, *Geschichte des Prager Theaters*, Prague, 1788, I, p. 237)
ording to a note of Gugitz in the Sirène edition VII, p. 312.

aiberti died in Turin on March 9, 1771, after retirement in that year. Details
upplementary to the *Memoirs* regarding these Turin personalities are
found in Baron Manno's manuscript "Patriziato Subalpino," now in the
Archivio di Stato, Turin.

8. In the *Memoirs* Casanova has represented the date of his expulsion as 1761,
when we know that it was November 1762.

9. Brézé's presence in Lugano to buy horses in 1769 is confirmed by a letter of
de la Perouse of October 19, 1769, to Casanova (*Casanova Gleanings*, II,
1959, p. 16). He was the author of numerous books on military subjects, and
was described by Gorani, who met him at Turin in 1769, as "very amiable
and witty" and as receiving "the men of greatest mark in science of the
locality and the most renowned foreigners who passed through this city."
(*Memorie*, Milan, III, 1942, p. 166.)

10. She has been identified as probably being Marie, wife of François Daniel
Borel, attorney of the parliament of Dauphiné in 1760. It will be recalled that
she was a sister of the mother of the famous Mlle. Roman who became a
mistress of Louis XV (P. Thevenot, "Séjour de Casanova à Grenoble,"
*Casanova Gleanings*, VIII, 1965.)

11. I have examined the Lisbon archives. The few items that remain of the
correspondence of Almada and Gama contain no allusion to Casanova nor,
for that matter, to the Augsburg Congress.

12. Translation from the German text of Schütz.

13. Haldenwang (*Casanova à Genève*, Paris, 1937, pp. 141, 153-157) has suggested
the identification of Hedwige and that of Mon Repos. If she were Anne May,
born in 1731, she would have been 31 in 1762, and not 22, the age given her
by Casanova, who almost invariably rejuvenated his heroines. Anne is
known to have married Gabriel de Wattenwyl or Watteville or Vatteville
(1734-92) at an unknown date. Casanova says she was the sister-in-law of
Sara Muralt, who also married a Wattenwyl.

14. B. Brunelli, "Avventurieri minori del Settecento, G. Passano," *Archivio
Veneto*, 1933.

15. His name appears as such from Lyons in the *Almanach général des
merchands, négocians et commercants de la France et de l'Europe* in 1772
and 1779, the only years available to us of this reference work.

16. For the text of the letters see F.L. Mars and Yves du Parc, "Casanova chez les
Lyonnais," *Casanova Gleanings*, VI, 1963, and VII, 1964.

17. The original text was published in *Pages Casanoviennes*, Paris, 1925, IV, pp.
15-23, with explanatory notes. The suggested date of the beginning of 1763
was ascribed to the letter, but it is evident from other correspondence that it
was dated early in November 1762.

18.  Casanova has presented the events of his life in Turin during his successive visits out of chronological order, which we have endeavored to restore in the account given of them.

## CHAPTER 10

1.  At least three others among his heroines, Esther, Mme. Dubois, and Pauline, shared his passion for literature.
2.  A. Giulini, *A Milano nel settecento*, Milan, 1926, pp. 99-106. The castle was burned in 1917.
3.  *Casanova Gleanings*, II, 1959.
4.  On May 30, 1768, she was accused of favoring gambling, which was prohibited by law. In 1772 she appears to have enjoyed the protection of Pastoret, King's advocate. The documents concerning her were found by M.J. Billoud, conservator of municipal archives at Marseilles, at the insistence of Ch. Samaran.
5.  As Pontarlier was not on the direct road from Geneva to Aix-en-Provence, it is possible that this is an error for Pont-de-Beauvoisin, on the former frontier between Savoy and France.

## CHAPTER 11

1.  Ch. Samaran, *op. cit.*, p. 267, and communication of Mr. Hardenberg, director of the National Archives of Holland to Ch. Samaran.
2.  Curiously enough, there seems to be a reference to Casanova in the same novel, according to Dr. Mars, to whom I am indebted for this discovery. Smollett attributes the following speech to one of his characters: "I know a low fellow of the same class who, being turned out of Venice for his impudence and scurrility, retired to Lugano, a town of the Grisons (a free people, God wot), where he found a printing press, from which he squirted his filth at some respectable characters in the republic, which he had been obliged to abandon. Some of these, finding him out of the reach of legal chastisement, employed certain useful instruments, such as may be found in all countries, to give him the bastinado; which, being repeated more than once, effectually stopt the current of his abuse." Casanova was in Lugano in 1769, occupied with the printing of his *Confutazione*. While there, he himself administered corporal punishment to a certain Marazzini, with whom he had quarreled at Madrid. It may have been a distorted echo of this on which Smollett based his material; it is certain that from what we know of the circumstances of Casanova's life in Lugano that, far from attacking Venice, he was busy endeavoring to gain the good graces of the Venetian authorities. The particular interest of this citation is the light it throws on Smollett's utilization of material, and the strong inference that parts of *Humphry Clinkier* may have been composed at Leghorn.

3. Casanova states, upon their meeting in Holland late in 1758, that he had had a brief liaison with the mother in Venice in May 1753 and that she gave birth to Sophie at Bayreuth "the last of the year." Sophie could have been a seven-months child, born at the end of December 1753 or in February 1754 at the end of the Venetian year. In either case, she would have been entering her sixth year, as Casanova remarks, when he met her in Holland, in December 1758. As no record has been found of the birth of Sophie Wilhelmine at Bayreuth, the question of Casanova's paternity cannot be answered. If he was her father, it must be assumed that Wilhelmine Friederike Imer, born February 15, 1753, had died.

4. Ch. Samaran, *op. cit.*, pp. 222-224.

5. Bleackley, *op. cit.*; I. Bloch, *Sexual Life in England*, London, 1938, p. 262; Casanova, *Memoirs*, 1903, II, notes pp. 137, 143; Horace Walpole's *Letters*; Archenholz, *A Picture of England*, Dublin, 1791, pp. 245-249; James Taylor, *Records of My Life*, London, 1832, New York, 1833.

6. J.P. Grosley, *Londres*, Lausanne, 1774, I, p. 352.

7. Walpoles, *Letters to Sir Horace Mann*, III, pp. 420-422.

8. *Gentlemen's Guide in His Tour Through France*, London, 1772, p. 214.

9. Archenholz, *A Picture of England*, Dublin, 1791, p. 194; he observes: "It is impossible to form an idea of the gravity with which everything is conducted even in these houses."

10. Archenholz, *op. cit.*, p. 194.

11. Archenholz, *op. cit.*, p. 191.

12. "Vincenzo Martinelli in England," in *Italian Studies*, XI, Cambridge, 1956, pp. 92-107; and a personal communication from Mrs. Thorne to the author.

13. Dresden, 1797, p. 53. Curiously enough, this meeting has escaped the notice of the most eminent of students of Johnson. The first of these to examine it critically has expressed astonishment at the manner in which Casanova succeeded in reproducing in French Johnson's strikingly characteristic manner of speech. (C.W. Stollery, "Casanova's Meeting with Samuel Johnson," *Casanova Gleanings*, VII, 1964.)

14. The author owes to Dr. and Mrs. Hübscher the suggested identification of Casanova with "Nehaus." *Boswell on the Grand Tour: Germany and Switzerland, 1764*, London, 1954, p. 76.

15. According to Archenholz (p. 144), in 1770, d'Eon was Deputy Grand Master of the French lodge of Freemasons.

16. Bleackley, *op. cit.*, p. 141.

17. Bleackley, *op. cit.*, p. 255.

18. Broglie, *Le secret du Roi*, Paris, 1878, II, pp. 556-557, which contains one of the most authoritative accounts of d'Eon, based on official documents. See also II, pp. 94-207, 557-582.

19. *Brinde aos senhores assignantes do diario de noticias em 1881*, Lisbon, 1882, pp. 51-64.

20. The arrests were made on December 12, 1758. One account gives their number as no less than 100, adding that the wives, daughters, and sisters of

the conspirators were sent to convents (Barbier, *Journal*, VII, pp. 124-125, February 1759).

21. For the history of this family of prostitutes of three generations, see Ch. Samaran, *op. cit.*, p. 270, and P. Grellet, *Casanova en Suisse*, Lausanne, 1919, pp. 149-166.

22. The letter refers to Monday the 12th of the month. In 1763 this date fell on a Monday only in September and December. By December there had been a rupture between them.

23. *The Life and Work of Sir John Fielding*, London, 1934.

24. In writing in his *Memoirs* the name "Maisonneuve" instead of the correct name "Chateauneau," Casanova was obviously seeking to reconstitute "new chateau" which he converted into "new house."

25. Marianne Charpillon became in 1773 for four years mistress of the famous John Wilkes, who also assumed financial responsibility for her mother, her grandmother, and one of her aunts. More than a hundred letters from the Charpillon to Wilkes and other correspondents are at the British Museum, Mss. 30880A.

26. *L'espion françois à Londres*, 1780, II, p. 255, where numerous amusing examples are given.

27. A satisfactory account of his life and works remains to be written. That of A. Ademollo, *Un avventuriero francese in Italia* (Bergamo, 1891), is almost exclusively concerned with his life in Italy. Its merit is its bibliography, which is inevitably incomplete. A far more definitive one is F.L. Mars, *Ange Goudar, cet inconnu, Essai bio-bibliographique sur un adventurier polygraphe du XVIII$^e$ siècle*, offprint from *Casanova Gleanings*, IX, 1966, p. 64.

28. *L'espion anglais*, London, 1779, II, p. 363; Louvet de Couvray, *Une année de la vie du chevalier de Faublas*, 1787 (ed. Garnier, p. 89); G.W.M. Reynolds, *The Mysteries of the Court of London*.

29. The three Goudar pamphlets were entitled: *Lettre d'un Français à M. le Duc de Nivernois à Paris, Contre-note ou Lettre à Monsieur le Marquis L. à Paris*, and *Examens des lettres, memoires et negotiations particulieres du Chevalier d'Eon, Ministre Plénipotentiaire de France auprès du Roi de la Grande Bretagne, dans une lettre à M. N.* For this pamphleteering war, see J.B. Telfer, *The Strange Career of the Chevalier d'Eon*, London, 1885, pp. 118, 138, 155. These pamphlets are not in Ademollo's biography.

30. See Telfer, as well as a letter of d'Eon, October 30, 1780 (Catalogue Pierre Cornuau, *Autographes anciens et modernes*, Paris, 1960, p. 17). A large lot of original d'Eon correspondence was sold on June 16, 1960, in Paris, and acquired, for the most part, by the Bibliothèque Nationale. According to d'Eon, a letter of Beaumarchais, purportedly addressed to d'Eon and published by Goudar in his *L'espion françois* (I, p. 264), was the work of Goudar.

31. Grellet, *Casanova en Suisse*, pp. 168-179; Ch. Samaran, *J. Casanova*, pp. 226-228.

32. Chr. Lerch, archivist of the Canton of Berne, has assured us that while there is nothing in the Berne archives to confirm Muralt's return to London, there

is, on the other hand, nothing that would invalidate such a supposition.

33. In at least two other instances women in the *Memoirs* are described as widows, namely Cecilia "Monti" in 1744 and "Henriette" in 1763, when their husbands appear to have been alive. This device may have been adopted for their better disguise.

34. Remarked also by J.P. Grosley, *Londres*, I, p. 124.

35. Bleackley, *Casanova in England*, pp. 41-43; Walpole, *op. cit.*, II, p. 480; Casanova, *Memoirs*, London, 1902, II, p. 156, note, an edition republished by the Navarre Society in 1922 and very useful for its annotations.

## CHAPTER 12

1. Restif de la Bretonne, *Les contemporaines*, XXXVII, Paris, 1784, p. 362. According to Dr. Mars, this practice seems to have been employed in order to prevent knowledge being gained by others of a treatment that was highly personal to the physician in the eighteenth century.

2. Casanova presumably had access to the French translation of Pope's *Iliad* in 1758, with notes.

3. J.F. Malcolm, *Anecdotes of the Manners and Customs of London in the Eighteenth Century*, II, p. 348.

4. Ilges, "Casanova in Berlin," *Mitteilungen des Vereins für die Geschichte Berlins*, Berlin, 1931, p. 90.

5. D. Thiebault, *Frédéric le Grand*, Paris, 1826, IV, pp. 94-95.

6. Lalande, *Voyage en Italie*, 1769, VIII, p. 516; Goldoni, *Mémoires*, 1822, I, p. 168; P. Molmenti, *Venice*, part III, vol. I, London, 1908, p. 173.

7. *Mon voyage en Prusse*, Paris, 1807, pp. 82-83. Dutens was an international figure similar to Paterson and Keith. Although French (a Protestant), he represented Great Britain for a time at the Sardinian court in Turin (*Mémoires d'un voyageur qui se repose*, London, 1806, 3 vols.)

8. E. Robins, *Our First Ambassador to China*, p. 21.

9. Mooser, *Annales*, II; Sirène ed. X, p. 327.

10. Princess Dashkov in her *Memoirs* confirms that Catherine did not care for music: *Memoirs of Princess Dashkov*, edited by Kyril Fitzlyon, London, 1958, p. 91, the latest and most complete edition.

11. It remains still unpublished, and the author has been informed by Mr. F.A. Brockhaus that there is no present intention to print it.

12. Moszynski, Grand Master of Polish Freemasons, alchemist, and architect, was a grandson of August II (1697-1733) of Poland through the latter's natural daughter, the celebrated Countess Cosel. See T. Mankowski, *August Moszynsky*, Cracow, 1928. [sic]

13. "Further Light on Casanova from Polish Archives," *Casanova Gleanings*, VIII, 1965, pp. 16-21; V. Cerný, "Les 'Polonica' du fond Casanova en Bohême," extract from *Mélanges de littérature comparée et de philologie, offerts à Mieczslaw Brahmer*, Paris-Warsaw, 1967, pp. 119-126.

14. It was Moszynski's father-in-law, Count Potocki, whom Casanova visited at

Christianpol, although Moszynski makes no reference to this in his report to the King.

15. The translation is that of Sir John Harington, *Orlando Furioso*, London, 1607, 18th Book, stanzas 1 and 2, p. 137.

16. The full text of the five documents cited will be found in *Casanova Gleanings*, IV, 1961, and VII, 1965.

17. Also see *Wienerisches Diarium*, April 9, 1766; *Vossische Zeitung*, No. 37, 1766; *Kaiserliche Reichs-Oberpostamtszeitung* of Cologne, March 29, 1766; *Ordinario Relationis Diariae Continuatio*, Cologne, Nos. 25 and 27, 1766.

18. E. Massi, *La vita, i tempi, gli amici di Francesco Albergati*, Bologna, 1878, p. 197; Cesarotti, *Epistolario*, Florence, 1811, I, pp. 41, 47.

## CHAPTER 13

1. Thiebault, *op. cit.*, II, p. 247.

2. Commentators—in particular, Gugitz—have seized on Casanova's account of Schwerin's arrest in 1766 and his subsequent incarceration at Spandau as an example of his untrustworthiness. It is evident that the arrest to which Casanova refers in 1766 was quite other than that of 1767.

3. *Pages Casanoviennes*, Paris, 1925, III, pp. 67-69.

4. Sirène ed. X, p. 349.

5. Wraxall, *Memoirs*, 1799, II, p. 320.

6. Carra, *Mémoires historiques et authentiques sur la Bastille*, London, 1789, III, pp. 202-211.

7. Ilges, *Aachener Geschichtvereins-Zeitschrift*, Aachen, 1932, vol. 53, pp. 80-117.

8. *Tableau de Spa*, 1782, n.p., pp. 16, 19-21, 30, 33-39, 46, 52.

9. That Croce did proceed to Warsaw appears indicated by a letter from Baron Boussoni from that city on June 8, 1768, to Casanova.

10. *L'Espagne éclairée*, Paris, 1954.

11. *Mémoires*, Paris, 1944, I, p. 326.

12. *Pages Casanoviennes*, IV, p. 39.

13. A. Hamilton, *A Study of Spanish Manners*, p. 37.

14. Both Beliardi and Olivades are the subject of notices in the *Mémoires* of Dufort de Cheverny, which confirm many of Casanova's details.

15. The duke was the famous Biron, father of the Prince de Courland, and when Casanova met him was aged seventy-four. After having been the lover of the Empress Anna of Russia, he became briefly Regent of Russia on her death in 1740, but that same year was exiled to Siberia. Recalled by Czar Peter III in 1762, he was restored to his title of duke in 1764. Such was the glamour he conveyed that his memory was still fresh in Russia before World War I, as evidenced by the eighteenth-century verses commemorating him, which the author's wife was taught as a child by her mother: "Quand Biron voulet danser, / Sa chemise fut apportée, / Sa chemise de Venise, / Ses manchettes,

mignonettes, / Ses souliers tout ronds. / Nous danserons Biron." ("When Biron wanted to dance, / They brought him his shirt, / His shirt from Venice, / His sleeves of lace, / His round shoes. / We dance Biron.")

16. For these various projects see *Pages Casanoviennes*, III, pp. 24-27; IV, p. 25; E. von Schmidt-Pauli, *Der andere Casanova*, Berlin; 1930, pp. 303-331; and for the Sierra Morena colony, the references given in Sirène ed. XI, p. 315.

17. Gorani, *Mémoires*, Paris, 1944, I, pp. 298, 300-302.

18. Letter from the Casanova archives in possession of the author.

19. The discovery of this hitherto unknown and unpublished document is due initially to the remarkable flair of Dr. F.L. Mars. Observing reference to it in Bono's holograph letter, he appealed to Count du Parc, of Lyons, to endeavor to track it down. M. du Parc, eminent man of letters and adept at research, was so intrigued by the problem that he resolved to find it if he had to turn over the records of every notary in Lyons. However, these were so well classified in the Rhône departmental archives that the document was found in half an hour. For the original, see *Casanova Gleanings*, VIII, 1964.

20. Of Passano's end we know only that he died in misery at Genoa after 1770.

21. P.N. Chantreau, *Lettres écrites de Barcelone*, Paris, 1792, p. 171, republished in Ch. Samaran, *Jacques Casanova*, p. 410.

22. For the text of the letters see *Casanova Gleanings*, II, 1959.

23. Thanks are due to P.E. Reeks, deputy chief passport officer, London, who kindly caused extensive researches to be made of past British passport practices. For a more extended examination of these, see *Casanova Gleanings*, II, 1959.

24. Another example is offered by Norman Himes, who has stated that it is from Casanova alone that we learn of the use in the eighteenth century of a gold ball as a contraceptive (*Medical History of Contraception*, Baltimore, 1936, cited by H. Bergues, *La Prévention des naissances dans la famille*, Paris, 1960, pp. 62-63). The reliance these two scholarly publications place on Casanova's testimony is a reflection of the growing recognition of his historical accuracy.

## CHAPTER 14

1. For the correspondence see *Casanova Gleanings*, II, 1959, and IV, 1961.

2. According to *The Pembroke Papers (1734-1780), Letters and Diaries of Henry, Tenth Earl of Pembroke* (London, 1942, p. 71), Lynch served as minister to Turin from 1768 to 1779. Lady Pembroke described him as having "a very light character, improper to guide young men."

3. Unpublished letter from the Casanova archives.

4. For text see *Le Livre*, Paris, 1881, p. 45; and Sirène ed., XI, p. 330.

5. E. Mola, *Le Livre*, 1884, p. 68.

6. N.W. Wraxall, *Mémoires historiques*, Paris, 1817, I, p. 187. Archenholz also confirms this detail and adds that, charged by Orloff with outfitting the

Russian fleet, Dick made a profit of half a million pounds.

7.　P. Molmenti, *Carteggi Casanoviani*, Milan, 1916.

8.　The incident is found in B. Croce, *Aneddoti e profili*, Milan, 1922, p. 73; H. Swinburne, *Courts of Europe*, London, 1841, I, p. 134. Count Lamberg mentions it in a letter dated August 4, 1787, to Casanova.

9.　The question has been examined at some length in my *Casanoviana*, Vienna, 1956, pp. 37-42.

10.　Gorani, *Mémoires secrets*, I, p. 18. The King's predeliction for tossing his subjects in blankets is confirmed also by Mann (II, p. 213) and Wraxall, *Mémoires historiques*, p. 143, and others.

11.　My thanks are due to C.R. Dowes for the reference. See his *Marquis de Sade*, London, 1927, p. 95. The episode is found in *Juliette*, 1797, IX, p. 308 (ed. Pauvert, 1954, V, p. 234).

12.　Sirène, ed. XI, p. 340, and the references therein cited; D'Ancona, *Nuova antologia*, 1882, p. 423; Lamberg, *Mémorial d'un mondain*, 1774, p. 126; and Tipaldo, *Biog. del sec. XVIII*, II, p. 104.

13.　Letter of June 14, 1774, to Prince Lubomirski (*Patrizi e avventurieri*, p. 171). The *Correspondance inédite du roi Stanislas Auguste* (Paris, 1875, pp. 304-305) mentions that Lee left Warsaw in 1767.

14.　Michael Kelly, who met her at Palermo some years later, described her as "one of the most beautiful women of her day, and a fine singer" (*Reminiscenses*, I, p. 83.)

15.　Valeri, *Casanova a Roma*, pp. 39-41. See Sirène ed. XII, pp. 241-242.

16.　John Taylor, *Records of My Life*, London, 1832, pp. 14, 19-23 (grandson of the oculist).

17.　Doran, *"Mann" and Manners at the Court of Florence, 1740-1786*, London, 1876, II, p. 232; C. Bandini, *Roma e la nobilità romana*, 1914, p. 151; Gorani, *Mémoires secrets*, II, pp. 149, 186-190; Cheke, *The Cardinal de Bernis*.

18.　Von Gleichen, *Souvenirs*, Paris, 1868, p. 32; Cheke, *op. cit.*, p. 224.

19.　Valeri, *op. cit.*, p. 50; Ademollo, *Fanfulla della Domenica*, March 18, 1885. There is an excellent account of the academy in H.C. Chatfield-Taylor's *Goldoni*, New York, 1913, p. 153.

20.　Published in "Roma per il Casaletti" under the title of *I pregi delle belle arti celebrati in Campidiglio del solenne concorso tenuto dall' insigne accademia del disegno in San Luca li 21 Aprile 1771. Reggendone il principato il Sig. Cavaliere D. Antonio Rafaele Mengs*, p. 84.

21.　*Supplément a l'exposition raisonnée*, pp. 28-29.

22.　Doran, *op. cit.*, II, p. 234.

23.　*Mémoires secrets*, II, pp. 210-214.

24.　A. Baschet, *Les archives de Venise*, Paris, 1870, p. 641.

25.　The manuscript text of a fourth volume of 154 pp. has recently come to light in the Casanova archives in Czechoslovakia.

26.　In the eighteenth century, the appearance of the author's name on the title page of a published work was the exception rather than the rule. Of Casanova's twenty-odd published works, his name appears on only six of those published during his lifetime.

27. *Katherina II*, Berlin, 1897, I, pp. 231-235.
28. It must be remembered that in the eighteenth century the territory of the Venetian Republic comprised not only the present lagoons but extended some distance into the mainland.

## CHAPTER 15

1. Faro, said to date from the thirteenth century, had reached its apogee of popularity in Casanova's day. It was played between a banker and an unlimited number of players, and wagers might be laid on one or more cards. The banker drew successively two at a time, one of which he placed face-up to his right, and the other to his left. If two cards, thus exposed, were not representative of the same figure or number, the card exposed on the banker's right entitled him to all the wagers made on that while having to make good those bets on the left. If the two cards were the same figure or number, the banker was entitled to all the wagers made on the card to his right and half of the sum risked on his left.
2. Ange Goudar, *Histoire des Grecs ou de ceux qui corrigent la fortune au jeu*, The Hague, 1757, p. 4.
3. Brandes, *Voltaire*, New York, 1930, II, p. 37.
4. *Boswell on the Grand Tour: Germany and Switzerland*, p. 111.
5. *Casanova Gleanings*, I, 1958, p. 19.

## CHAPTER 16

1. For this letter see *Pages Casanoviennes*, III, pp. 34-37.
2. For full text see *Pages Casanoviennes*, VIII, p. i-vii.

## CHAPTER 17

1. The first was a *Lettre historico-critique* published under date of May 12, 1784. A series of unsigned articles by Casanova followed, on the same subject, in the *Osservatore Triestino* between January 22 and February 26, 1785. Shortly thereafter, he published *Exposition raisonnée, Lettre à Messieurs Jean et Étienne L(uzac)*, editors of the *Gazette de Leyde*, who had defended the official Dutch viewpoint, and finally *Supplément á l'Exposition raisonnée*.
2. *Histoire de la vie et des aventures de la Duchesse de Kingston . . . À* laquelle on a joint une notice curieuse sur Stefano Zannovich, *prétendu Prince Castriotto d'Albanie*, London, 1789; E. Van Biema, "Stiepan Annibale, Prince d'Albanie, Un aventurier, au XVIII$^e$ siècle," *La Nouvelle Revue*, Paris, 1898, pp. 488-518, 683-700; 1899, pp. 88-107.

3.  Commentators of Da Ponte's memoirs have almost without exception remarked upon their untrustworthiness. The best edition of Da Ponte in English is that edited by A. Livingston, Philadelphia, 1929; a very readable biography is that of A. Fitzlyon, *The Libertine Librettist*, London, 1955.
4.  The most detailed examination is that of Paul Nettl, "Casanova and 'Don Giovanni'" in the *Saturday Review*, New York, January 28, 1956.
5.  The vast accumulation of his other manuscripts, comprising in the neighborhood of 8,000 pages, was preserved for many years in the Waldstein castle at Dux. With the nationalization decrees of the Czechoslovakian state they passed into possession of that government and are now deposited in the Czechoslovakian archives at Mnichové Hradiště near Prague.

# *Selected Bibliography*

This bibliography includes works by Casanova and important publications concerning Casanova. It does not include all of the many works to which ad hoc reference is made in the text and in the (more than 250) footnotes.

## 1. BIBLIOGRAPHY

Childs, J. Rives, *Casanoviana, An Annotated World Bibliography of Casanova and of Works Concerning Him,* Vienna, 1956. Supplements have been published in *Casanova Gleanings,* Nice, beginning in 1958.

## 2. PRINCIPLE PUBLISHED WORKS OF CASANOVA

### a. *Individual Publications*

*Zoroastro, Tragedia tradotta del francese,* Dresden, 1752.
"Camille Veronese" (Madrigal) in *Mercure de France,* April 1757.
*Confutazione della storia del Governo Veneto d'Amelot de la Houssaie,* Amsterdam [Lugano], 1769, 3 vols.
"Sonetto sulla statua in Campidoglio" in *I pregi delle belle arte,* Rome, 1771.
*Lana Caprina,* Bologna, 1772. French translation in *Pages Casanoviennes.* V, Paris, 1925.

*L'armonia*, Trieste, 1773. Occasional poem.

*Applausi*, Trieste, 1773. Occasional poem.

*À l'occasion de la fête du glorieux Saint Adolphe*, Trieste, 1773.

*Felicità di Trieste. Cantata a tre voci*, Trieste, 1774.

*Istoria delle turbolenze della Polonia dalla morte di Elisabetta Petrowna fino alla pace fra la Russia e la Porta Ottomana*, Gorizia, 1774, 3 vols. Including a 4th vol. that Casanova left as ms., published in Padua (Marsilio), 1974.

"Sonetto" in *Gazetta Goriziana*, December 8, 1774.

*Dell'Iliade de Omero, tradotta in ottava rima*, Venice, 1775-78, 3 vols.

*Scrutinio del libro "Éloges de M. de Voltaire,"* Venice, 1779.

*Opuscoli miscellanei*, January 1779 (1780) to July 1780, 7 parts. The French translation of "Il Duello" (June 1780) reprinted in *Pages Casanoviennes*, II, 1925.

*Lettere della Nobil Donna Silvia Belegno alla Nobil Donzella Laura Gussoni*, Venice, 1780. Adaptation by Mme. Riccobin, *Lettres de miladi Catesby*. New ed. by Fogola Ed., Turin, 1975, 8 vols.

*Le messager de Thalie*, Venice, October 1780 to January 1781, 11 numbers. Reprinted in *Pages Casanoviennes*, I, 1925.

*Di aneddoti Veneziani*, Venice, 1782. Adaptation by Mme. de Tencin, *Le siège de Calais*, 1739.

*Né amori, né donne, ovvero la stalla ripulita*, Venice, 1783. French translation in *Pages Casanoviennes*, VIII, 1925.

*Vers publiés à Spa*, August 19, 1783.

*Lettre historico-critique . . .* , Hamburg, May 12, 1784.

Six untitled and unsigned articles in *L'Osservatore Triestino*, January 22 to February 26, 1785, concerning a dispute between Holland and Venice.

*Exposition raisonnée du différend qui subsiste entre les deux républiques de Venise et d'Hollande*, 1784. Reprinted 1785. Italian translation, *Esposizione ragionata . . .* , 1785.

*Lettres à Messieurs Jean et Étienne L.*, 1785. Italian translation; *Lettere ai Signori Giovanni e Stefano Luzac*, 1785. French text reissued in the Hague, 1785. Dutch translation: *Brief van eenen Venetiaan aan de Heeren J. en E. L.*, Utrecht, 1785.

*Supplément à l'Exposition raisonnée*, 1785. Italian translation: *Supplemento alla esposizione ragionata . . .* , 1785.

*Soliloque d'un penseur*, Prague, 1786. Reprinted in *Pages Casanoviennes*, VII, 1925.

*Histoire de ma fuite des prisons de la République de Venise, qu'on appelle les Plombs*, Leipzig [Prague], 1788 [1787].

*Icosameron ou l'histoire d'Edouard et Elisabeth qui passèrent quatre vingt un ans chez les Megamicres habitans aborigènes du Protocosme dans l'intérieur de notre globe*, Prague, 1790 [1788]. Recent English translation: *Icosameron, or the Story of Edward and Elizabeth Who Spent 81 Years in the Land of the Megamicres, Original Inhabitants of Protocosmos in the Interior of*

*Our Globe* (translated by Rachel Zurer), Jenna Press, New York, 1985.
*Solution du problème déliaque,* Dresden, 1790.
*Corollaire à la duplication de l'hexaèdre,* Dresden, 1790.
*Démonstration géometrique de la duplication du cube,* Dresden, 1790.
*À Leonard Snetlage,* Dresden, 1797. Casanova's etymological work.

## b. Coauthored Works

Goudar, Ange. *L'espion chinois,* Cologne, 1765, 6 vols. *The Chinese Spy,* London, 1765, 6 vols.; Dublin, 1766.
Piazza, Antonio. *Discorso all'orecchio di Monsieur Louis Goudar,* Venice, 1766.

## c. Memoirs

*Aus den Memoiren des Venetianers Jacob Casanova de Seingalt, oder sein Leben, wie er es zu Dux in Böhmen neiderschrieb,* ed. from the original French ms. by Wilhelm von Schütz, Leipzig (F. A. Brockhaus), 1822-28, 12 vols.
*Mémoires du Venitien J. Casanova de Seingalt,* Paris (Tournachon-Molin), 1825-29, 14 vols. Pirated and distorted translation of the (foregoing) Brockhaus edition.
*Mémoires de J. Casanova de Seingalt, écrits par lui-même,* Leipzig (F. A. Brockhaus), Paris (Ponthieu et Comp.), 1826-38, 12 vols. Adaptation by Jean Laforgue. Until 1960 the most popular and most reprinted text.
*Mémoires de Jacques Casanova de Seingalt,* Paris (Paulin), 1833-37, 10 vols. Reprinted by Rozez, Brussels, 1860-67, 6 vols., and by Flammarion, Paris, 1899-1928, 6 vols. The so-called Busoni text.
*The Memoirs of Jacques Casanova Written by Himself, Now for the First Time Translated into English* (by Arthur Machen), privately printed, London, 1894, 12 vols. Numerous reprints.
*Erinnerungen,* translated and introduced by Heinrich Conrad, Munich and Leipzig (Müller), 1907-13, 15 vols. Invaluable for the notes and supplements, a monument of German erudition.
*Mémoires de J. Casanova de Seingalt, Nouvelle édition publiée sous la direction de Raoul Vèze, d'après le texte de l'édition princeps,* Leipzig-Brussels-Paris, 1826-38. *Variantes et commentaires historiques et critiques,* Paris (La Sirène), 1924-35, 12 vols. The introductions to each volume and the copious notes, however outmoded some of these have become in the light of subsequent research, will always give value to this monument of French erudition. The text and notes, in part, were published, in a translation by Arthur Machen, by the Limited Editions Club, New York, 1940, 8 vols.
*Histoire de ma vie, Édition intégrale,* Wiesbaden (F. A. Brockhaus), Paris (Librairie Plon), 1960-62, 12 vols. The first publication of the original text of Casanova.

*History of My Life,* first translation into English (by Willard R. Trask) in accordance with the original French ms., New York, 1966-71, 12 vols.
*Life and Memoirs of Casanova* (translated by Arthur Machen, ed. by George Gribble), New York, 1984, 1985. Not the authentic text.

## 3. CORRESPONDENCE

No attempt has ever been made to unify Casanova's correspondence. The most important collections of his letters are noted below.
*Briefwechsel* (vol. 15 of *Erinnerungen;* see under "Memoirs" above), ed. by Aldo Ravà and Gustav Gugitz, Munich, 1913.
*Carteggi Casanoviani,* Palermo, 1916, 1919, 2 vols., ed. by Pompeo Molmenti.
*Casanova Gleanings,* Nice, ed. by J. Rives Childs from 1958 to 1973, by F. L. Mars since 1974.
*Casanova und Graf Lamberg,* Vienna, 1935, ed. by Gustav Gugitz; Otten, 1935.
*Correspondance avec J. F. Opiz,* Leipzig, 1913, 2 vols., ed. by František Khol and Otto Pick. German translation: Berlin, 1922.
*Epistolario, 1759-1798,* Milan (Longanesi), 1969, ed. by Piero Chiara.
*Lettere di donne a G. Casanova,* Milan, 1912, ed. by Aldo Ravà. Incomplete French translation (by Édouard Maynial): *Lettres de femmes à J. Casanova,* Paris, 1912.
*Pages Casanoviennes,* Paris, 1925-26, III-VIII ed. by Joseph Pollio and Raoul Vèze.
*Patrizi e avventurieri,* Milan, 1930, ed. by Carlo L. Curiel, Gustav Gugitz, and Aldo Ravà.
*Vermischte Schriften,* Berlin (Propyläen-Verlag), 1971, ed. by E. Straub.

## 4. WORKS CONCERNING CASANOVA

### a. Biographies and Appreciations

Bàccolo, L. *Casanova e i suoi amici,* Milan, 1972.
Buck, Mitchell. *The Life of Casanova,* Studies in Italian Literature No. 46, New York (Haskell), 1977.
Childs, J. Rives. *Casanova, A Biography Based on New Documents,* 1961. Translated into German (1960), Italian (1962), French (1962—a revised and enlarged edition of the original English text), and Japanese (1968).
Childs, J. Rives. *Casanova, Eine Biographie,* Munich (Blanvalet Verlag), 1977.
Childs, J. Rives. *Casanova Gleanings* (see under "Correspondence" above).
Dobrée, B. *Giacomo Casanova, Chevalier de Seingalt,* London and New York, 1933. German translation: Hamburg, 1934.
Ellis, Havelock. *Affirmations,* London, 1898.
Endore, S. Guy. *Casanova, His Known and Unknown Life,* New York, 1929.

Frenzi, Giulio de. *L'Italiano errante*, Naples, 1913.

Furlan, F. *Casanova et sa fortune littéraire*, Saint-Médard-en-Jalles, 1971.

Gamba, B. *Biografia di Giacomo Casanova*, Venice, 1835.

Gervaso, Roberto. *Casanova*, Milan, 1974.

Guède, A. *Casanova*, Paris, 1912.

Gugitz, Gustav. *Giacomo Casanova und sein Lebensroman, Historische Studien zu seinen Memoiren*, Vienna, 1921.

Haeuptner, Gerhard. *Giacomo Casanova, Versuch über die abenteuerliche Existenz*, Meisenheim, 1956.

Kesten, Hermann. *Casanova*, Munich, 1952.

Kesten, Hermann. *Die Lust am Leben*, Munich, 1970.

Koch, Thilo. *Casanova, Ein Versuch*, Munich, 1959.

Le Gras, Joseph, and Raoul Vèze. *Casanova*, Paris, 1930 ("Les grandes vies aventureuses").

Le Gras, Joseph. *Le véritable Casanova*, Paris, 1950.

Marceau, Félicien. *Casanova ou l'anti-Don Juan*, Paris, 1949.

Masters, John. *Casanova*, New York, 1969.

Maynial, Édouard. *Casanova et son temps*, Paris, 1910. English translation: *Casanova and His Time*, London, 1911.

Nettl, Paul. *Casanova und seine Zeit, Zur Kultur- und Musikgeschichte des 18. Jahrhunderts*, Esslingen, 1949.

Nettl, Paul. *The Other Casanova*, New York, 1950.

Ottmann, Viktor. *Jacob Casanova von Seingalt, Sein Leben und seine Werke, nebst Casanovas Tragikomödie "Das Polemoskop,"* Stuttgart, 1900.

Perrault, Gilles. *Casanova*, Paris, 1963.

Polišensky, Josef (ed.). *Giacomo Casanova histoire mého zivota*, Prague, 1968.

Powell, L. C. G. *Casanova*, Pasadena, 1948. Reprinted in *Islands of Books*, Los Angeles, 1951.

Samaran, Charles. *Jacques Casanova, Une vie d'aventurier au XVIII$^e$ siècle*, Paris, 1914. Reissued 1931.

Schmitz, Oscar A. H. *Don Juan, Casanova und andere erotische Charaktere*, Munich, 1913.

Schnitzler, Arthur. *Casanova's Homecoming*, New York (AMS Press), reprint of 1930 (translated by Eden Paul and Paul Cedar).

Zottoli, Angelandrea. *Giacomo Casanova*, Rome, 1945, 2 vols.

Zweig, Stefan. *Drei Dichter ihres Lebens: Casanova, Stendhal, Tolstoy*, Leipzig, 1928. Reprinted in Zweig, *Baumeister de Welt*, Frankfurt, 1951.

## b. Individual Studies

Abirached, R. *Casanova ou la dissipation*, Paris, 1961.

Ademollo, A. *Corilla Olimpica*, Florence, 1887.

Ademollo, A. "Testo dell'Histoire de ma vie del Casanova e la veracità dell sue Memorie" in *Fanfulla della Domenica*, December 17, 1882.

Adnesse, J. F. M. *Casanova après ses mémoires*, Bordeaux, 1919.

Ambesi, A. C. *Storia della massoneria,* Milan, 1971.

Ancona, Alessandro d'. "Un avventuriero del secolo XVIII" in *Nuova antologia,* I, 1882. Reprinted in d'Ancona, *Viaggiatori e avventurieri,* Florence, 1911.

Bàccolo, L., and P. Chiara. *Casanova erotico, illustrato dal Chauvet,* Milan, 1975.

Bàccolo, L. *Casanova e i suoi amici,* Milan, 1972.

Bailly, A. *La Sérénissime République de Venise,* Paris, 1958.

Barthold, Friedrich Wilhelm. *Die geschichtlichen Persönlichkeiten in Jacob Casanovas Memoiren,* Berlin, 1846, 2 vols.

Barzini, L. *Gli italiani,* Milan, 1965.

Baschet, Armand. "Preuves curieuses de l'authenticité des Mémoires de Jacques Casanova" in *Le Livre,* 1881.

Beck, Art. *Enlightenment: Shorthand for a Scurrilous Life (The Rediscovered Poems of Giacomo Casanova),* (Invisible-Red Hill) 1977.

Belgrano, L. T. *Aneddoti e ritratti casanoviani,* Turin, 1889.

Bleackley, Horace. *Casanova in England,* London, 1923.

Bocchi, A. *Brani di storia parmigiana,* Parma, 1922.

Botta, A. "Scoperto in Polonia un inedito de famoso avventuriero: Casanova racconta" in *L'Europeo,* December 14, 1967.

Bozzòla, A. *Casanova illuminista,* Modena, 1965.

Bozzolato, G. *Proposta per una revisione storiografica: Giacomo Casanova,* Bari, 1967.

Bozzolato, G. *Polonia e Russia alla fine del XVIII secolo,* Padua, 1964.

Brunelli, B. *Un'amica di Casanova,* Palermo, 1924. English translation: *Casanova Loved Her,* London, 1929.

Brunelli, B. "Il duello di Casanova" in *Fanfulla della Domenica,* March 29, 1914.

Brunelli, B. "I compagni di Giacomo Casanova sotto i Piombi," in *Rivista italiana,* June 1914.

Brunelli, B. "Figurine Padovane" and "Un mistero Casanoviano svelato" in *Atti e memorie della R. Ac. di Padova,* 1933-34, 1938.

Brunetti, M. "La fuga di G. Casanova in una narrazione contemporanea" in *Nuovo archivio,* Venice, 1917.

Bruno, F. *La scapigliatura napoletana e meridionale,* Naples, 1971.

Bull, Tage. "La véracité des Mémoires" in *Pages Casanoviennes,* II, Paris, 1925.

Bull, Tage. "Le style de Casanova" in *Pages Casanoviennes,* III, Paris, 1925.

Bull, Tage. "Le vrai texte des Memoires de Casanova" in *Pages Casanoviennes,* IV, Paris, 1925.

Capon, Gaston. *Casanova à Paris, Ses séjours par lui-même, avec notes, additions et commentaires,* Paris, 1913.

Cassirer, E. *La filosofia dell'illuminismo,* Florence, 1935.

Chiara, Piero. *Saggi, libelli e satire de Giacomo Casanova,* Milan, 1968.

Comisso, G. *Agenti segreti veneziani,* Milan, n.d.

Compigny des Bordes, A. *Casanova et la Marquise d'Urfé*, Paris, 1928.

Contini, Erman. "Uomo di teatro" in *Rivista italiana del dramma*, Milan, 1939.

Craveri, R. *Voltaire politico dell'illuminismo*, Turin, 1937.

Croce, Benedetto. "Un amico napoletano di Casanova" in *Fanfulla della Domenica*, November 12, 1890.

Croce, Benedetto. "Il falso Bellino" in *Letteratura*, V, No. 5, March 1, 1890.

Croce, Benedetto. "Sara Goudar a Napoli" in *Lettere e arti*, Bologna, June 14, 1890.

Croce, Benedetto. *Aneddoti di varia letteratura*, Naples, 1924, 3 vols.

Cucuel, Georges. "La musique et les musiciens dans les Mémoires de Casanova" in *Revue du dix-huitième siècle*, Paris, 1913.

Curiel, Carlo L. "Casanova le séducteur" in *Mercure de France*, 1921.

Curiel, Carlo L. *Trieste settecentesca*, Milan, 1922.

Curiel, Carlo L. "Friuli nei Mémoires di G. Casanova: in *Ce Fastu*, Udine, 1933.

Damerini, G. "Sulle orme di Giacomo Casanova" in *Gazetta di Venezia*, January 6, 1912.

Damerini, G. *Casanova a Venezia dopo il primo esilio*, Turin, 1957.

Da Ponte, L. *Memoirs*, Philadelphia, 1929.

Dewar, G. *The Unlocked Secret, Freemasonry Examined*, London, 1966.

De Wyzeva, T. "Un épisode de la vieillesse de Casanova" in *Revue des deux mondes*, Paris, March 1914.

Dobrée, B. *Three Eighteenth Century Figures: Sarah Churchill—John Wesley—Giacomo Casanova*, London, 1962.

Dolcetti, G. "La Fuga di G. Casanova dai Piombi di Venezia" in *Nuovo archivo veneto*, 1914.

Eustache, E. *Casanova et ses Mémoires, Étude medico-historique*, Paris, 1929.

Fay, B. *La massoneria e la rivoluzione intellettuale del secolo XVIII*, Turin, 1945.

Fleuret, F. "Autour de Casanova" in *Pages Casanoviennes*, IV, Paris, 1925.

Frati, L. "Lana Caprina di G. Casanova" in *Letteratura*, 1890.

Frati, L. *Il Settecento a Bologna*, Milan, 1913.

Frati, L. "Casanova a Bologna" in *Nuova antologia*, August 1, 1922.

Fulin, Rinaldo. *Cinque scritture di G. Casanova*, Venice, 1869.

Fulin, Rinaldo. "Casanova e gl'Inquisitori di Stato" in *Atti dell'istituto veneto*, 1877.

Giacomo, Salvatore di. "Casanova a Napoli" in *Nuova antologia*, 1922.

Giardini, C. *I grandi avventurieri*, Milan, 1966.

Giulini, A. *A Milano nel settecento*, Milan, 1926.

Givry, G. de. "La Kabbale de J. Casanova" in *La Sirène*, III, 1916.

Glaser, Hugo. *Der Fall Casanova*, Vienna, 1946 ("Bibliophile Zeit- und Streitfragen," 3).

Grellet, Pierre. *Un amis vandois de Casanova* (L. de Bravois), Montreux, 1940.

Grellet, Pierre. *Les aventures de Casanova en Suisse*, Lausanne, 1919.

Haldenwang, Georges. *Casanova à Genève*, Paris, 1937.

Henry, Charles. *Les connaissances mathématiques de Jacques Casanova de Seingalt*, Rome, 1883 (1882).

Henry, Charles. "J. Casanova de Seingalt et la critique historique" in *Revue historique*, 1889.

Ilges, F. Walter. *Casanova in Köln*, Cologne, 1926.

Jonard, N. *La vie quotidienne à Venise au XVIII$^e$ siècle*, Paris. 1965.

Lancey, C. ver Heyden de. "Les portraits de Jacques et de François Casanova" in *Gazette des beaux-arts*, 1934.

Lanza, M. *Di G. Casanova e delle sue Memorie*, Venice, 1877.

Le Gras, J. *L'extravagante personnalité de Jacques Casanova*, Paris, 1923.

Ligne, Charles de. "Fragment sur Casanova" and "Aventuros" in *Oeuvres*, Vienna, 1795-1809. Reprinted in *Mélanges anecdotiques, littéraires et politiques*, Paris, 1933, and as appendixes of many editions of the *Mémoires*.

Mahler, A. "Catalogue des manuscripts de Casanova conservés au Château de Dux" in *Revue des bibliothéques*, Paris, 1905, vol. 15.

Marsan, Eugène. *Les femmes de Casanova*, Paris, 1924.

Marsan, J. *Sur le pas de Casanova à Venise*, Paris 1962.

Maynial, Édward, and Raoul Vèze. *La fin d'un aventurier: Casanova après les Mémories*, Paris, 1952.

Meccoli, S. "Ritrovato vicino a Praga un manoscritto di Casanova storico" in *Corriere della sera*, August 1, 1967.

Messadaglia, L. "Giacomo Casanova e Merlin Cocai" in *Nuovo archivo veneto*, 1938.

Meucci, C. *Casanova finanziere*, Milan, 1932.

Mola, E. "Giacomo Casanova e la Repubblica di Venezia" in *Rivista europea*, 1881, vol. 23.

Molmenti, Pompeo. *Epistolari veneziani nel secolo XVIII*, Milan, 1914.

Monnier, P. *Venise au XVIII$^e$ siècle*, Paris, 1907.

Morgulis, Gregoire. "Musset et Casanova" in *Revue des études italiennes*, 1956.

Nettl, Paul. "Casanova and 'Don Giovanni'" in *Saturday Review*, No. 4, New York, January 28, 1956.

Nettl, Paul. "Casanova and the Dance" in *Dance*, New York, 1945.

Nettl, Paul. "Casanova and Music" in *The Musical Quarterly*, New York, 1929.

Nicolini, Fausto. "Giacomo Casanova e il Cardinale Acquaviva d'Aragona" in *Artusa*, 1945.

Ottmann, Viktor. "Casanovas Werke und seine literarische Hinterlassenschaft" in *Zeitschrift für Bücherfreunde*, 1897-98.

Pollio, Joseph. *Casanova et la Révolution*, published by the Société de l'Historie de la Révolution Française.

Poritzky, E. "Jakob Casanova" in *Zeitgeist, Beilage zum Berliner Tagblatt*, Berlin, April 22, 1907.

Parti, L. *Il settecento a Bologna*, Milan, 1913.

Ramperti, Marco. *Casanova réhabilité*, Paris, 1961.

Ravà, Aldo. *La musa dialettale di Giacomo Casanova*, Venice, 1911.

Ravà, Aldo. "Casanova a Lugano" in *Bollettino storico della Svizzera italiana*, 1911.

Ravà, Aldo. "Come furono pubblicate le Memorie di Casanova" in *Marzocco*, November 13, 1910.

Ravà, Aldo. "Novissimi studi casanoviani" in *Marzocco*, May 10, 1914.

Ravà, Aldo. "Le opere pubblicate da G. Casanova" in *Marzocco*, October 9, 1910.

Ravà, Aldo. "Studi cassanoviani a Dux" in *Marzocco*, September 18, 1910.

Regnier, H. de. "Voltaire et Casanova" in *Revue des deux mondes*, Paris, 1928, vol. 42.

Ricci, C. Burney. *Casanova e Farinelli*, Milan, 1900.

Rollestone, J.D. "The Medical Interest of Casanova's 'Memoirs'" in *Janus*, Leyden, 1917. French translation in Sirène ed. VII.

Rostand, M. *La vie amoureuse de Casanova*, Paris, 1924.

Samaran, Charles. "Casanova" in *Dictionnaire des lettres françaises, dix-huitième siècle*, Paris, 1960.

Sarfatti, M.G. *Casanova contro Don Giovanni*, Milan, 1950.

Schmidt-Pauli, Edgar von. *Der andere Casanova, Unveröffentlichte Dokumente aus dem Duxer Archiv*, Berlin, 1930.

Spini, G. *Ricerca dei libertini, La teoria dell'impostura delle religioni nel seicento italiano*, Rome, 1950.

Steiner, G. "Songs of Experience" in *The Reporter*, New York, October 15, 1959.

Symons, Arthur. "Casanova at Dux" in *North American Review*, New York, September 1902.

Teza, E. "Di Giacomo Casanova traduttore dell'Iliade" in *Rivista dell'Accademia di Scienze, Lettere e Arti*, Padua, 1910.

Toffanin. "Casanova sanfedista" in *La critica e il tempo*, Turin, 1930.

Toth, Karl. "Jacques Casanova de Seingalt" in *Germanisch-Romanische Monatsschrift*, 5, 1913.

Uzanne, Octave. "Casanova et la postérité" in *Revue du XVIII$^e$ siècle*, Paris, 1917.

Valeri, A. "Casanova a Roma" in *Rivista d'Italia*, Rome, 1899.

Valeri, A. "Casanoviana" in *Fanfulla della Domenica*, June 25 and July 2, 1899.

Whibley, Charles. *Literary Portraits*, 1920. Facsimile ed. in Essay Index Reprint Series: Ayer Co. Publishers, Salem, NH.

Zardo, A. "Il maggior confidente di Giacomo Casanova" in *Nuova antologia*, Rome, 1919, vol. 202.

# *Index of Persons*

This index includes the Chronology and the Notes. If a name appears also in the Selected Bibliography, the page references are followed by *"also Bibl."*

# Index of Places

This index includes the Chronology and the Notes.